BOOKENDS
Objects of Art & Fashion

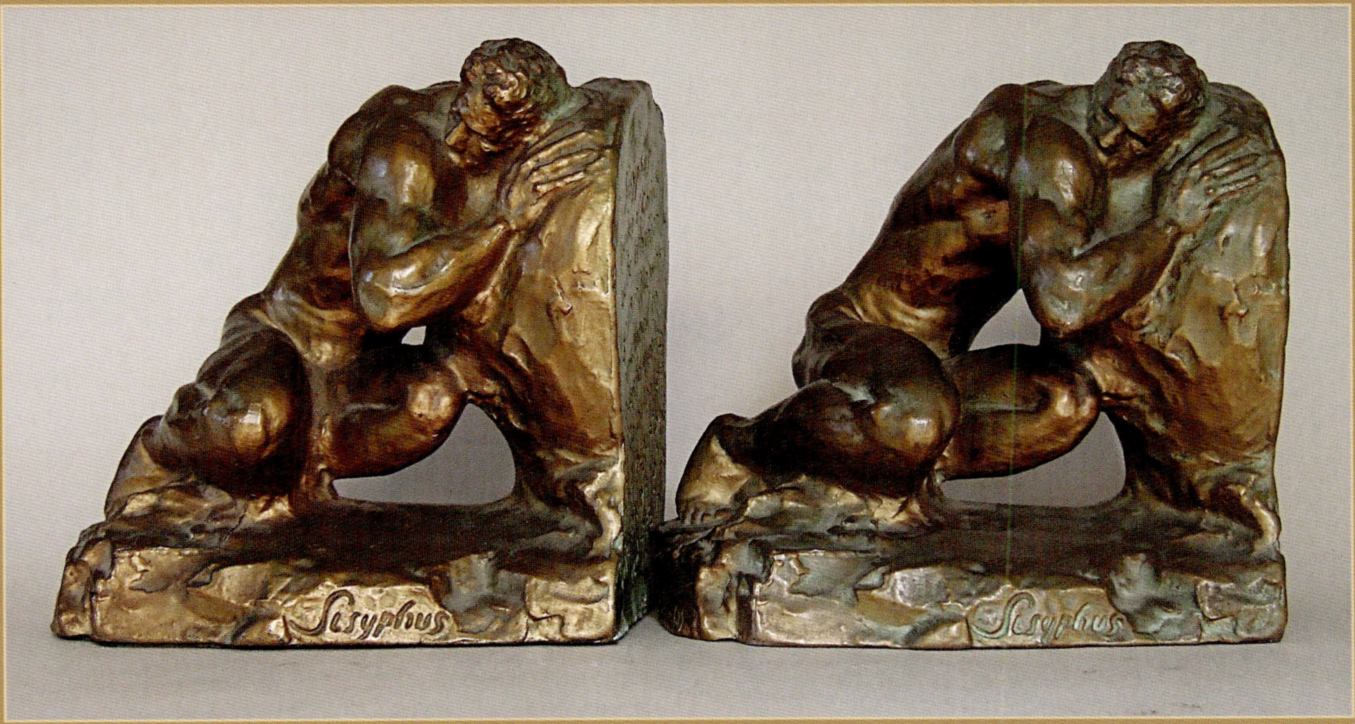

Robert Seecof, PhD, MD,
& Donna Seecof, MSN

Schiffer Publishing Ltd
4880 Lower Valley Road • Atglen, PA 19310

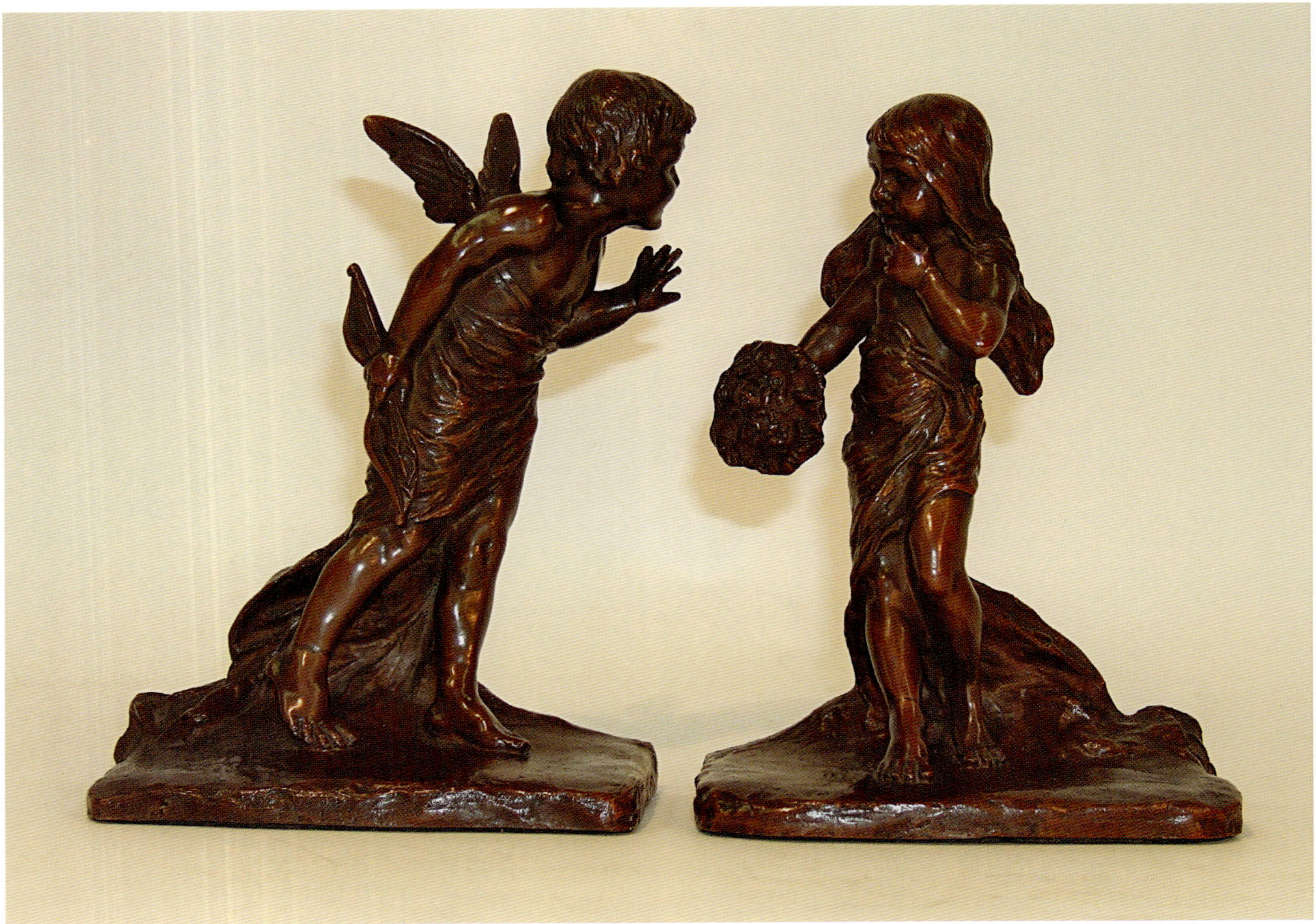

Library of Congress Control Number: 2012948105

Type set in Arrus BT

ISBN: 978-0-7643-4168-7
Printed in China

Published by Schiffer Publishing, Ltd.
4880 Lower Valley Road
Atglen, PA 19310
Phone: (610) 593-1777; Fax: (610) 593-2002
E-mail: Info@schifferbooks.com

In Europe, Schiffer books are distributed by
Bushwood Books
6 Marksbury Ave.
Kew Gardens
Surrey TW9 4JF England
Phone: 44 (0) 20 8392 8585; Fax: 44 (0) 20 8392 9876
E-mail: info@bushwoodbooks.co.uk
Website: www.bushwoodbooks.co.uk

Contents

Preface

Donna and I wrote the first book on bookends in 1995 (*Bookend Revue*, Schiffer Publishing Ltd., 1996). At that time we briefly addressed bookends as works of art. Since that time we have become more aware of bookends as a medium of art and fashion, and we have attempted to show these relationships to all bookend lovers in this volume.

— Robert Seecof

Acknowledgments

We owe special thanks to Gregory Seecof for assisting with all our computer operations for this book. Charles DeCosta generously allowed us to present some of the bookends from his outstanding collection, which can be seen at antiquebookendcollection.com

Chapter 1

Introduction to Bookends

Historically, bookends were always meant to be decorative. They were commercial products and always responded to the prevalent styles in order to sell. Today we find bookends that were designed in the popular fashions of their times – in Arts & Crafts style or in Art Deco style, for example, and changes in bookend styles reflect the major changes in decorative art fashions that took place in the United states, decade by decade in the twentieth century.

Art styles permeated society in America to varying degrees. American people lived with Victorian ideals and styles for generations and adopted them unthinkingly. The Art Nouveau style reached into all forms of art and design including commonplace personal belongings, and became a chosen way of life in England and Europe, with perhaps a smaller following in America. Art Deco fashions and lifestyle dominated American sensibilities and preferred life style in the 1920s and 1930s. 1940s fashions took a back seat to World War II in the United States. The 1950s, 1960s, and 1970s, which we now call mid-century modern style, prevailed in commercial fashions. After the 1970s, styling seemed to fragment and no single decorative style dominated, but Arts & Crafts styling survived though the entire century.

Thus, fashion dictated bookend styles and, today, vintage bookends document the fashion styles of past times. Bookends did not represent all of the high art styles of the 19th and 20th centuries, but they did reflect the major decorative styles, and these are the principal bookend styles that we review in this book. Furthermore, nearly all bookends, old or new are sculptures, and all were created by artists. Bookends are a medium of decorative art and we appreciate them as artwork to the present day.

Bookends may be identified as to art style by a typical design, as, for example, streamlining typifies American modern in Art Deco, or the identification may depend on subject material that was characteristic, like, for example, oak leaves and acorns for Arts & crafts era.

Not only do old bookends reflect bygone art styles, but many bookends document historical events as well. Some pairs commemorate individuals and historical events by directly illustrating them. For example, a bookend showing Charles Lindbergh's airplane – The Spirit of St. Louis – or his portrait commemorates his historic transatlantic flight. Other bookends establish a timeline by changes in their composition. For example, lead was used only until about 1915, and pressed woody material and chalk were used during World War II, when metal was diverted to the war effort. Decorative bookends also served as advertising leaders and tokens of fraternal societies.

Today there are thousands of different pairs of bookends available, but as recently as the nineteenth century there were very few. There needed to be an evolution of books before there could be an evolution of bookends, and a look backwards shows us how this came about.

Before there were books, there were scrolls. The first scrolls were introduced thousands of years ago and were probably made from papyrus; later scrolls used sheet copper or silver as well. Scrolls were presumably stored horizontally, so we must imagine that bookends would not have been created until codices arrived. Codices, primitive books with papyrus or wooden pages and wood or leather bindings came into use early in the common era. There is, however, no record of bookends used to support the codices. The printing press was invented in the fifteenth century and gave rise to books as we know them today, and we can guess there were bookends, but no bookends have been found from these early times.

Finally, in the early part of the nineteenth century, bookends appeared, probably in England, in the form we now call a bookrack – a pair of bookends connected at their bases by a single short shelf. Books rested on the shelf, and the bookends prevented them from falling sideways. The shelf was made of wood or of metal tubes and frequently fashioned from several pieces nested together so the length was adjustable. These adjustable bookracks are called bookslides or adjustable bookracks. The end pieces were frequently hinged and could be folded down against the shelf. Bookracks and bookslides remained popular in England during the nineteenth and the early part of twentieth century, and we can still find them today.

Gutenberg's techniques for printing were used until about 1800. The industrial revolution then brought successive improvements in the printing process. Inexpensive paper from wood pulp replaced expensive rag-based paper. In 1886, the linotype machine was invented and enabled whole lines of metal type to be set from a controlling keyboard. Books could then be manufactured more rapidly and inexpensively, so for the first time books were readily available to people who were not wealthy. Toward the middle of the nineteenth century, compulsory elementary education appeared in America, first in Massachusetts and then around the country. Not only did books become plentiful, but common people were enabled to read them. Books became desirable symbols of culture in American homes, and bookends were produced to support and embellish the new home libraries.

Here we come to an important matter. Large numbers of bookends were produced in the United States in the twentieth century because compulsory education generated a literate population who wanted to own and display books. Comparatively few bookends were produced in England and Europe, probably because of lesser demand, and the bookends that were produced were generally high-end items. Because the overwhelming majority of bookends were produced in the United States, bookends can be considered an American art form. All the bookends in this book are American-made except for the few that are identified as foreign made.

American bookend art styles and subject materials followed the popular fashions decade by decade and gave us a record of American interests in these matters throughout the twentieth century, as we will see.

Bookracks and bookslides appeared in American homes early in the twentieth century (Figures 1-3). Some of the first ones were sold as plain wooden blanks, and people decorated them at home with wood-burning equipment. The technique was called pyrography. From 1909 though 1913 the Sears catalogs offered wooden bookracks stamped with outlines of owls or other designs. The company advised the home buyer to decorate the bookracks by staining and burning, and offered an outfit for burning that featured torches with platinum tips for benzene, alcohol, or gas flames. These wooden relics are still available, but only dedicated collectors seem interested in them. Large numbers of bookracks and bookslides were produced early on, but they fell out of favor, probably because the decorated ends could not be seen well from the front. Whatever the true reasons, relatively few were produced after 1920.

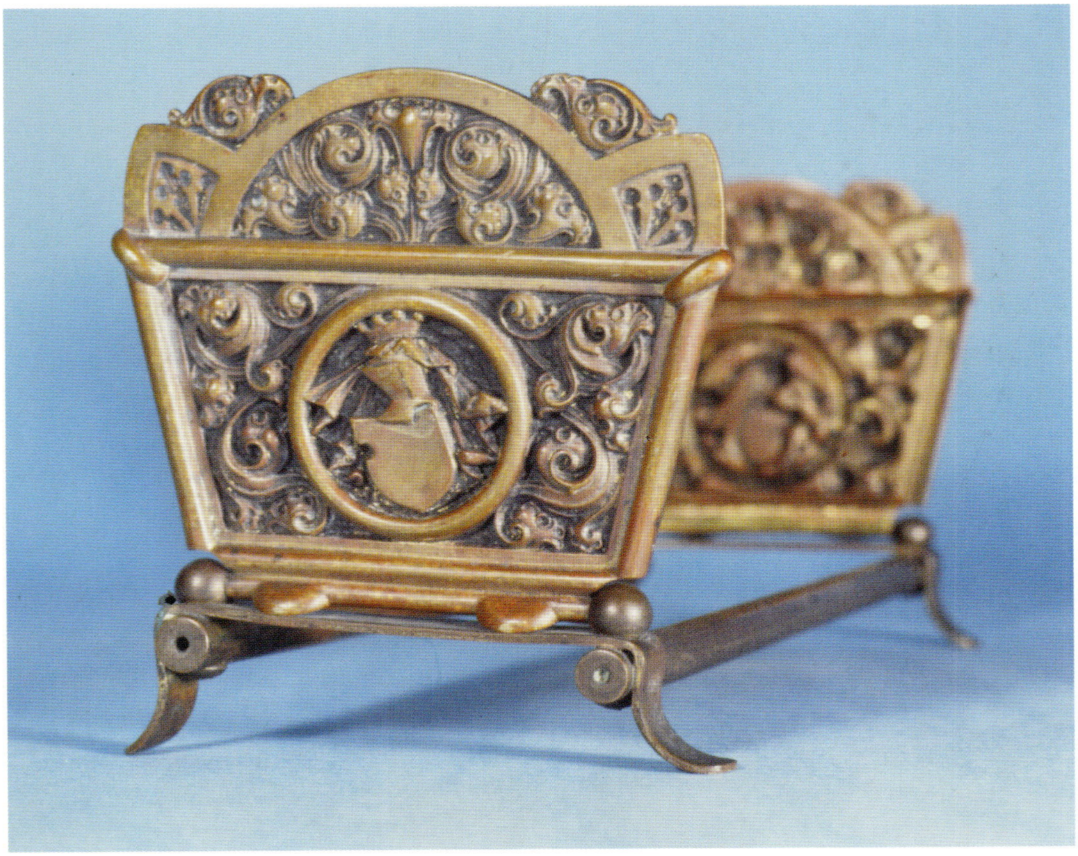

Figure 1. Heraldic Design. 5.75" brass. Circa 1900. Rarity 5 Foldable but non-adjustable bookrack $60-90.

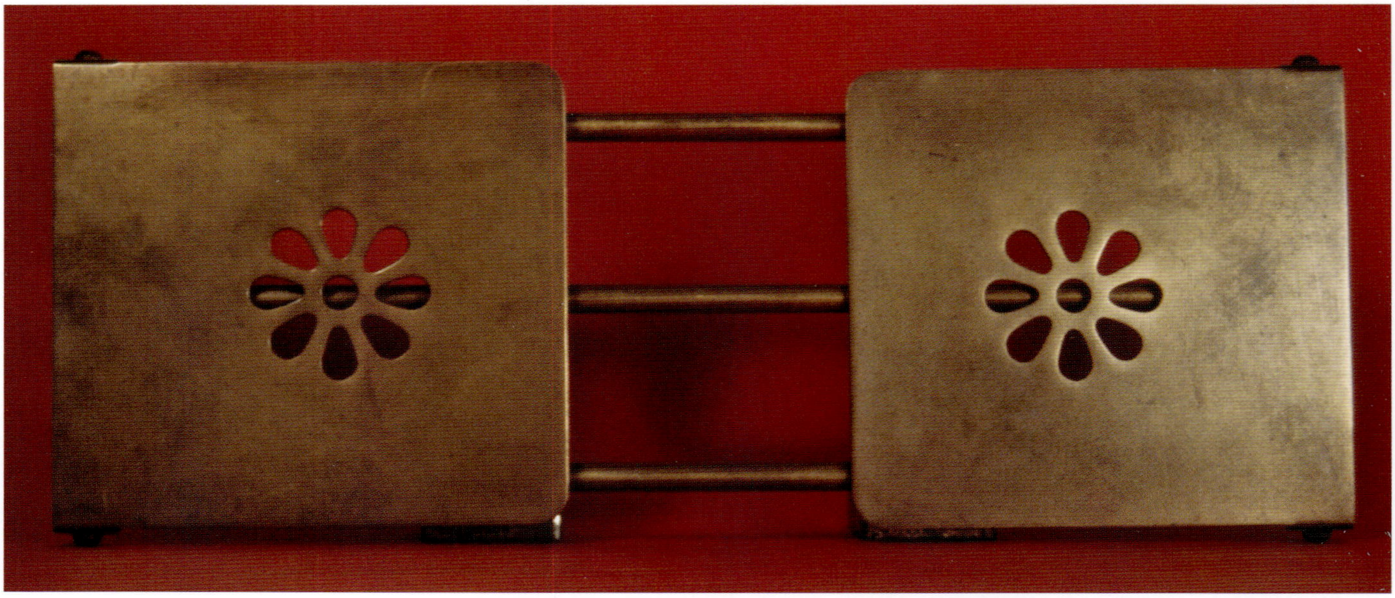

Figure 2. Eight Petals. 5.5", bronze, brass. Inscription: Shop mark of Bradley and Hubbard Inc. Circa 1915. Rarity 5. Arts & Crafts. Foldable bookslide. Ends are folded down. Brass tubes are visible. Smaller tubes slide into larger tubes to adjust length. $160-240.

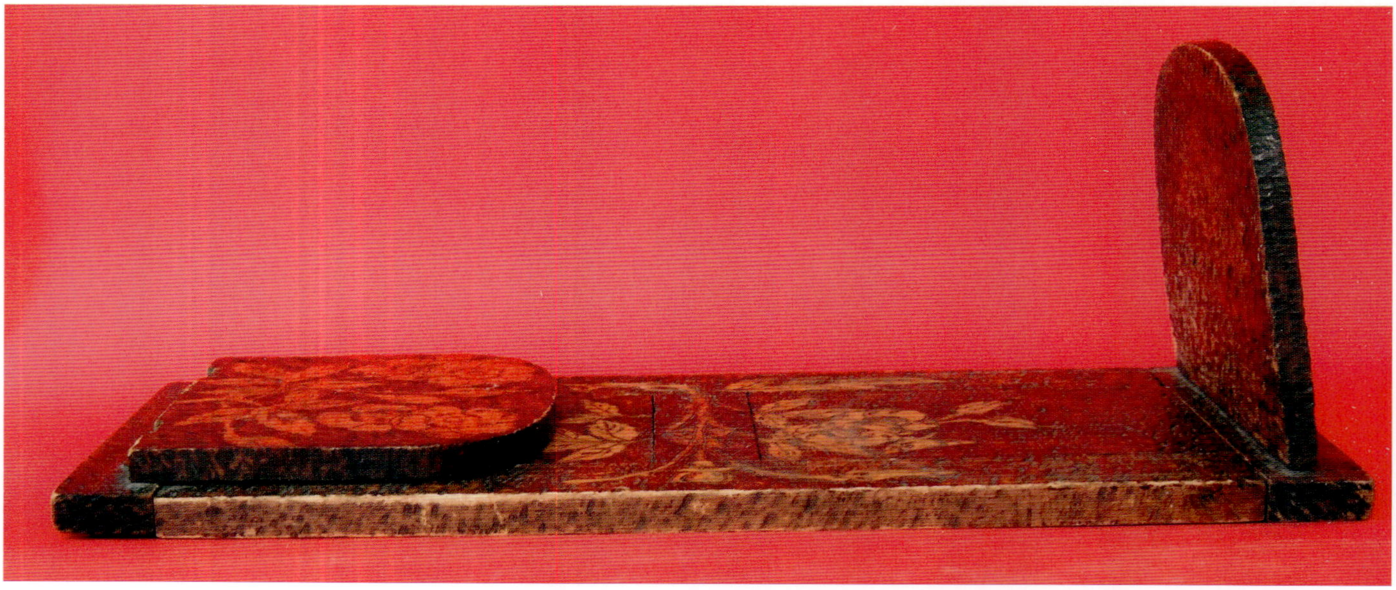

Figure 3. Floral Woodburn. Hand burned and stained wood bookslide. 6.5" Inscription: E. M. C. Merry Christmas, DEC. 25, '06. Rarity 5. Folk art. Decorated by pyrography (see text). $120-180.

By 1916, the Sears catalogue was already offering pairs of free-standing bookends and we know that such bookends were available elsewhere. This catalog illustrated bookends with wooden bases and uprights and with ornamental brass owls positioned on the bases. The early free-standing bookends were called "book rocks."

The earliest American bookends we have seen with documented dates were marked 1892 and the next earliest were 1903 (Figure 47), so earlier ones must have been very rare. By the 1920s, there was a flood of American bookends in great variety, and bookends have been manufactured ever since, although bookend production dropped noticeably in about 1930, apparently because of the Great Depression. Many foundries closed during the Depression and iron bookends were infrequently produced afterwards. Bookend production declined

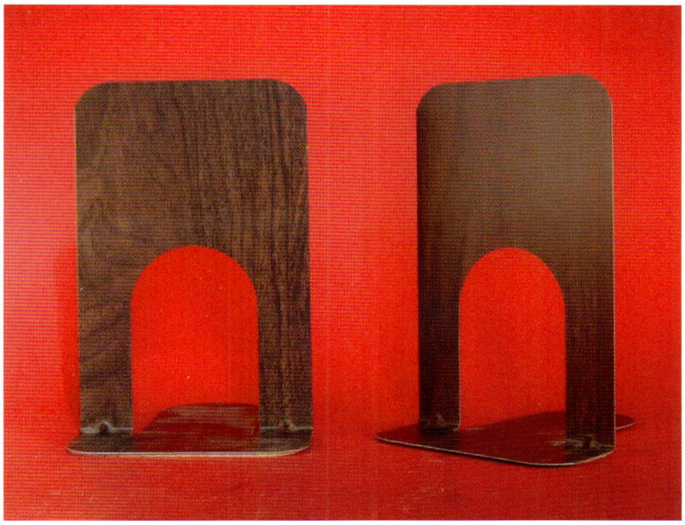

Figure 4. Dewey. 7.25", sheet steel. 1902 (recent version shown) Rarity 1. Modernist industrial design, but may not be related to the German school (see below). $2-4.

again during World War II and once again after 1950, when public television appeared and presumably cut into the number of readers.

By 1902, free-standing metal bookends were being marketed in the United States by Melvil Dewey, the originator of the Dewey decimal system for tracking library books. The Dewey bookend has a base with an upright section on it to hold books vertically, and a foot which projects behind the upright. Books rest on the foot and stabilize the bookend (Figure 4). We will use the terms base, upright, and foot to describe bookends in this text, although many bookends do not have a foot.

The period before 1920 is interesting because it contained a relatively large proportion of high-end bookends. For example, the prestigious Gorham foundries issued over 100 different pairs of bookends and most bore early dates. Apparently, high-end bookends led the fashion for bookends that blossomed in the 1920s.

Bookends have been manufactured from a large number of different materials and over a dozen are represented in this book. Metals have been most popular because they are heavy, readily cast, take a variety of finishes, and are durable. Metals, other materials, and casting procedures are discussed further in the Appendix.

For all bookends, the height from the bottom of the base is an important defining characteristic and tall ones are generally preferred. Bookends taller than about twelve inches appear to be too tall for most books, and those under about three and one half inches are hard to see and are not likely to sell. We cite the height with each bookend illustration and the weight, as well, if it exceeds eight pounds per pair. Heavy weight usually attests to expensive, durable construction.

Sometimes, a bookend bears the date of production. Otherwise the age must be estimated by the art style, the methods and materials of manufacture, the subject material, the identity of the foundry or the artist, and so on. We list the date of production for bookends if this is known. If the date is not certain, we give it as a circa date and this is usually accurate to within five years before or after the given date. Many pairs of vintage bookends are now more than 100 years old and should be considered antiques. The remainder are certainly collectibles.

The name of the foundry or its shop mark is frequently inscribed on a bookend, and several shop marks are illustrated in the appendix. The name of the foundry always appears on the attached company paper label, if one is present, so pictures of labels are not needed.

Price is determined by all the considerations that usually apply to antiques and collectibles, such as age, decorative quality, condition, artist, size, art style, foundry, materials of manufacture and, of course, supply and demand. Prices in this book are given for pairs of bookends, even when only one of a pair is shown. The price refers only to undamaged bookend pairs of the color and materials shown. The same pair in other colors or materials might command a different price. Single bookends usually sell for less than half the price for a pair. Bookend prices have been rising, on average, for the past several years. A pair of iron butterflies by the French artist Edgar Brandt sold for $24,000 at a Christie's auction in 2004, probably a record high price for bookends, but prices in the thousands are not unusual today.

Rarity is important to bookend value, and we have ranked them by how often we have seen them, in shops, in collections, or on eBay. Thus, bookends seen every few months, usually on eBay, are ranked 1, very common. Those seen every one, two, or three years are ranked 2, common. Those seen every four, five, or six years are ranked 3, uncommon. Those seen about once every seven, eight, or nine years are ranked 4, rare. Those we have seen only once in our eighteen years of collecting are ranked 5, extremely rare.

Four abbreviations are used in the captions:

- c. stands for circa, meaning near the stated year.
- Attrib. stands for attributed to.
- Pounds are shown as lbs.
- " stands for inches.

Chapter 2

Victorian Style Bookends

The original American colonies were English colonies, of course, and Americans were English subjects. England dominated our economy and our culture. After the Revolutionary War, English influence persisted, especially among the well-to-do, throughout the Victorian era (1837-1901). Furthermore, Victorian sensibilities persisted in America into the beginning of the twentieth century.

After bookend production began here, in about 1900, some bookends showed Colonial figures (Figures 5-12), and many showed Victorian images. Thus, we generated bookends in Victorian style after the Victorian era closed. Victorian images persisted here until the 1920s, and afterwards were only infrequently used.

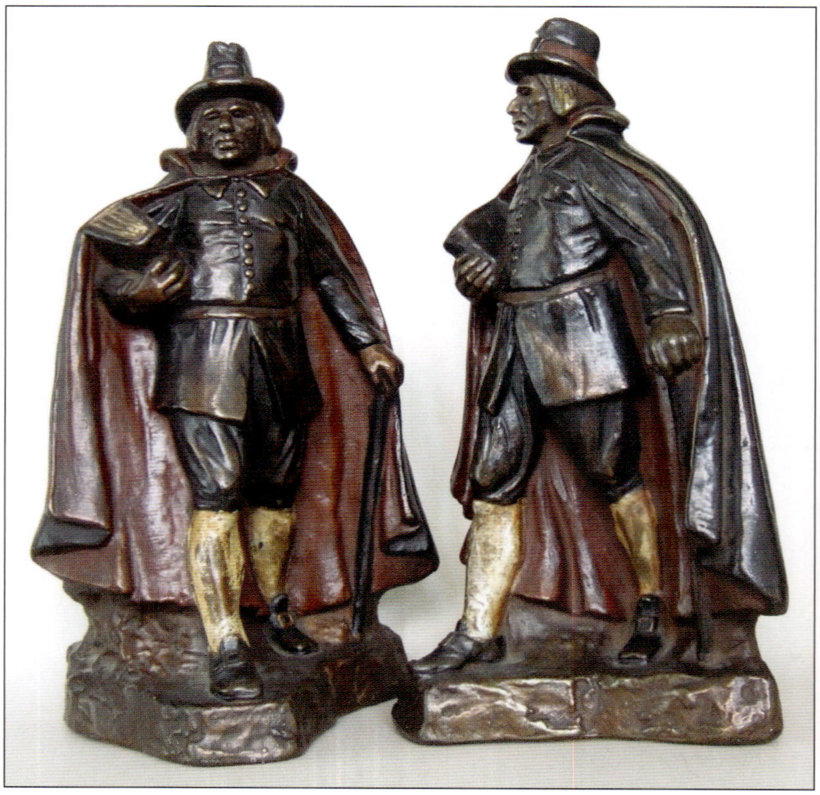

Figure 5. Pilgrim. 10.5", electroformed. Inscription: artist Ruhl signature, Bradley and Hubbard shop mark. Circa 1919. Rarity 3. Colonial revival. These are large, heavy bookends, 9 lbs./pair. $400-600.

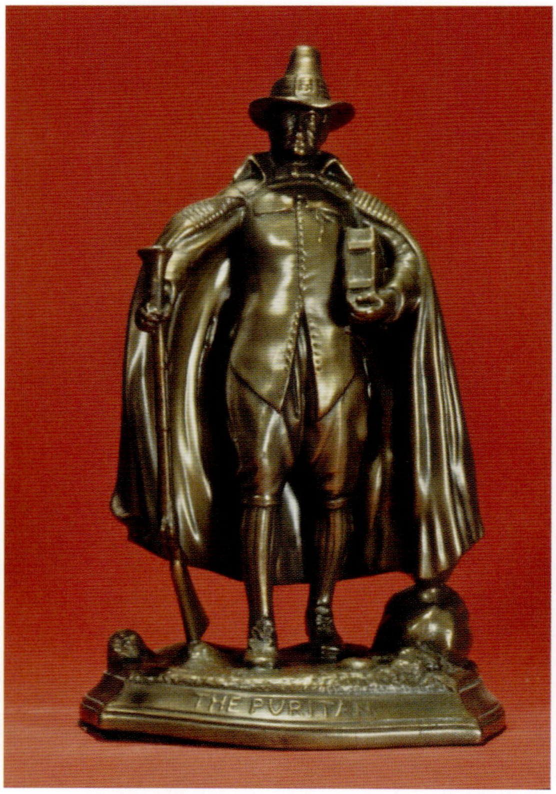

Figure 6. Puritan. 9.25", bronze plating over gray metal. Inscription: Puritan, Jennings Brothers shop mark. Circa 1919. Rarity 3. Colonial revival. $240-360.

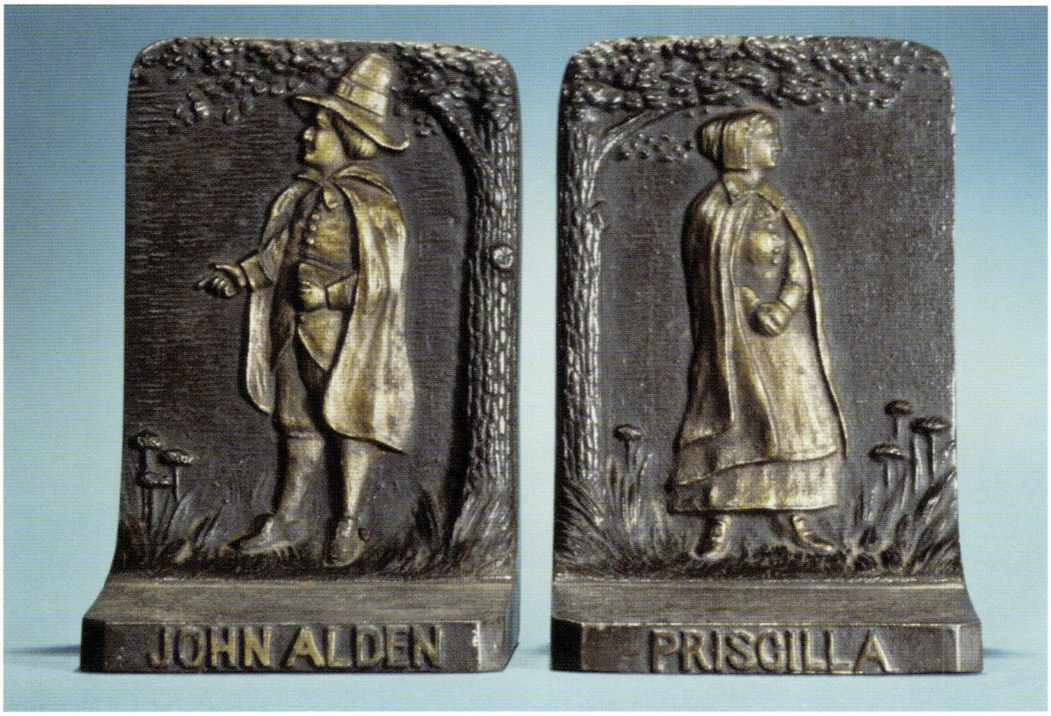

Figure 7. Priscilla and Alden. 5", iron. Inscription: Shop mark of Bradley and Hubbard. Circa 1925. Rarity 2. Colonial revival. $100-150.

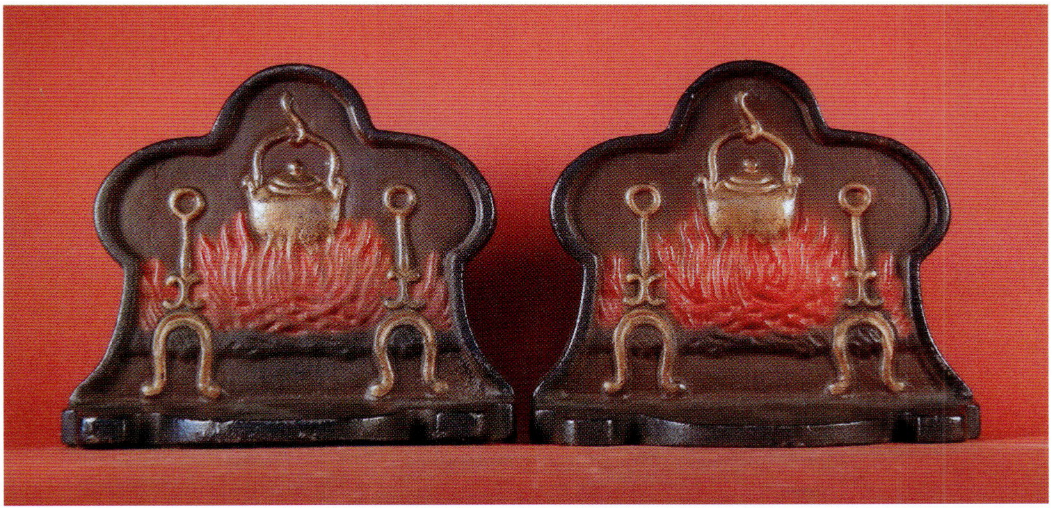

Figure 8. Colonial Cooking Fireplace. 5.75", iron. Foundry: Attrib. Albany. Circa 1910 Rarity 2. $56-84. Colonial revival. In Colonial times, some fireplaces were used for cooking and heating. $60-80.

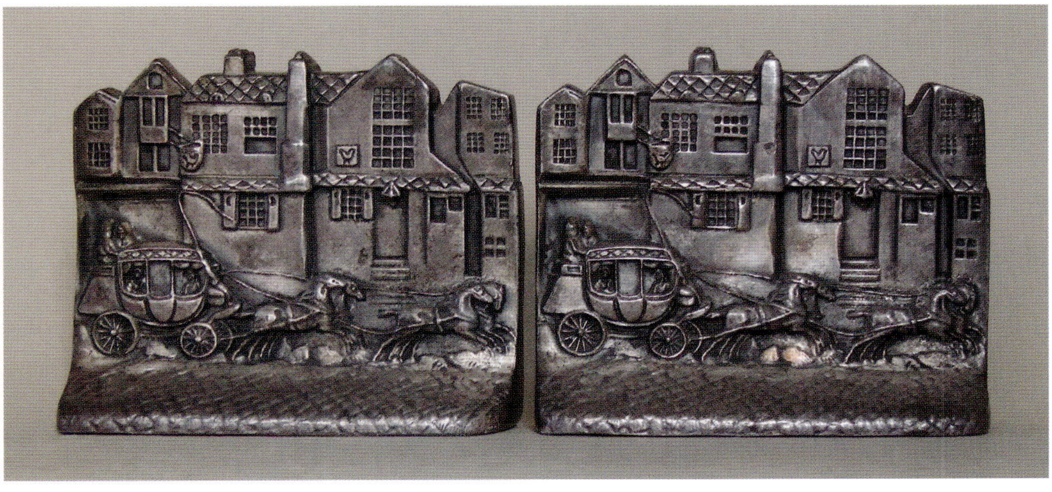

Figure 9. The Old Stagecoach. 4", silver, 66 oz. per pair. Circa 1915. Rarity 5. Colonial revival. The value is inflated by the price of silver. $3100.

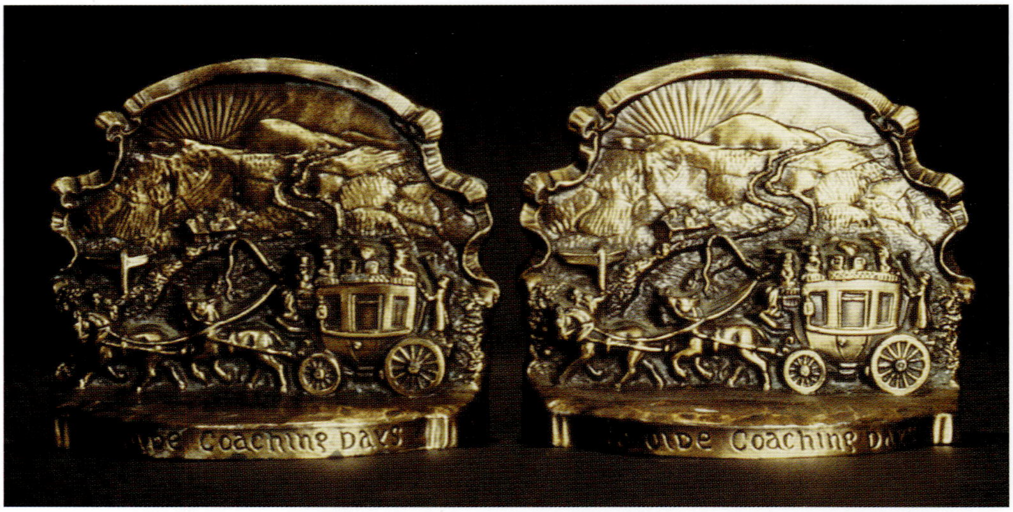

Figure 10. Ye Olde Coaching Days. 4.25", bronze plating over gray metal. Inscription: Jennings Brothers, shop mark, 2385. Circa 1916. Rarity 4. Colonial revival. $100-150.

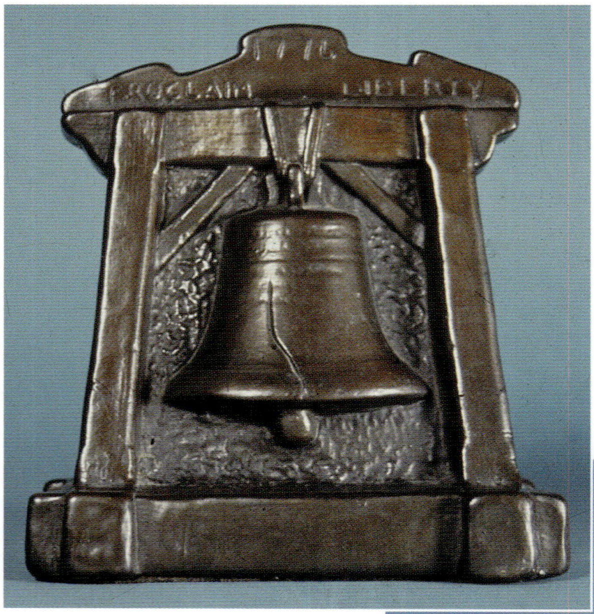

Figure 11. Liberty Bell. 6.75", Electroformed Bronze. Inscription: 1776, proclaim liberty. Shop mark of Armor Bronze. Circa 1924. Rarity 3. Colonial revival. $100-150.

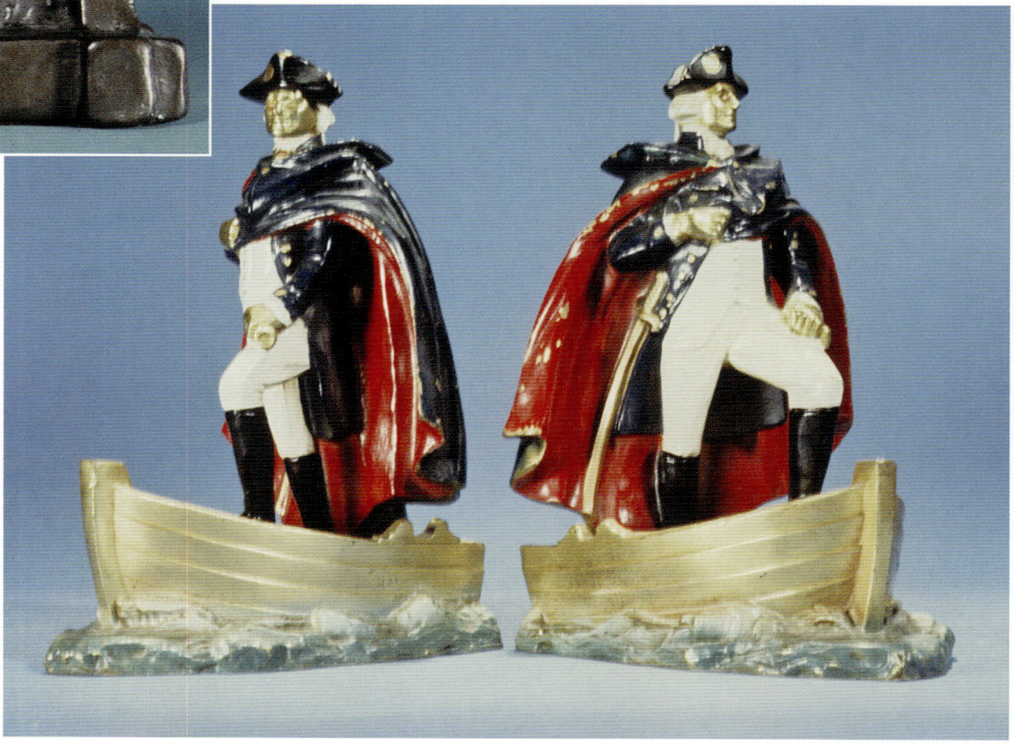

Figure 12. Washington Crossing the Delaware. 6.75", gray metal. Inscription: Shop mark of K&O, signed by J. Ruhl. Circa 1930. Rarity 3. Colonial revival. $160-240.

Revival Style Bookends

Throughout the Victorian period in England, no new, dominant Victorian art style emerged. Rather, the century was principally one of revivals – Greek, Elizabethan, Italian Renaissance, and Gothic – and many bookends featured these revivals. Because the Victorian era was so long and so important, a large variety of bookends were produced that can be considered Victorian in style.

Bookends appeared that featured Greek-revival subjects like columns and pediments from Greek ruins, people in Greek togas, and characters from Greek myths, as well as bookends showing Elizabethan subject materials like busts of Shakespeare, jesters, and people in Elizabethan dress. Reproductions of paintings and portraits of Italian Renaissance figures were produced. Revival-style bookends are shown in Figures 13-33. Additional bookends of Gothic revival style are shown in Figures 135-139.

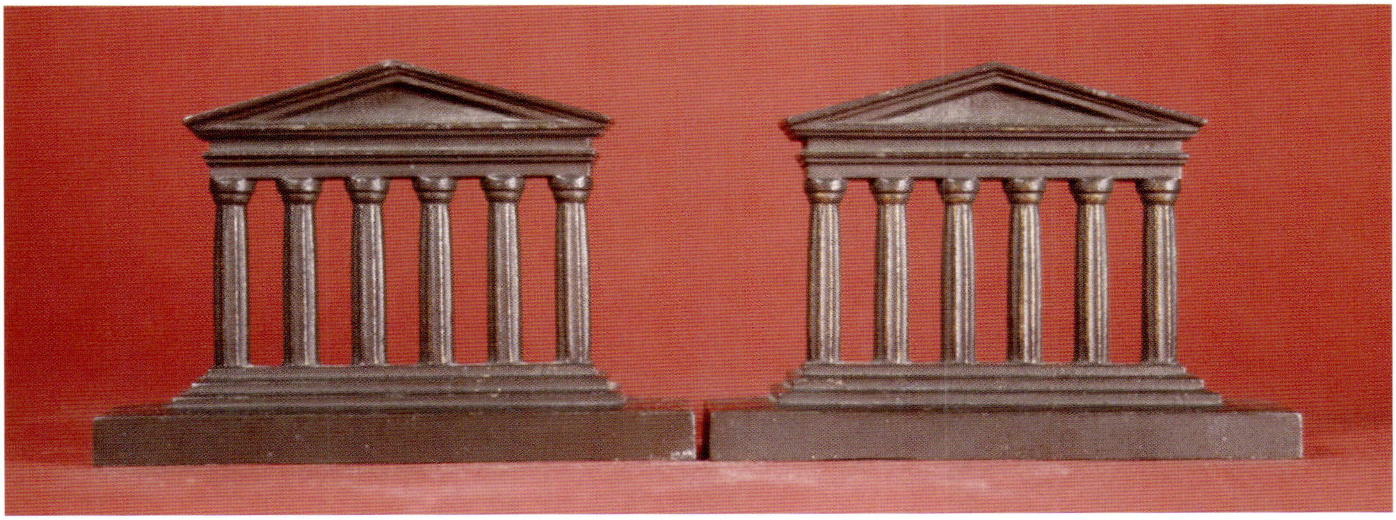

Figure 13. Athens. 3.5", iron. Inscription: Shop mark of Bradley and Hubbard. Circa 1922. Rarity 2. Greek revival. $60-90.

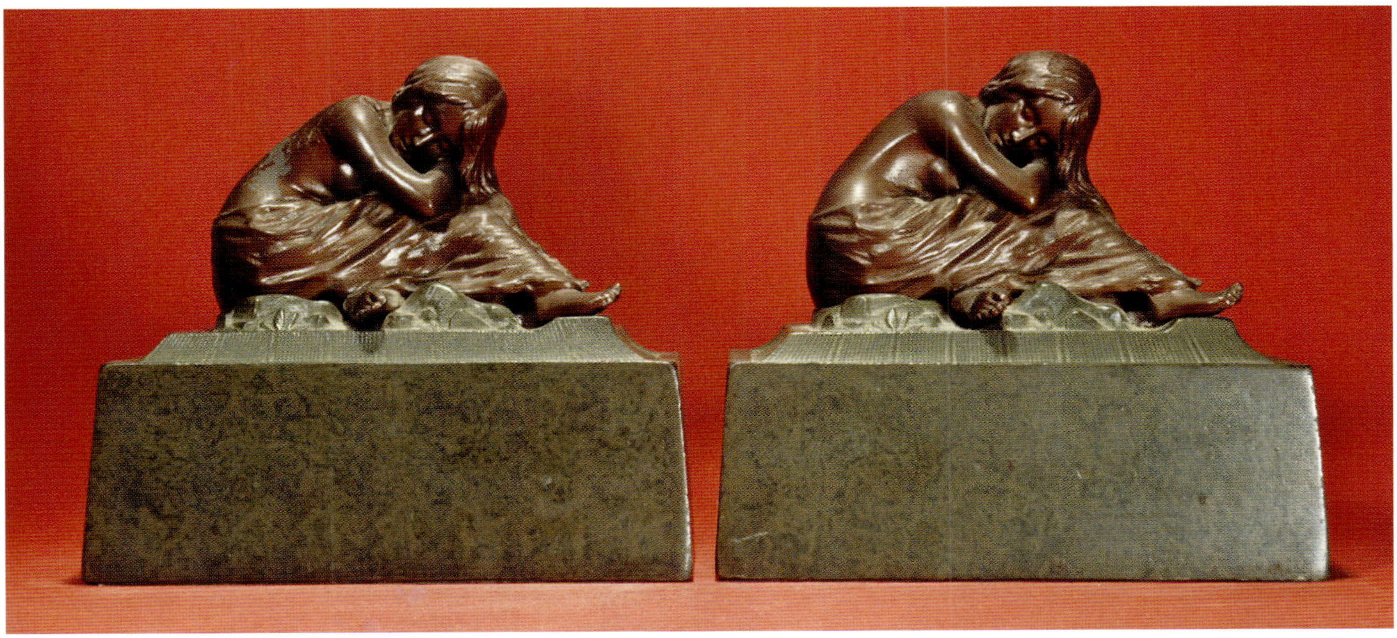

Figure14. Niobe. 6.5", iron, gray metal, Inscription: A paper tag on the felt identifies the goddess Niobe who was turned to stone but continues to weep for her lost offspring. Foundry: Judd. Circa 1925. Rarity 2. Greek revival. These are large bookends. $280-420.

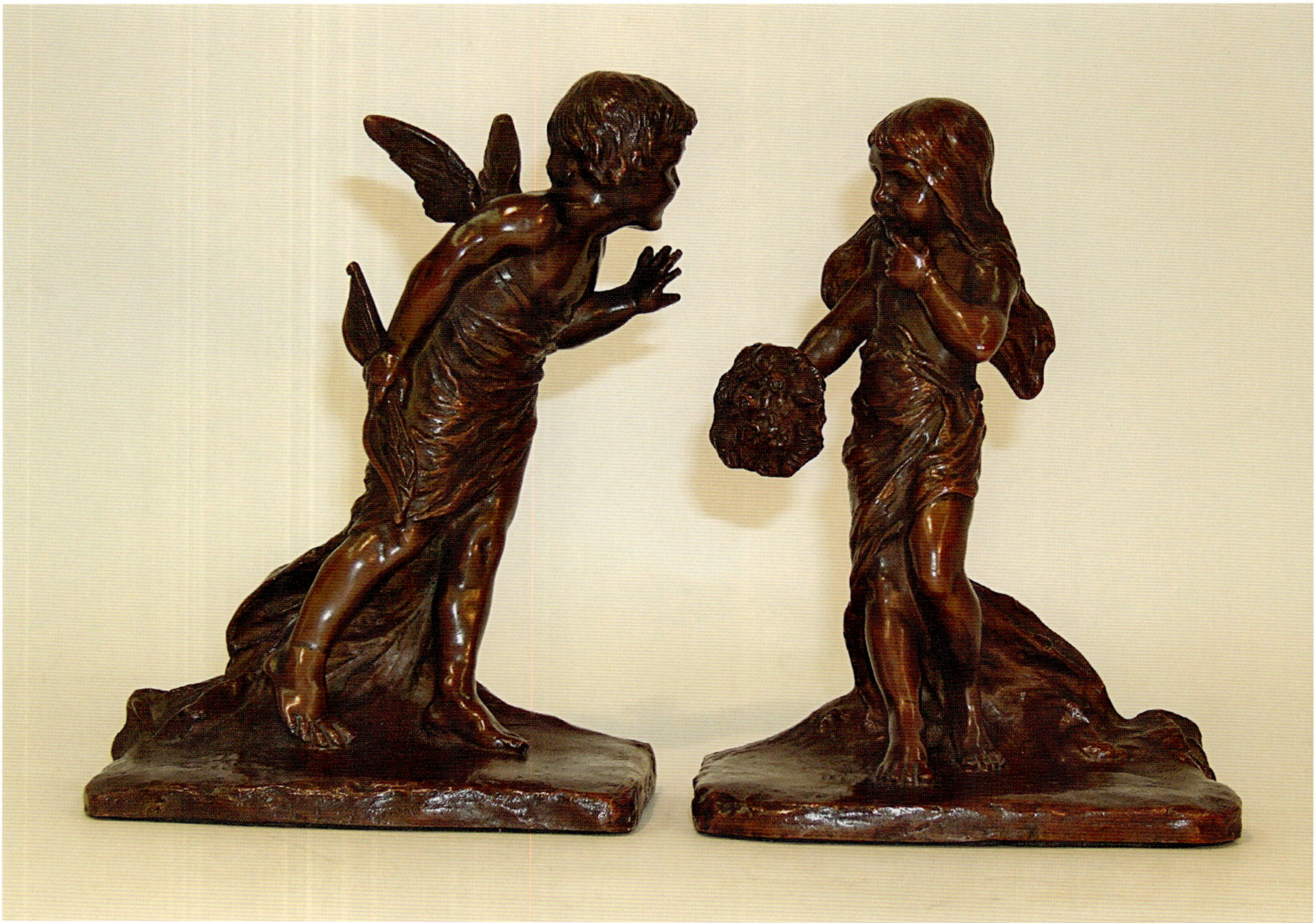

Figure15. Cupid and Girl. 6.75", solid bronze. Inscription: Cast by Griffoul N.J., Sold by Theodore B Starr Inc. N.Y., signed M. Peinlich, Scp. Circa 1920. rarity 5. Greek revival *By courtesy of Charles DeCosta, from his collection.* $1800-2000.

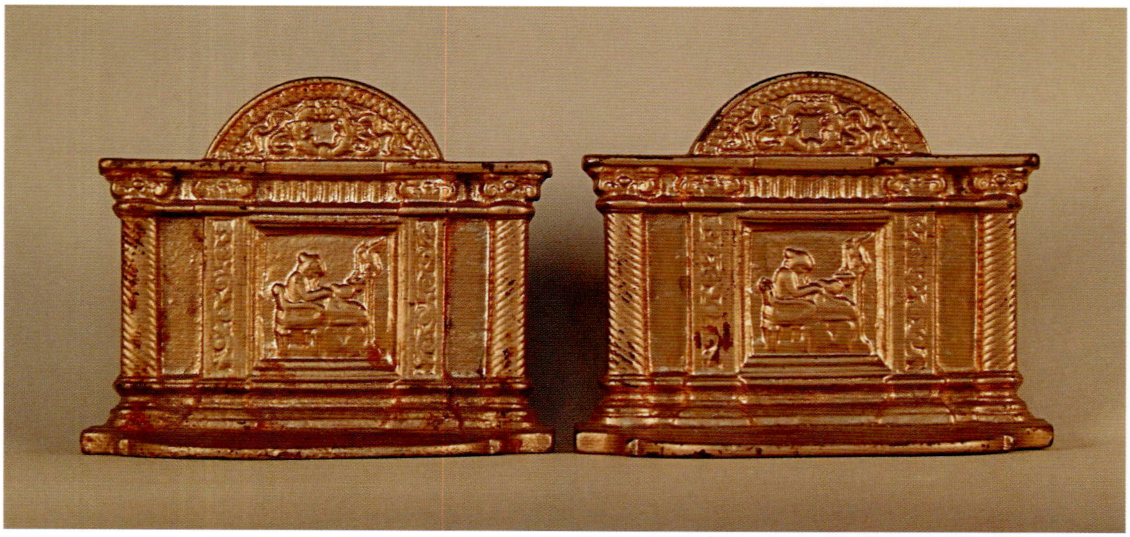

Figure 16. Penelope Unravels the Shroud. 4", gray metal. Circa 1920. Rarity 1. Greek revival. Penelope refuses marriage until she completes the weaving of a shroud. She weaves by day and unravels her work by night in order to postpone marriage. *Bookend interpretation by Emmanuel P. Papadakis, Ph.D.* $50-70.

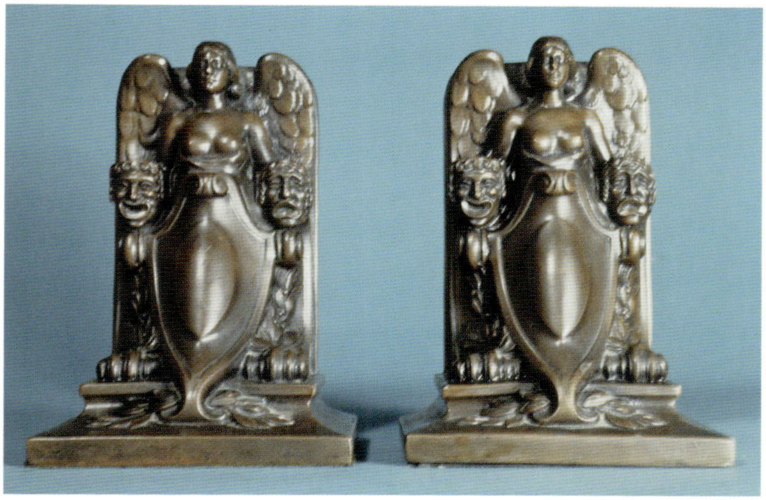

Figure17. Lady of the Theater. 5", bronze plating over gray metal. Inscription: Shop mark of Jennings Brothers, 1529. Circa 1925. Rarity 3. Greek revival. The masks are comedy and tragedy. $220-330.

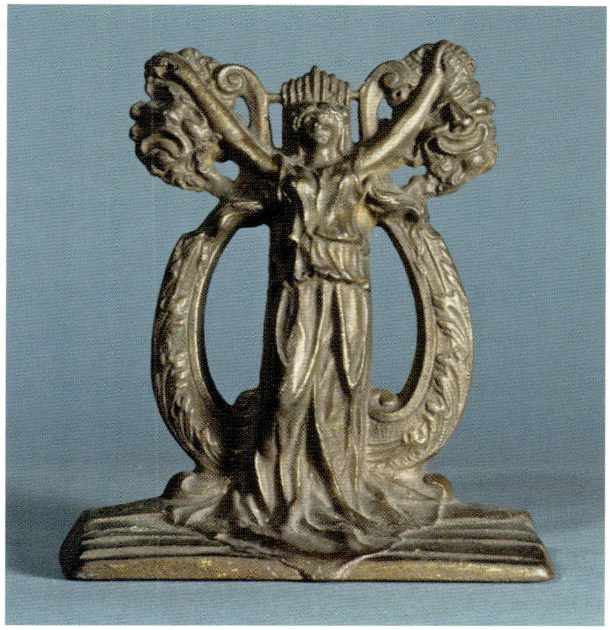

Figure 18. Thesbian. 5.5", iron. Circa 1925. Rarity 3. Greek revival. $100-150.

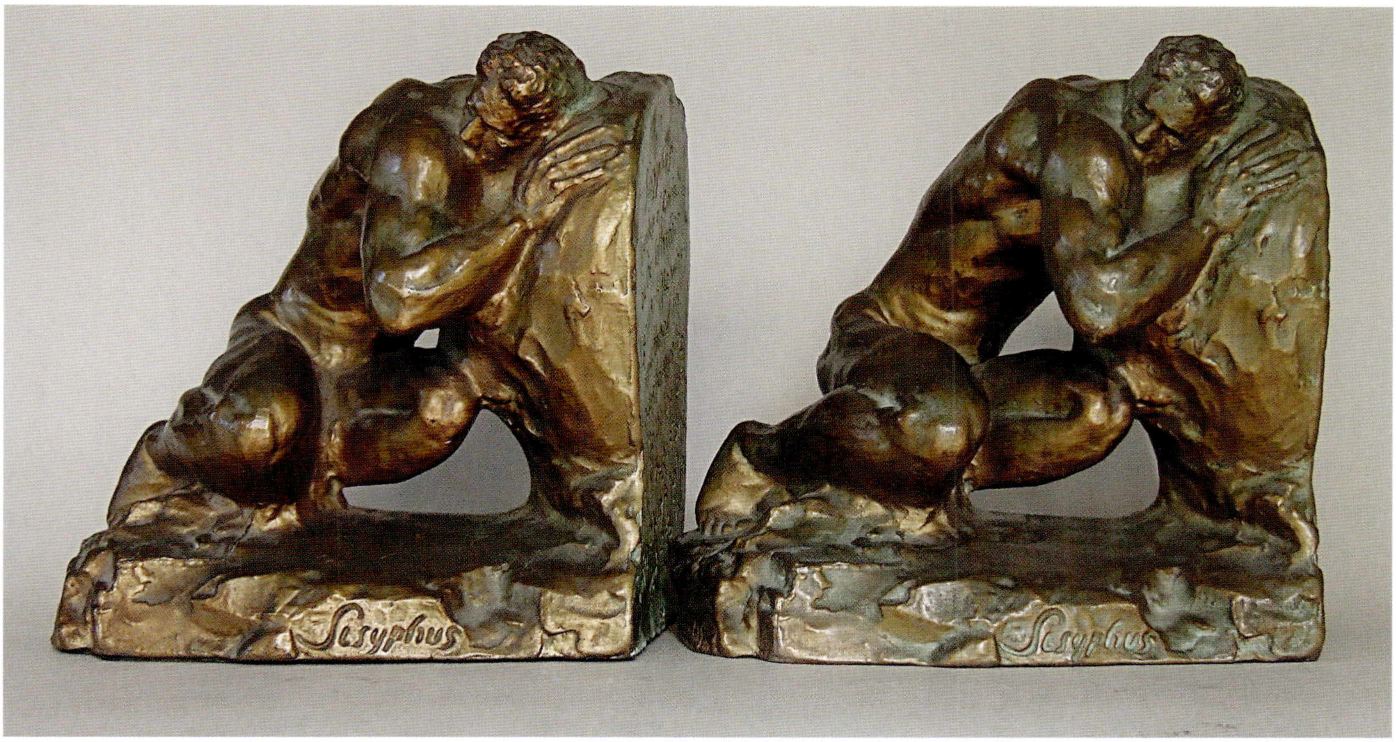

Figure 19. Sisyphus. 6.5", gray metal. Inscription: Signed by the artist McClelland Barclay. The legend of Sisyphus is inscribed on the rear of the upright. Foundry: Attrib. Dodge Inc. Circa 1930. Rarity 2. Greek revival. These are large, heavy bookends, 12 lbs./ pair. $320-480.

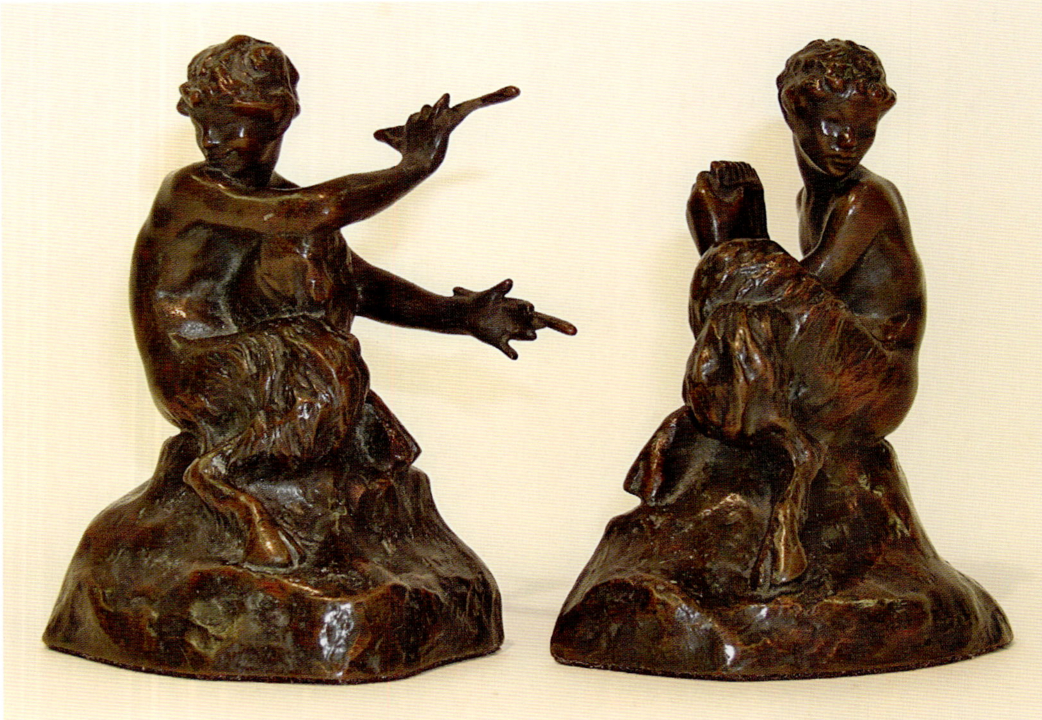

Figure 20. Fauns. 5.5", solid Bronze. Inscription: Gorham Co. New York, A.M. Wright, 1914. Rarity 5. Greek revival. *By courtesy of Charles De Costa, from his collection. $2,500-3,000.*

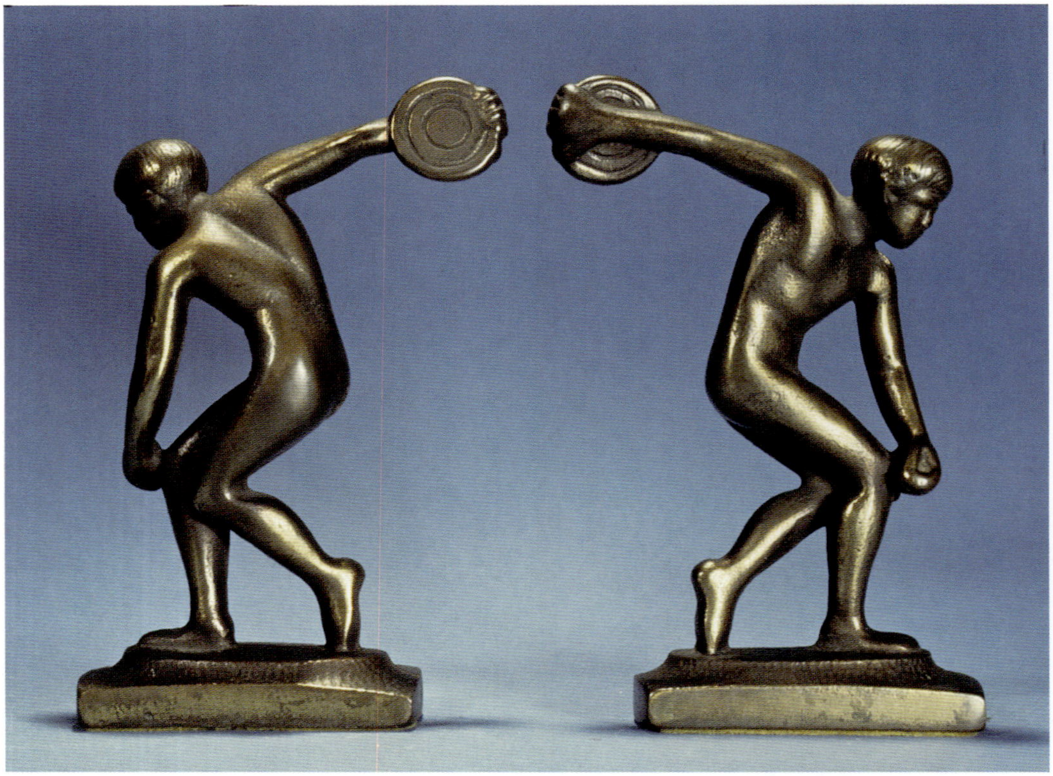

Figure 21. Discus Thrower. 7", iron. Foundry: Attrib. Littlestown. Circa 1920. Rarity 3. Victorian. Greek revival. $100-150.

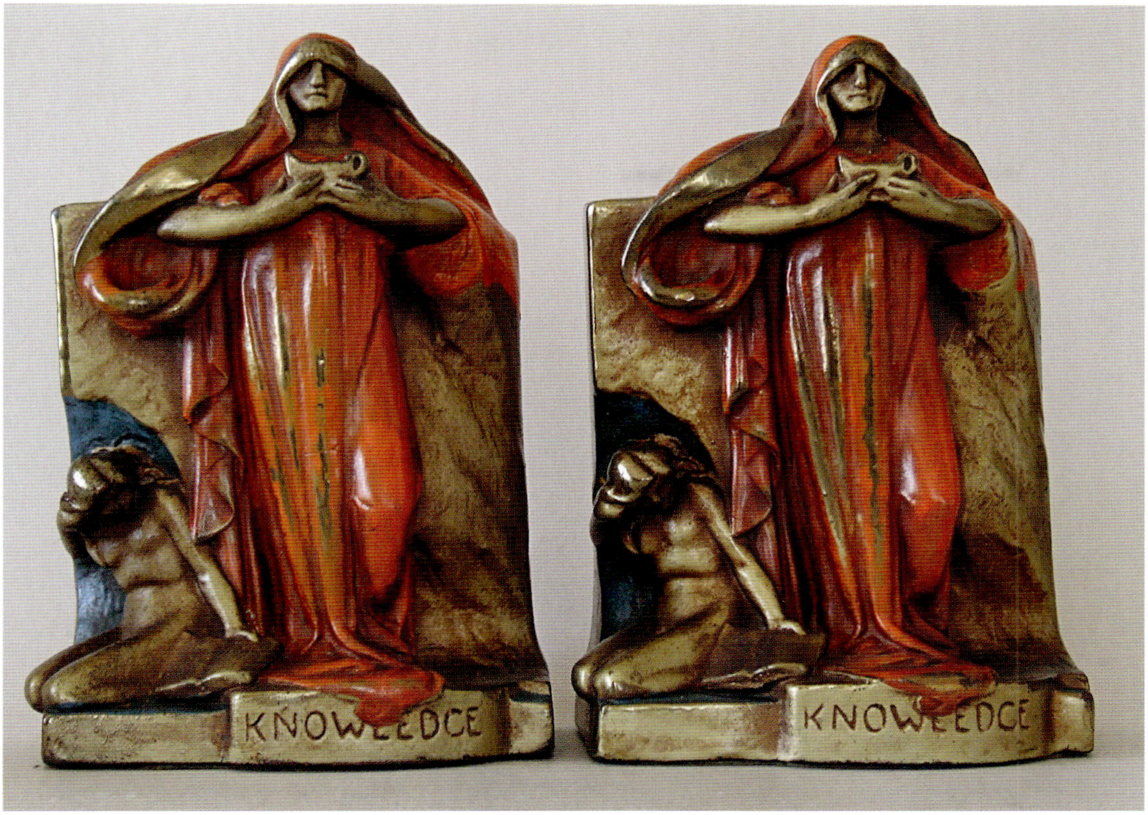

Figure 22. Knowledge with Lamp. 7.5", gray metal. Inscription: Knowledge. Foundry: Pompeian Bronze. Sculptor V. Carano. Circa 1920. Rarity 2. Greek revival. A mysterious figure in a Greek gown holds an oil lamp while a nude acolyte crouches below. A lamp of knowledge is a prevalent motif among bookends. Attributed to Greek mythology, possibly to the Diogenes story. $220-420.

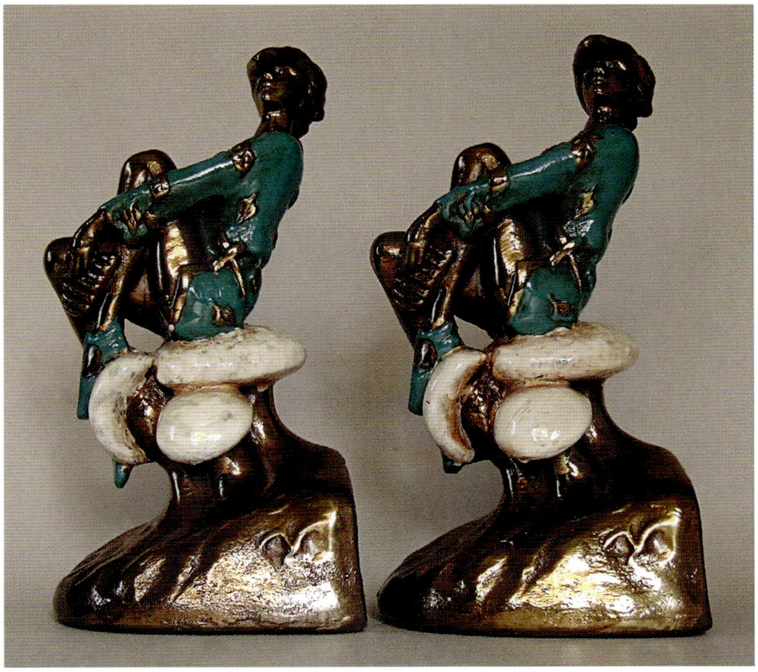

Figure 23. Peter Pan on mushrooms. 7.25", electroformed bronze. Inscription: shop mark of Marion Bronze. Circa 1950. Rarity 4. Victorian. Concern for children. This is a copy. The original foundry is unknown. $200-300.

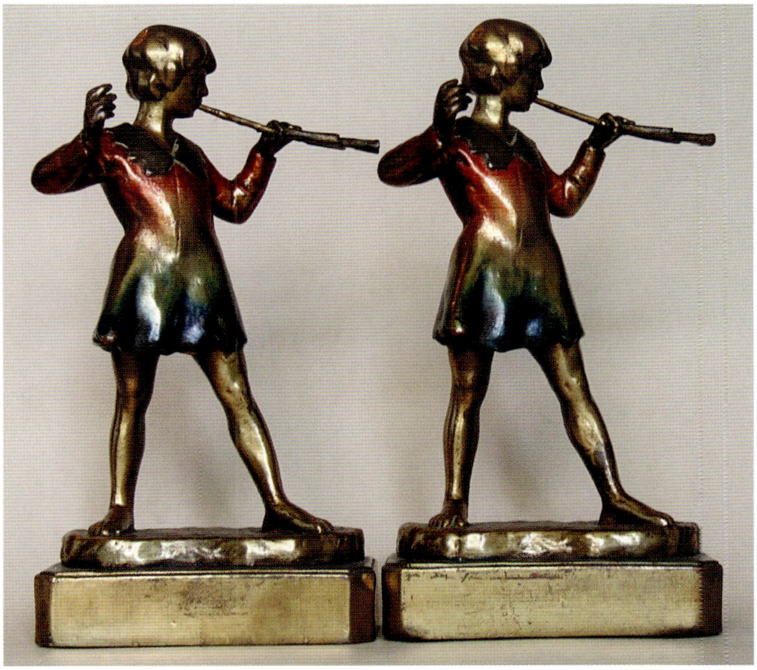

Figure 24. Peter Pan. 9.25", electroformed bronze. Inscription: Pompeian Bronze, and signature of the artist Herzel. Circa 1917. Rarity 2. Victorian. Concern for children. This figure is a copy of Peter Pan from a sculpture by Sir George Frampton in 1912, standing in Kensington Gardens, London. $240-360.

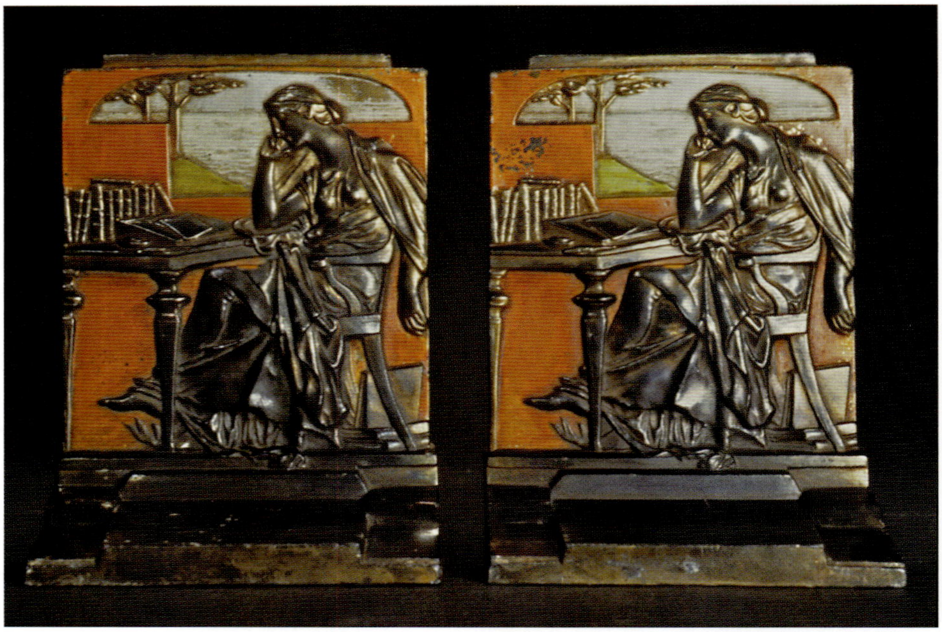

Figure 25. Knowledge. 4.25", gray metal. Inscription: Knowledge, Pompeian Bronze, 1925. Rarity 3. Victorian. $160-240.

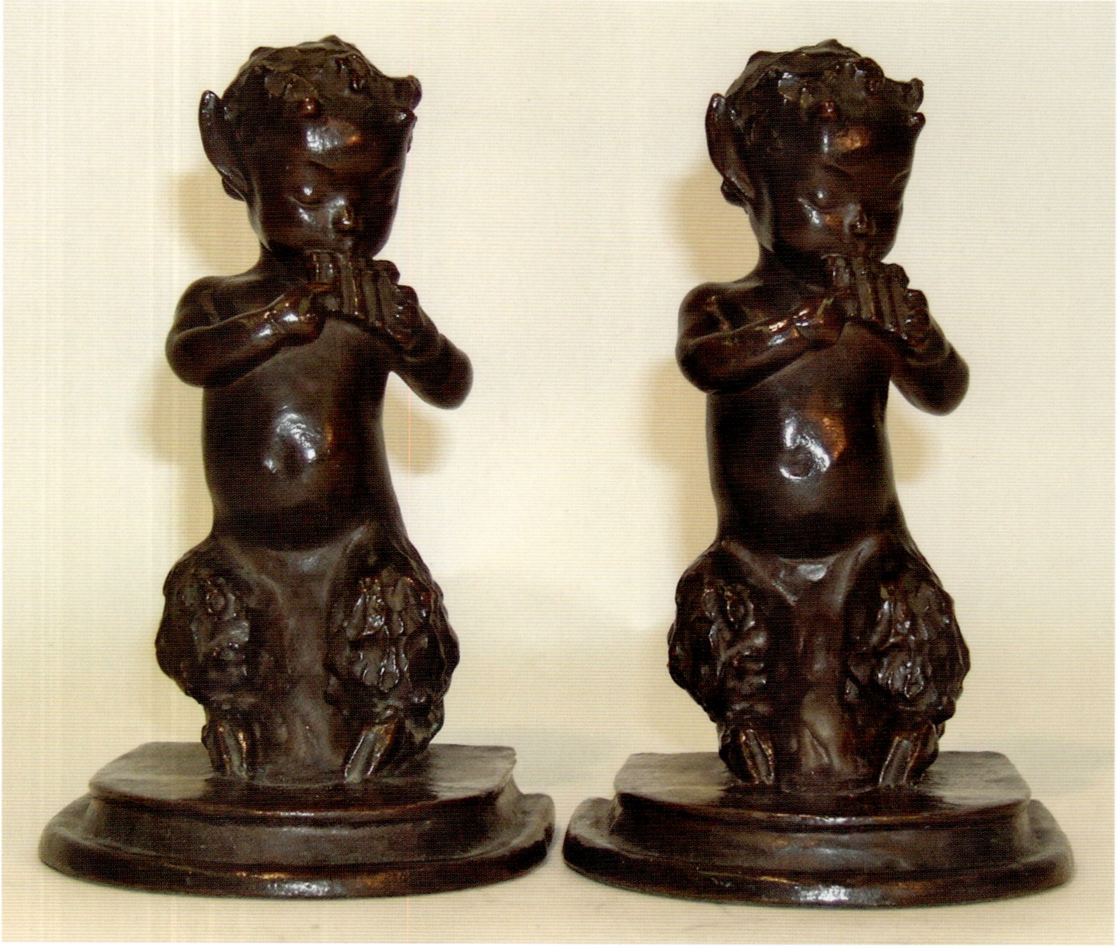

Figure 26. Musical Pan. 6.25", solid Bronze. Inscription: Cast by Griffoul, Newark, N.J., signed by B. Putnam 1914. Rarity 5. Victorian. *By courtesy of Charles DeCosta, from his collection.* $2,000-2,500.

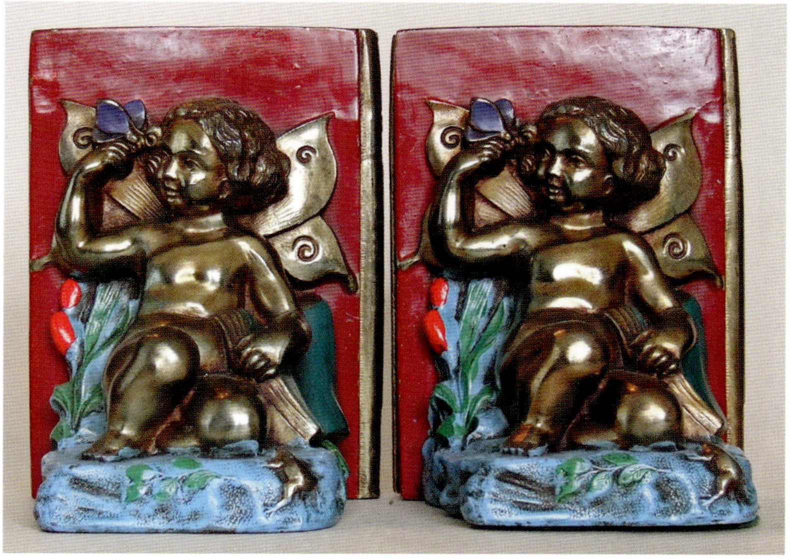

Figure 27. Cherub and Butterfly. 6", gray metal. Inscription: Ronson label. Circa 1925. Rarity 4. Victorian. Italian renaissance revival. More frequent in black. $340-520.

Figure 28. Musician Cherubs. 6.75", bronze. Circa 1916 Rarity 5. Victorian. Italian renaissance revival. These are large, deep bookends. $400-600.

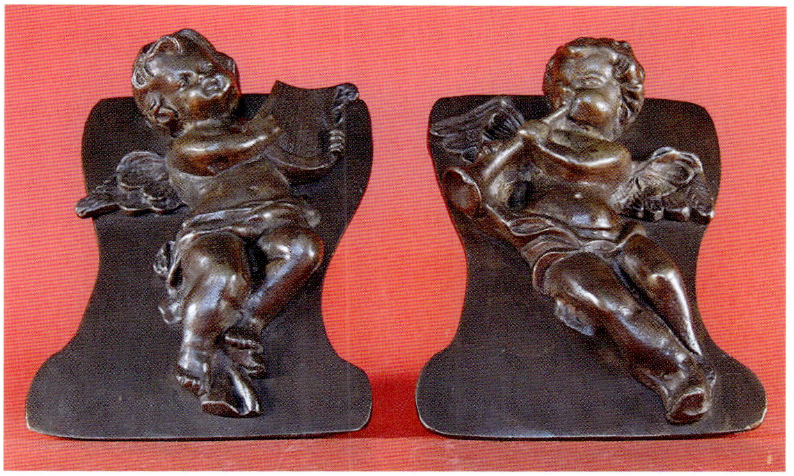

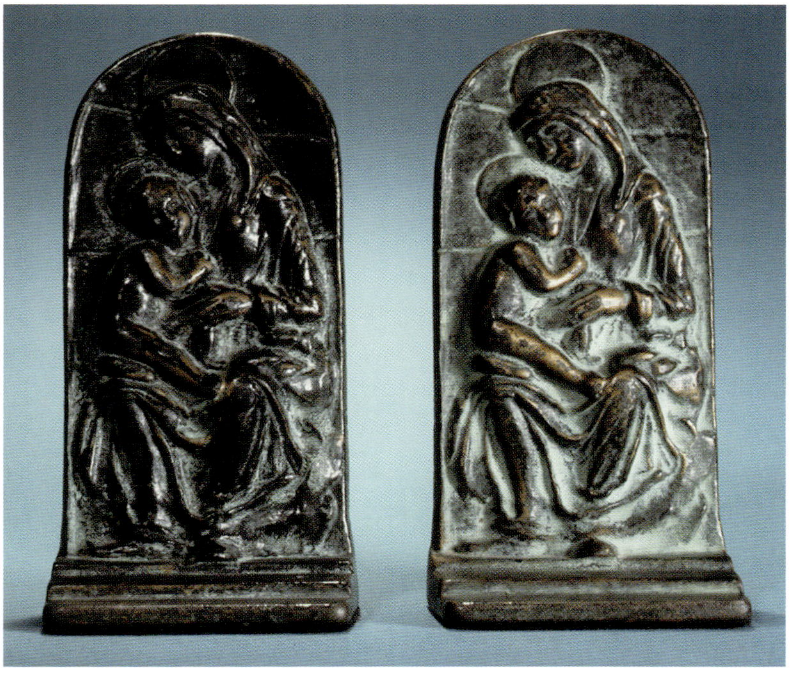

Figure 29. Holy Mother and Child. 4.75", iron. Circa 1920. Rarity 3. Foundry: Snead Ironworks. Victorian. Renaissance revival. These could have been called Medieval revival. $100-150.

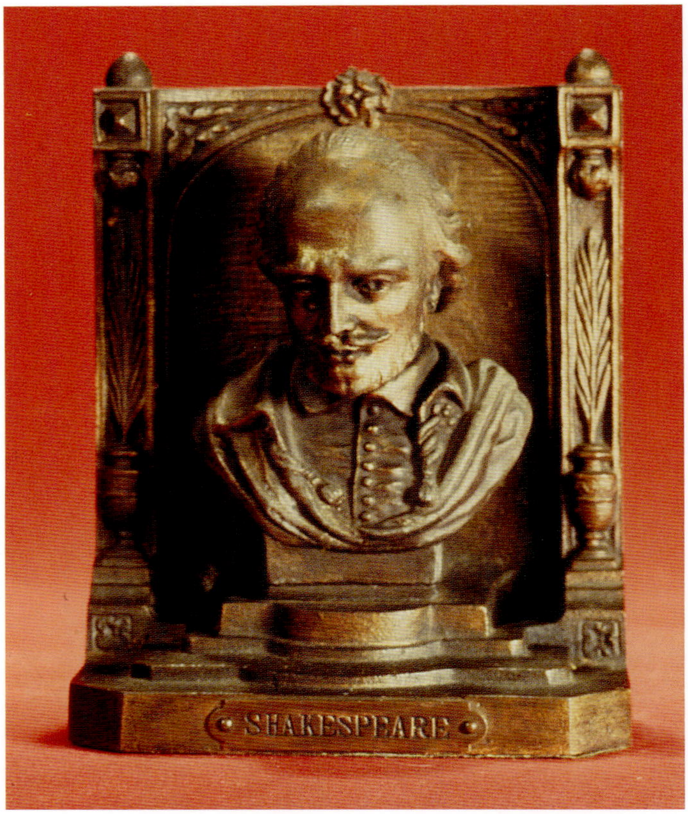

Figure 30. Shakespeare. 4", iron. Inscription: Shop mark of Bradley and Hubbard. Circa 1915. Rarity 3. Elizabethan revival. $160-240.

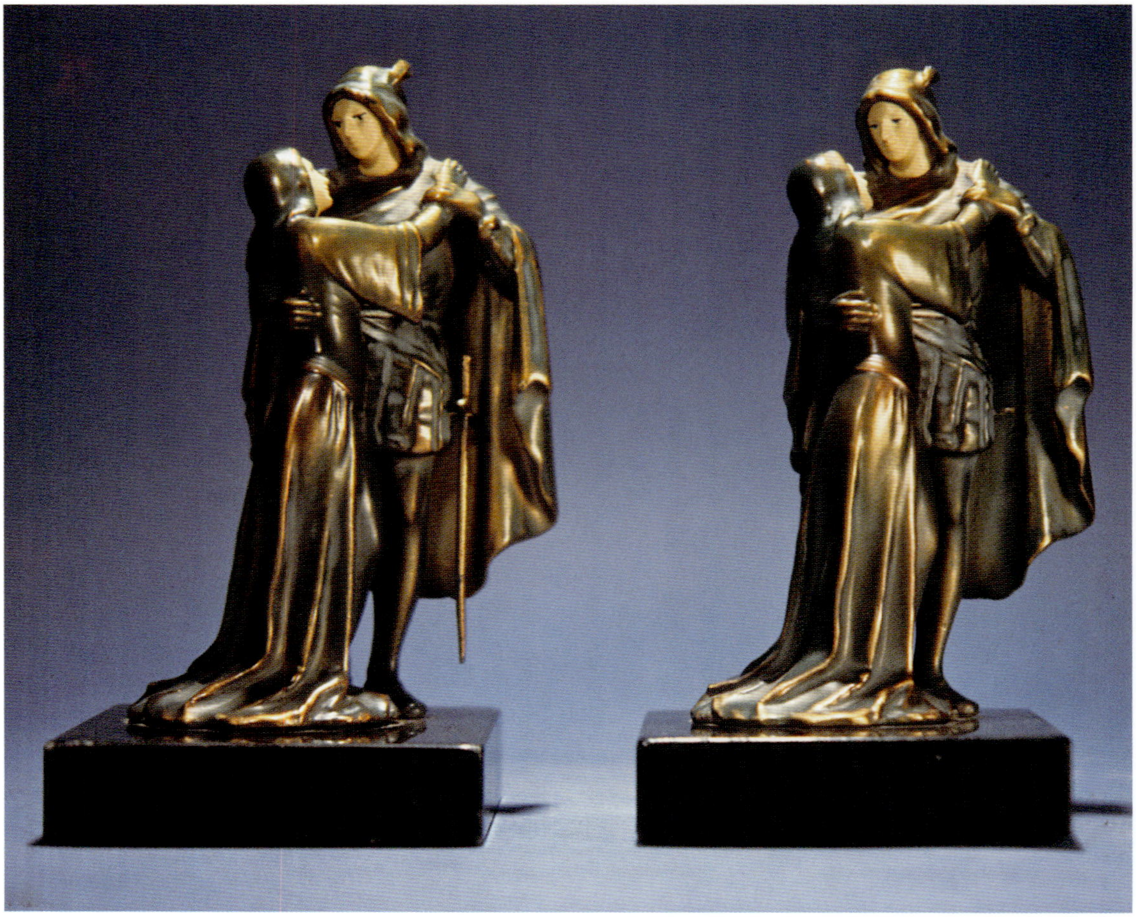

Figure 31. Romeo and Juliet. 7", gray metal, celluloid, Bakelite. Foundry: JB Hirsch. Circa 1920. Rarity 3. Elizabethan revival. $240-360.

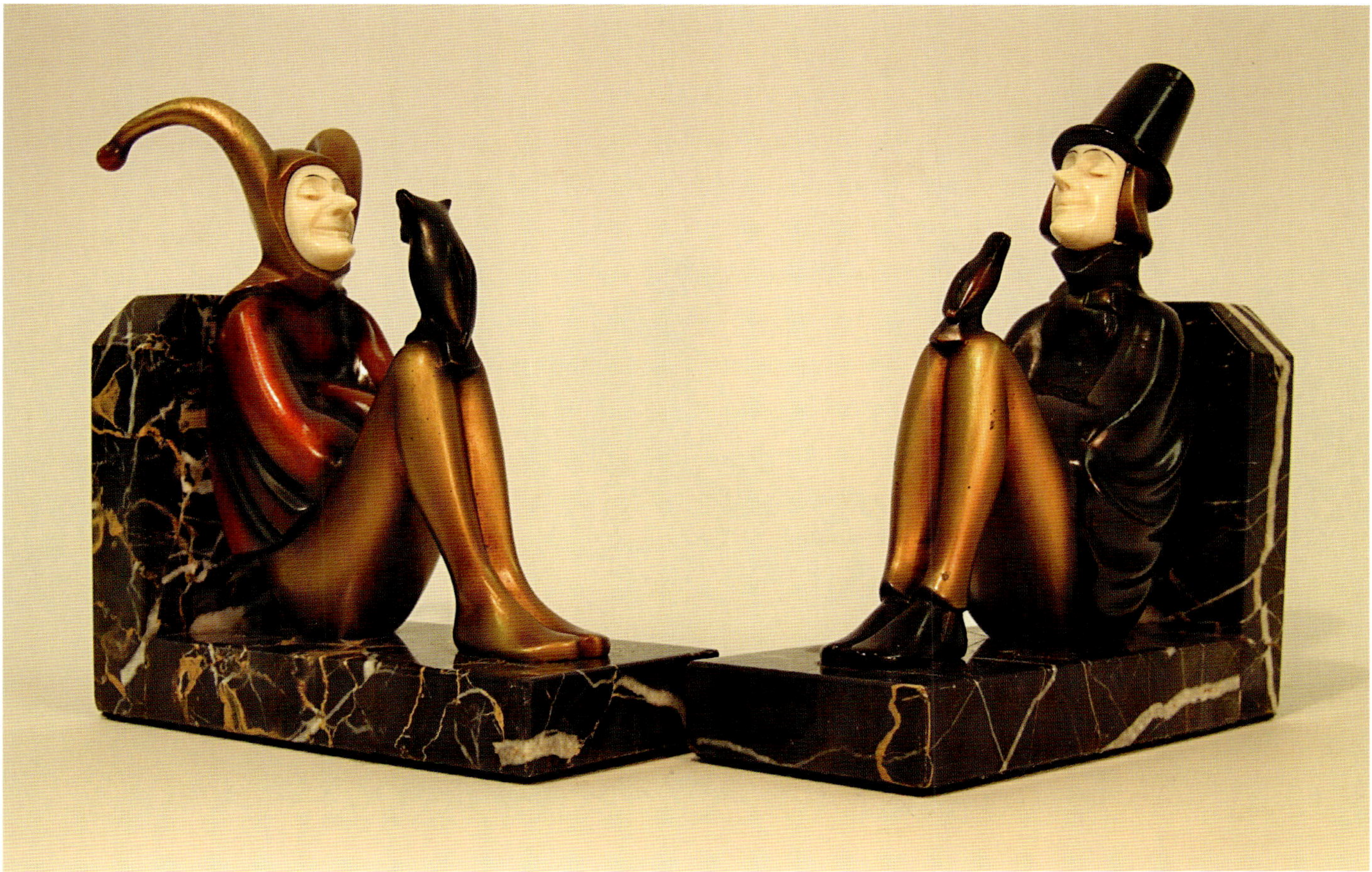

Figure 32. Bird Watchers. 6.5", bronze, ivory, marble. Inscription: Signature of the sculptor-Roland Paris. Circa 1913. Rarity 5. Victorian, Elizabethan revival, Jesters performed in medieval, renaissance and Elizabethan times. *By courtesy of Charles DeCosta, from his collection.* $5,000-6,000.

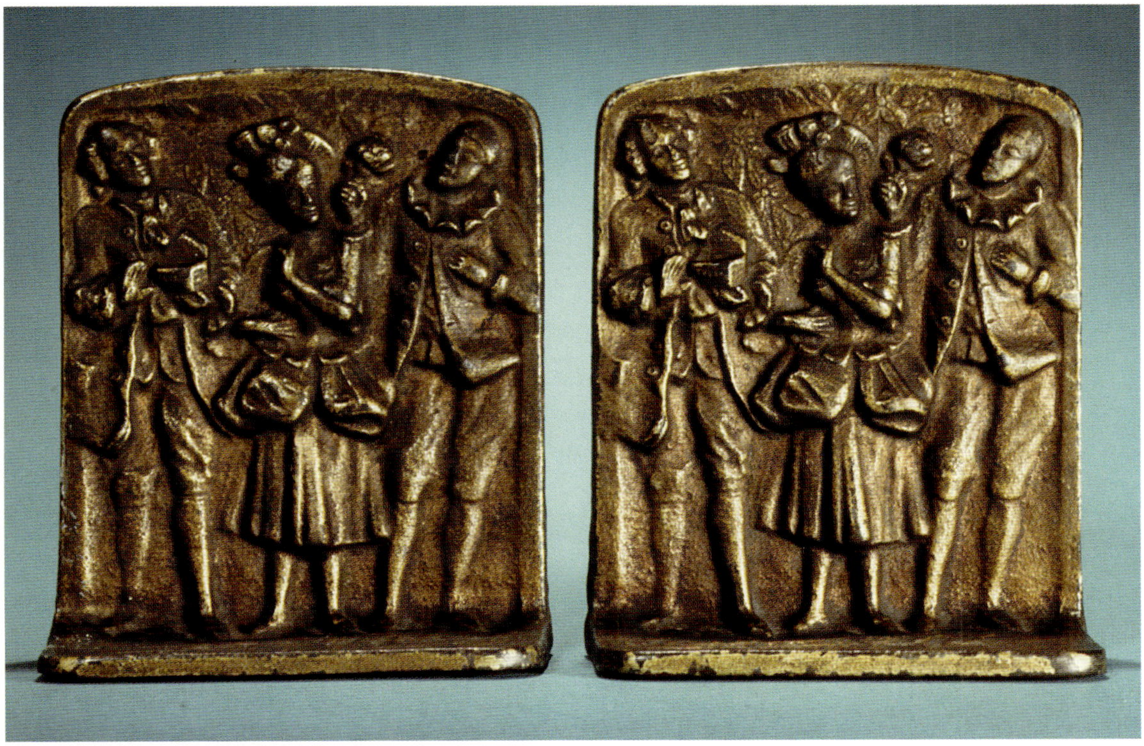

Figure 33. Entertainers. 5", iron. Circa 1916. Rarity 5. Victorian. Elizabethan revival.$64-86.

English Lifestyles and Attitudes Bookends

In addition to revival-style bookends, American foundries produced bookends that illustrated aspects of English Victorian lifestyles and attitudes. For example, Victorians aimed for cozy homes and close-knit domestic life, especially children and family, and these things were very important to them. This gave rise to many bookends that portrayed children and pets. Bookends also showed houses, sometimes just hearths, or even just gates, all symbolizing home and domesticity. Workers yearned for homes in the countryside, away from the grimy city in which they worked, just like American workers, then and now, and bookends showing country homes became popular.

Victorians brought the countryside into their homes in another way too. Naturalistic decoration was favored on all manner of objects. Representations of leaves, flowers, small animals, birds, and seashells embellished many Victorian household objects. So, bookends appeared with background or primary subject materials featuring a variety of plants, animals, and people, frequently in outdoor settings.

Victorians are well known for sentimentality, and this too is reflected in bookends. One sees loving mothers reading to adorable children, and, again, many bookends featuring children alone. Children apparently evoked sentimentality, family, and domesticity, in addition to being cute, so it is not surprising that many bookends show them.

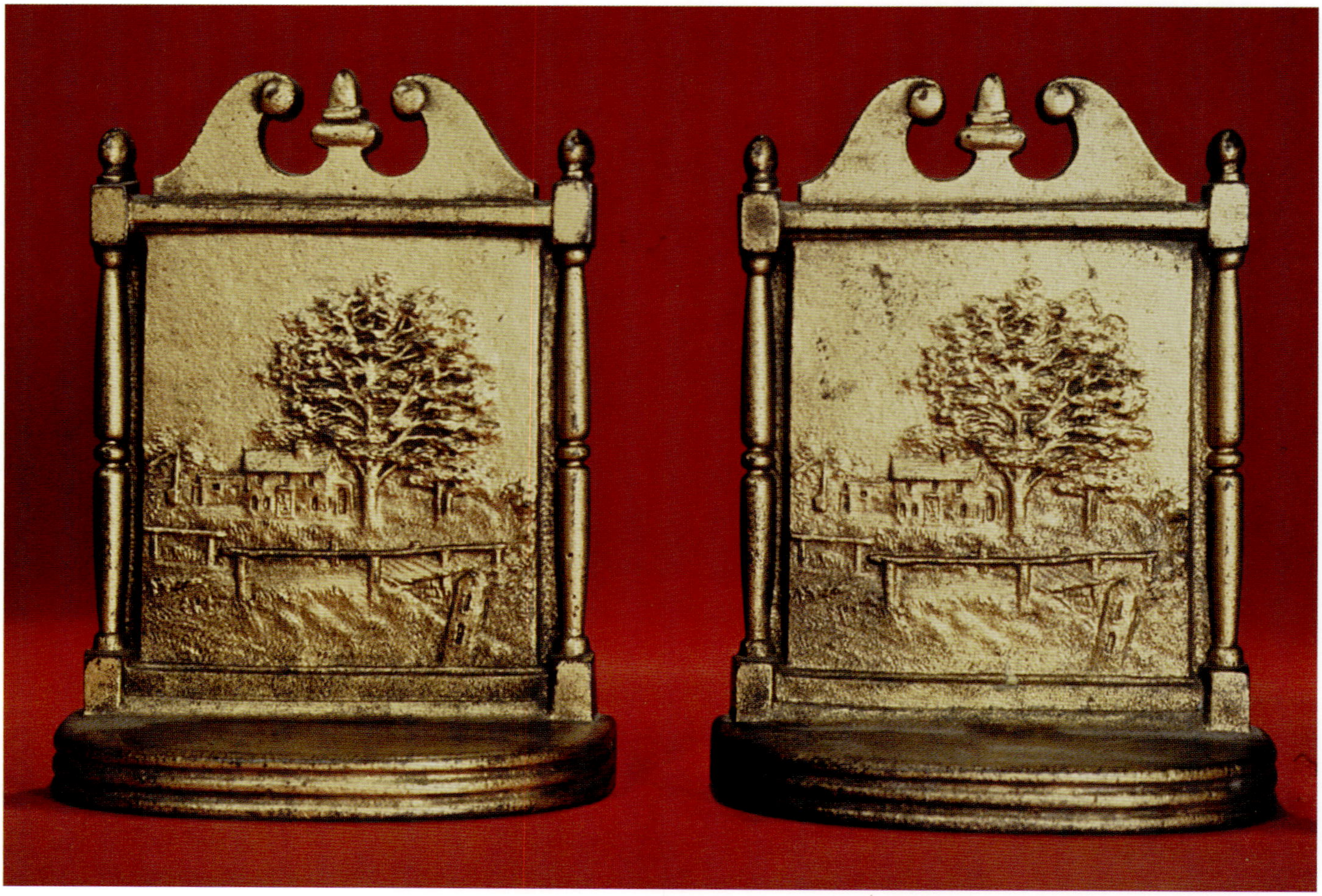

Figure 34. Farm Scene. 5", iron. Circa 1920. Rarity 2. Victorian. $60-90.

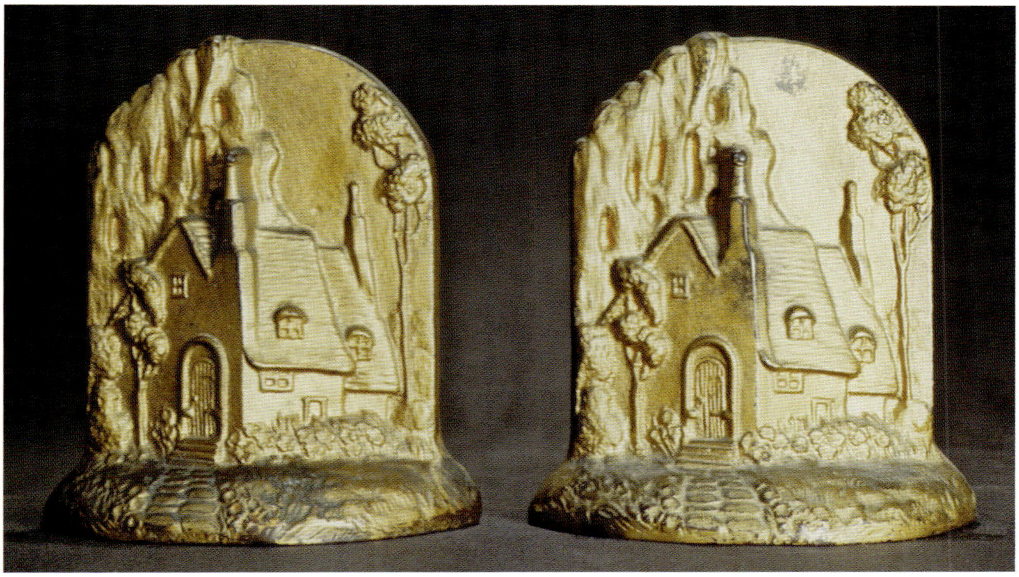

Figure 35. Country Cottage. 5", iron. Foundry : Hubley. Circa 1920. Rarity 4. Victorian. $60-90.

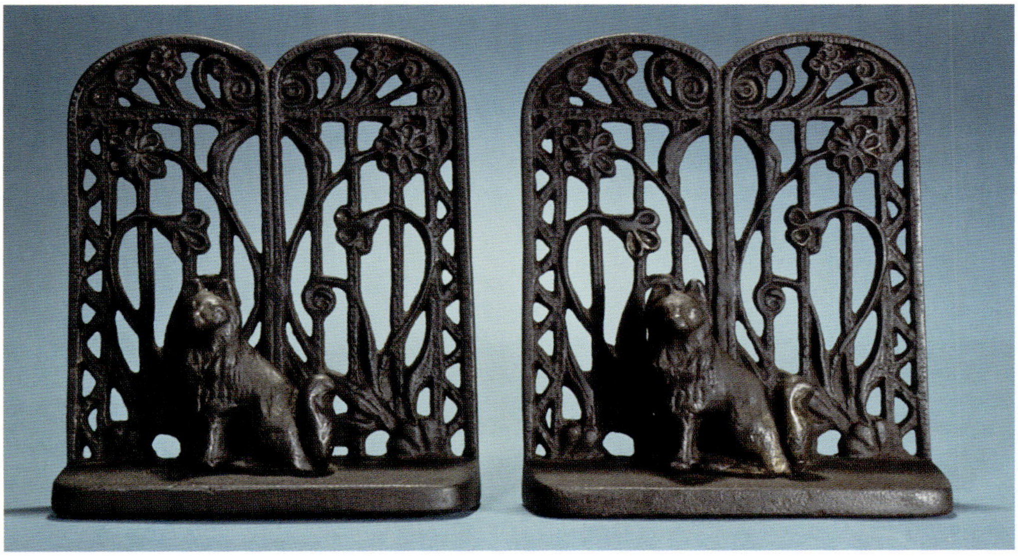

Figure 36. Dog at Gate. 6", iron. Inscription: C co. Foundry: Creation Company. Circa 1920. Rarity 5. Victorian. $100-150.

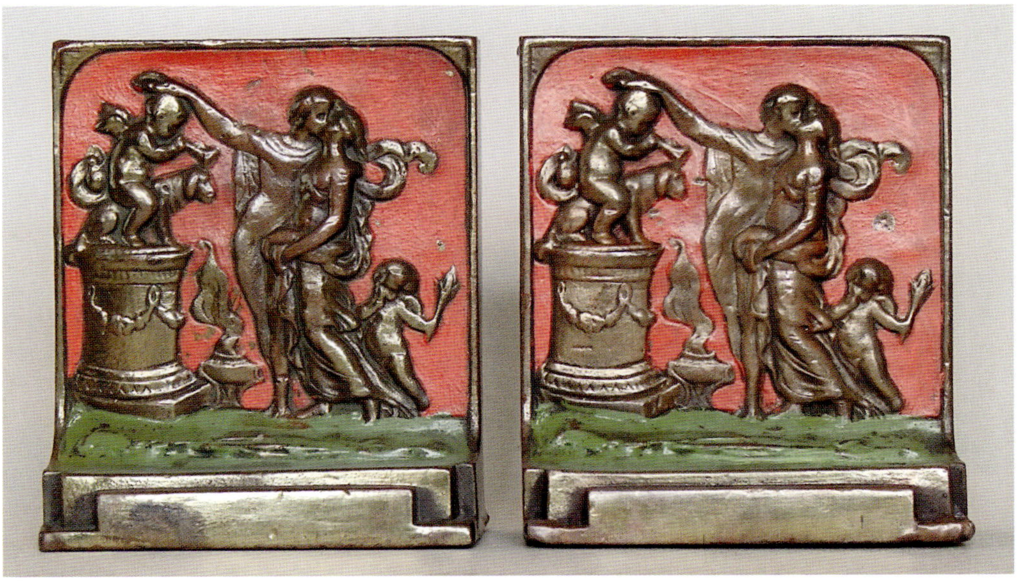

Figure 37. Altar of Love. 5.5", gray metal. Inscription: Altar of Love, Pompeian Bronze Co. Circa 1925. Rarity 2. Victorian. A pinnacle of domesticity and sentimentality. A couple vows enduring love before a mystic flame while the loyal family dog watches and cherubim represent angels on the scene. $160-240.

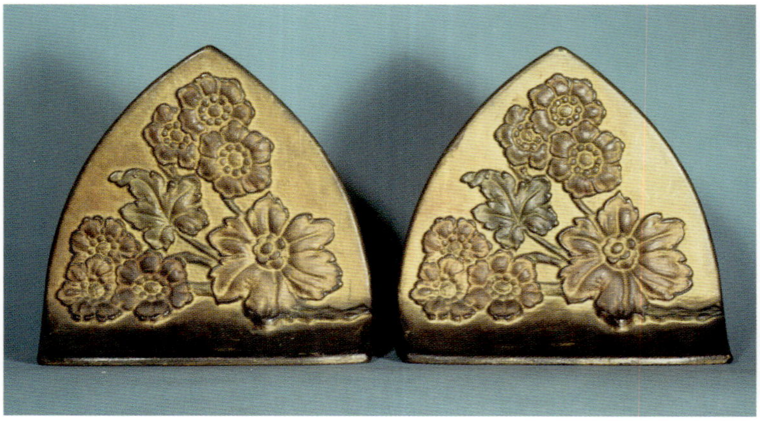

Figure 38. Flowers. 9", iron. Inscription: Albany, N.Y., 1922. Rarity 3. Victorian. $80-120.

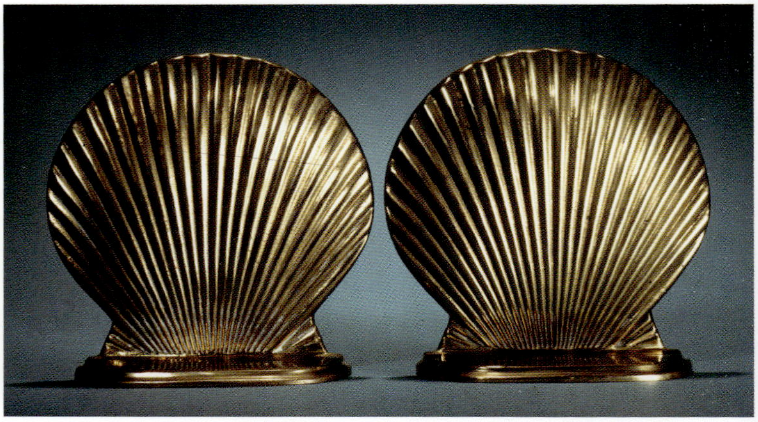

Figure 39. Shell. 5", brass. Circa 1980. Rarity 3. Victorian. $20-30.

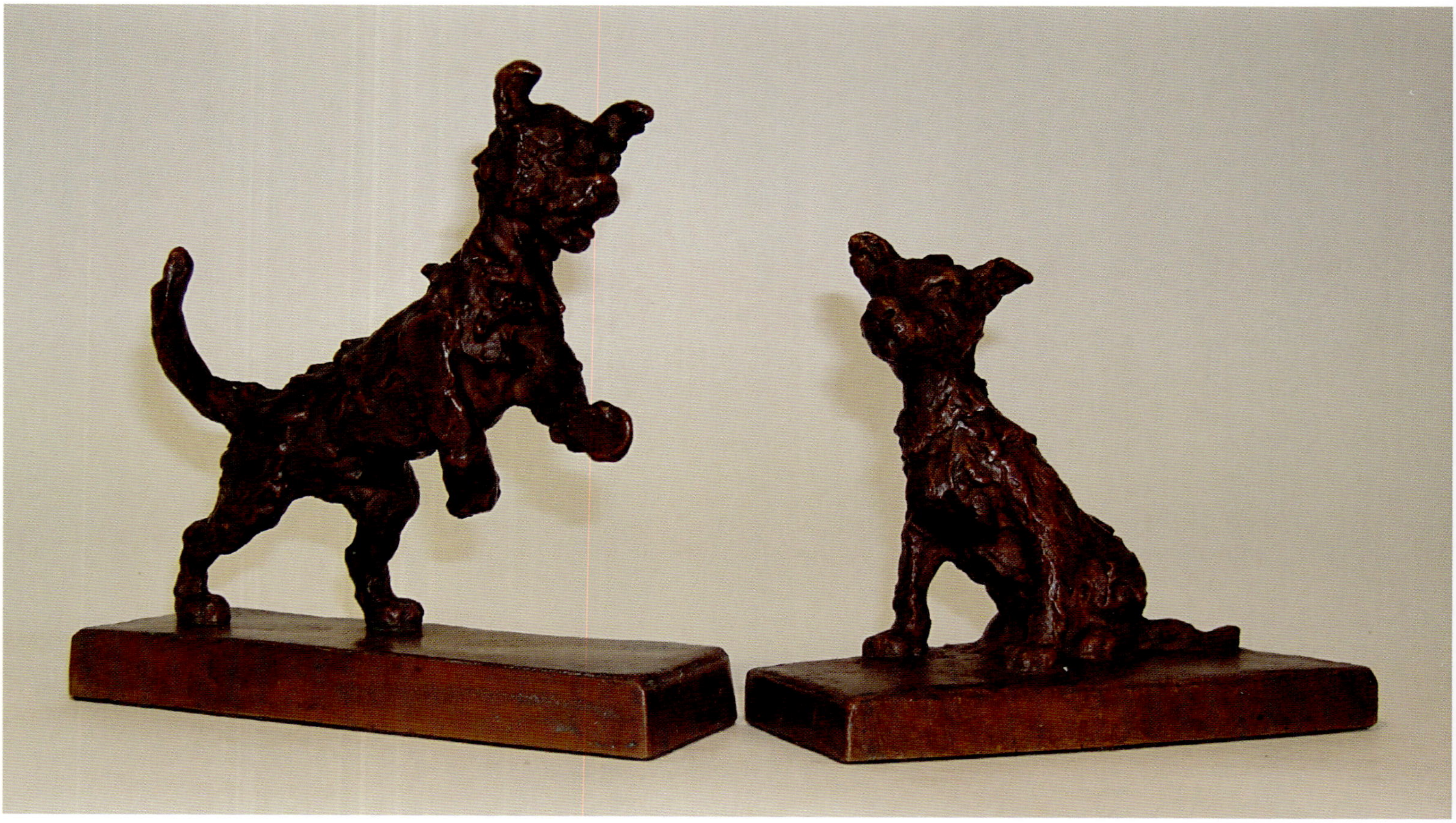

Figure 40. Playful Terriers. Solid bronze. Inscription: Kunst Foundry N.J., signed E.B. Parsons. Circa 1914. Rarity 5. Victorian. *By courtesy of Charles DeCosta, from his collection.* $2,000-2,500.

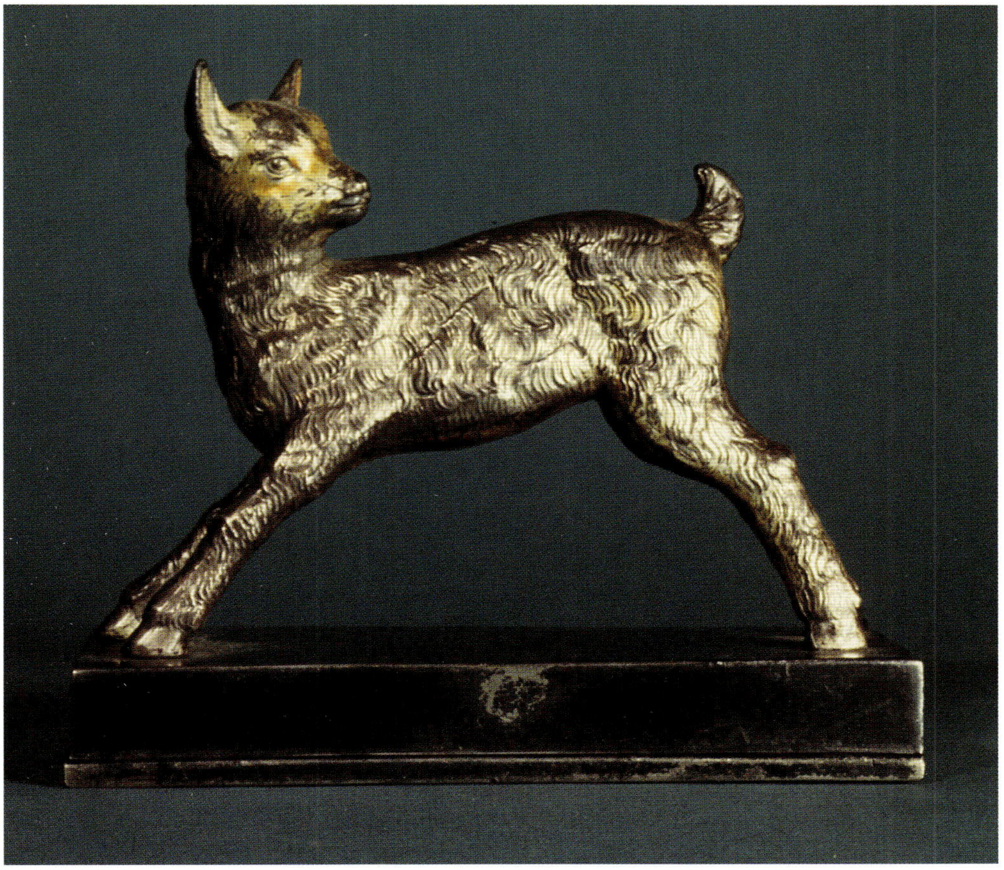

Figure 41. Goat. 5", bronze plating over gray metal. Inscription: Shop mark of Jennings Brothers. Circa 1928. Rarity 4. $100-150.

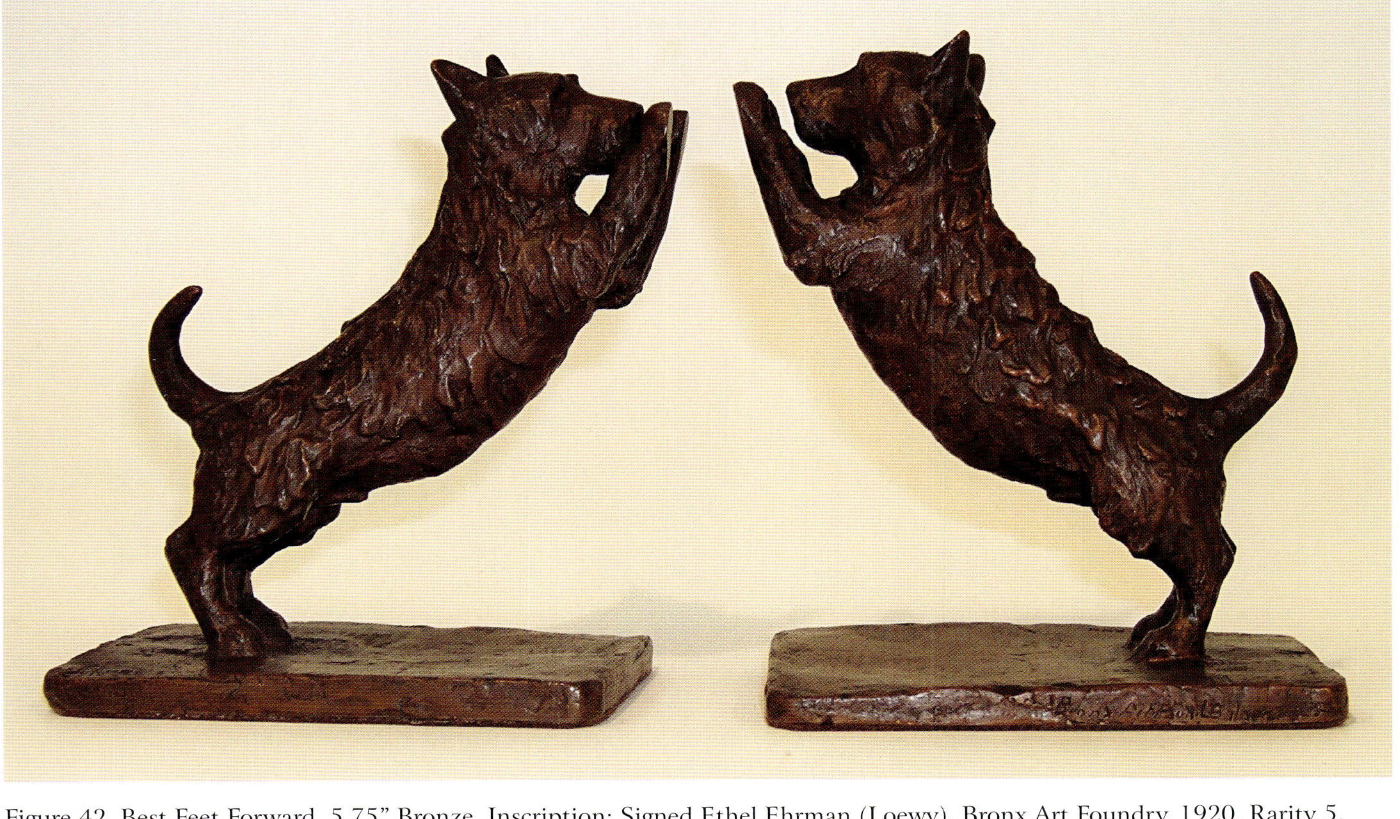

Figure 42. Best Feet Forward. 5.75" Bronze. Inscription: Signed Ethel Ehrman (Loewy), Bronx Art Foundry, 1920. Rarity 5. Victorian. *By courtesy of Charles DeCosta, from his collection.* $1,800-2000.

Figure 43. Reading a Story. 5.75", bronze plating on gray metal. Inscription: Shop mark of Jennings Brothers, 1565. Circa 1920. Rarity 3. Victorian. $120-180.

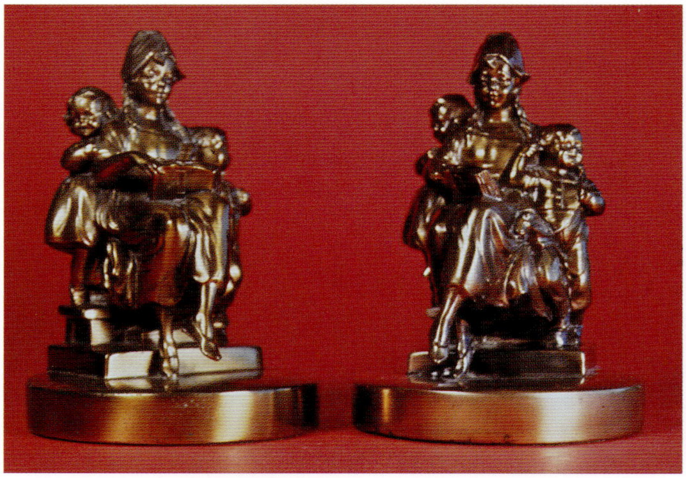

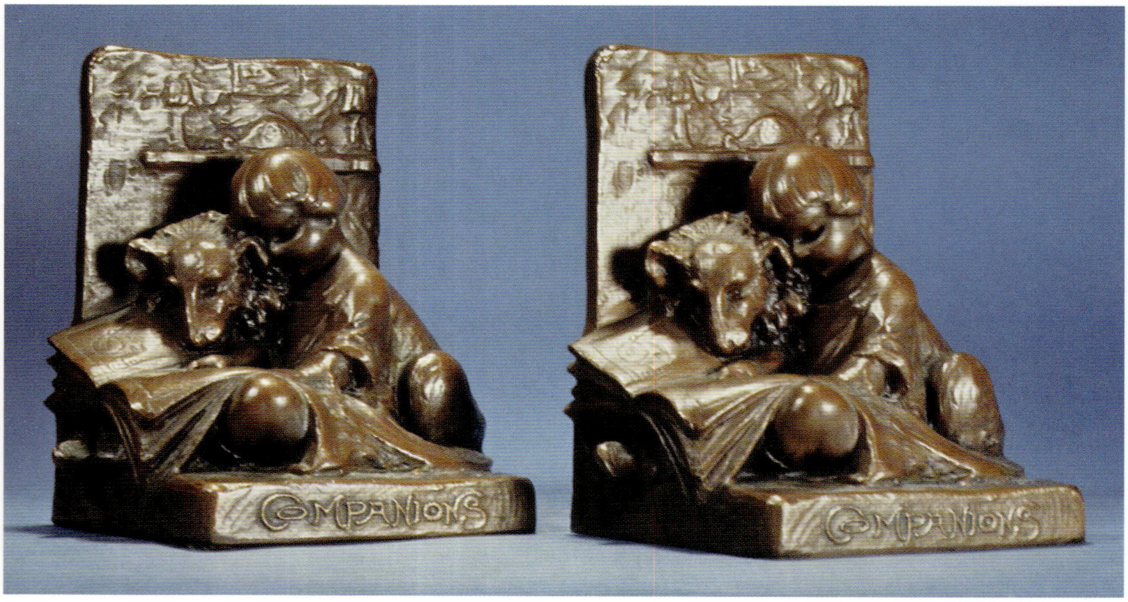

Figure 44. Companions. 7", bronze plating on gray metal. Inscription: Shop mark of WB. Circa 1920. Rarity 3. Victorian. $140-210.

Figure 45. Child Reading. 6.5", gray metal. Inscription: Frankart Inc. Circa 1923. Rarity 4. Victorian. $240-360.

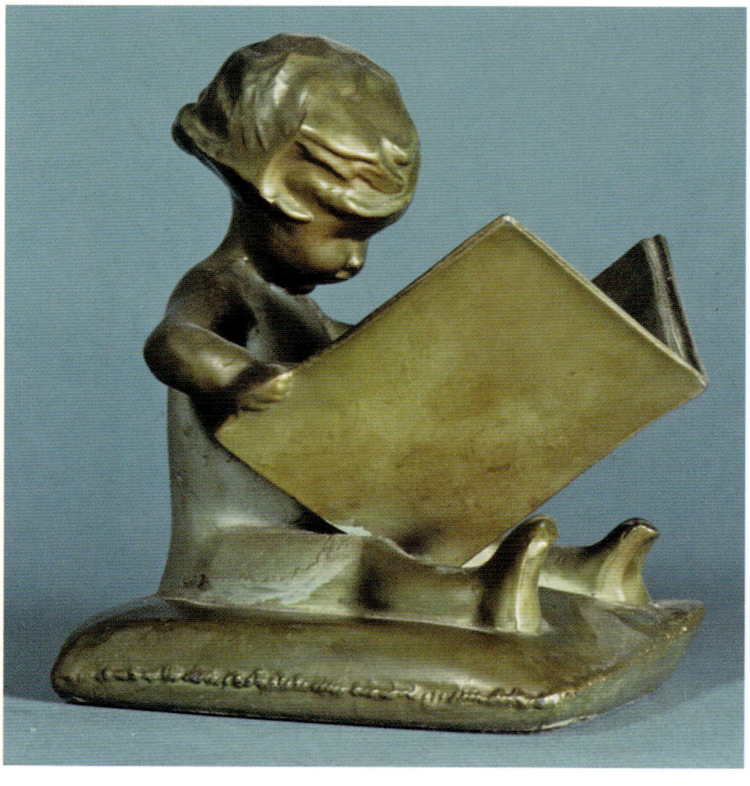

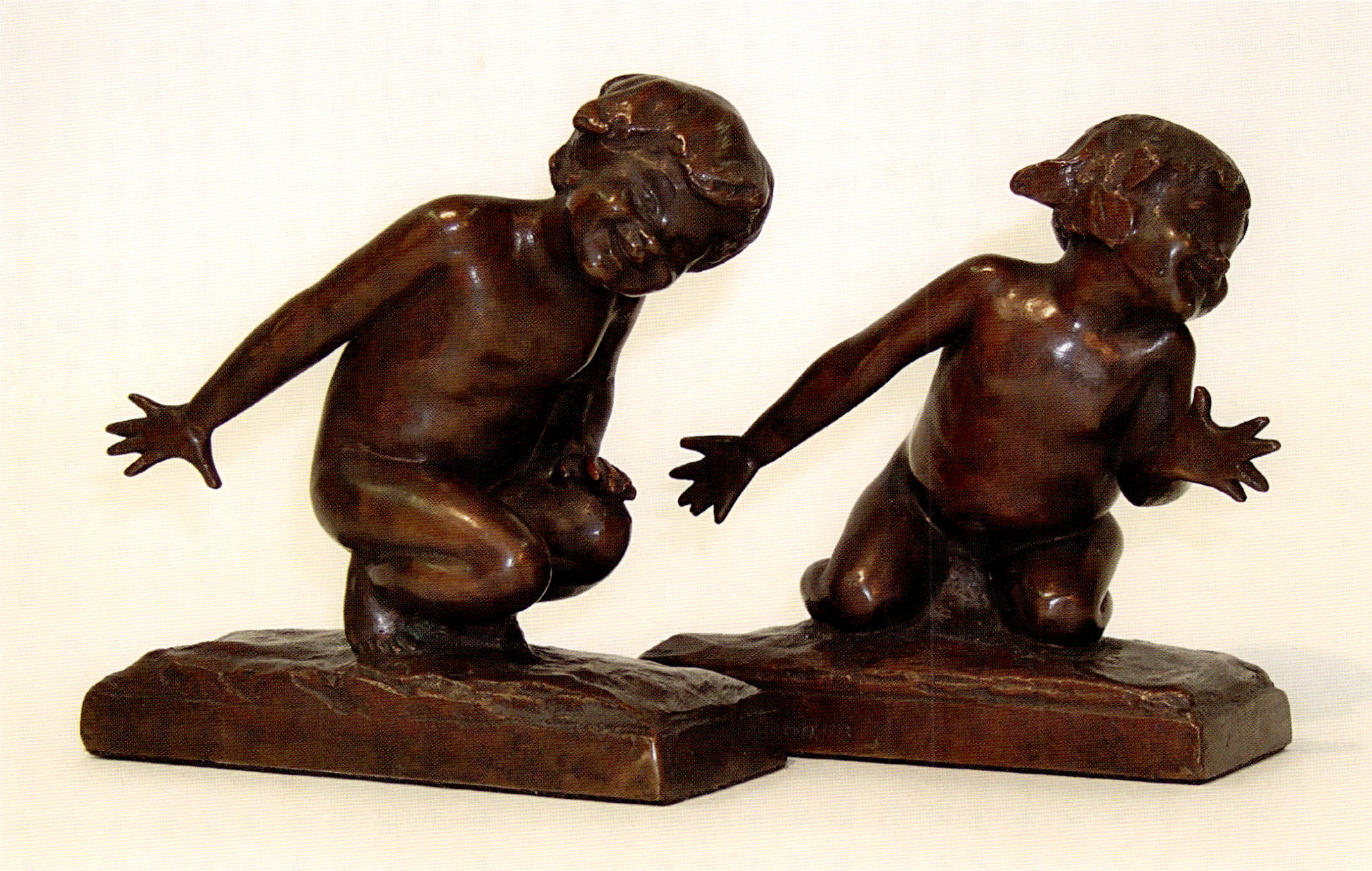

Figure 46. Hide and Seek. 6.5", solid bronze. Inscription: Gorham Co. Founders, signed E. B. Parsons, 1913. Rarity 5. Victorian. *By courtesy of Charles DeCosta, from his collection.* $1,800-2,000.

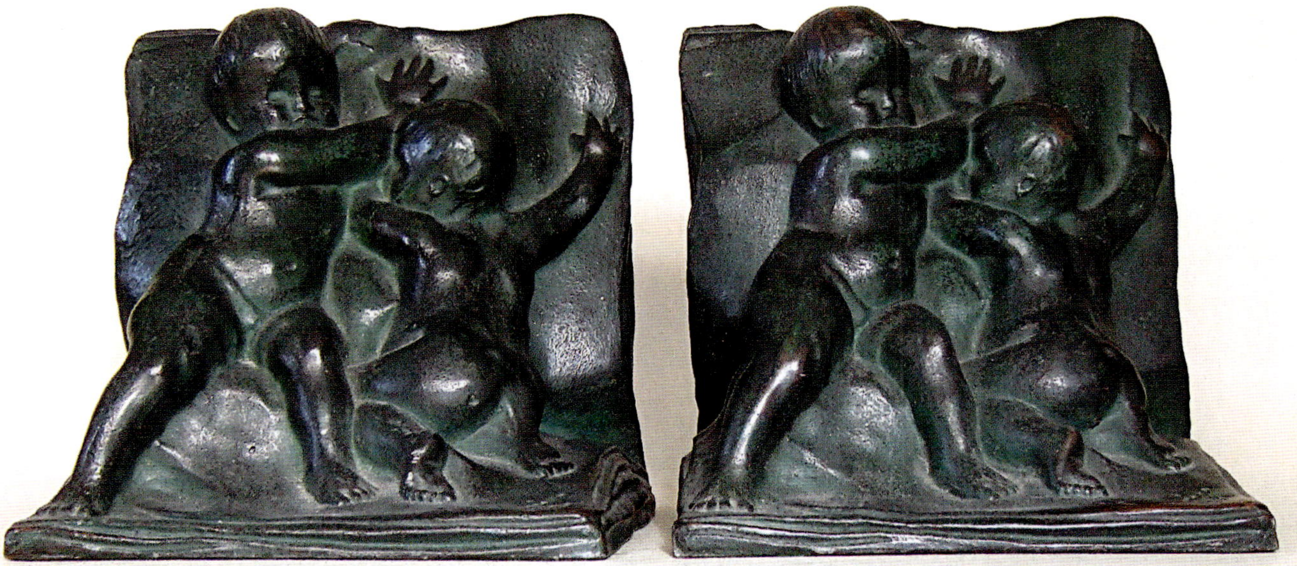

Figure 47. Infants on Book. 5", bronze plating on gray metal. Inscription: NAL Co. Signed by Henri Crenier, 1903. Rarity 5. Victorian. These are heavy bookends, 9 lbs./pair. Copies, undated and unsigned by Crenier, were issued by several foundries and are seen regularly. $960-1,440.

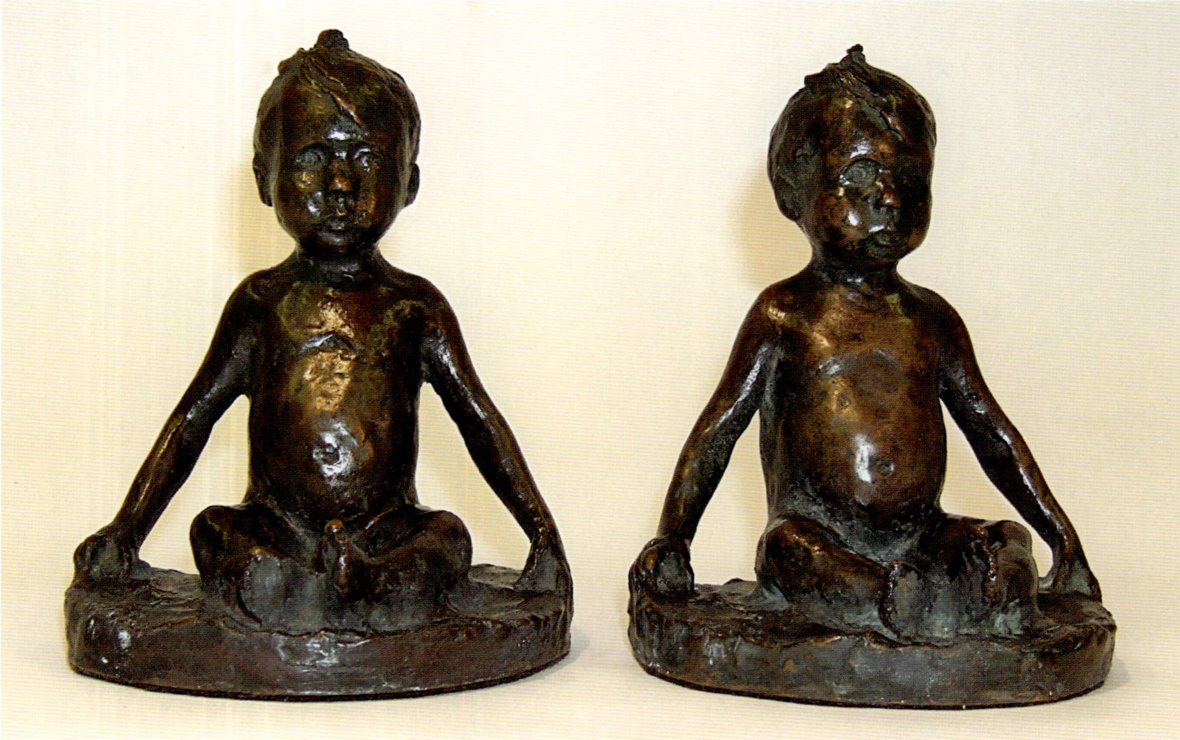

Figure 48. First Bath. 6", bronze. Inscription: Roman Bronze Works. Circa 1915. Rarity 5. Victorian. *By courtesy of Charles DeCosta, from his collection.* $1,800-2,000.

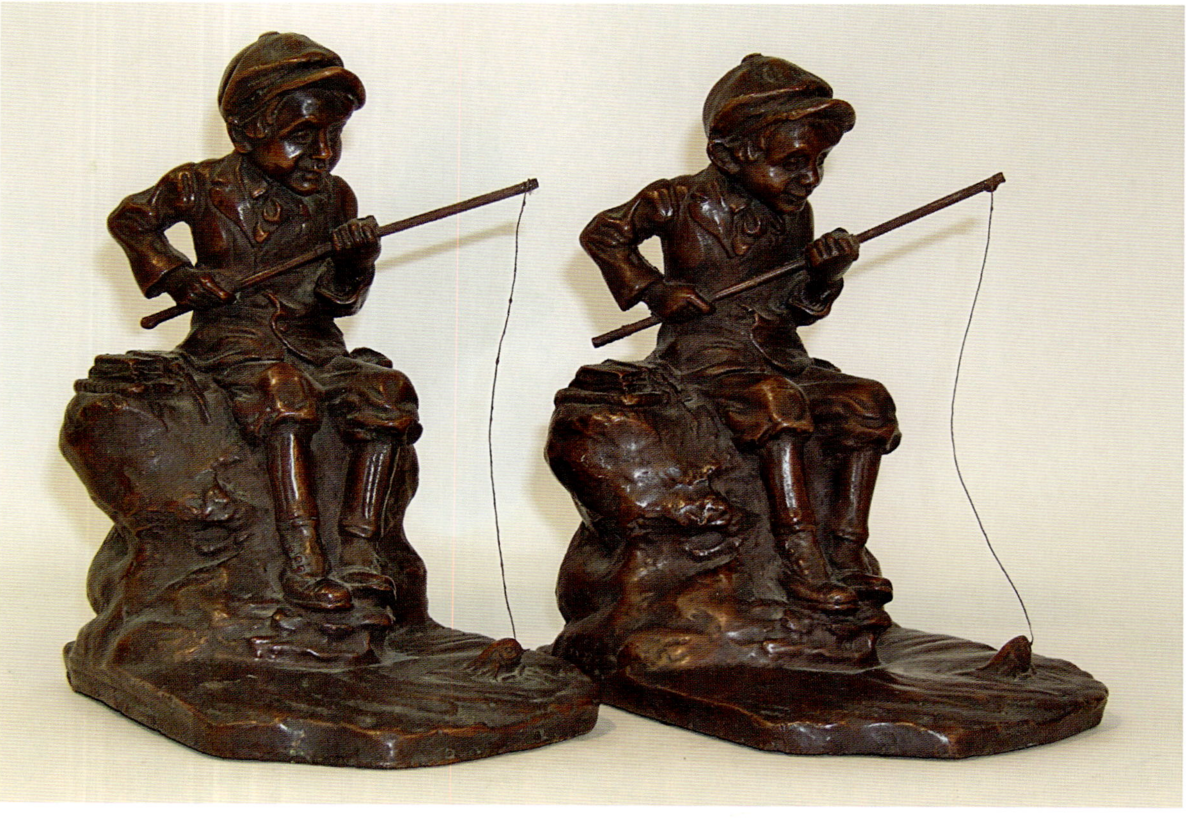

Figure 49. Boy Fishing. 8.75", electroformed bronze. Inscription: KBW (Kathodian Bronze Works). Circa 1910. Rarity 5. Victorian. *By courtesy of Charles DeCosta, from his collection.* $1,500-1,800.

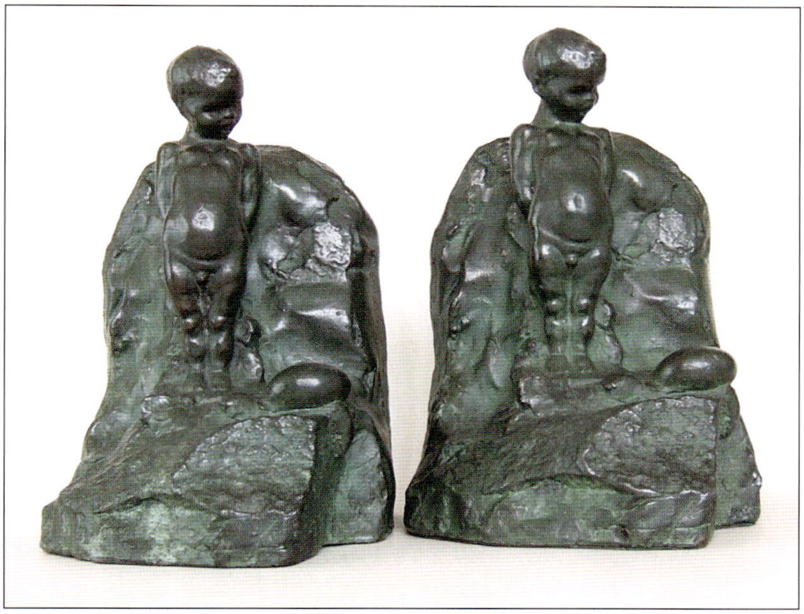

Figure 50. Boy and Snail. 8", electroformed bronze. Inscription Ghiglia. Foundry: Attrib. Paul Mori. sculptor Ghiglia. Circa 1915. Rarity 5. Victorian, Children, animals, outdoors. $400-600.

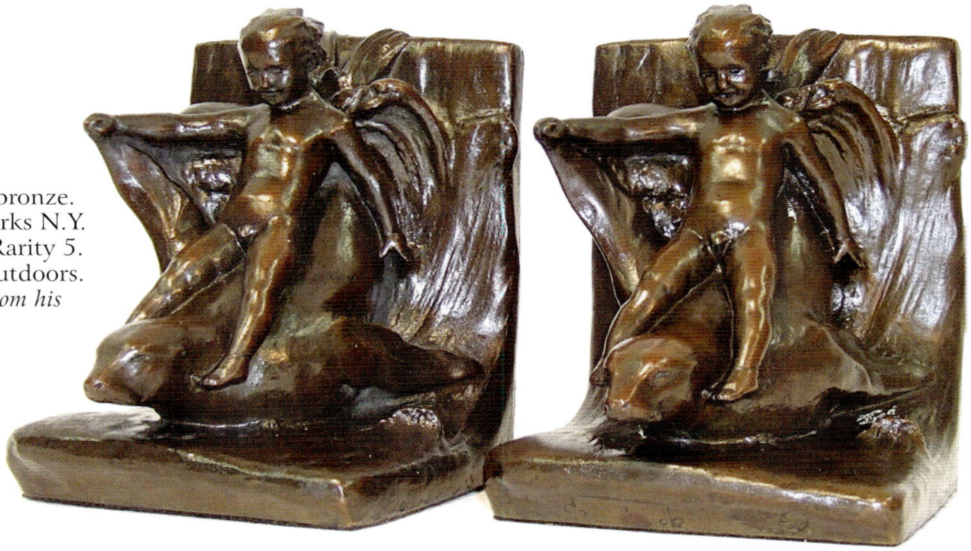

Figure 51. Boy on Seal. 6.25", bronze. Inscription: Roman Bronze Works N.Y. signed L Maraffi. Circa 1910. Rarity 5. Victorian. Children, animals, outdoors. *By courtesy of Charles DeCosta, from his collection.* $2,500-3,000.

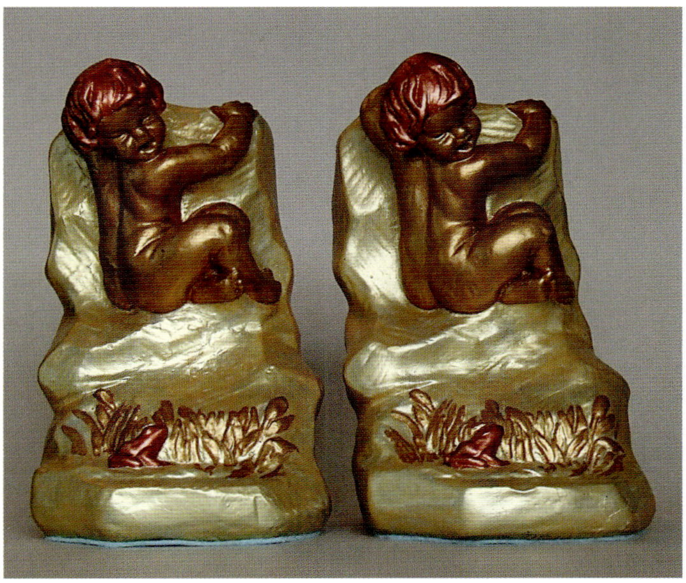

Figure 52. Infant and Frog. 7.5", electroformed bronze. Inscription: Armor Bronze shop mark, Morani signature. Circa 1914. Rarity 3. Victorian. Children, animals, outdoors. $216-324.

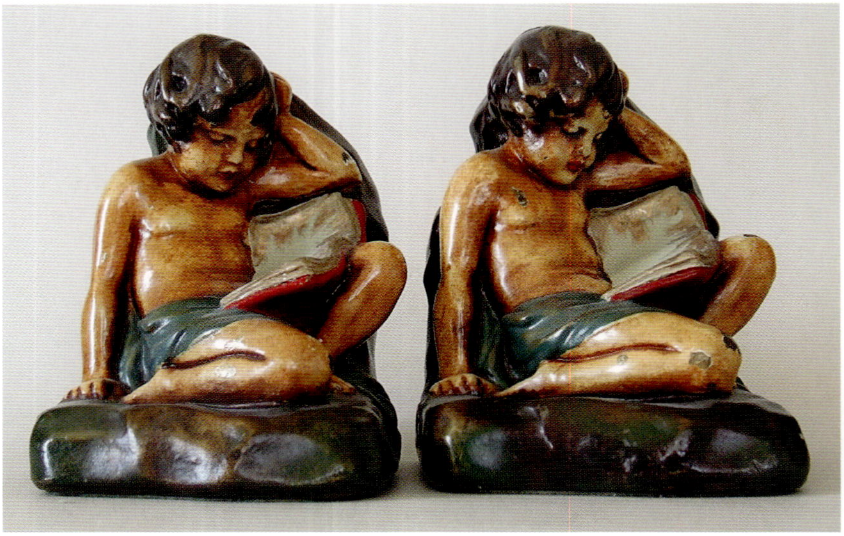

Figure 53. Boy & Book. 6.25", electroformed bronze. Inscription: Armor Bronze shop mark, Morani signature. Circa 1914. Rarity 2. Victorian. Children, animals, outdoors. $200-300.

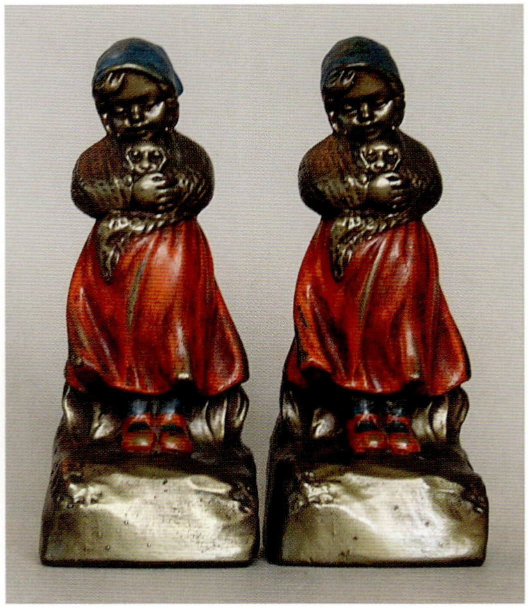

Figure 54. Girl and Puppy 6", electroformed bronze. Inscription: Pompeian Bronze company label. Circa 1915. Rarity 2. Victorian. Children and animals. $200-300.

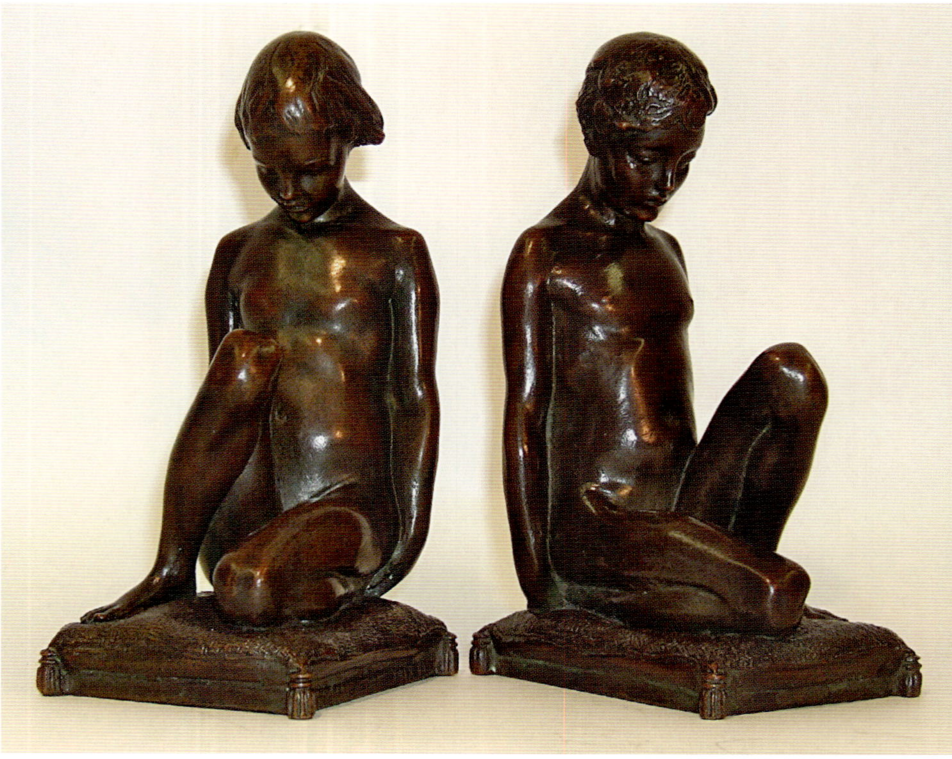

Figure 55. Boy and Girl. 8.25", hollow bronze. Inscription: Roman Bronze Works N.Y., Karl H. Gruppe (sculptor) 1918. Rarity 5. Victorian. Only a few copies are thought to exist. *By the courtesy of Charles DeCosta, from his collection.* Victorian. $9,000-10,000.

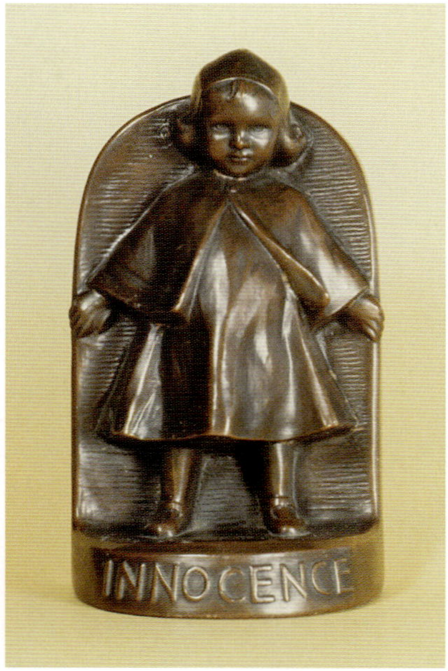

Figure 56. Innocence. 7", bronze plating on gray metal. Inscription: Innocence, Shop mark of Jennings Brothers, 1702. Circa 1916. Rarity 3. Victorian. $200-300.

Dante and his unattainable soul mate Beatrice (see Figure 57) are found on bookends from many different foundries, and these recall profound Victorian sentiment. The story of Dante and Beatrice is told in Elbert Hubbard's book, *Little Journeys*:

> Dante Alighieri (1265-1321) spent his youth in the city of Florence in the early years of the Italian Renaissance. He was a student, a troubadour, a political activist, and, above all a distinguished writer and poet who can be considered the father of modern literature.
>
> Dante met Beatrice at a party when they were both nine years old, and he was so transfixed by her presence that he underwent a mystical experience and loved her thereafter for the remainder of his life. They met face to face only one more time, very briefly, when they were both eighteen, and she was already married, but Dante remained true to her memory afterwards. He married later and raised a family, but always considered Beatrice to be the bride of his soul. He worshiped her publicly and immortalized her in poetry, but she never responded to him. He was fated to love her in absentia, so to speak, until he died, when he believed they would be joined in heaven.
>
> At the turn of the century, Dante was considered a tragic figure. His love for Beatrice transcended sex and worldly considerations, and was therefore pure. The fact that his love was unrequited was considered all the more admirable. Today, pure love gets no respect, as we know.

Another example of Victorian sentimentality is illustrated by bookends devoted to the Lion of Lucerne (see Figure 58). The actual lion is a colossal figure in the side of a sandstone cliff in Lucerne, Switzerland. It is a tribute to 760 slain Swiss guards, who were hired to protect King Louis XIV of France during the French Revolution. In Victorian times, death in the line of duty was considered a noble outcome.

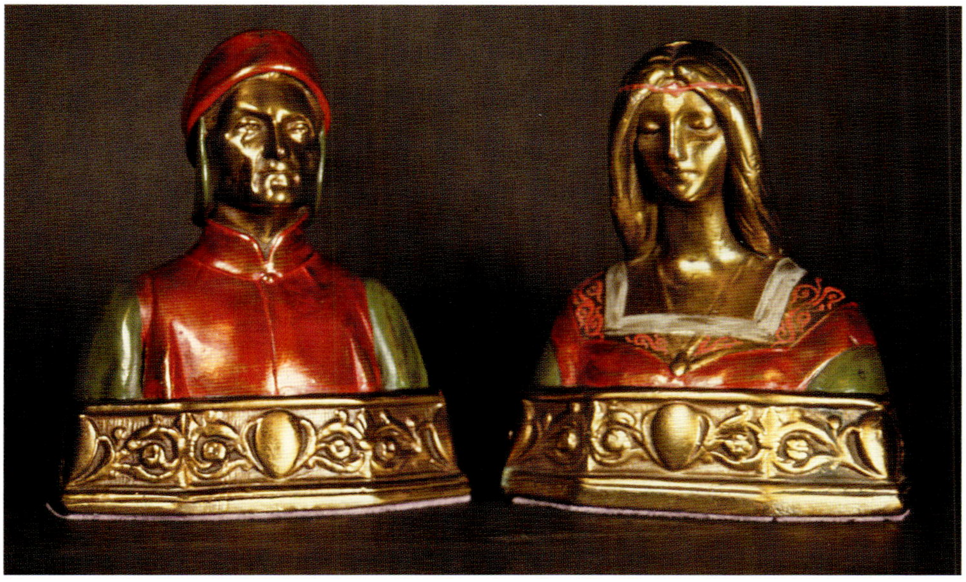

Figure 57. Dante and Beatrice. 7", electroformed bronze. Inscription: Shop mark of Armor Bronze. Circa 1920. Rarity 3. Victorian. Dante and Beatrice bookends, or Dante alone, have been issued by many foundries in many colors. $200-300.

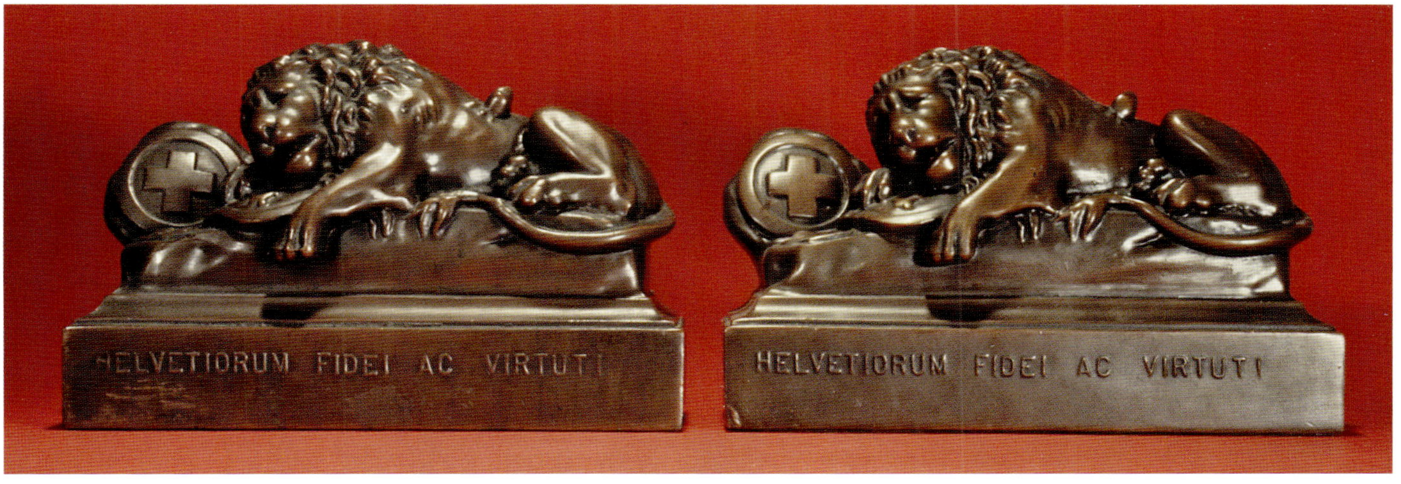

Figure 58. The Lion of Lucerne. 6", bronze plating over gray metal. Inscription: Shop mark of Jennings Brothers,1258. Circa 1925. Rarity 2. Victorian. $160-240.

Figure 59. A Girl Scout, 6.25", iron. Inscription: A Girl Scout. Circa 1927. Rarity 3. Victorian. Portraiture, sentimentality. $200-300.

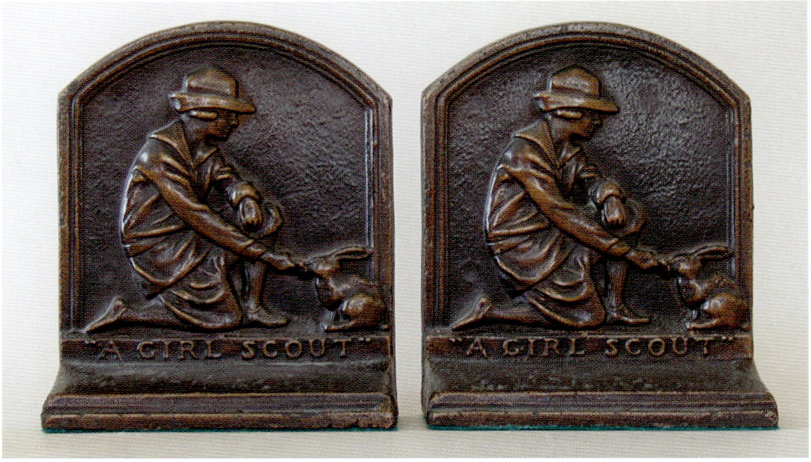

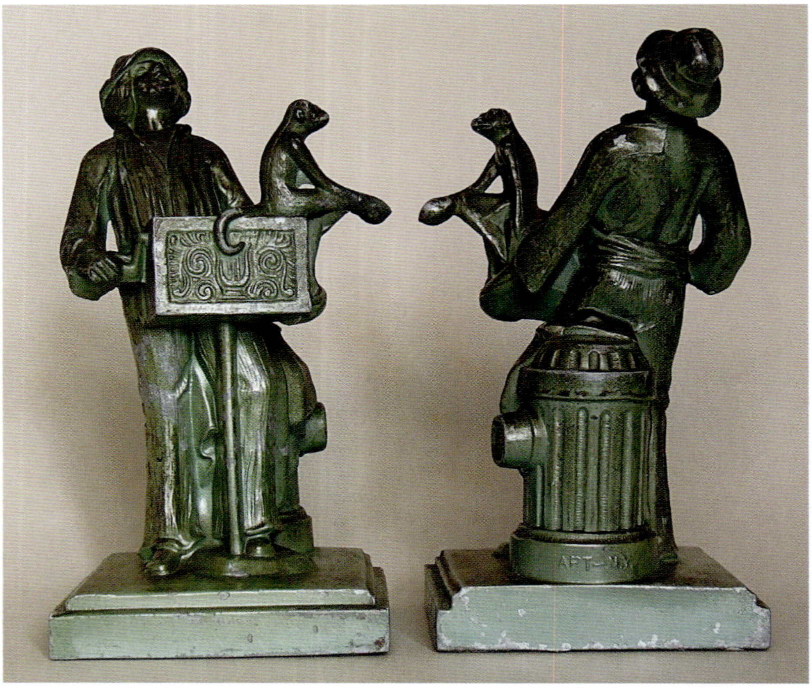

Figure 60. Organ Grinder. 7.5", gray metal. Circa 1900. Rarity 5. Victorian style. Sentimentality. $500-750.

Figure 61. Forest Nymph and Frog. 7.5", electroformed bronze. Inscription: Armor Bronze shop mark, artist Morani signature. 1914. Rarity 3. Victorian. Nude female desexed by showing her as a classical forest nymph. $275-410.

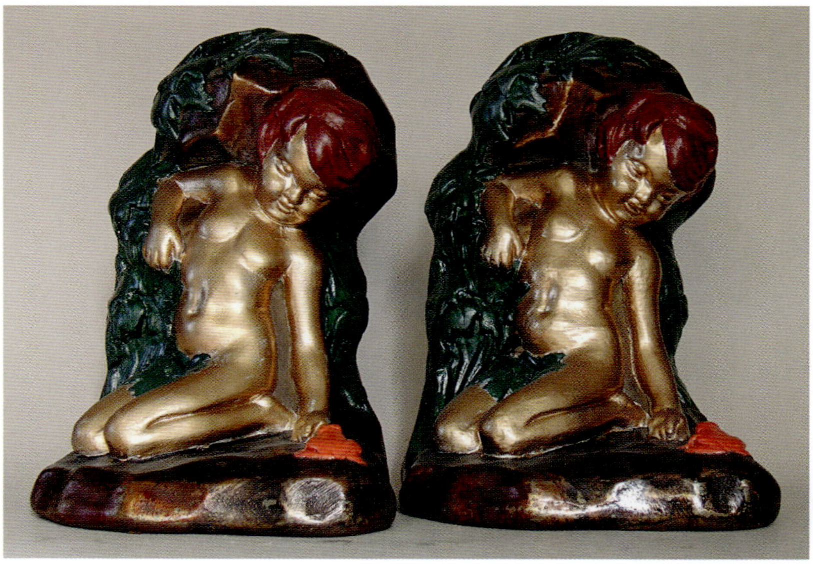

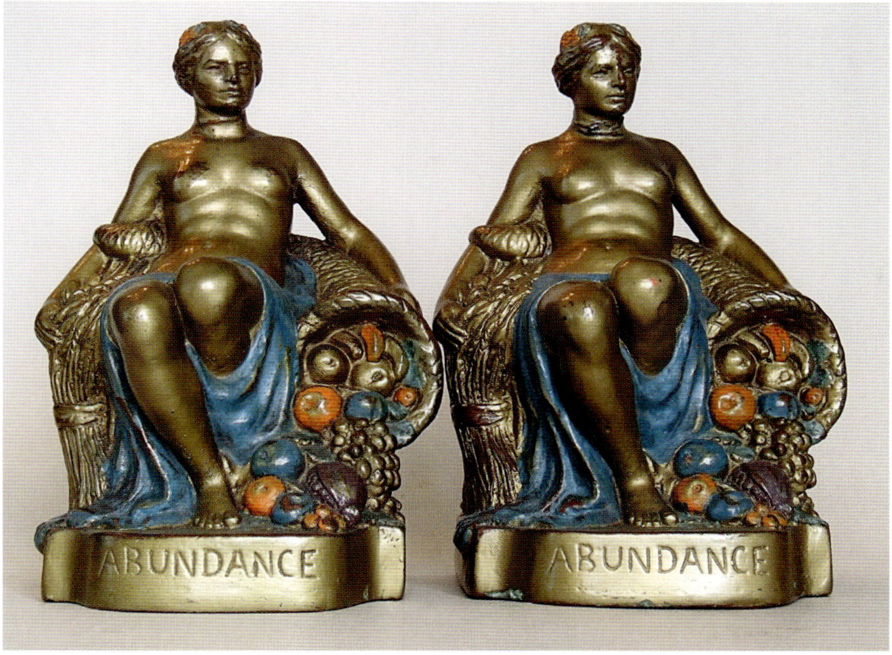

Victorians were also known for their professed strict morality. They would not sanction statuettes of contemporary nude men or women in their homes, but appreciated nudes if they were representations of gods or goddesses or other classical personages and therefore of academic and not prurient interest. It was common for Victorian sculptures and portraits to bear titles. Thus, we have many Victorian-style bookends of nudes, frequently bearing titles to make their classical origins clear.

Figure 62. Copia. 7.25", electroformed bronze. Inscription: Abundance. Signed by M. Rotellini. Attrib. Pompeian Bronze Co. Circa 1915. Rarity 3. Victorian style. The Roman goddess of abundance is shown with her cornucopia. She is nude but classical and, therefore, not lewd. $240.-360.

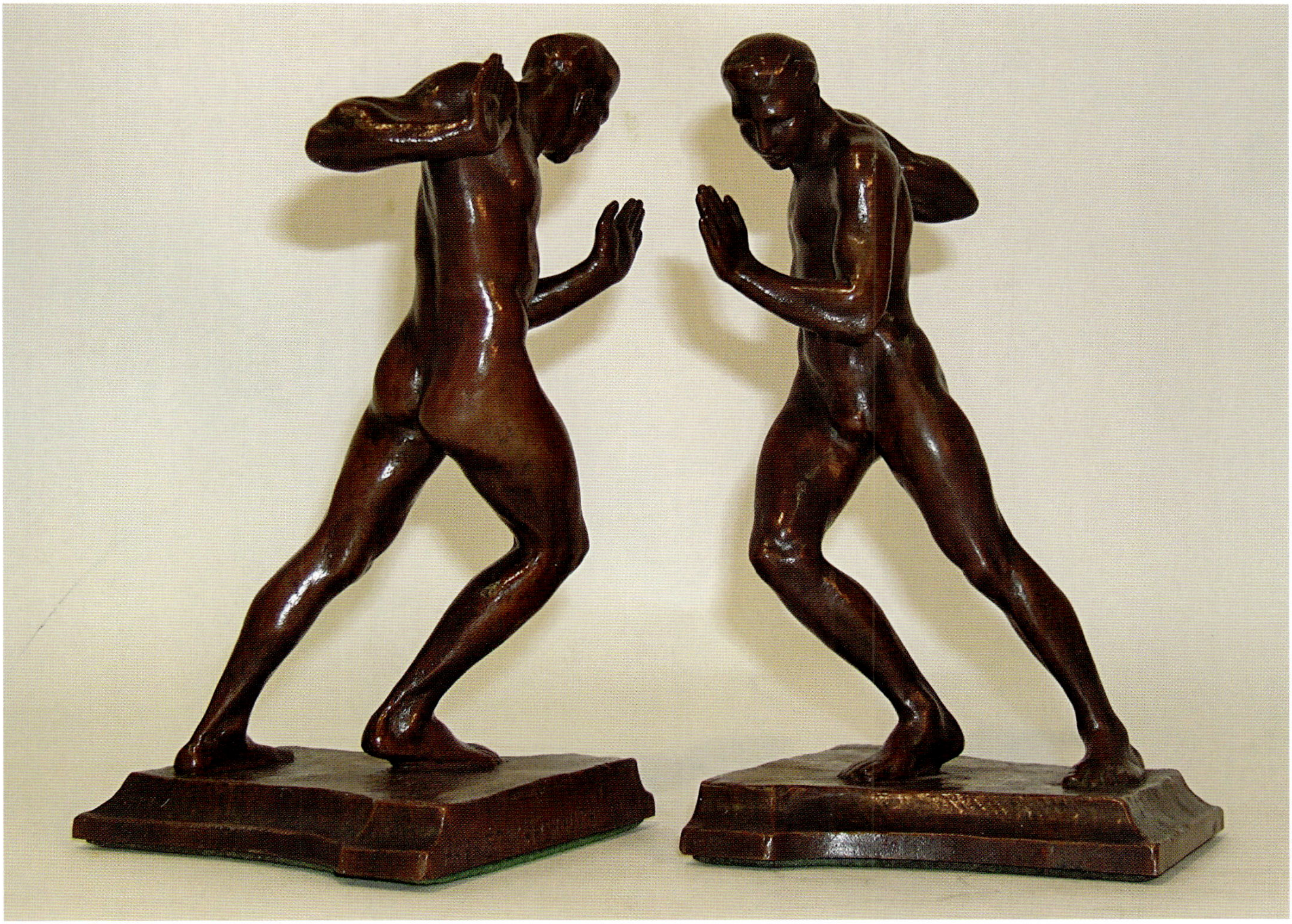

Figure 63. Pushing Men. Bronze. Inscription: Gorham Founders. Signed Harriet W. Fishmuth, 1912. Rarity 5. Victorian. These are not anatomically correct, so they are chaste. *Courtesy of Charles DeCosta, from his collection.* $9,000-10,000.

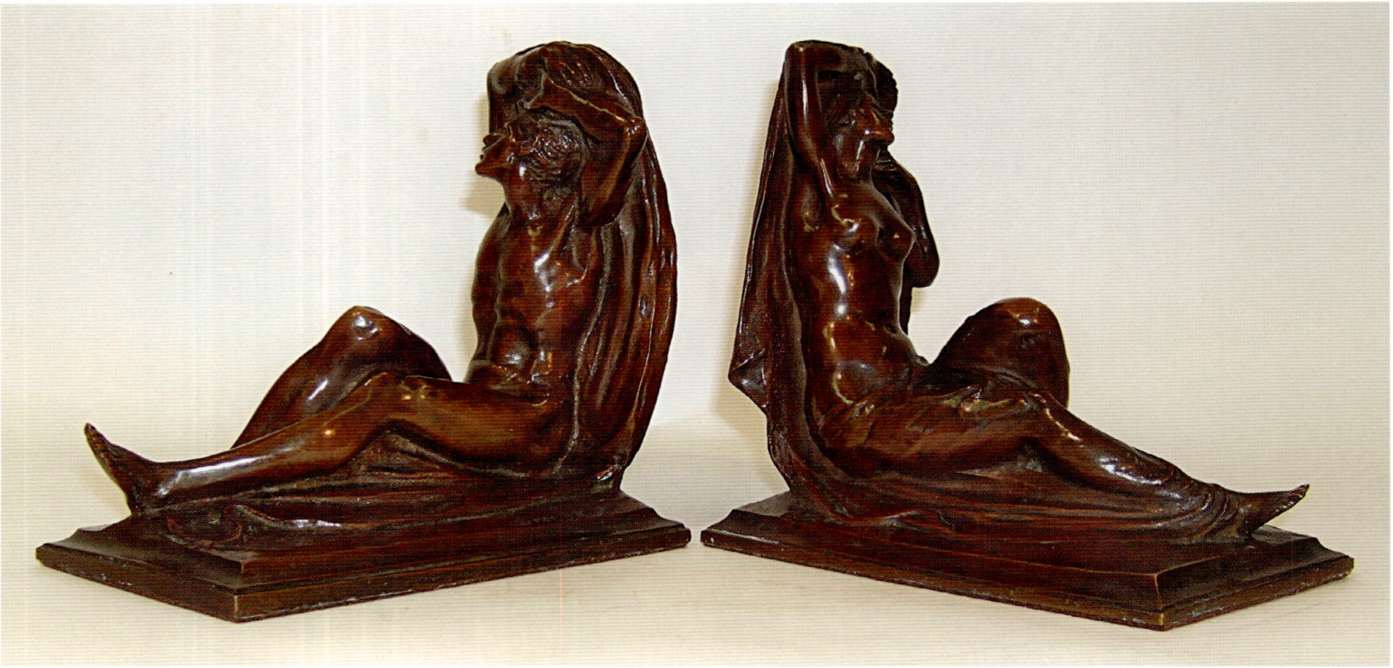

Figure 64. Man and Woman. 7.5", bronze. Inscription: signed I. Konti (sculptor), 1914. Rarity 5. Victorian, classical style. *Courtesy of Charles DeCosta, from his collection.* $6,000-8,000.

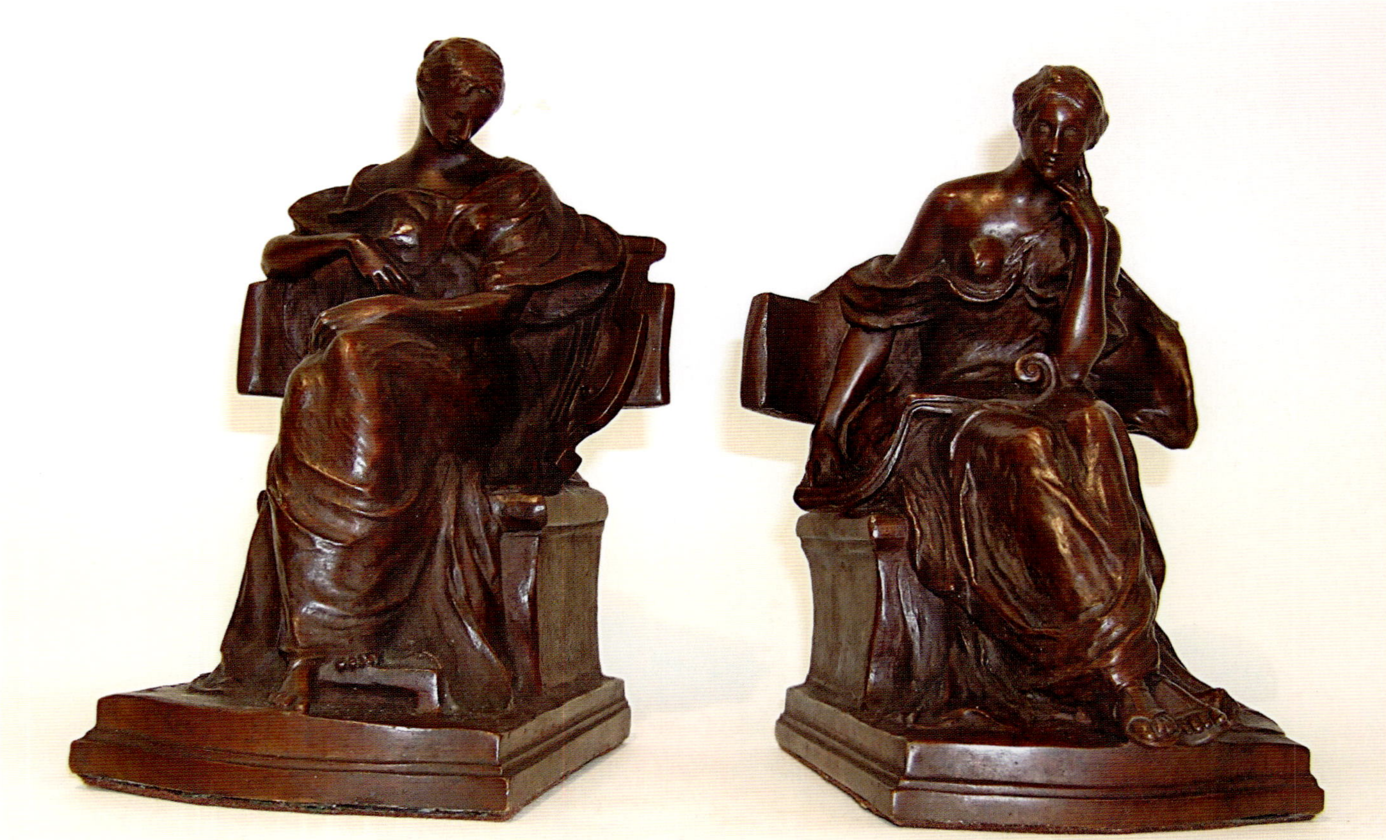

Figure 65. Poetry and Thought. Solid Bronze 9" Inscription: Attrib. Roman Bronze Works, signed I. Konti (sculptor), 1911. Rarity 5. Victorian, classical style. *Courtesy of Charles DeCosta, from his collection.* $8,000-10,000.

Portraits were very popular in Victorian times and they found their way onto American bookends. Engaging portraits abound of Englishmen like Charles Dickens, Americans like Walt Whitman, Henry Wadsworth Longfellow, Ralph Waldo Emerson, or Edgar Allen Poe, and notables from classical antiquity. Clothing styles resembling the English were popular here too, especially in antebellum times. For instance, we can now find bookends showing American antebellum ladies dressed in 19th century bonnets and voluminous skirts (Figures 78, 79).

The fact that very many bookends with Victorian imagery were fashionable in the early twentieth century, many more than we can show here, attests to our persistent Victorian sensibilities at that time.

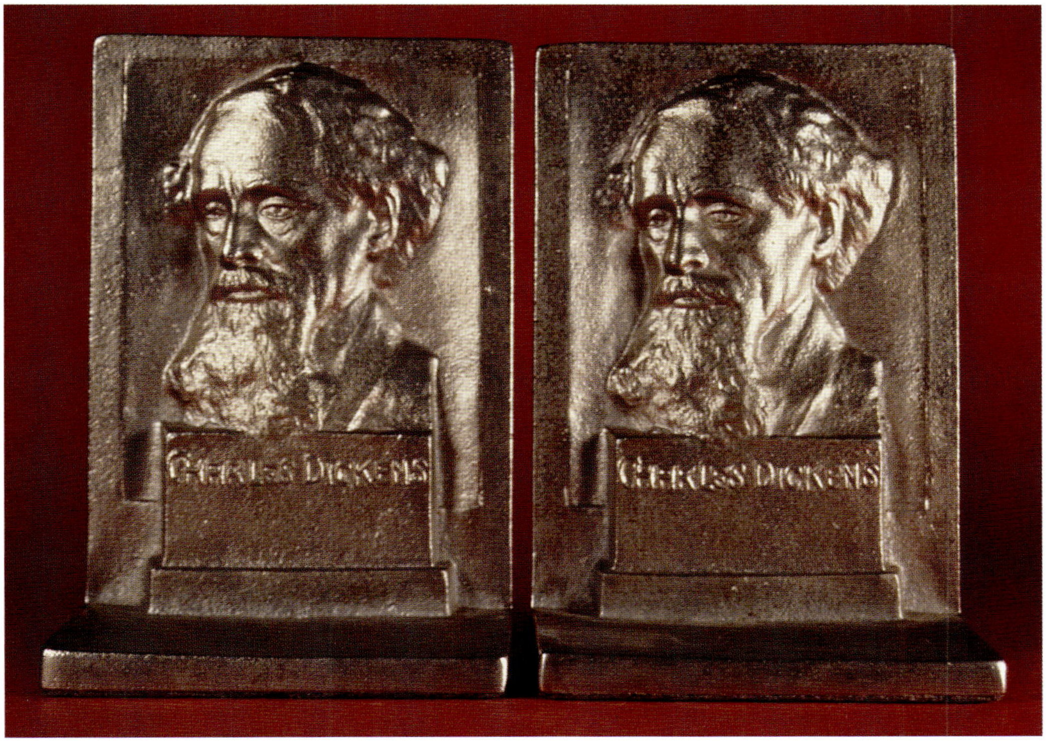

Figure 66. Charles Dickens. 6", iron. Circa 1920. Rarity 4. Victorian portraiture. $80-120.

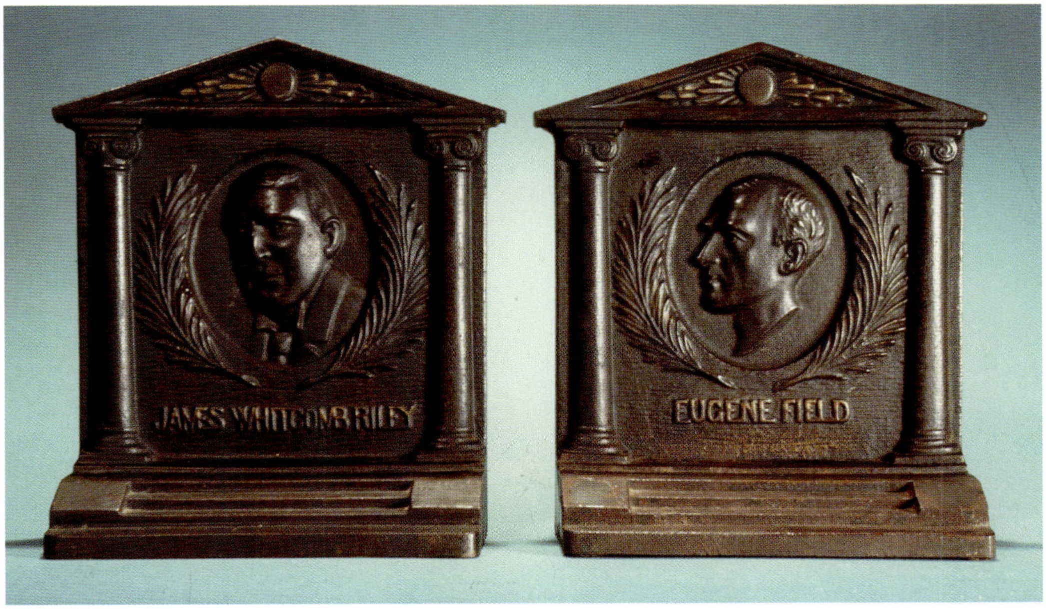

Figure 67. Field and Riley. 5.5", iron. Inscription: Shop mark of the Bradley and Hubbard. Circa 1920. Rarity 3. Victorian portraiture. $160-240.

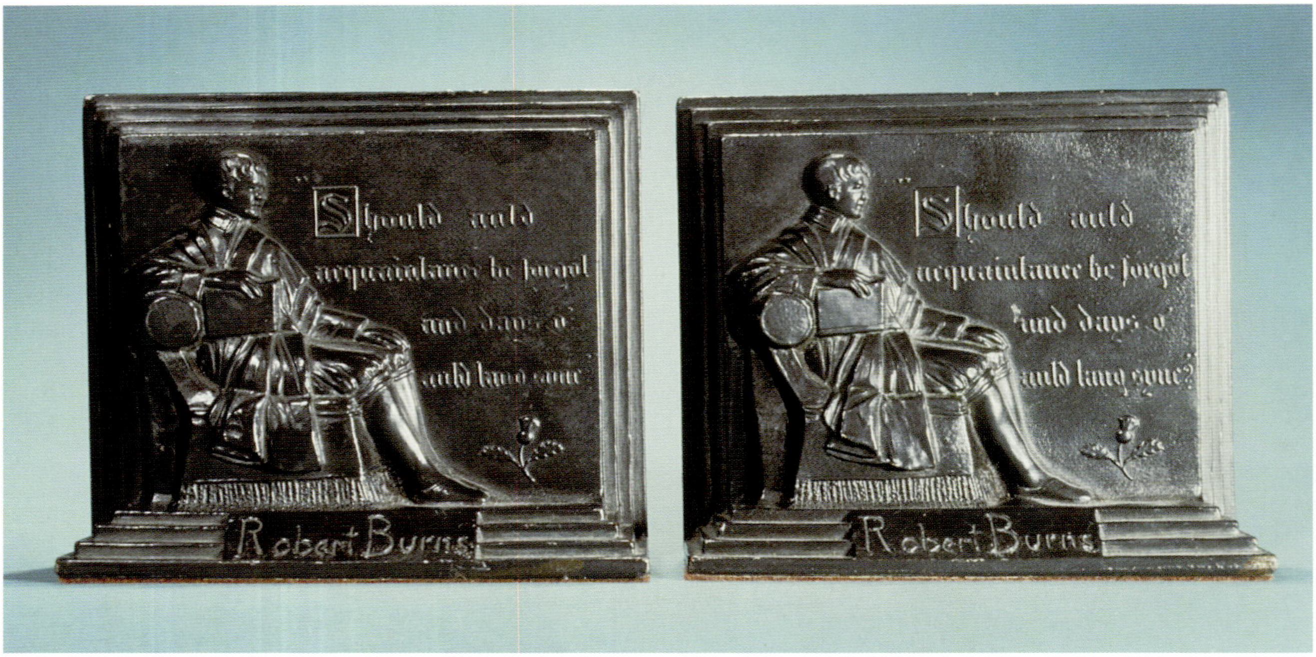

Figure 68. Robert Burns. 4.75", gray metal. Inscription: Shop mark of K&O. 1926. Rarity 3. Victorian portraiture. $100-150.

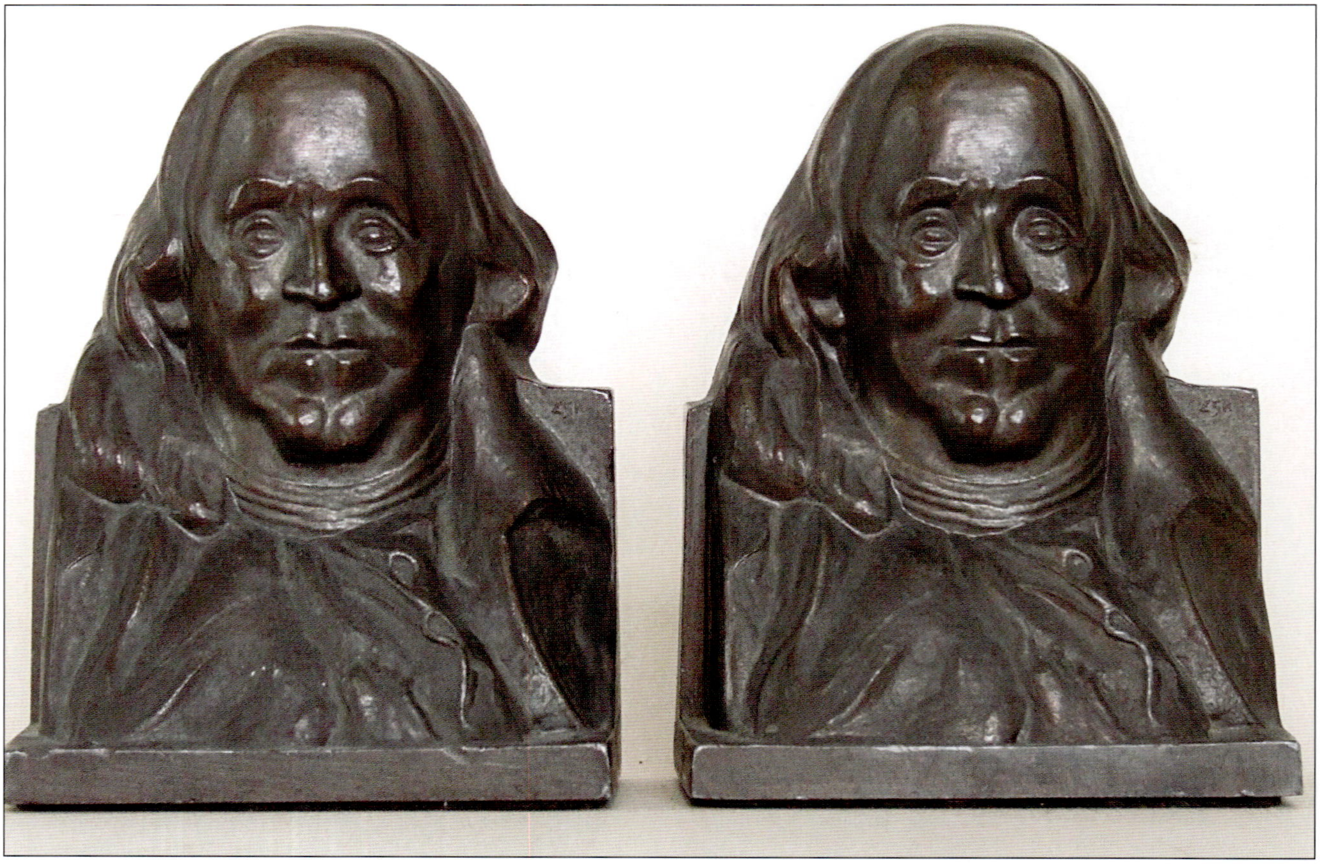

Figure 69. Benjamin Franklin. 4.75", print metal. Inscription: Barnmart Brothers and Spindler. Circa 1920. Rarity 3. Victorian portraiture. $200-300.

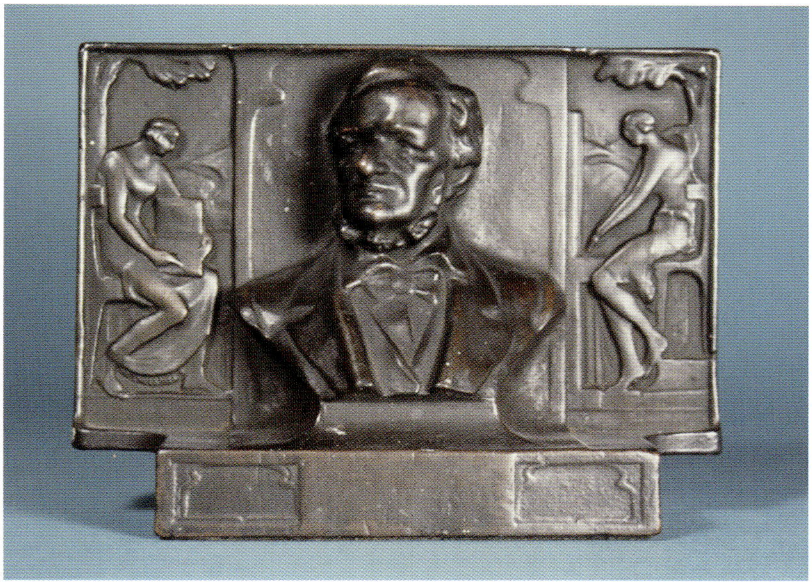

Figure 70. Richard Wagner. 4.5", electroformed bronze. Inscription: Pompeian Bronze, 1921. Rarity 3. Victorian portraiture. $200-300.

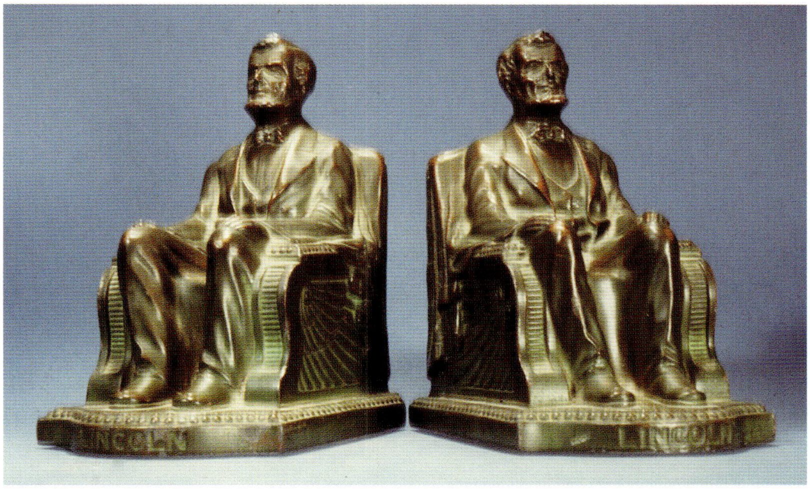

Figure 71. Abraham Lincoln. 6.5", gray metal. Inscription: Nuart, 1924. Rarity 3. Victorian portraiture. Bookends showing Lincoln are very frequently seen. $80-120.

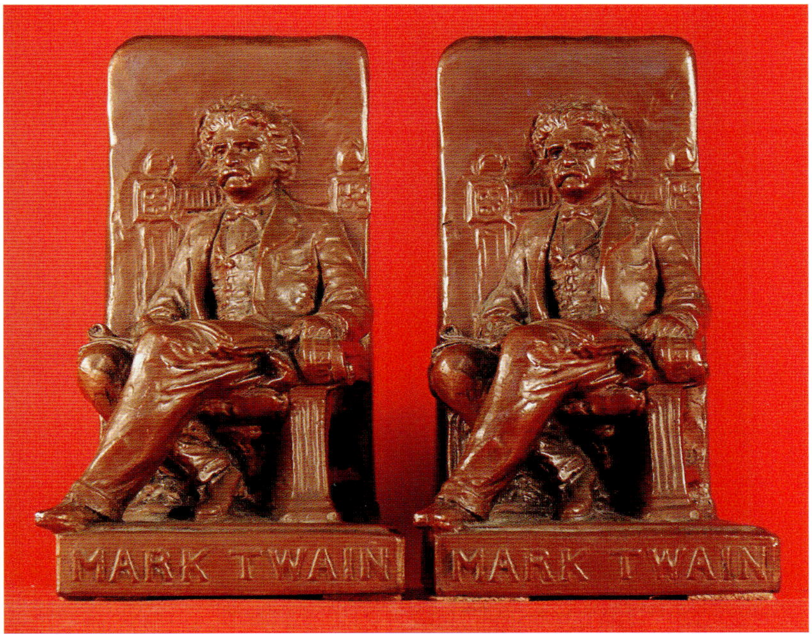

Figure 72. Mark Twain Sitting. 6.5", bronze plating on gray metal. Inscription: Mark Twain, WB shop mark. Circa 1915. Rarity 3. Victorian. Portraiture. $200-300.

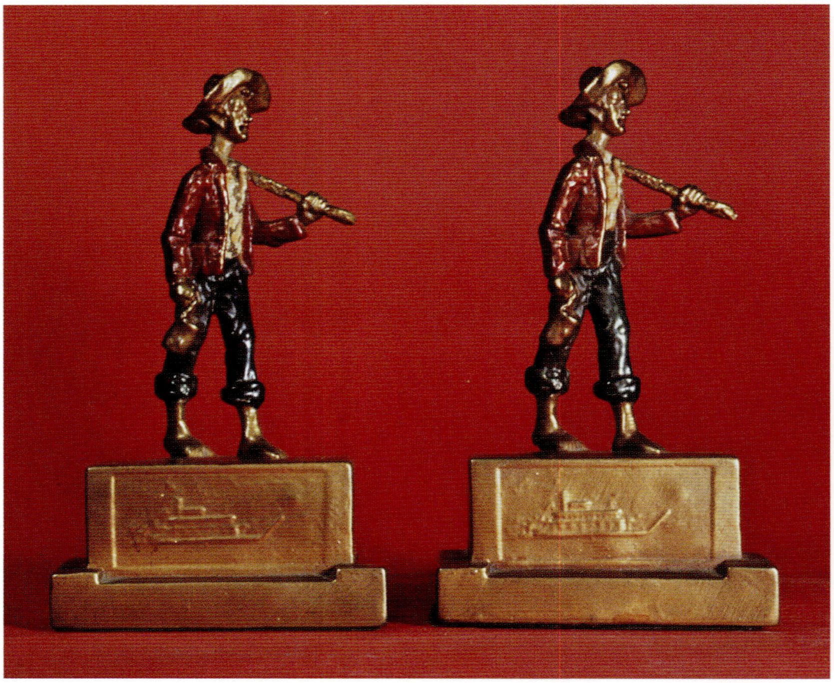

Figure 73. Huck Finn. 7.25", electroformed bronze. Shop mark of Armor Bronze. Circa 1914. Rarity 3. Victorian era. $240-360.

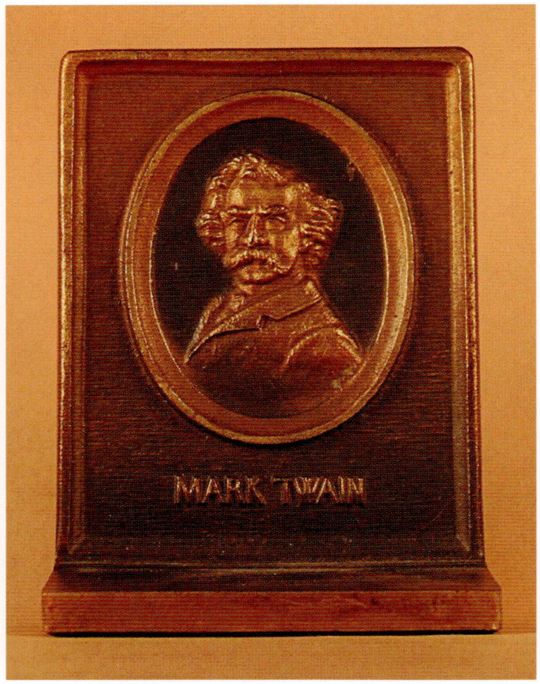

Figure 74. Mark Twain Bust. 5.5", iron. Inscription: Mark Twain and shop mark of Bradley and Hubbard. Circa 1915. Rarity 4. Victorian. Portraiture. $200-300.

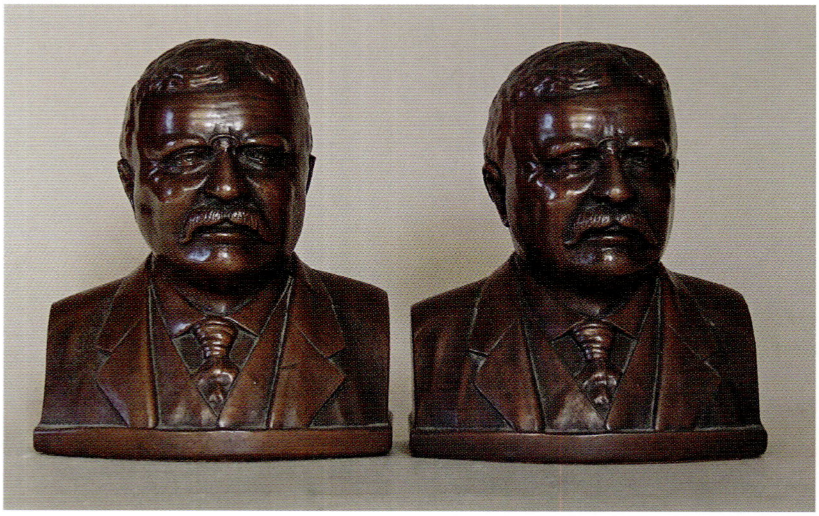

Figure 75. Theodore Roosevelt Bust. 4.75", bronze plating on gray metal. Inscription: Shop mark of Jennings Brothers. Circa 1924. Rarity 3. Victorian. Portraiture. $200-300.

Figure 76. Theodore Roosevelt Profile. 5" Bronze. Attrib. Judd. Circa 1919. Rarity 4. Victorian. Portraiture. $275-420.

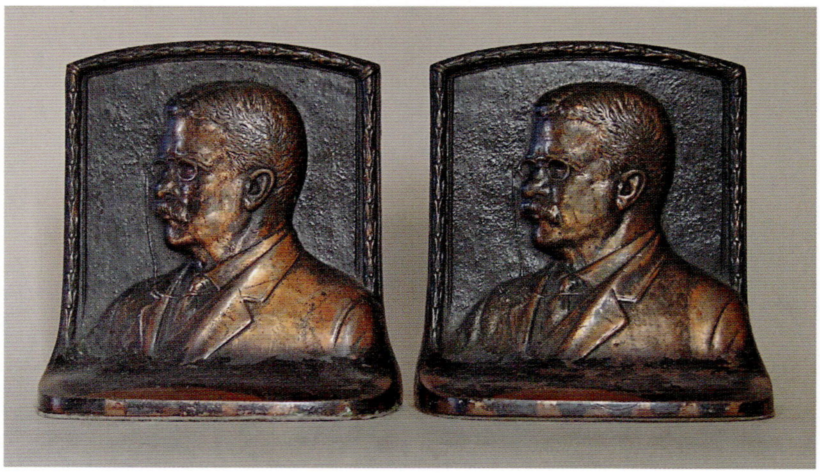

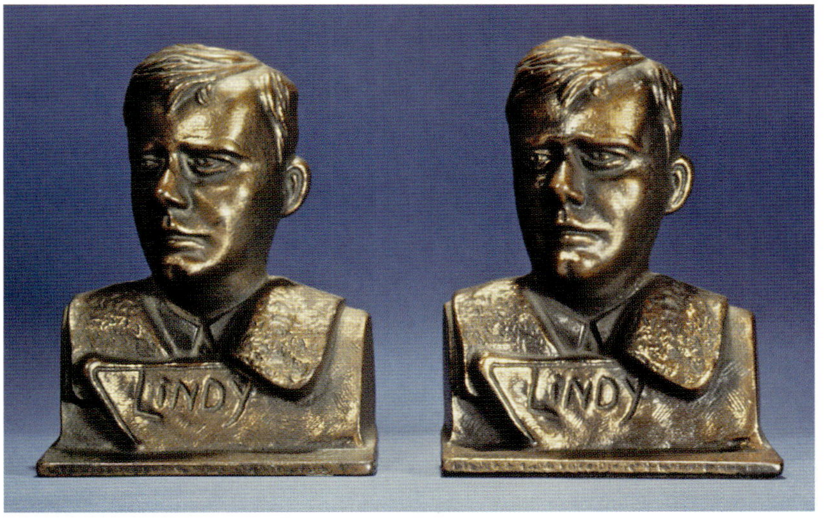

Figure 77. Lindy (Charles Lindbergh). 6", iron. Inscription: Lindy, Verona. Circa 1929. Rarity 3. Victorian. Portraiture. $120-180.

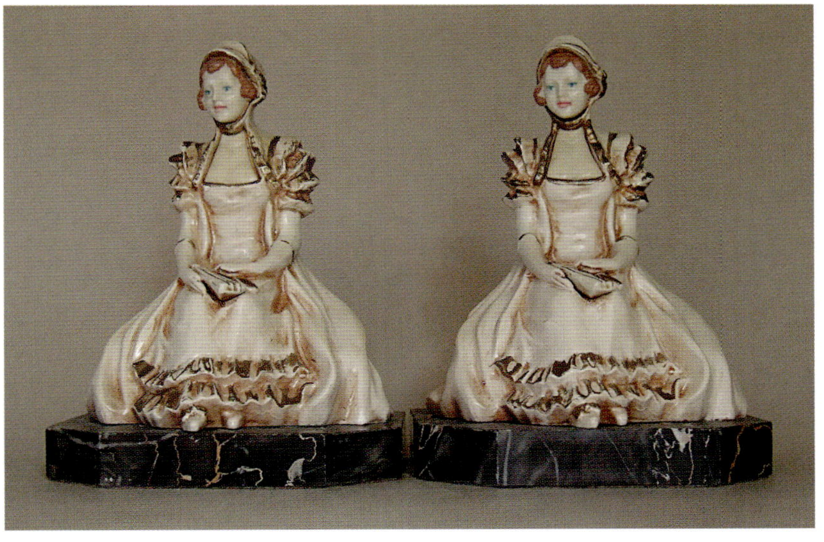

Figure 78. Sit and Wait. 6.5", gray metal, celluloid, marble. Foundry: Attrib. Hirsch. Circa 1910. Rarity 2. Victorian. Antebellum era. $240-360.

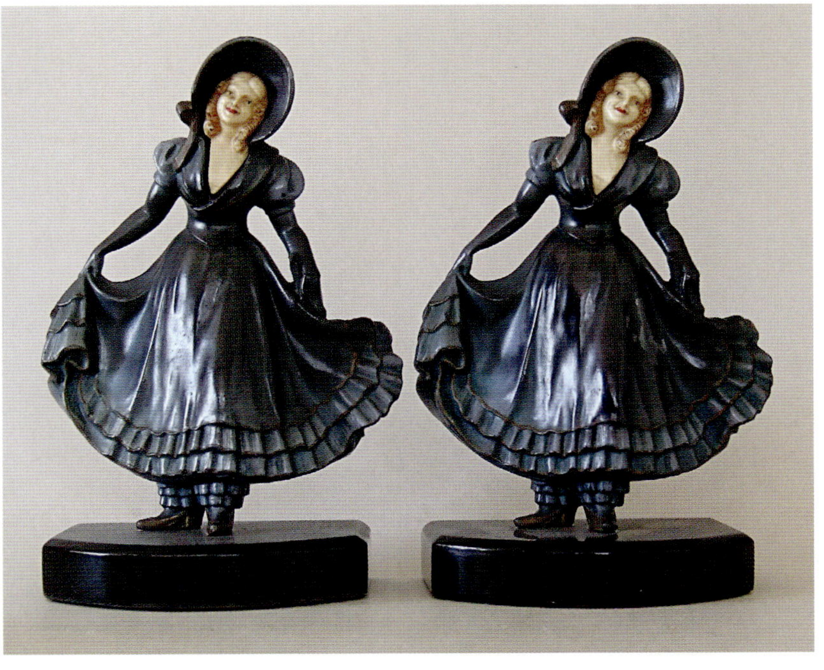

Figure 79. Southern Belle. 8.25", gray metal, celluloid, Bakelite. Foundry: Attrib. Hirsch. Circa 1910. Rarity 3. Victorian. Antebellum era. $260-390.

Chapter 3

Aesthetic Style Bookends

There are numerous bookends that do not fit neatly into a popular art style from the past century. We will attribute them to the Aesthetic art style which carried on in England during the last half of the nineteenth century. The Aesthetic style eschewed philosophy, morality, or any other socio-political basis for art work and embraced beauty for beauty's sake. This chapter is devoted to a random collection of bookends, all beautiful. Aesthetic-style bookends are shown in Figures 80-134.

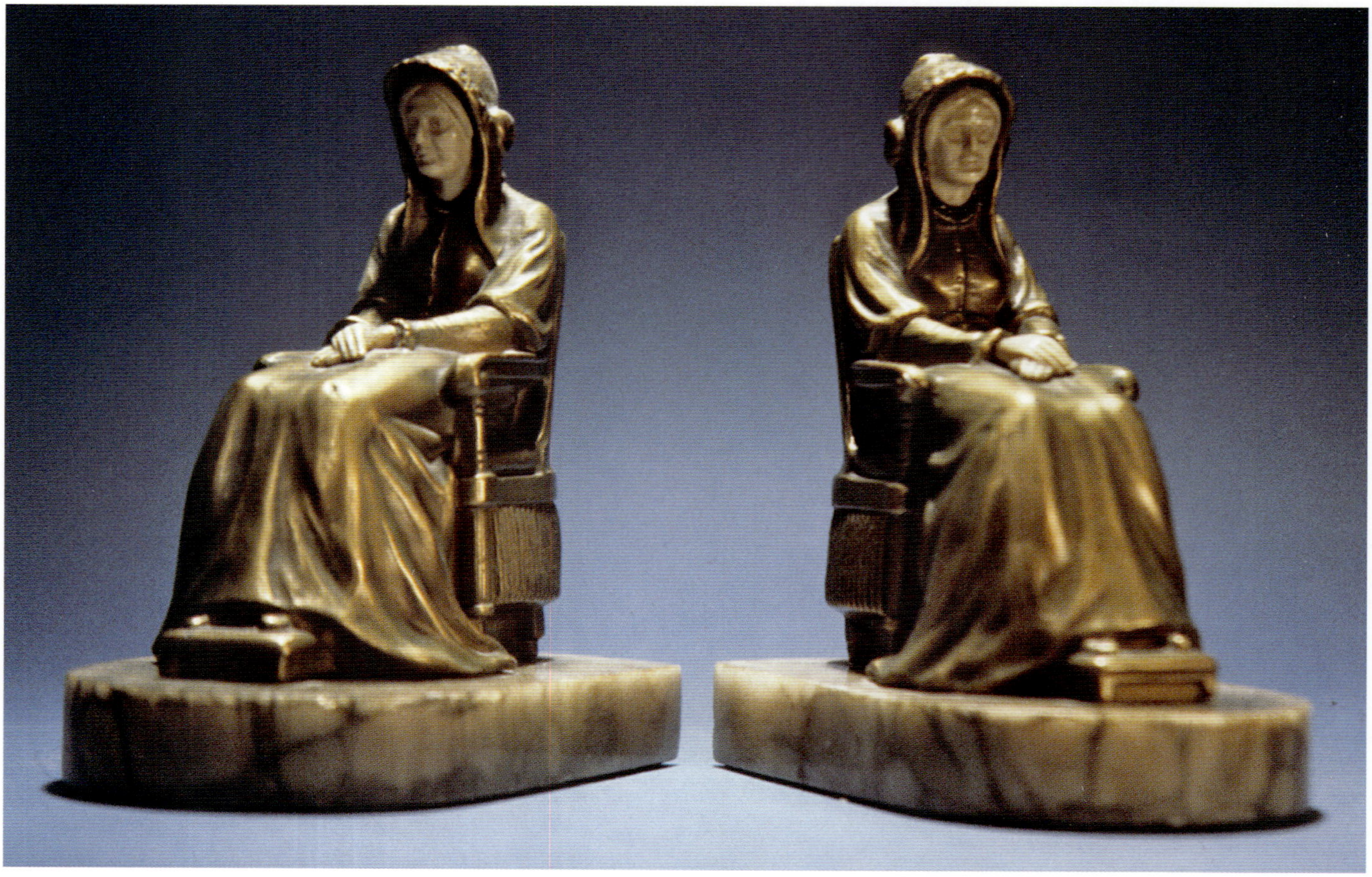

Figure 80. Whistler's Mother. 6.5", gray metal, celluloid. Foundry: Hirsch. Circa 1931. Rarity 3. Taken from an Aesthetic-style painting by James Whistler. $200-300.

Figure 81. Mephistopheles. 4", lead. Circa 1910. Rarity 5. Aesthetic. $500-750. These bookends are small, but lead is heavy, 8 lbs./pair. $500-750.

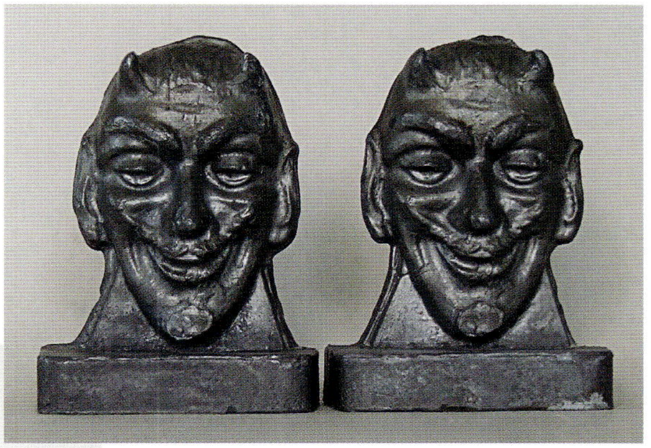

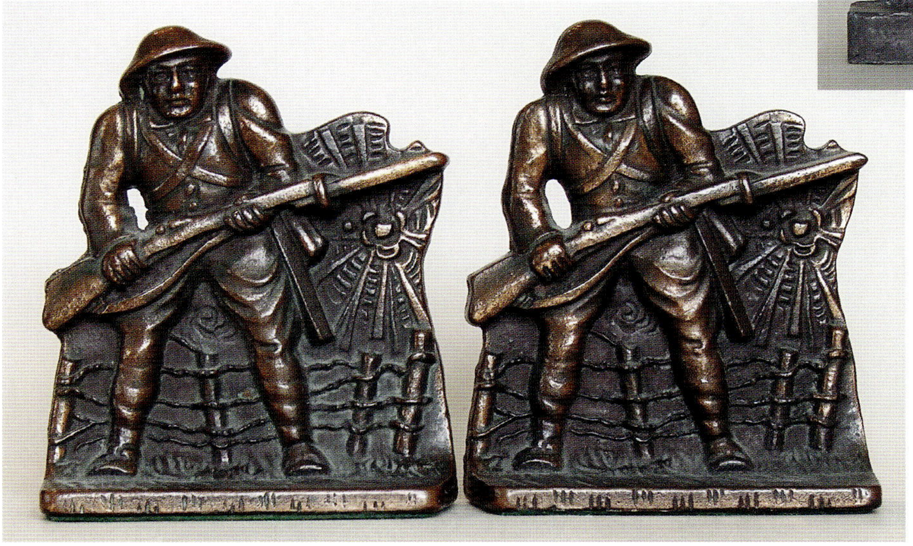

Figure 82. Doughboy. 5.5", iron. Foundry: Hubley. Circa 1918. Rarity 4. Aesthetic.$200-300.

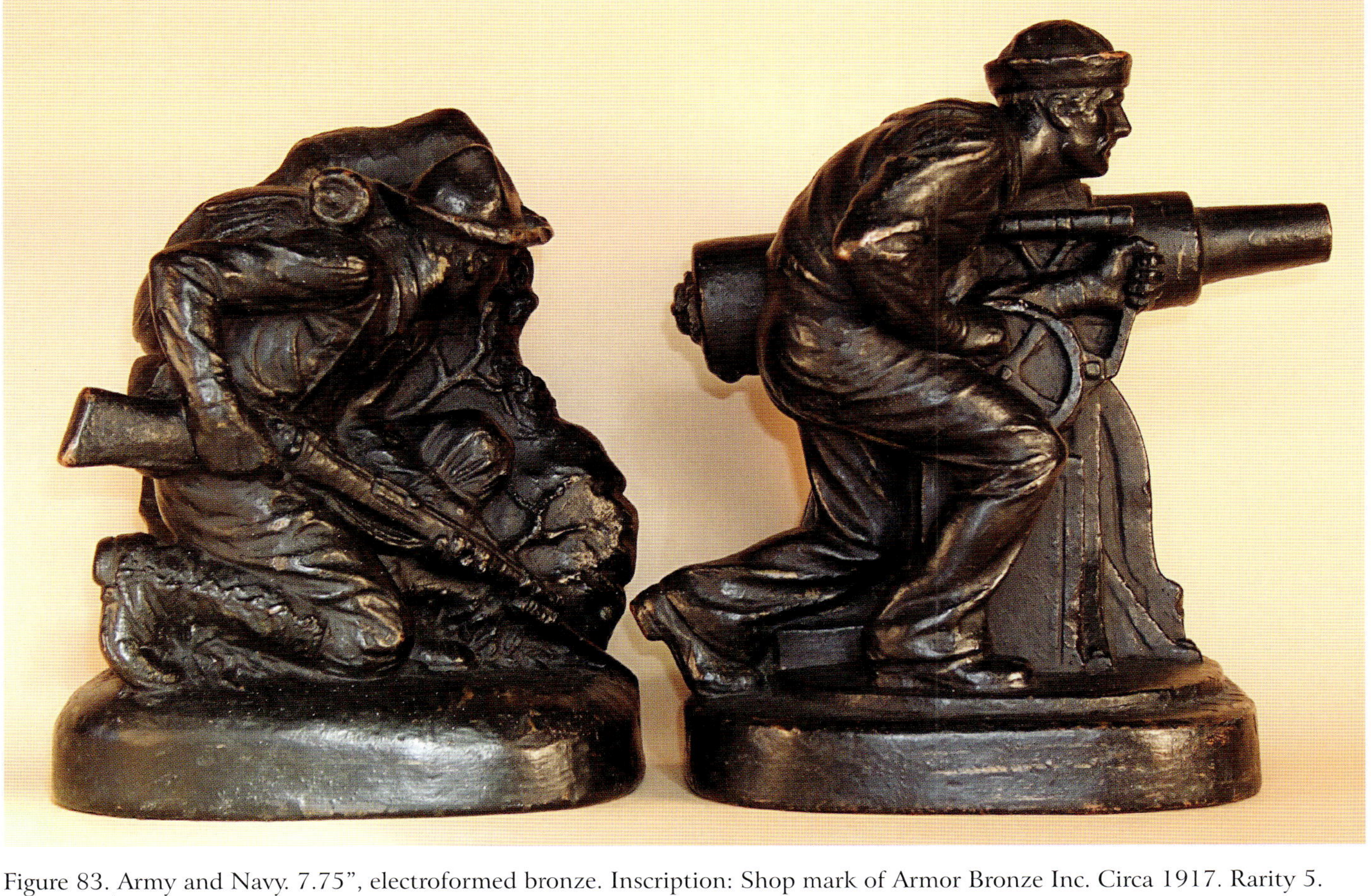

Figure 83. Army and Navy. 7.75", electroformed bronze. Inscription: Shop mark of Armor Bronze Inc. Circa 1917. Rarity 5. Aestheic. $500-750.

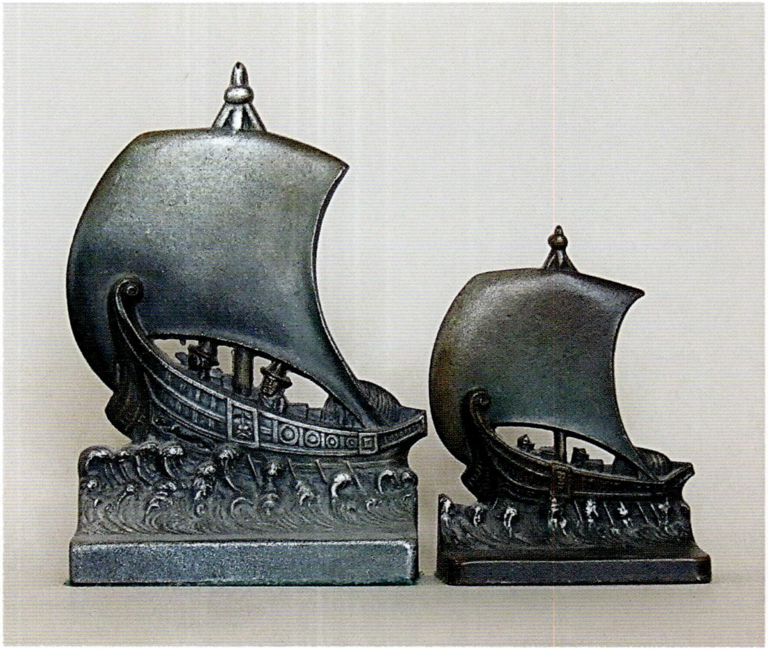

Figure 84. Viking Ship doorstop (l) and bookend (r). 8.5" & 6.5", iron. Bookend inscription: Shop mark of Bradley and Hubbard. Circa 1925. Rarity 1. Aesthetic. $80-120. Doorstop inscription: Shop mark of Bradley and Hubbard Mfg. Co. Circa 1925. Rarity 4. Aesthetic. $275-420.

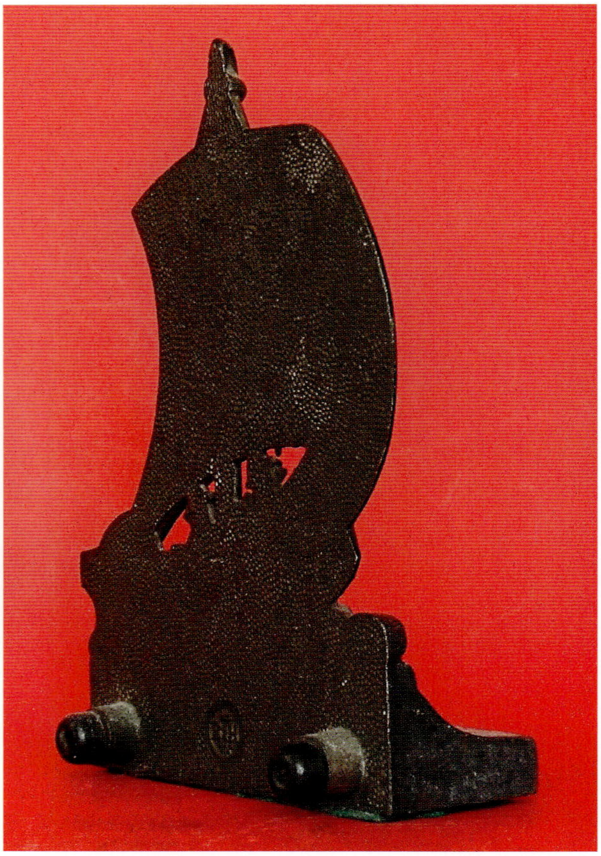

Figure 85. Viking Ship doorstop. Mate to the Viking Ship bookends. The bumpers on the rear are featured on Bradley and Hubbard doorstops.

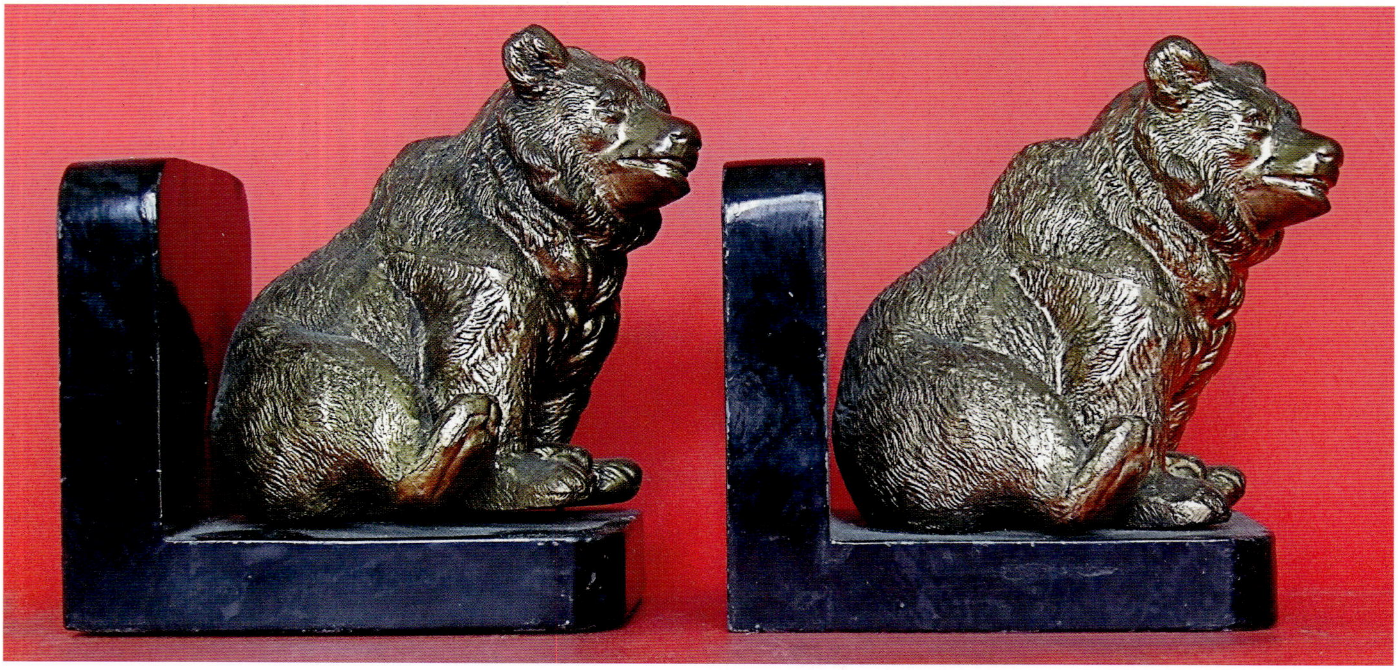

Figure 86. Sitting Bear. 5", gray metal. Inscription: Ronson company label. Circa 1930. Rarity 4. Aesthetic. $240-360.

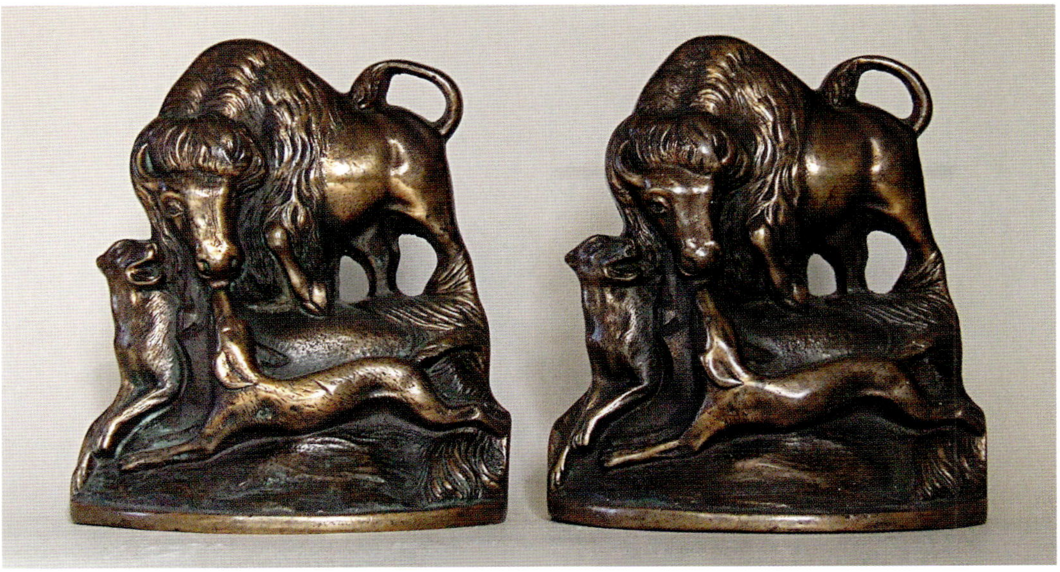

Figure 87. Buffalo Hunt. 6", bronze. Inscription: Buffalo Hunt, Copyright 1926, Gift House Inc. Solid Bronze. Rarity 3. Aesthtic.$275-420. Wolves on bookends are very infrequent. $275-420.

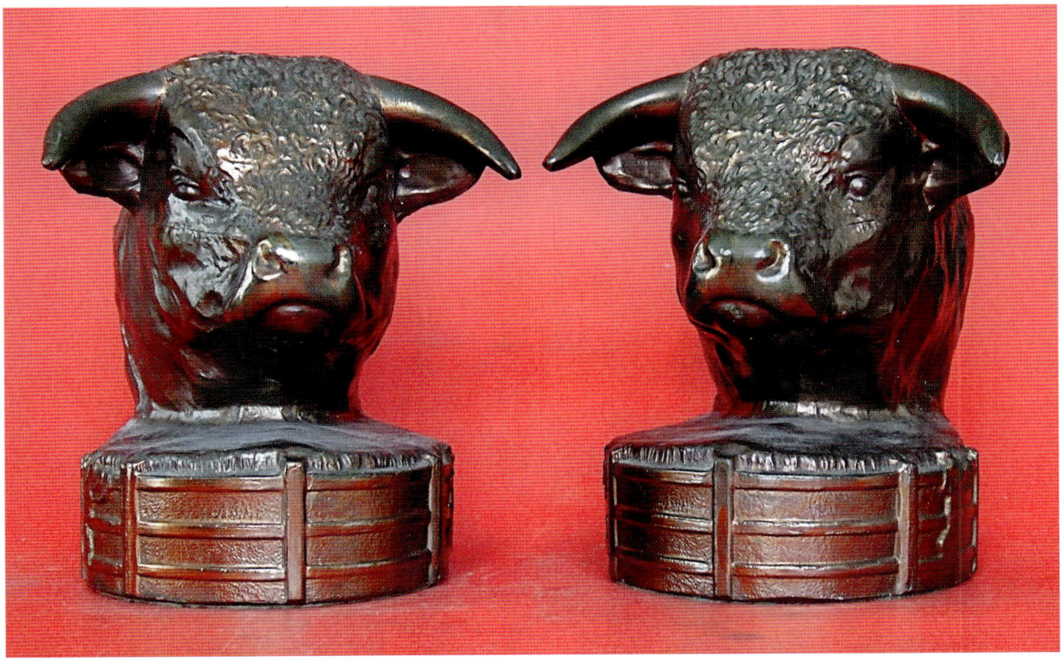

Figure 88. Steer. 6", gray metal. Inscription: Company label for Dodge Inc. Sculptor: Attrib. Gladys Brown. Circa 1947. Rarity 2. Aesthetic. $160-240.

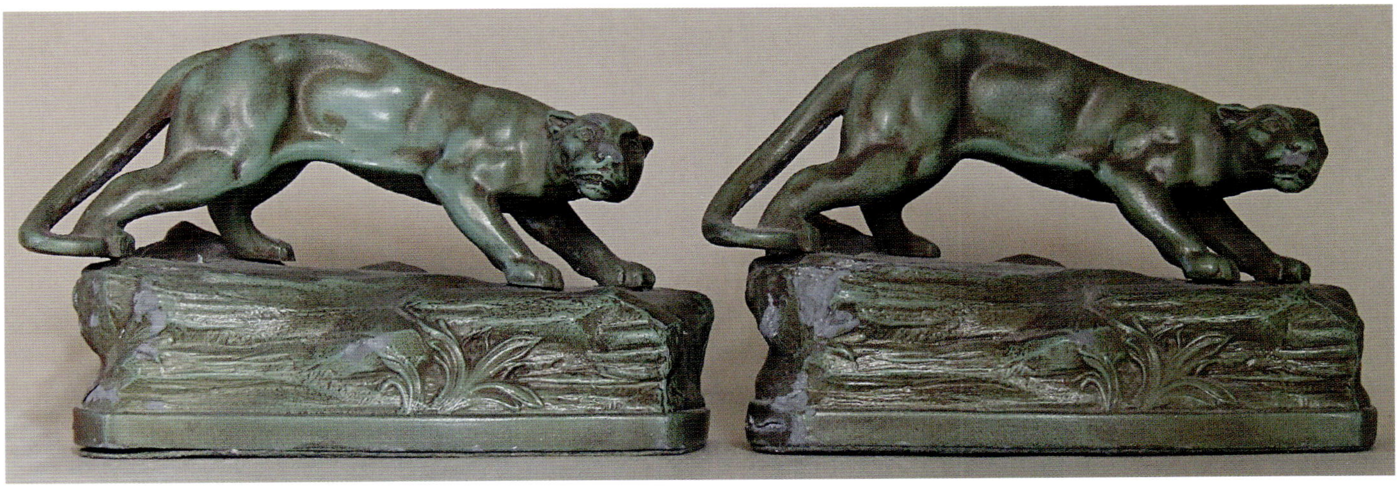

Figure 89. Cougar. 4.25", gray metal. Inscription: Shop mark for K&O. Circa 1920 Rarity 3. Aesthetic. $160-240.

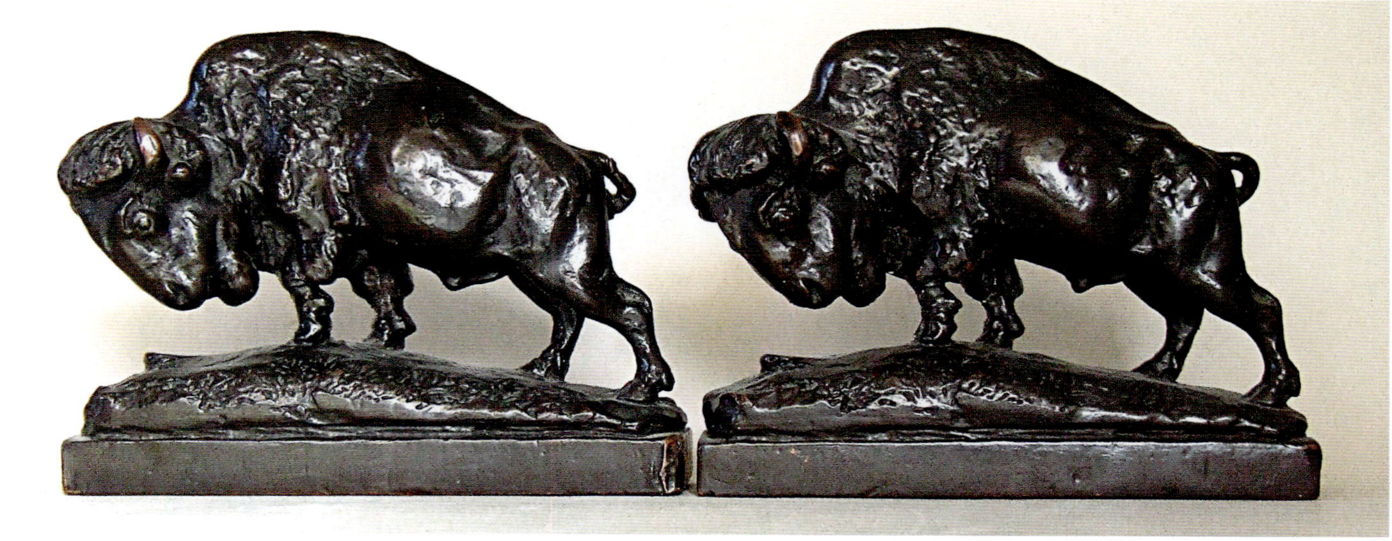

Figure 90. Prairie Bison. 5.5", electroformed bronze: Foundry: Attrib. Armor Bronze. Circa 1925. Rarity 2. Aesthetic. $256-384.

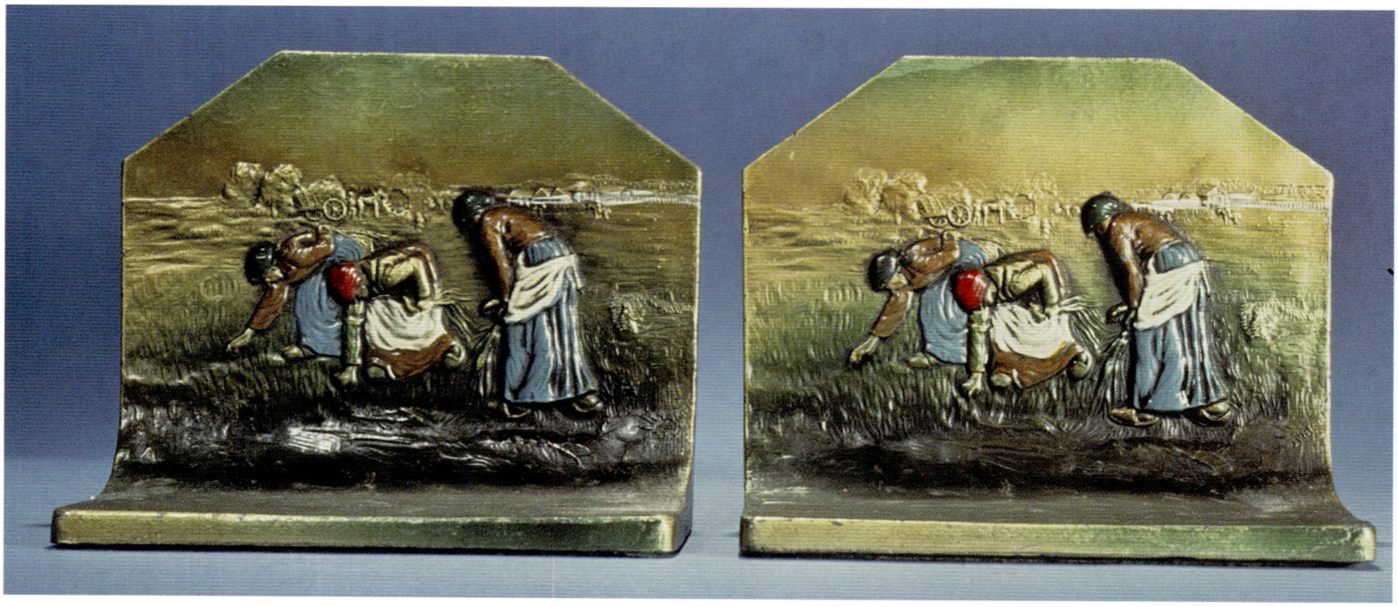

Figure 91. The Gleaners. 4.25", gray metal. Inscription: K&O. Circa 1925. Rarity 3. Aesthetic. Copied after a painting by Jean-Françoise Millet. 1925. $120-150.

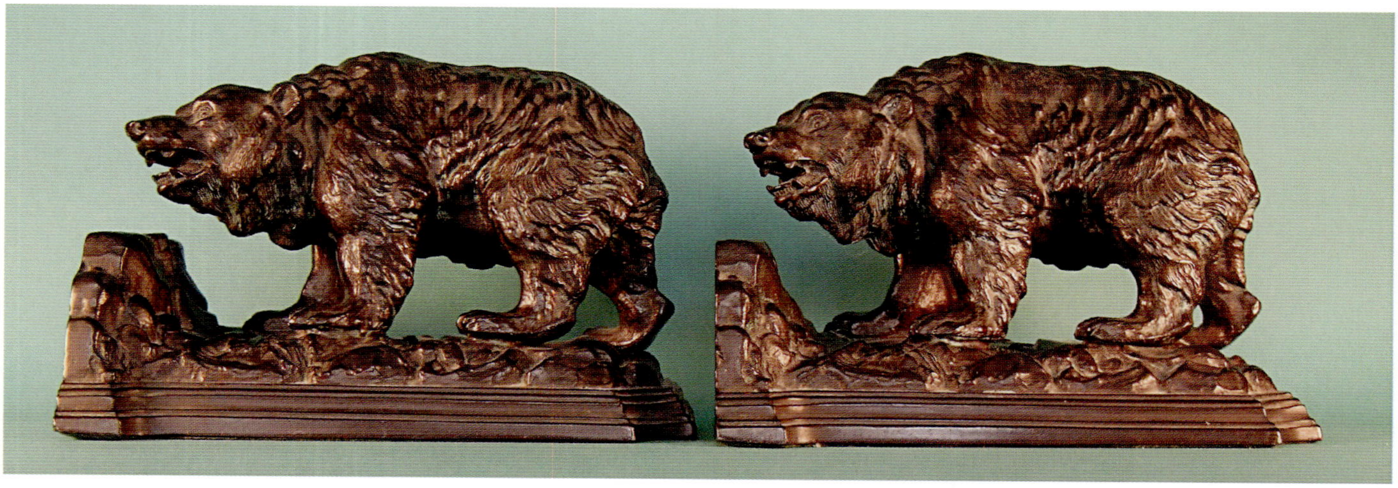

Figure 92. Grizzly Bear. 5", gray metal. Foundry: Attrib. Ronson. Sculptor: Attrib. A. Barye., here copied. Circa 1925. Rarity 4. Aesthetic. $224-334.

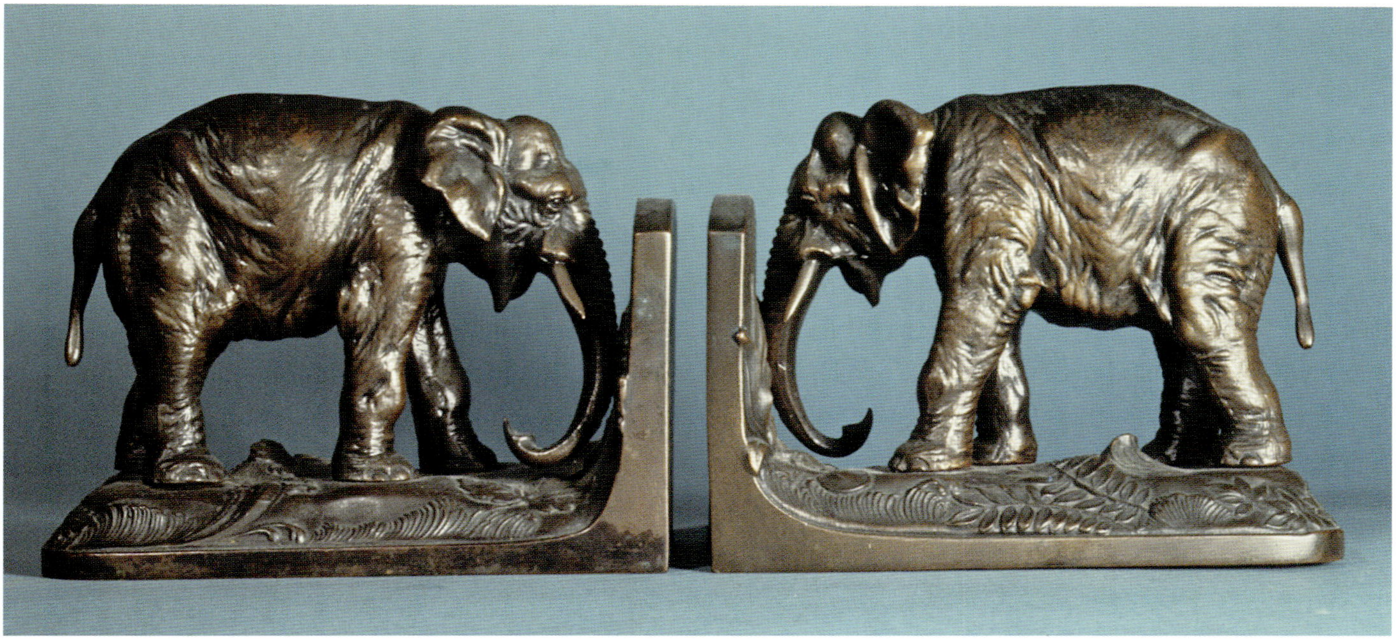

Figure 93. Jumbo. 5", gray metal. Inscription: Shop mark of Jennings Brothers. Circa 1919. Rarity 4. Aesthetic $80-120.

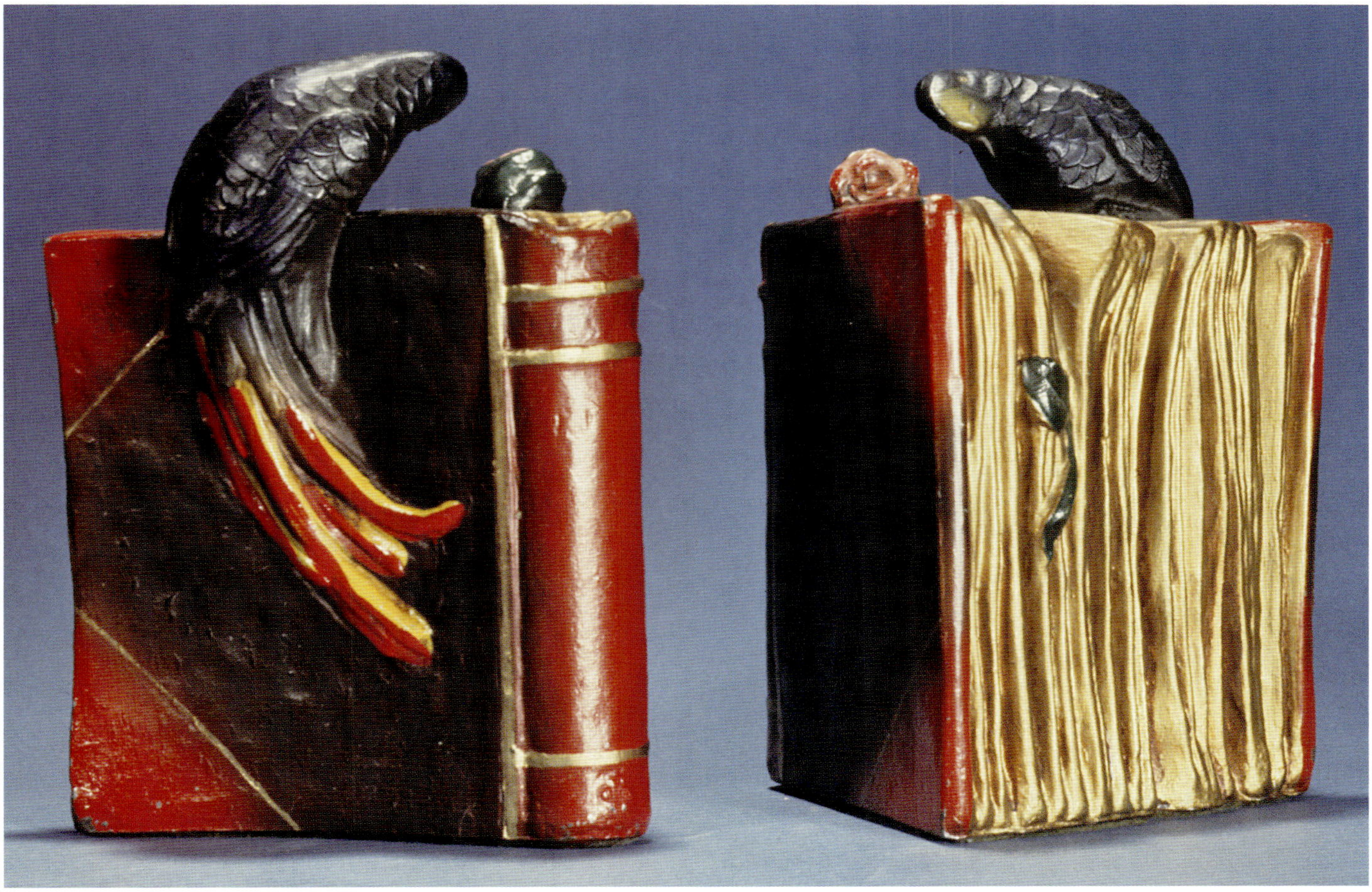

Figure 94. Parrot on Book. 6", gray metal. Inscription: AMW, 1927. Rarity 4. Aesthetic. $240-360.

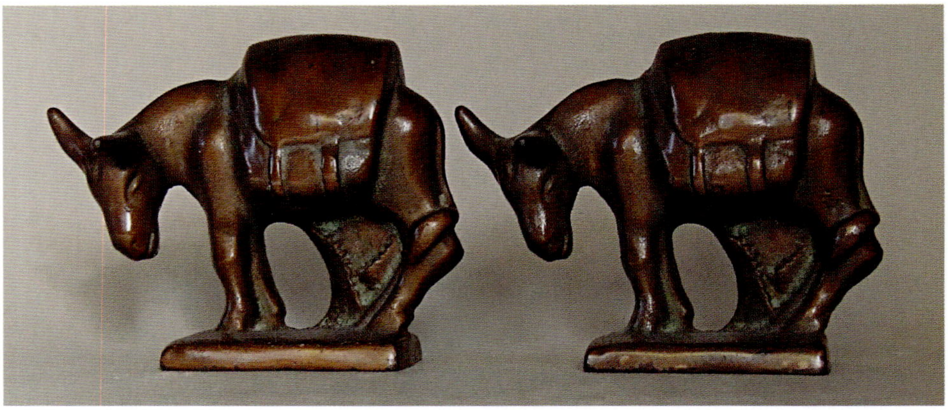

Figure 95. Pack Mules. 4", iron. Inscription: 492 Foundry: Hubley. Circa 1925. Rarity 2. Aesthetic. $80-120.

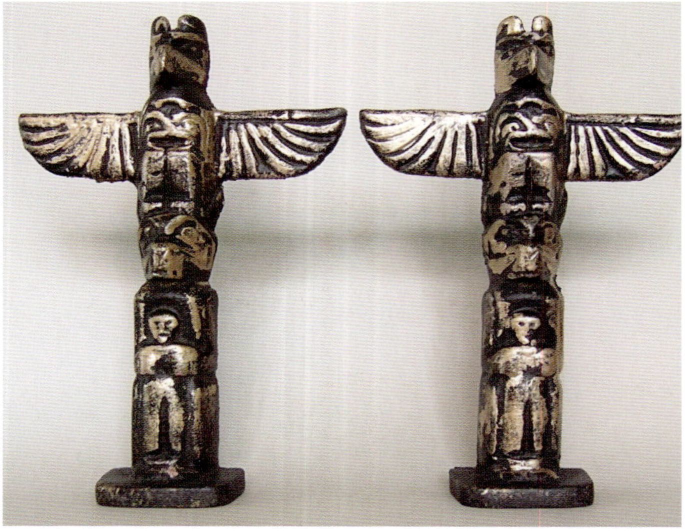

Figure 96. Eagle Totem Pole. 11.5", iron. Circa 1925, Rarity 5. Aesthetic. $275-420.

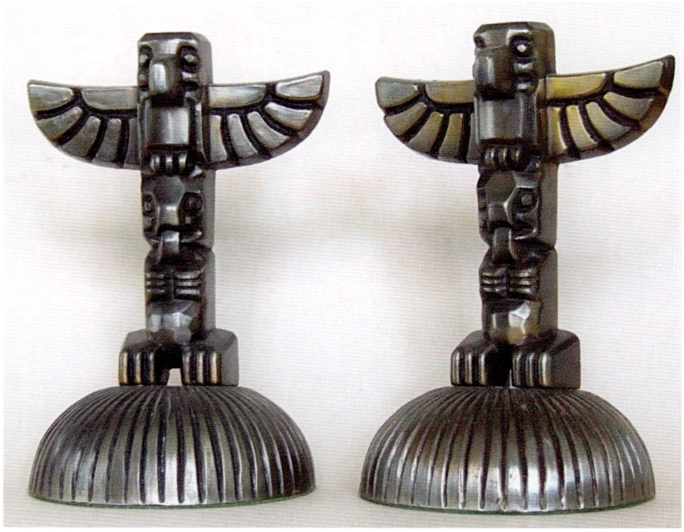

Figure 97. Raven Totem Pole. 6", bronze. Inscription: Cygnus Inc, Edmonds, Washington. Circa 1935. Rarity 2. Aesthetic. Northwest Coast Indian totem pole with Deco features. $200-300.

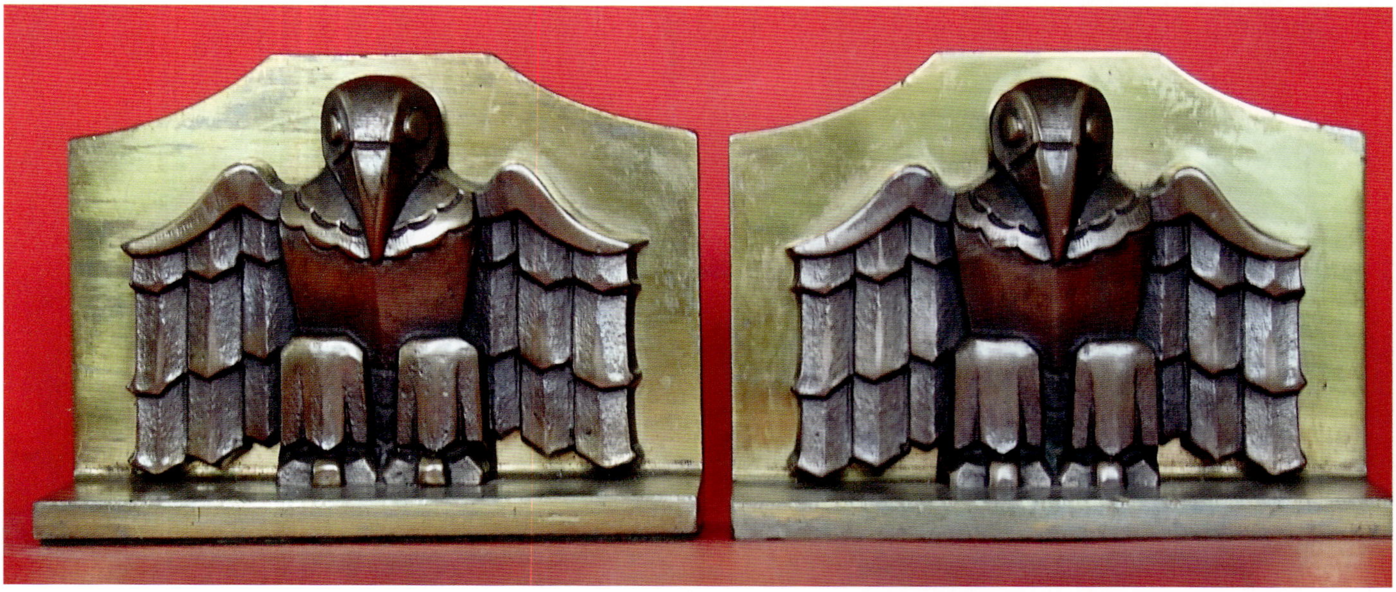

Figure 98. Raven Totem Figure. 4", bronze. Foundry: Attrib. Cygnus Inc. Circa 1935. Rarity 5. Aesthetic. Northwest Coast Indian totem figure with Deco features. $275-420.

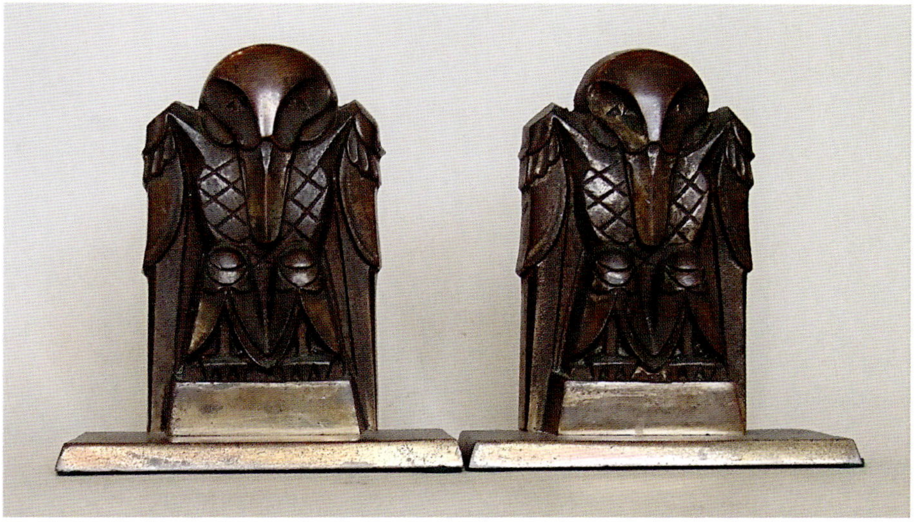

Figure 99. Raven Spirit. 6", bronze. Foundry: Attrib. Cygnus Inc. Circa 1935. Rarity 3. Aesthetic. Northwest Coast Indian totem figure with Deco features. $256-284.

Figure 100. Raven Figure. 5", lead. Circa 1915. Rarity. 4. Aesthetic. These are somewhat small, but lead is heavy, 9.Lbs./pair. $400-600.

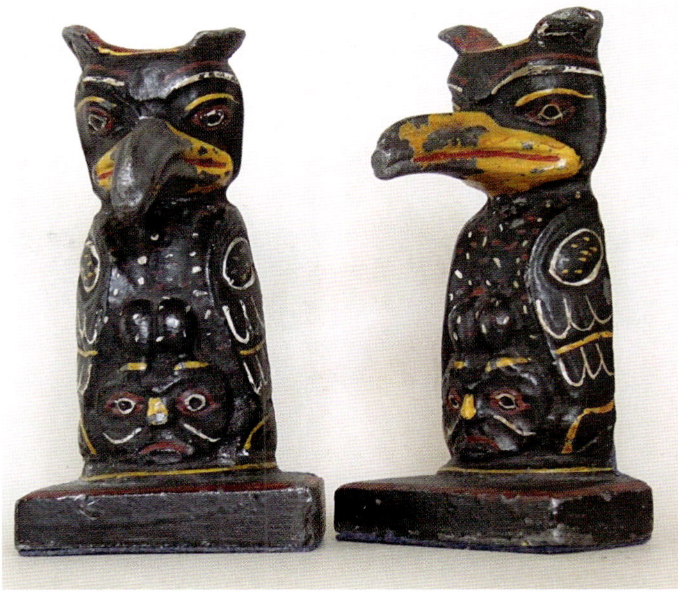

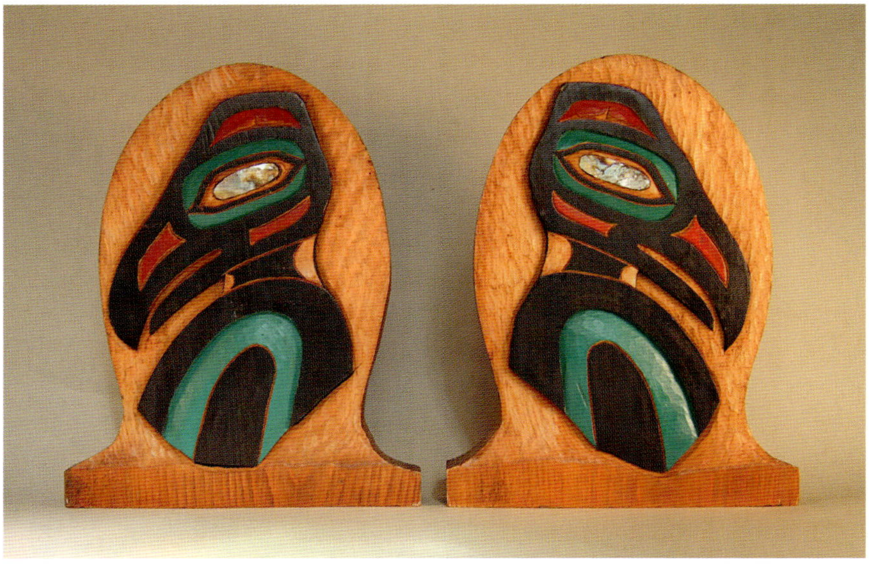

Figure 101. Raven with Abalone Shell Eye. 10", red cedar, abalone shell eye. Circa 1930? Rarity 5. Aesthetic. Folk art. Carved in low relief with hand tools. $200-300.

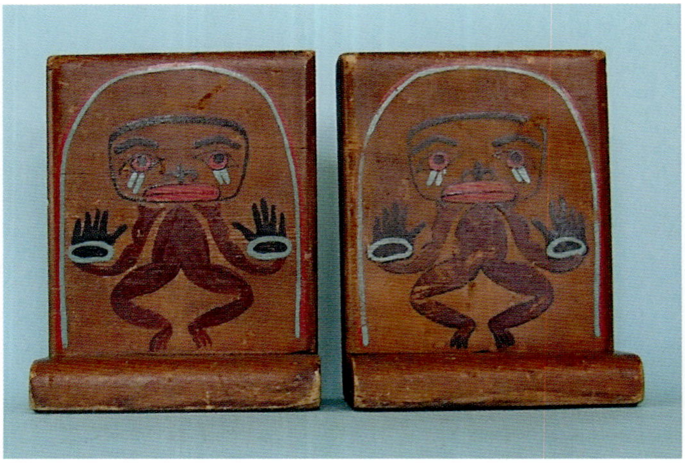

Figure 102. Guardian Spirit. 6.75", red cedar. Circa 1930? Rarity. 5. Aesthetic. Folk art presentation of a traditional guardian figure. $200-300.

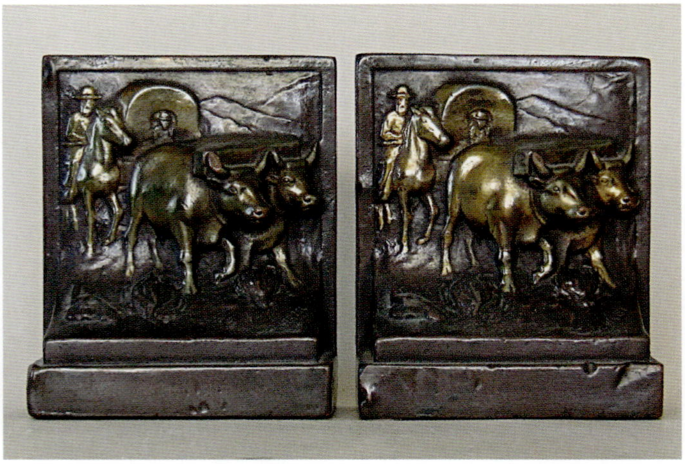

Figure 104. The Covered Wagon. 5.5", electroformed bronze. Inscription: The Covered Wagon, Paul Herzel. Foundry: Attrib. Pompeian Bronze. Circa 1920. Rarity 2. Aesthetic. $200-300.

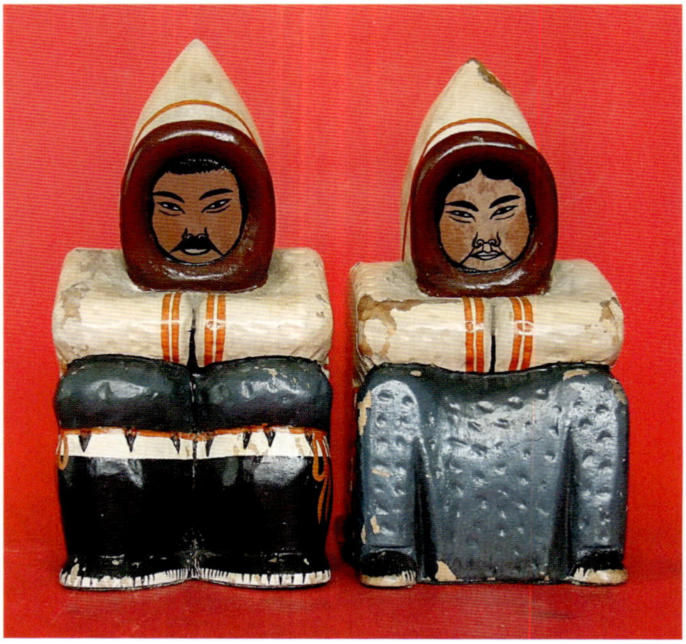

Figure 103. Grenfell Eskimos. 5.75", wood. Foundry: Grenfell Missions. The first production was as early as 1909, but this pair may be later. Circa 1909. Rarity 3. Aesthetic. Folk art presentation of Eskimos. $400-600.

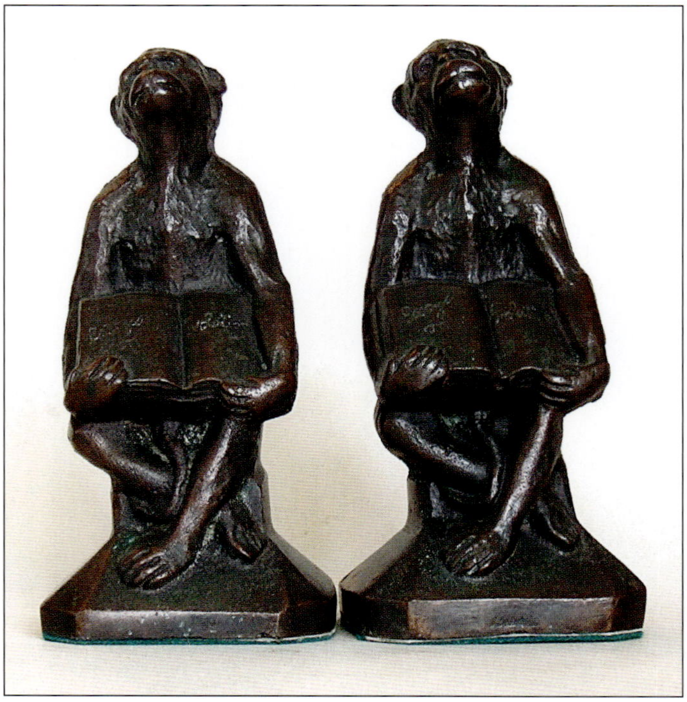

Figure 105. Scopes Monkey (Chimpanzee). 6.75", iron. Inscription on the book: Essays in evolution. Foundry: Howe Co., Chicago. Circa 1928. Rarity 3. Aesthetic. $240-360.

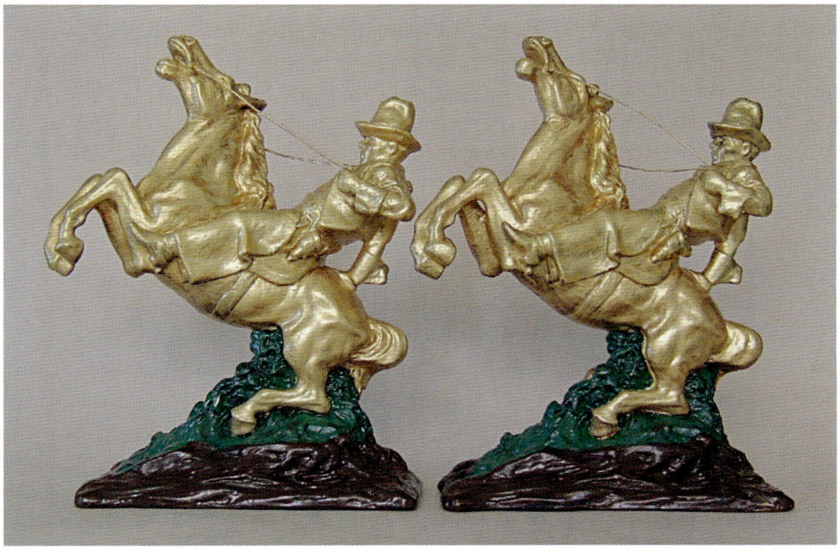

Figure 106. Working Cowboy. 9", electroformed bronze. Inscription: Armor Bronze 1928. Rarity 3. Aesthetic. The hat is battered so he is not a movie cowboy hero. $400-600.

Figure 107. Rodeo Rider. 6.5", gray metal. Inscription: Ronson, Newark NJ, 1942. Rarity 5. Aesthetic. A PMC copy is available. $200-300.

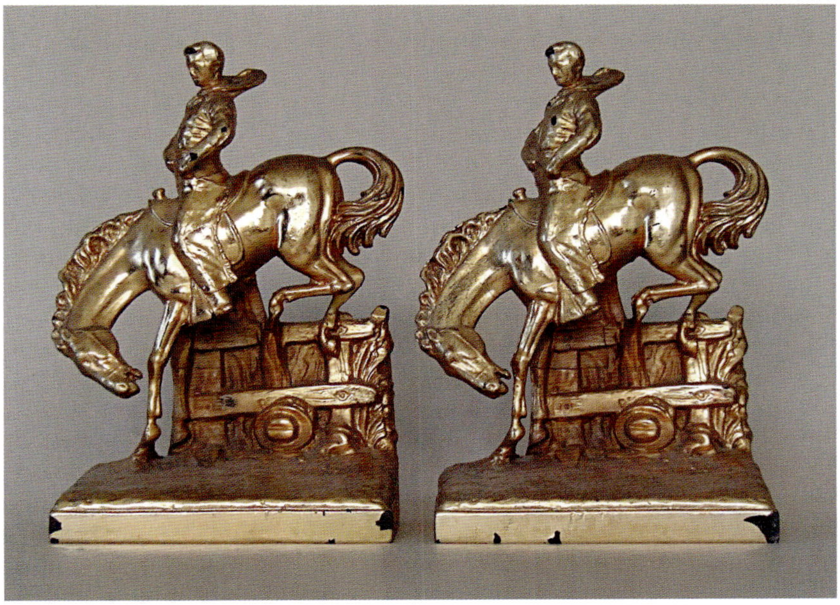

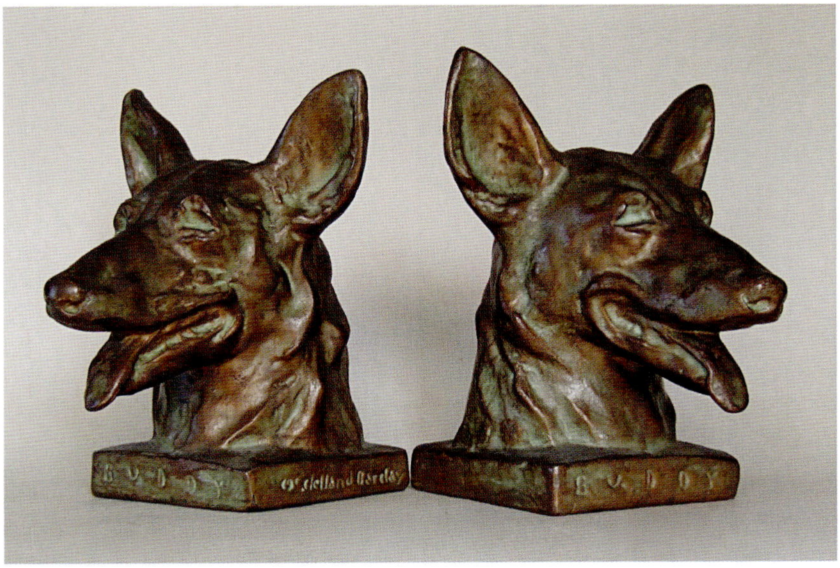

Figure 108. Buddy. 7.75", gray metal. Inscription: Buddy and McClelland Barclay. Foundry: Dodge Co. 1931. Rarity 2. Aesthetic. Buddy was the first trained seeing-eye dog. $200-300.

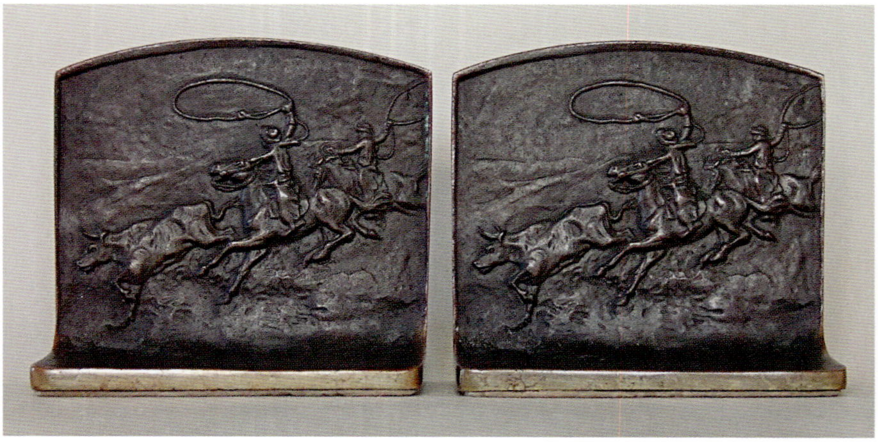

Figure 109. Roundup. 5", bronze. Circa 1920. Rarity 1. Aesthetic. $160-240.

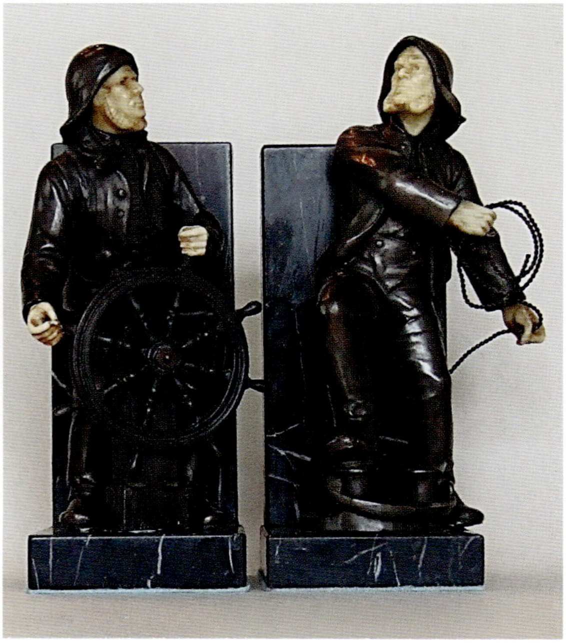

Figure 110. Busy Mariners. 9", gray metal, celluloid, and marble. Inscription: Germany. Circa 1930. These are large, heavy, bookends, 10 Lbs./pair. $500-750.

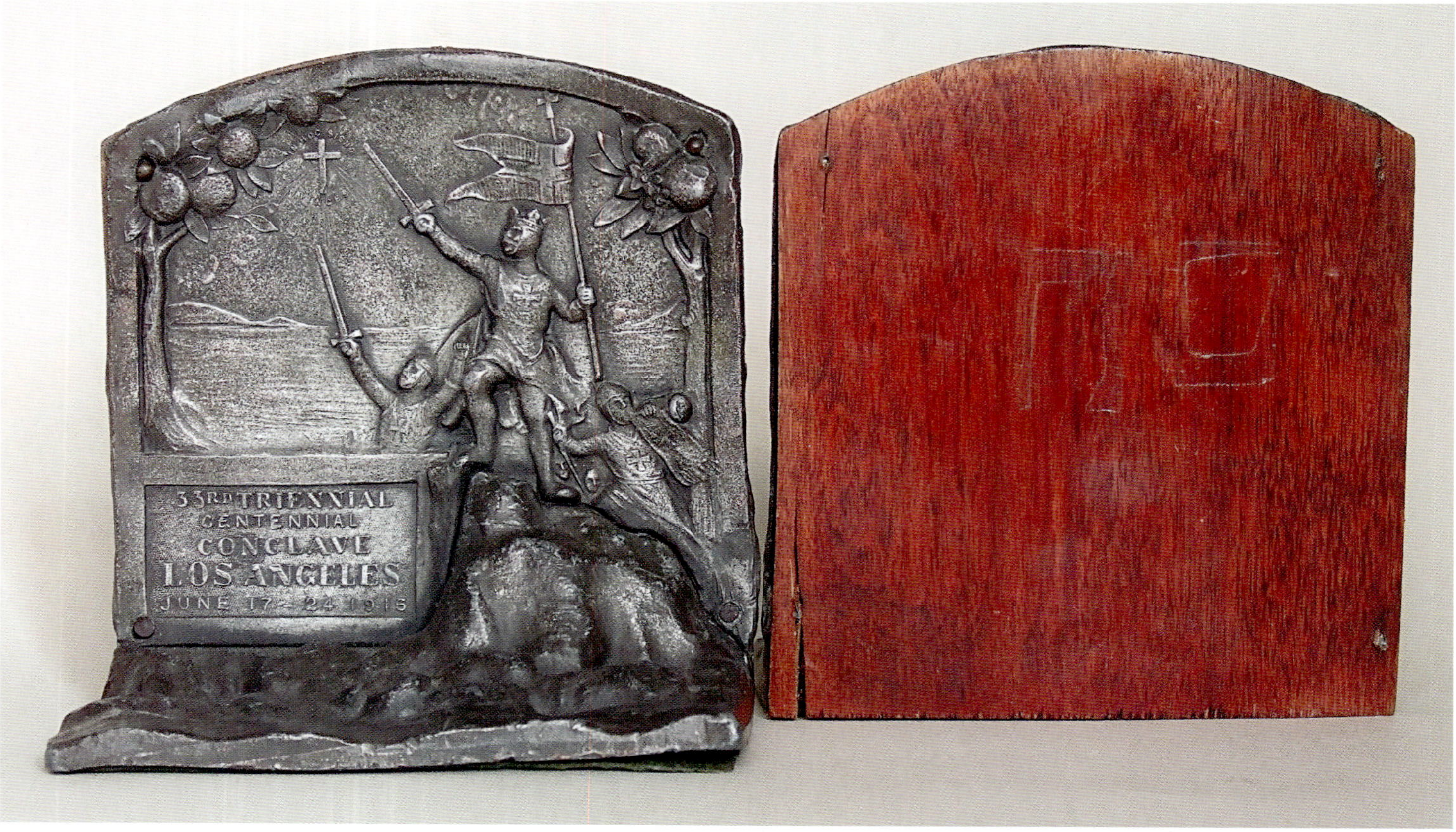

Figure 111. Knights Templar. 5.25", lead backed by wood. Inscription: 33rd triennial centennial conclave Los Angeles June 17-24 1916. Rarity 4. Aesthetic. From the Masonic Society. $270-420.

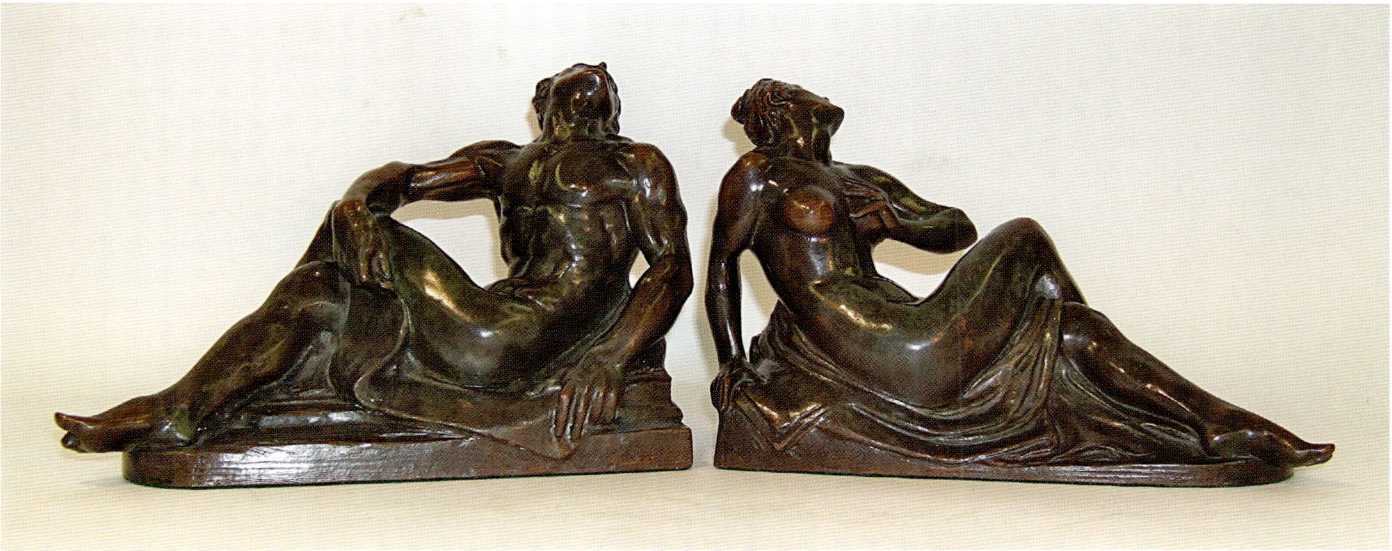

Figure 112. Man and Woman. 7.75", solid bronze. Inscription: Gorham Co. founders OBPG, signed R. Aitken. Circa 1915. Rarity 5. Aesthetic. *By courtesy of Charles DeCosta, from his collection.* $9,000-12,000.

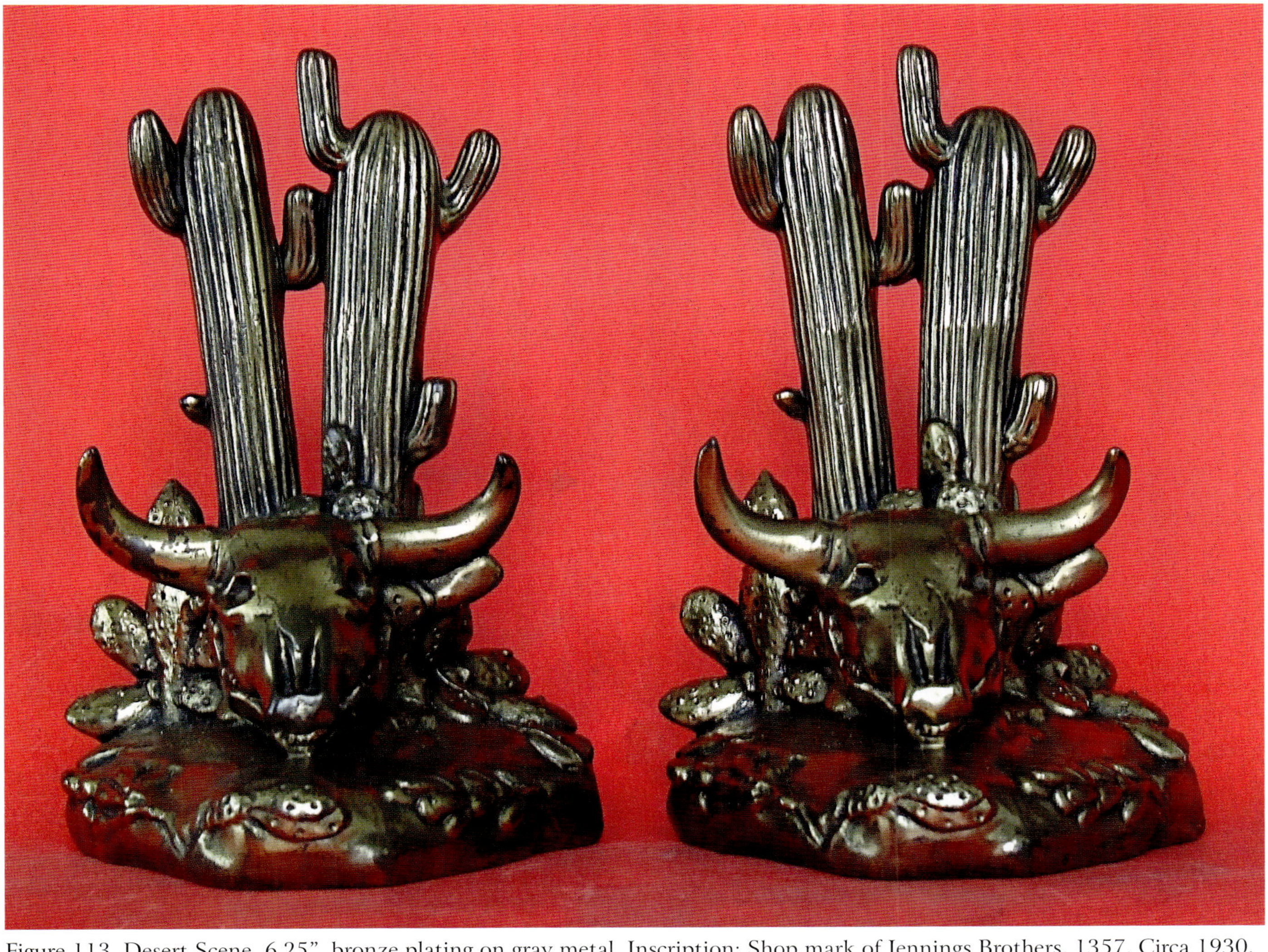

Figure 113. Desert Scene. 6.25", bronze plating on gray metal. Inscription: Shop mark of Jennings Brothers, 1357. Circa 1930. Rarity 4. Aesthetic. $240-360.

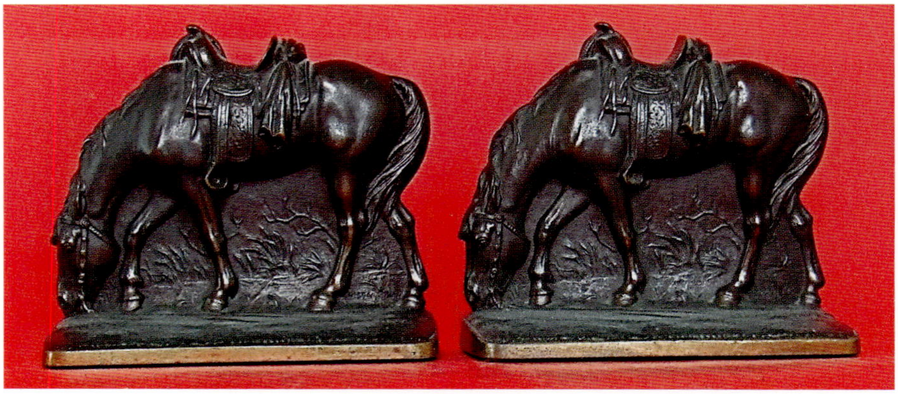

Figure 114. Empty Saddle. 4.25", bronze. Inscription: 9694, bronze, Signature of Gregory Allen. Foundry: Judd. 1929. Rarity 4. Aesthetic. Pictured in the Sears catalog, 1929. Unsigned iron reproductions are very common. $200-300.

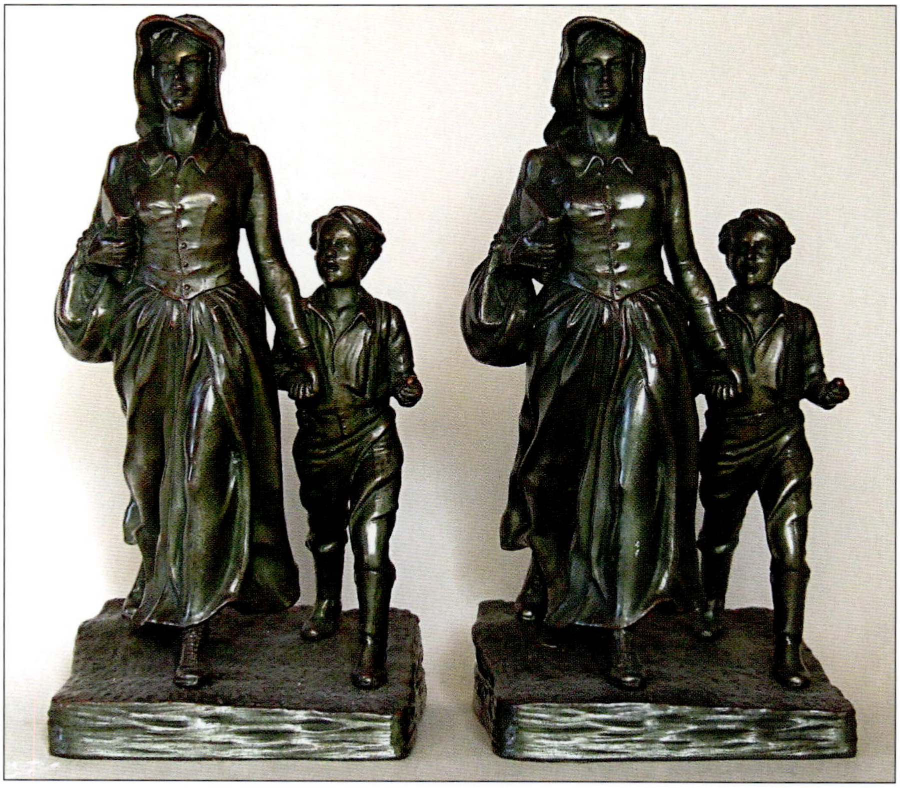

Figure 115. Pioneer Woman. 9", bronze plating on gray metal. Inscription: Shop mark of Jennings Brothers, 8855. Circa 1930. Rarity 3. Aesthetic. Reproduction of a statue in Ponca City, Oklahoma, by sculptor Bryant Baker in 1929. $400-600.

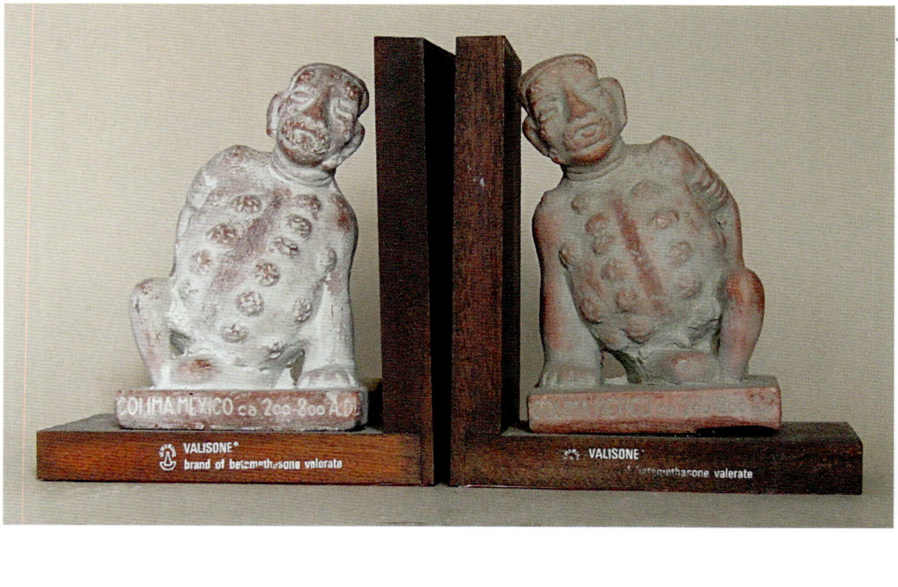

Figure 116. Itch and Scratch. 5.25", pottery and wood. Inscription: Valisone, brand of beta methasone valerate. Colima, Mexico, ca 200-800 AD, Shering. Foundry: Spanish. Circa 1950. Rarity 5. Advertising leader. Colima Indians made pottery figures representing ill people. These have a skin disorder which presumably would be alleviated by the Shering skin cream. Aesthetic. $200-300.

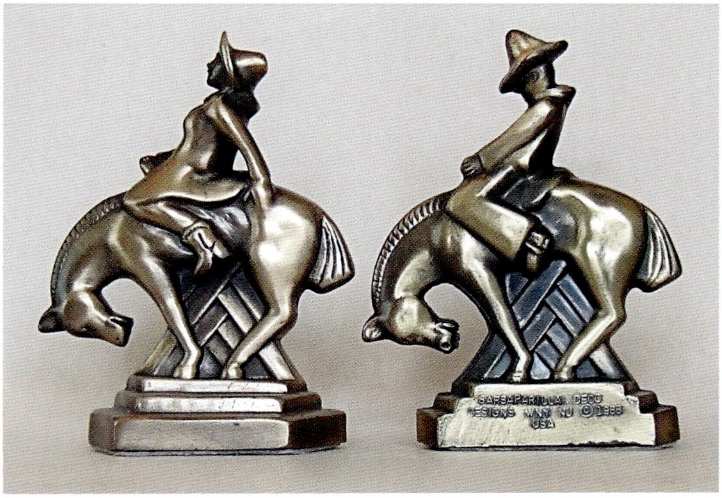

Figure 117. Dude Riders. 6.5", gray metal. Inscription: Sarsaparilla, Deco designs, WNY. NJ, 1988. Rarity 2. Aesthetic. (Art Deco?). Reproduction of bookends from the Art Deco era. Original foundry unknown. $100-150.

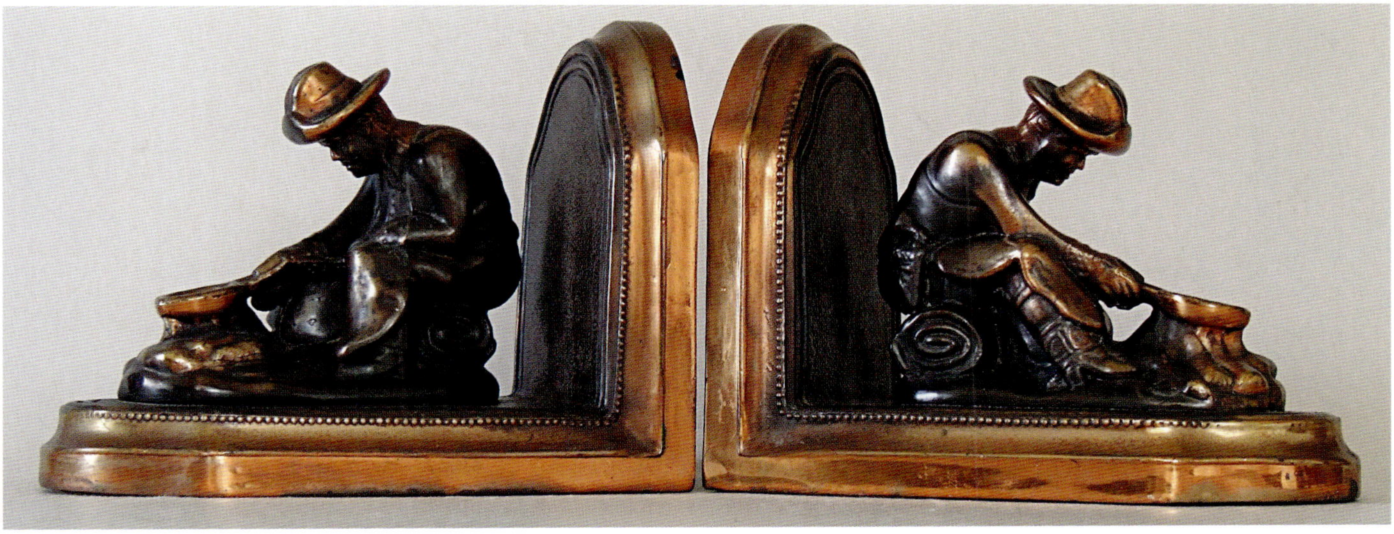

Figure 118. Prospector Cooking. 4.25", gray metal. Foundry: Attrib. Dodge. Inc. Circa 1939. Rarity 4. Aesthetic. $100-150.

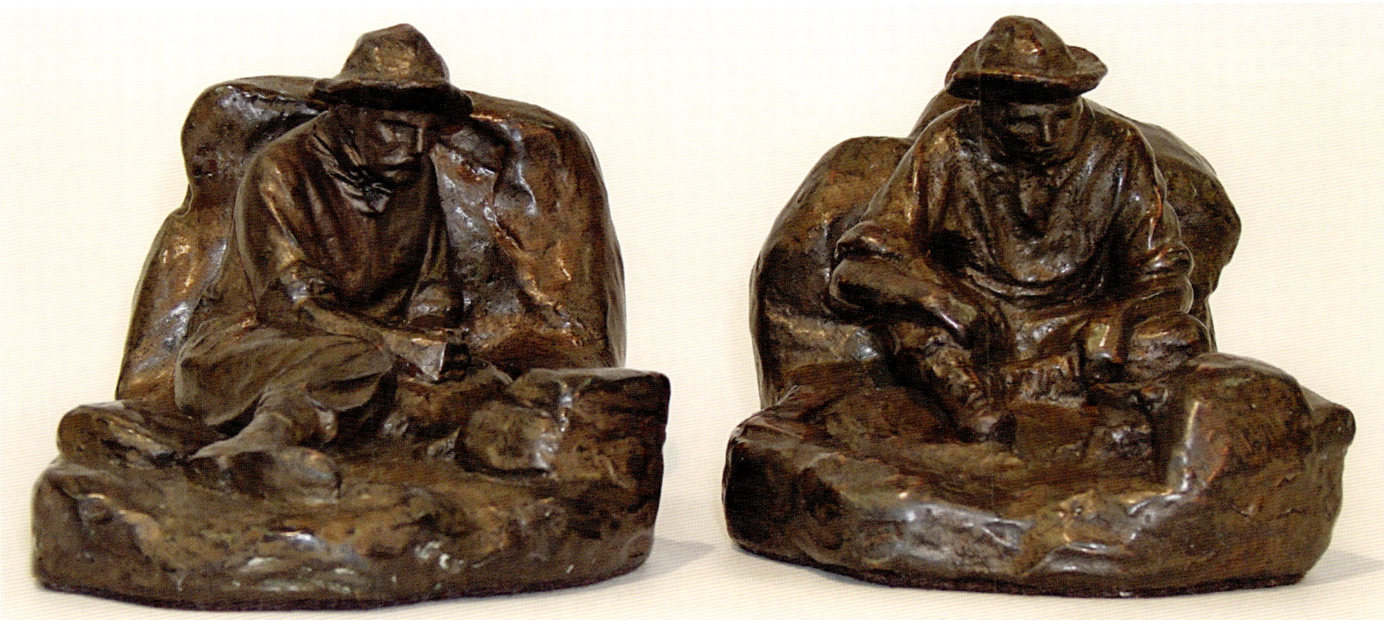

Figure 119. Prospector. 4.5", electroformed bronze. Inscription: signed D. Franklin. 1913, 1914. Rarity 5. *Aesthetic. By courtesy of Charles DeCosta, from his collection.* $1,600-1,800.

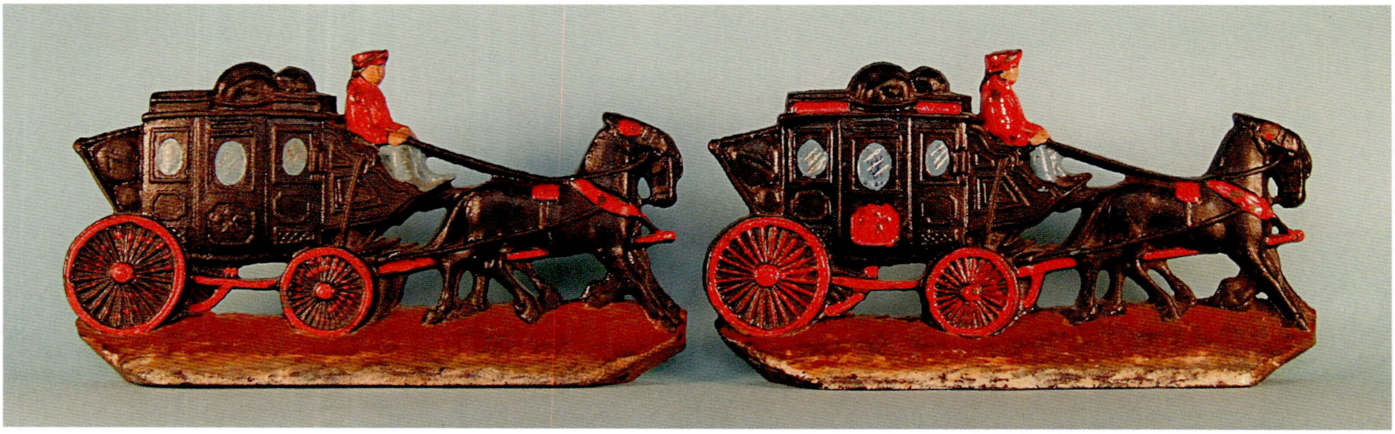

Figure 120. Stage Coach Trip. 4.5", iron. Inscription: W.H. Howell Co., '06. Rarity 4. Aesthetic. This inscription establishes W.H. Howell Co. as an early bookend foundry. $200-300.

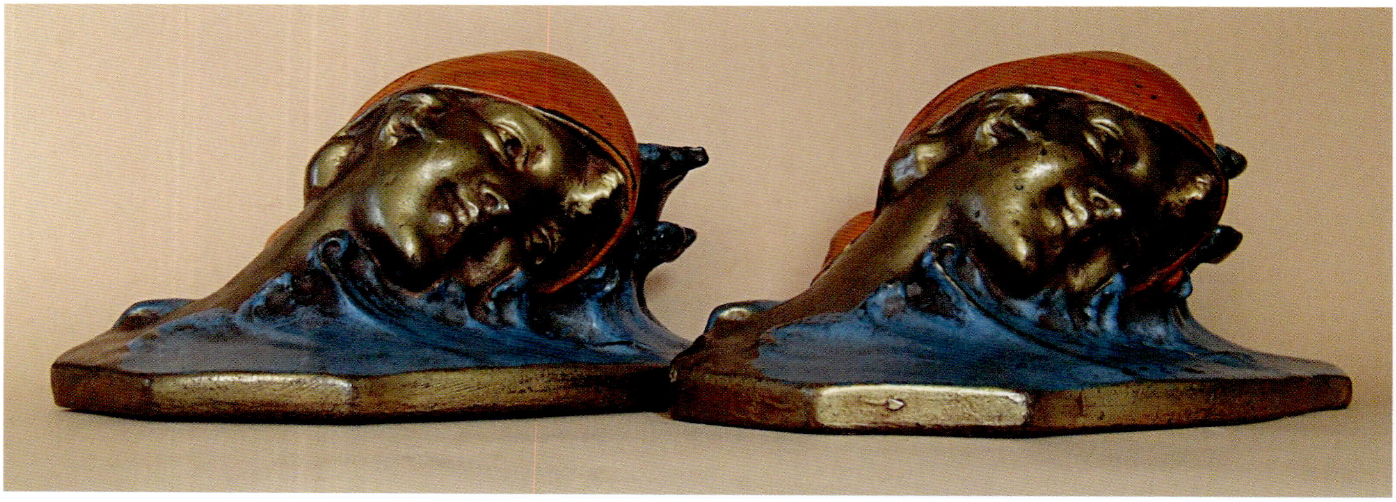

Figure 121. Gertrude Ederle. 4", electroformed bronze. Foundry: Attrib. Armor Bronze. Circa 1927. Rarity 4. Aesthetic. Gertrude Ederle was an internationally-known celebrity for her record-breaking swimming. She was and is a feminist icon. $500-750.

Figure 122. Water Fowl. 7", aluminum. Inscription: Ernst. Circa 1955. Rarity 4. Aesthetic. $80-120.

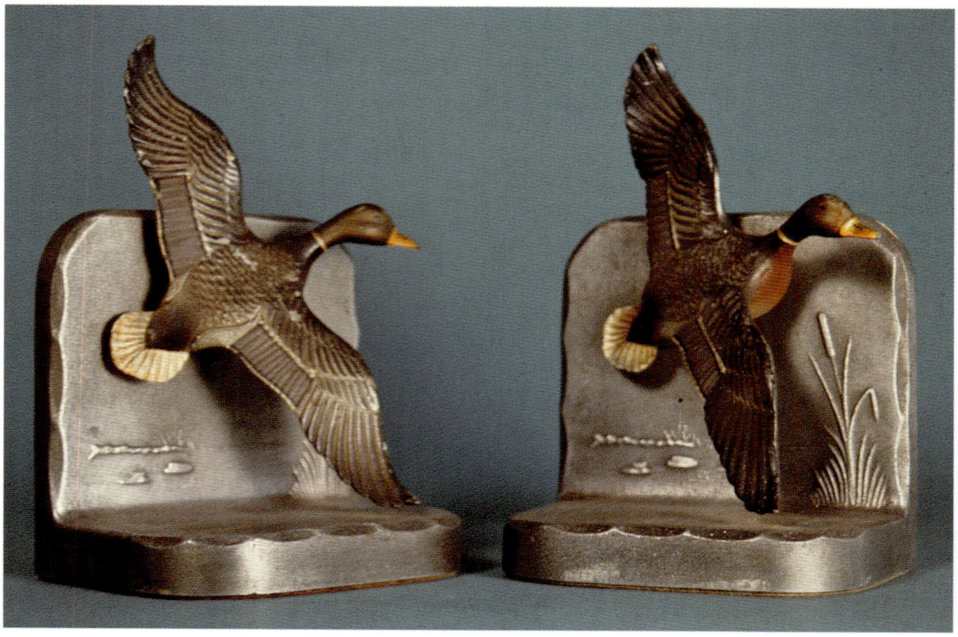

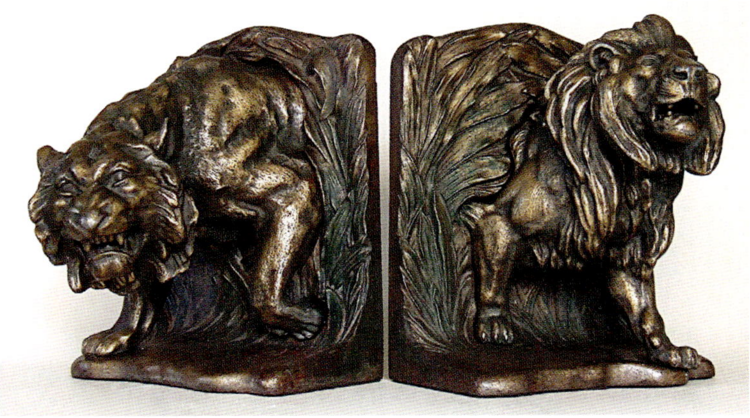

Figure 123. Lion and Tiger. 7", iron and gray metal. Inscription: Shop mark of Bradley and Hubbard. Circa 1915? Rarity 3. Aesthetic. These are large, heavy bookends, 18 lbs./ pair. $500-750.

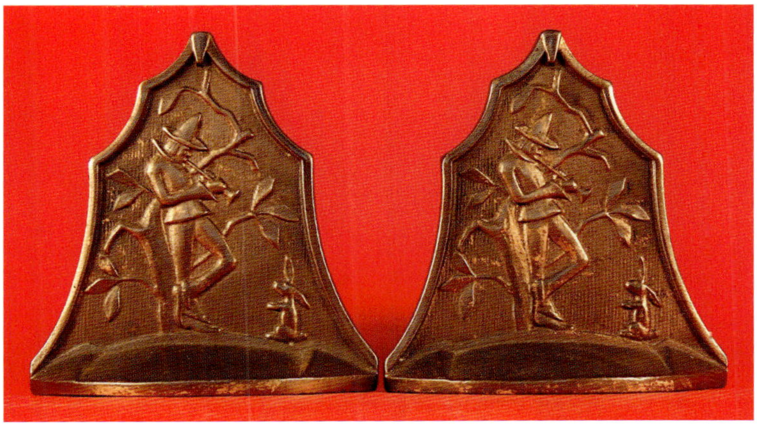

Figure 124. The Wanderer. 5.75", iron. Inscription: The Wanderer, 1928 and shop mark of Connecticut foundry. Rarity 2. Aesthetic. (Art Nouveau?) Possibly related to an old English poem with this title from the tenth century or perhaps earlier. $120-180.

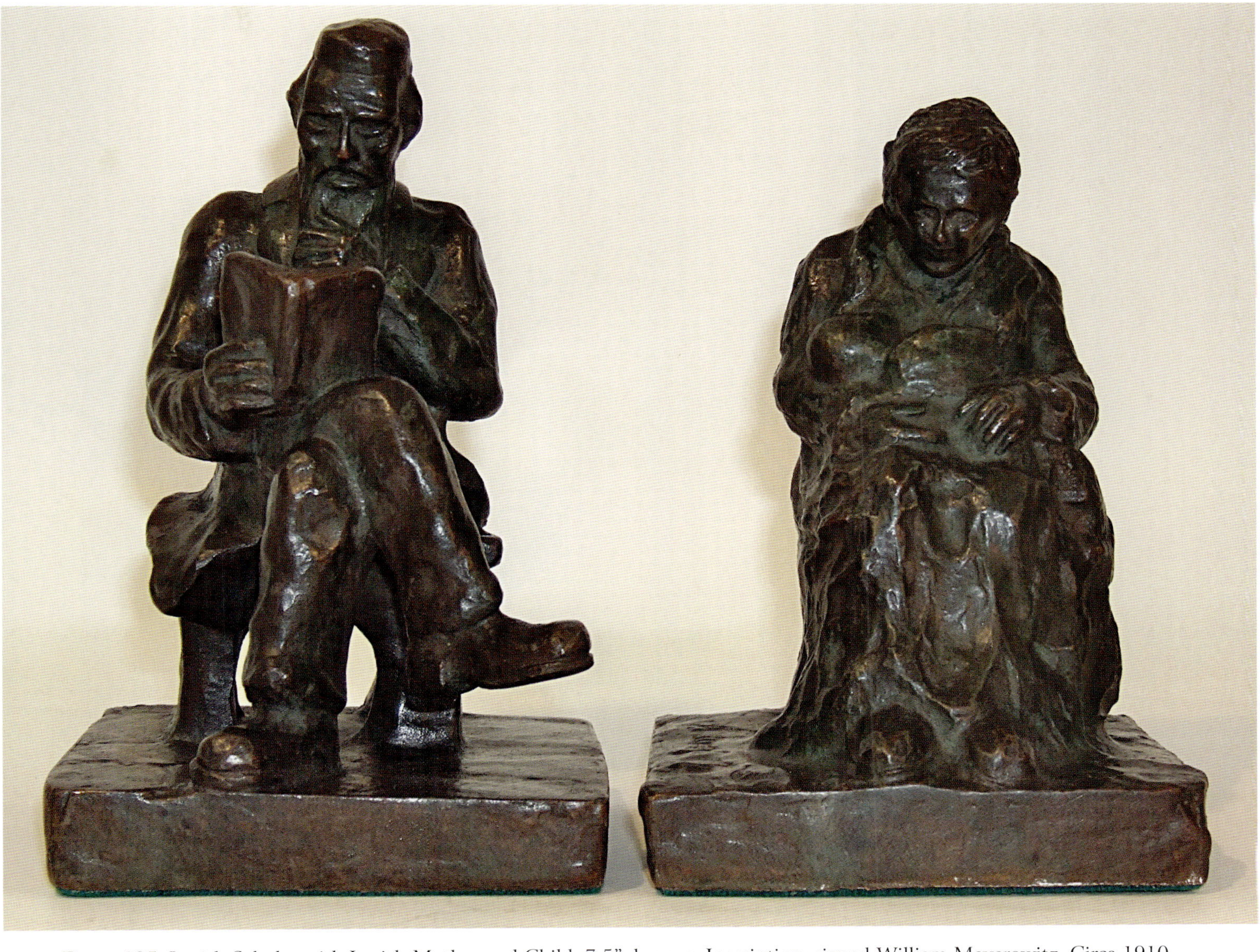

Figure 125. Jewish Scholar with Jewish Mother and Child. 7.5", bronze. Inscription: signed William Meyerowitz. Circa 1910. Rarity 5. Aesthetic. *By courtesy of Charles DeCosta, from his collection.* $4,000-5.000.

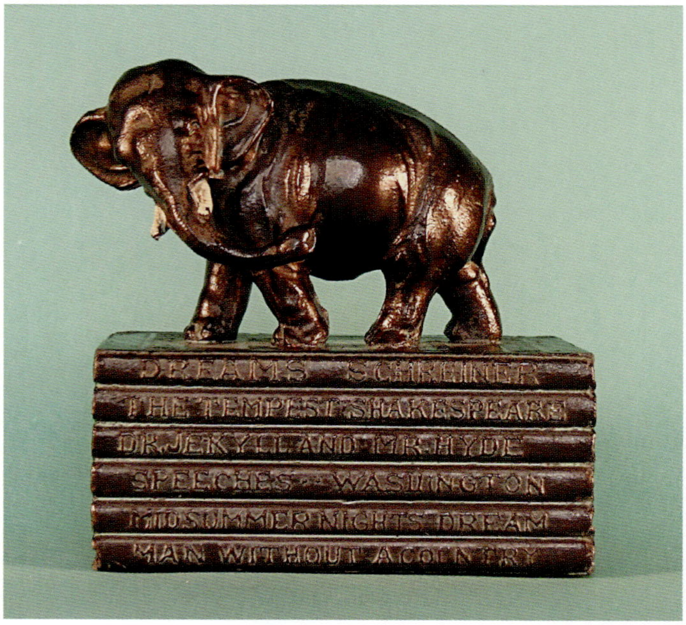

Figure 126. Elephant and Books 4.5", gray metal. Foundry: Attrib. Ronson. Circa 1922. Rarity 3. Aesthetic. Small *Little Leather Library* books were sold in the early nineteen twenties, and these bookends were meant to support those books. This elephant stands on reproductions of the books. $100-150.

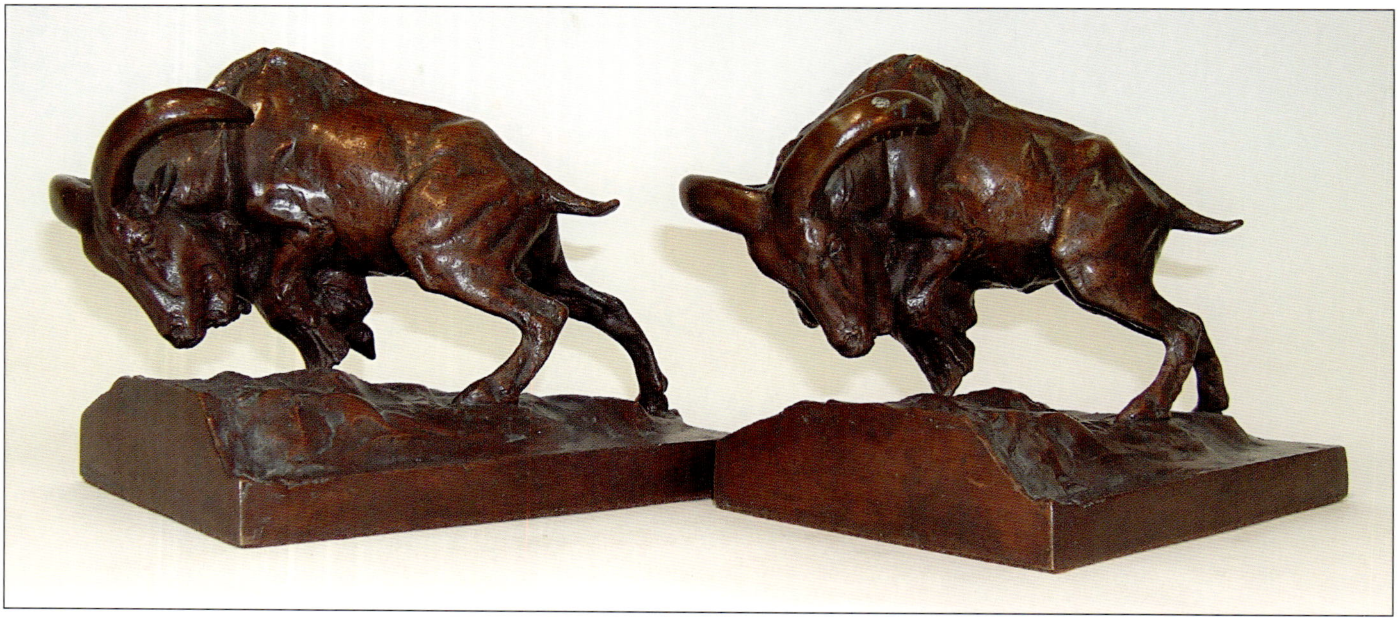

Figure 127. Dall Sheep. 6", bronze. Inscription: Gorham Co. Founders, signed Anna V. Hyatt. 1928. Rarity 5. Aesthetic. *By courtesy of Charles DeCosta, from his collection.* $7,000-8,000.

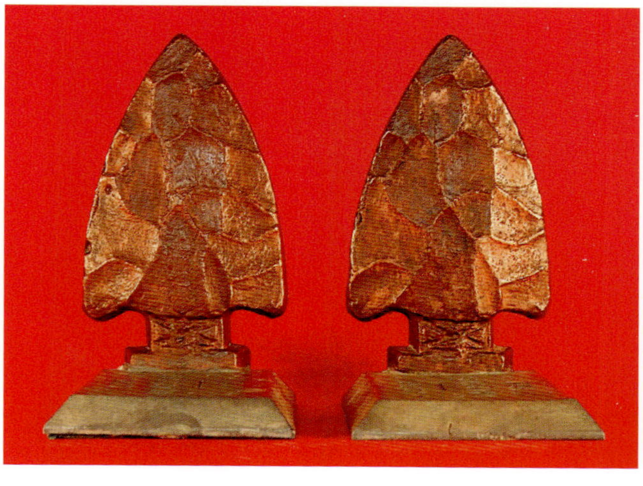

Figure 128. Arrowhead. 4.25", gray metal. Inscription: Rotary, Anaconda, 1931. Rarity 5. Aesthetic. This arrowhead is the trademark of the Anaconda Copper Co. $120-180.

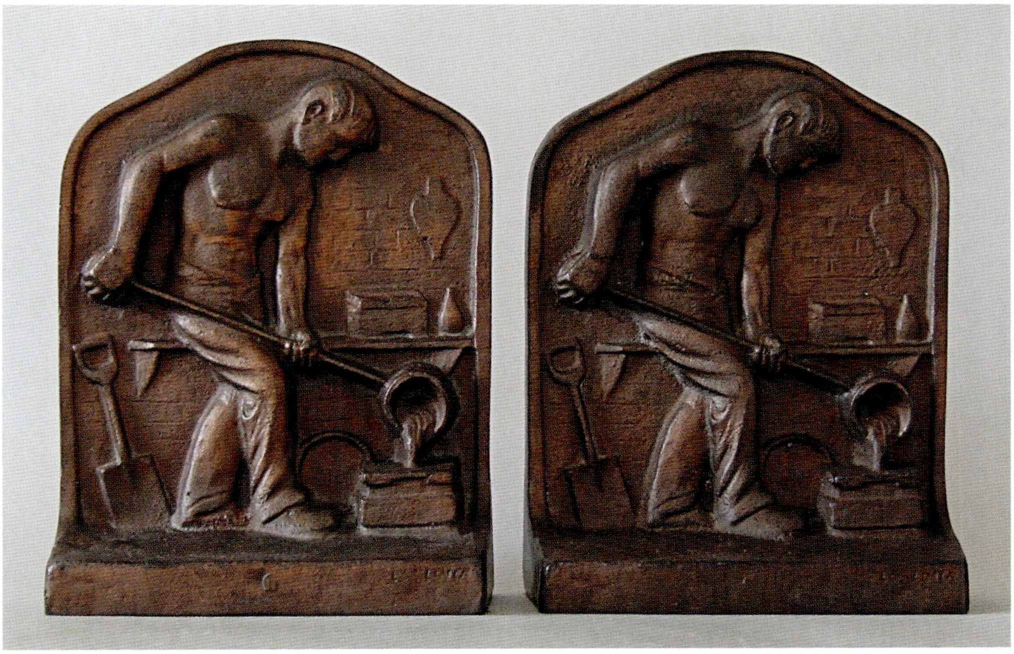

Figure 129. Foundry Worker. 7.25", iron. Inscription: Forest City Foundries, L C Lynn. Sculptor: Louis Linn. Circa 1931. Rarity 4. Aesthetic. (Promotional?) In this time of labor union growth, the laborer is pictured, not the foundry. $200-300.

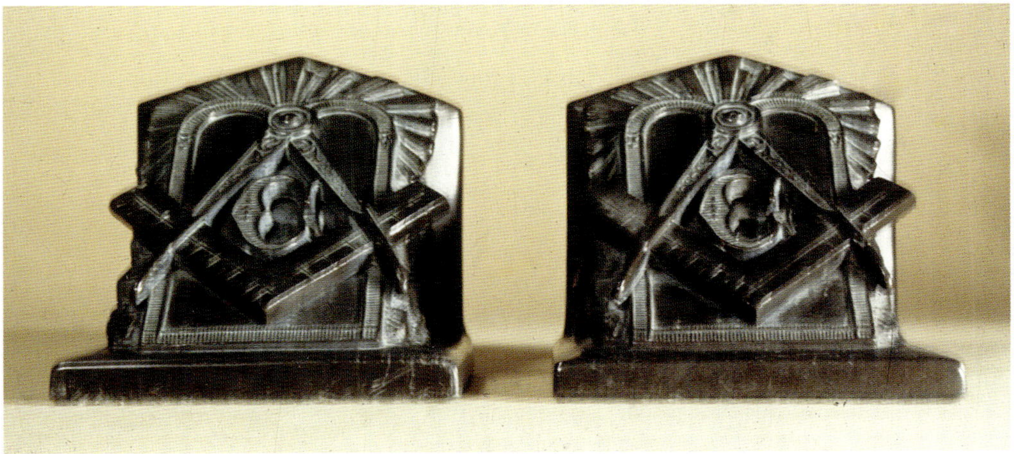

Figure 130. Shriners. 4.75", iron. Circa 1925. Rarity 4. Aesthetic. Promotional. $60-90.

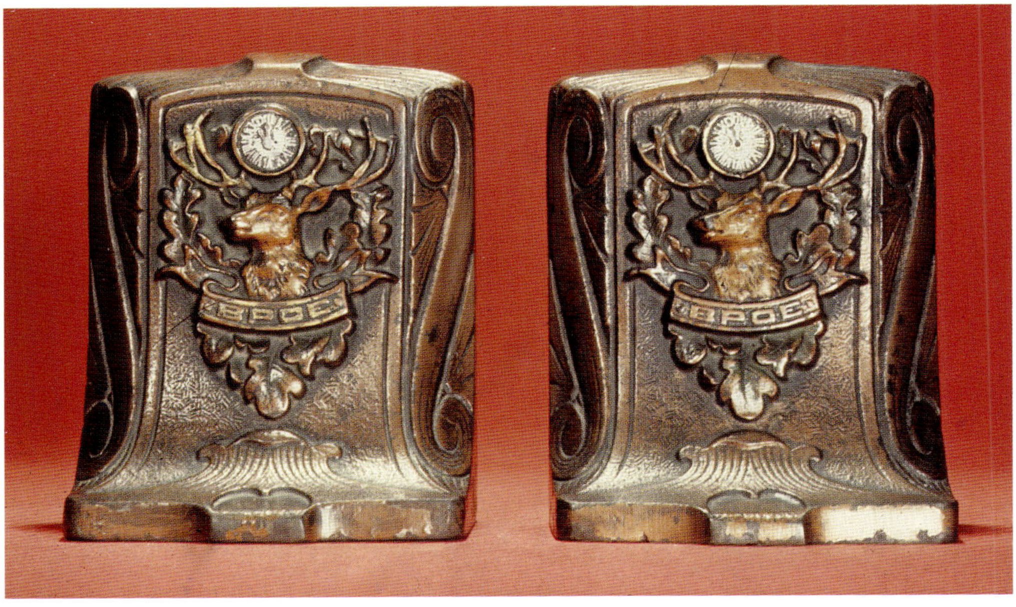

Figure 131. Benevolent and Protective Order of Elks. 5.25", iron. Inscription: BPOE. Circa 1928. Rarity 5. Promotional. $80-120.

Figure 132. Masonic Lodge. 3.5" gray metal. Inscription: L.V Aronson (Ronson), 1922. Rarity 4. Aesthetic. $75-115.

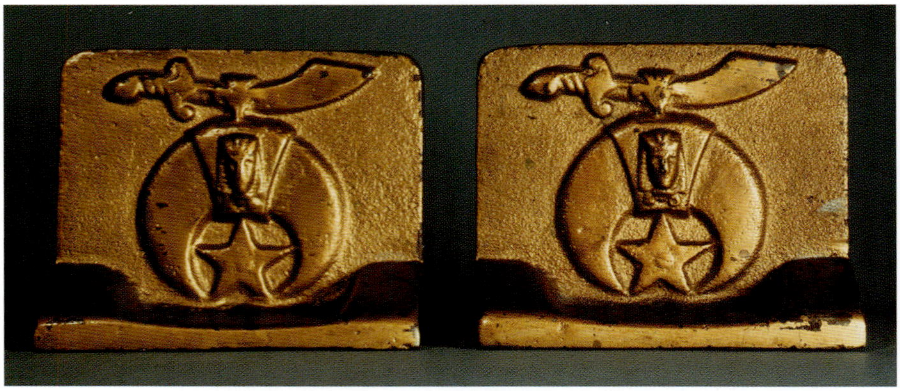

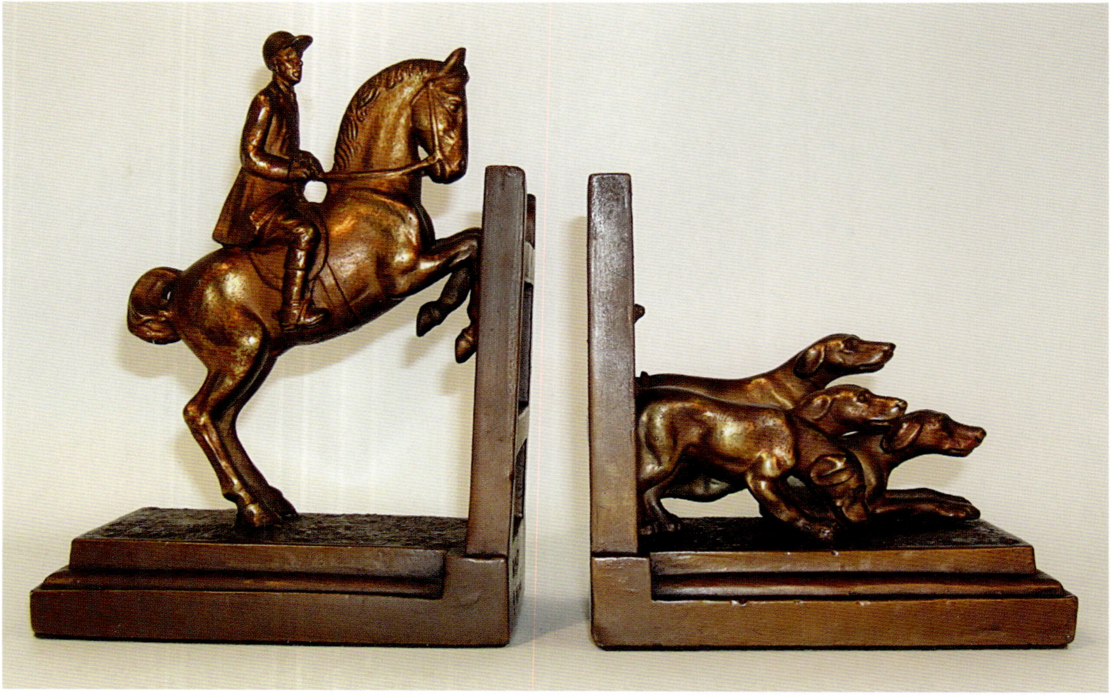

Figure 133. Fox Hunt. 8.25", electroformed bronze. Inscription: Armor Bronze company label, Signature of D. Martini (sculptor), 1937. Rarity 5. Aesthetic. *By courtesy of Charles DeCosta, from his collection.* $900-1,000.

Figure 134. Wilderness Cabin. 7", iron. Foundry: Attrib. Albany. Circa 1935. Rarity 3. Aesthetic. $100-150.

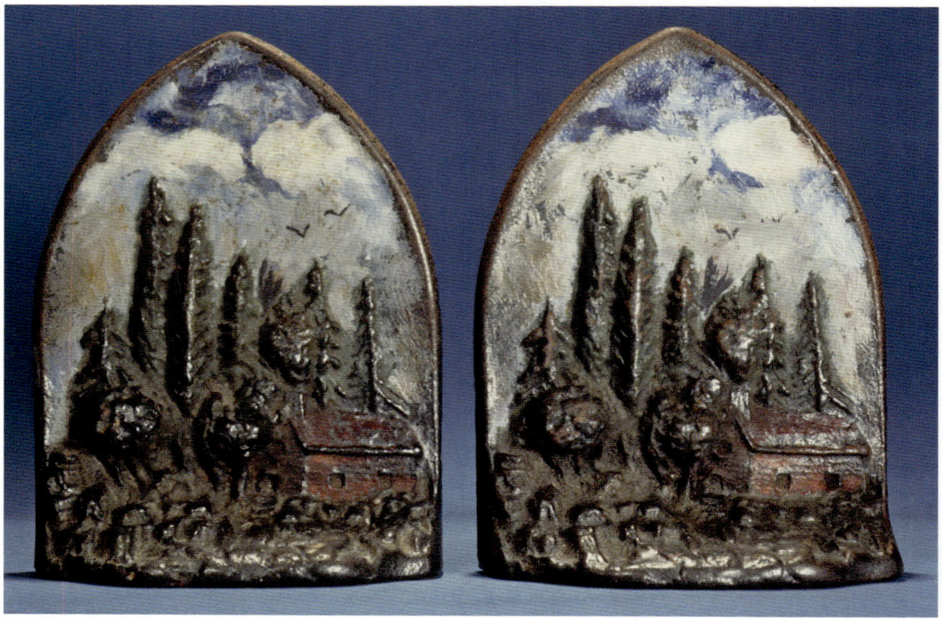

Chapter 4

Arts & Crafts Style Bookends

The Arts & Crafts Movement began in the last half of the nineteenth century in England. It began as a protest against the impersonal and often shoddy goods produced in the beginning of the industrial revolution in that century. The protest was popularized by the well-known art critic and poet, the mystical John Ruskin, who railed against the loss of artistic merit and creativity in machined goods, and the conversion of skilled artisans into machine operators. He promoted organic, naturalistic images in art and looked to medieval times and Gothic architecture for inspiration.

The style we know today as Arts & Crafts derives its name from an art conference in England in 1888. This style had been developed by the brilliant poet William Morris and his colleagues beginning in about 1860. Morris accepted the philosophy promoted by Ruskin, including the admonition that utilitarian objects as well as art objects should be beautiful. Morris is credited with the quotation "Have nothing in your house that you do not know to be useful or believe to be beautiful." We will accept that for bookends.

The Arts & Crafts style drew upon the Arts & Crafts Movement and became part of it. It was not simply an endorsement of Gothic art, although it overlapped Gothic material. Gothic art was chiefly architectural and the Gothic style bookends can be described as Victorian Gothic revival (Figures 135-139). The Arts & Crafts style of the time drew rather upon the idealized medieval community, especially of the fourteenth century. It used motifs such as knights and their beautiful ladies, minstrels, castles, fools, and medieval dress (Figures 140-147), and met the philosophy of the movement by promoting objects that were functional, unadorned, serviceable, and hand-produced by artisans. The Arts & Crafts style grew to include not only medieval subject material but any material produced by Arts & Crafts criteria. For example, American art pottery from about 1900 is considered in the Arts & Crafts genre regardless of subject material. The style could be credited to the Victorian era, but it did not become fully developed until somewhat later.

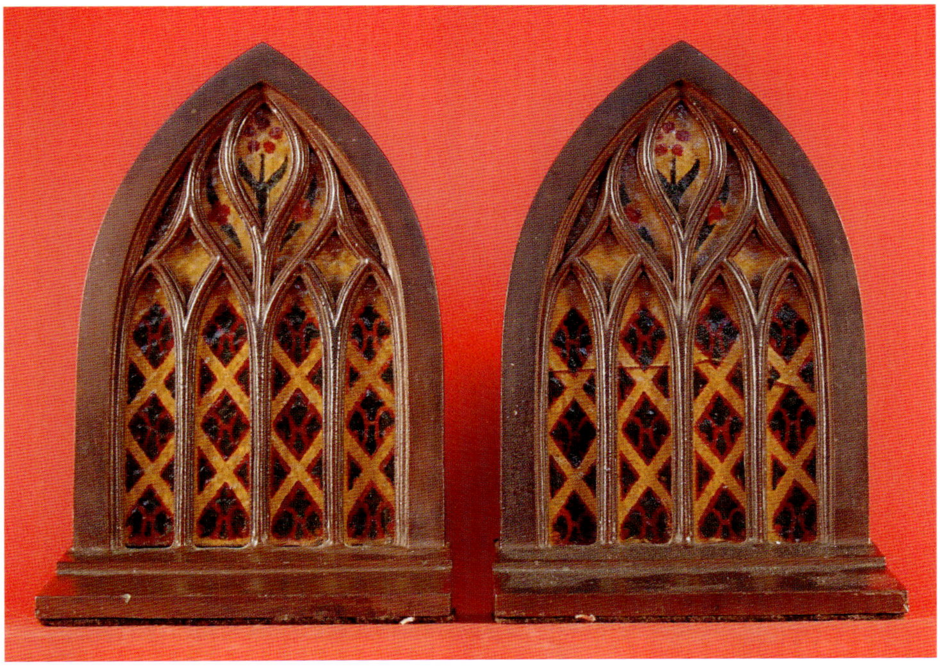

Figure 135. Stained Glass Window. 7.25", iron, glass, painted paper. Inscription: Bradley and Hubbard shop mark. Painted paper behind slag glass, and faced with an iron grill, gives the appearance of a Gothic arch with a stained glass window. Circa 1915. Rarity 5. Victorian. Gothic revival. $500-600.

Figure 136. Gothic Arch. 6", gray metal. Circa 1915. Rarity 3. Victorian. Gothic revival. $60-90.

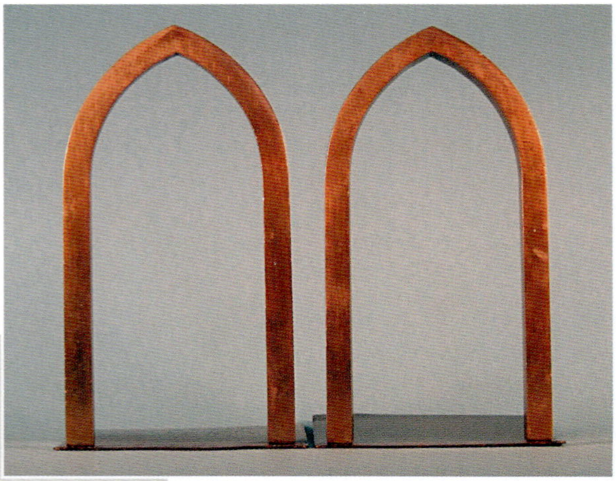

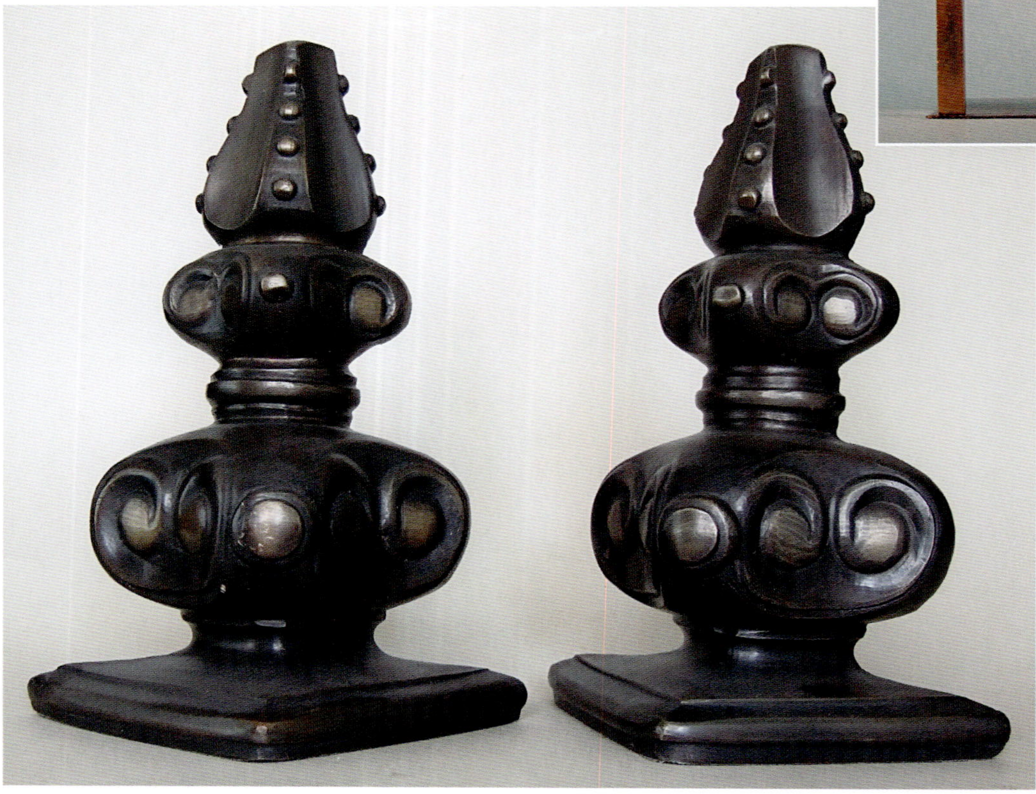

Figure 137. Gothic Tower. 9.75", bronze. Circa 1919. Rarity 5. Victorian. Gothic revival. These are large, tall bookends. $270-420.

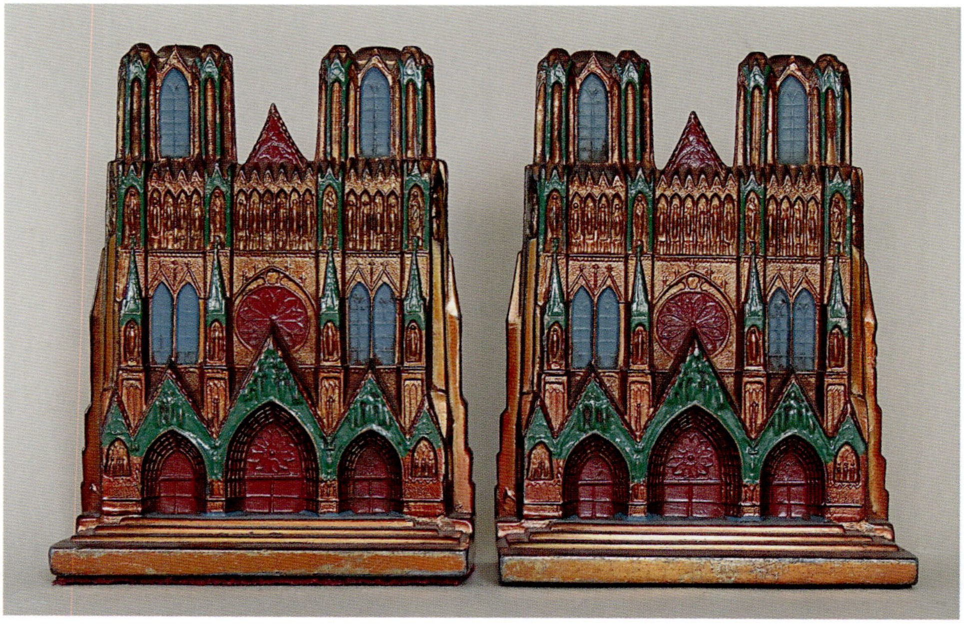

Figure 138. Reims Cathedral, West Facade. 5.5", gray metal. Inscription: Ronson company label. Circa 1919. Rarity 2. Victorian. Gothic revival. $240-360.

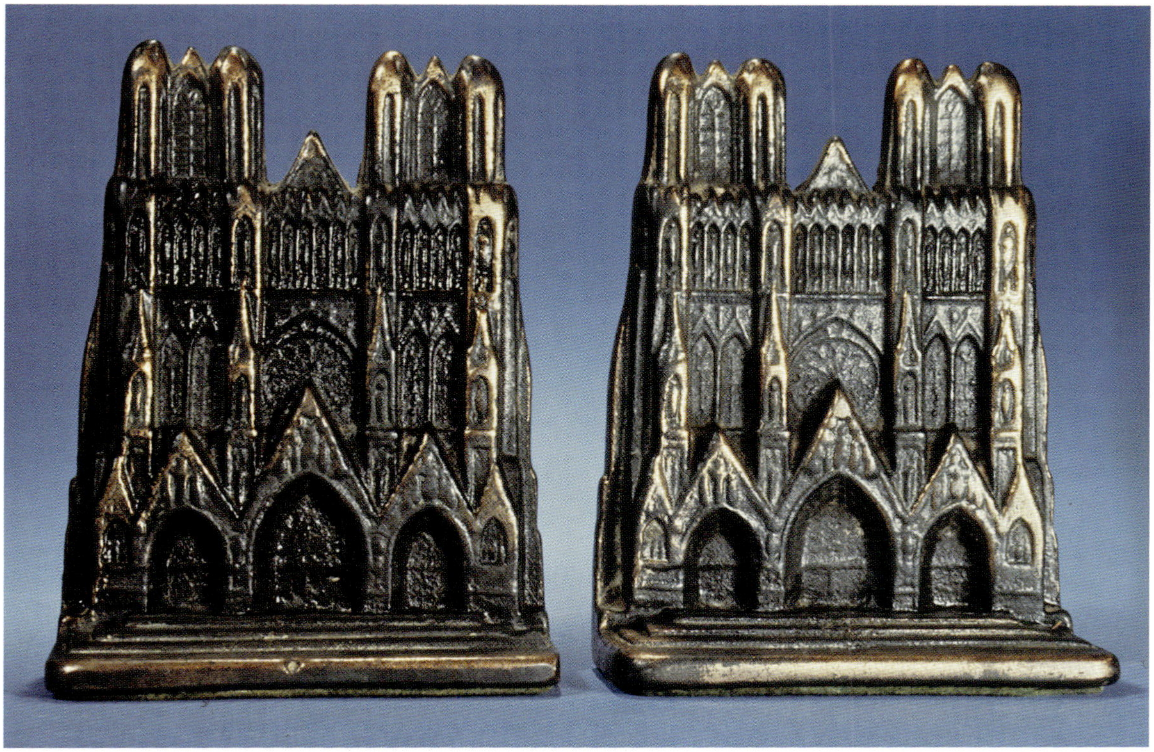

Figure 139. Reims Cathedral, West Facade. 5.5" Iron. Circa 1920. Rarity 3. Victorian. Gothic revival. $60-90.

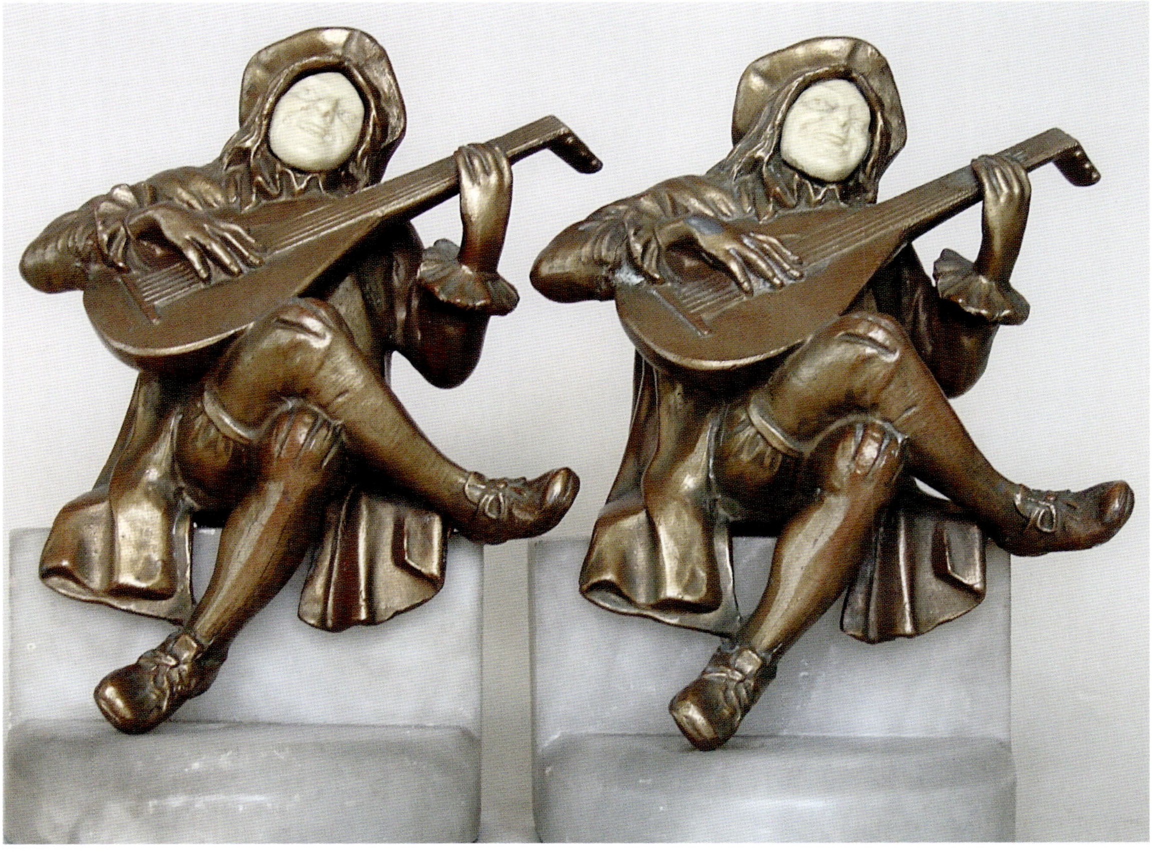

Figure 140. Minstrel. 7.25", gray metal, celluloid, and marble. Attrib. Hirsch Foundry. Circa 1930. Rarity 4. Arts & Crafts. $240-360.

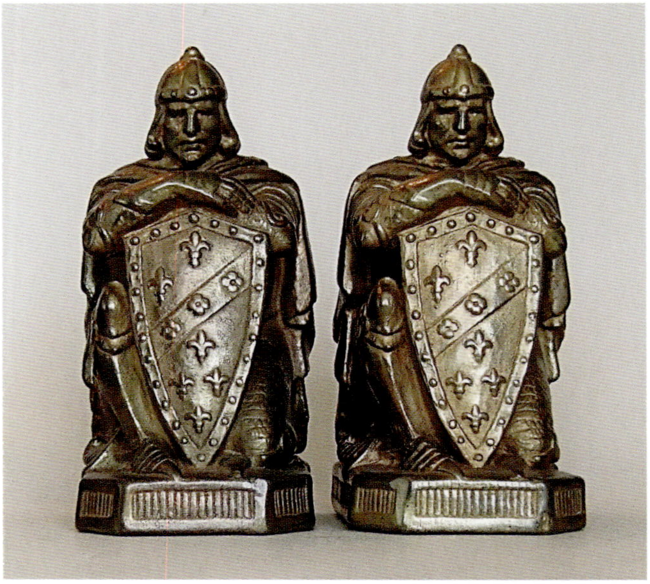

Figure 141. Kneeling Knight. 7.5", gray metal Inscription: Armor Bronze shop mark, label, 1922 and signature Gregory Allen. Rarity 3. Arts & Crafts. Polychrome Marion Bronze copies are more frequently seen. $256-384.

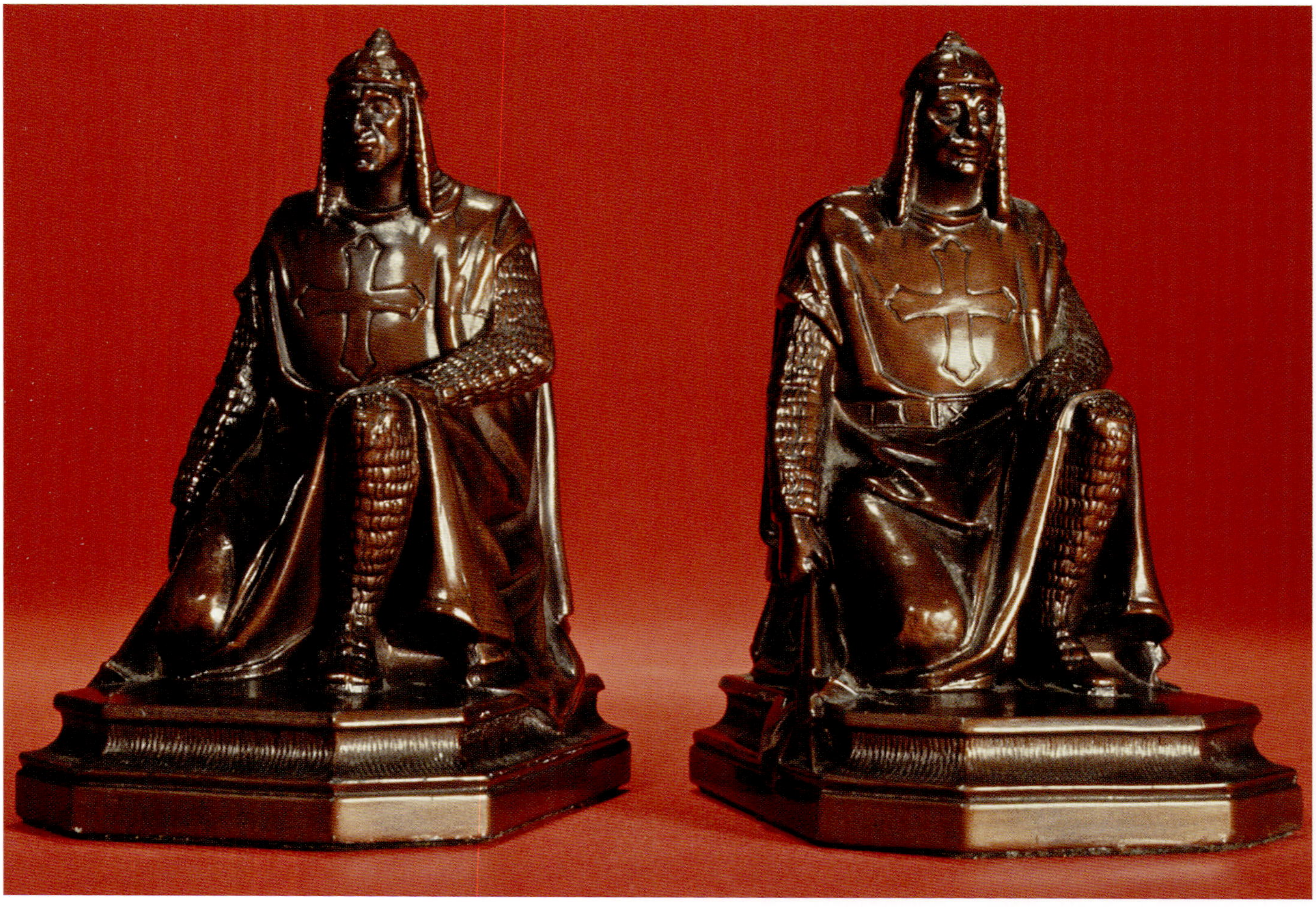

Figure 142. Knight Kneeling. 5", gray metal. Inscription: shop mark of K&O., signature of Ruhl. Circa 1924. Rarity 3. Arts & Crafts. $200-300.

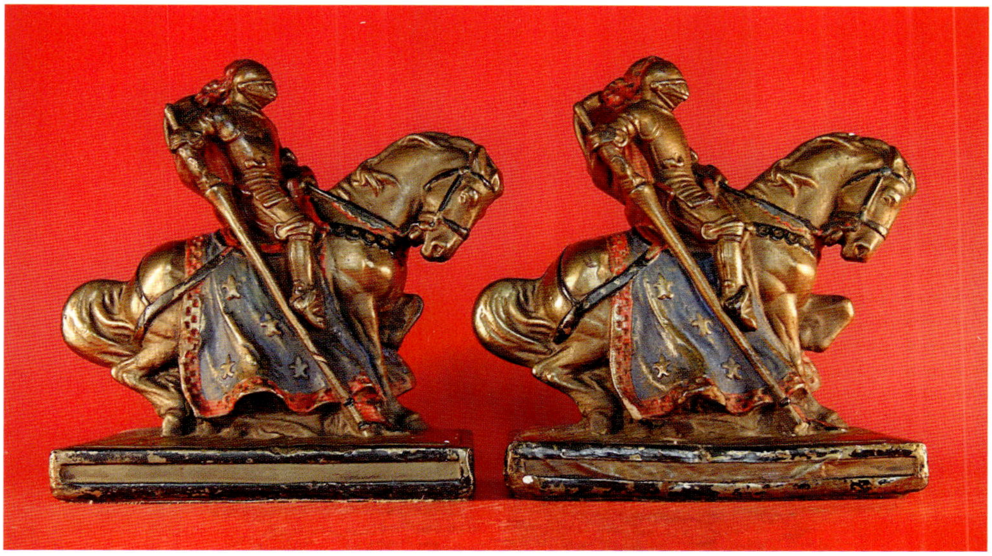

Figure 143. Knight on Horseback. 7", electroformed bronze. Inscription: Armor Bronze shop mark., signature of Gregory S. Allen. Circa 1922. Rarity 5. Arts & Crafts. A Marion Bronze copy is seen more frequently. $260-400.

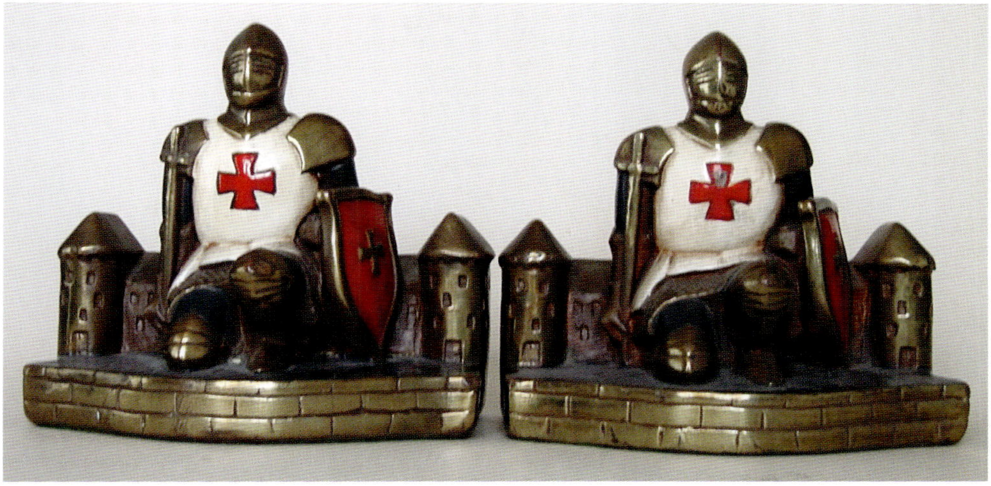

Figure 144. Knight Templar and Castles. 6", gray metal. Attrib. Armor Bronze Inc. Circa 1922. Rarity 5. Arts & Crafts. $280-420.

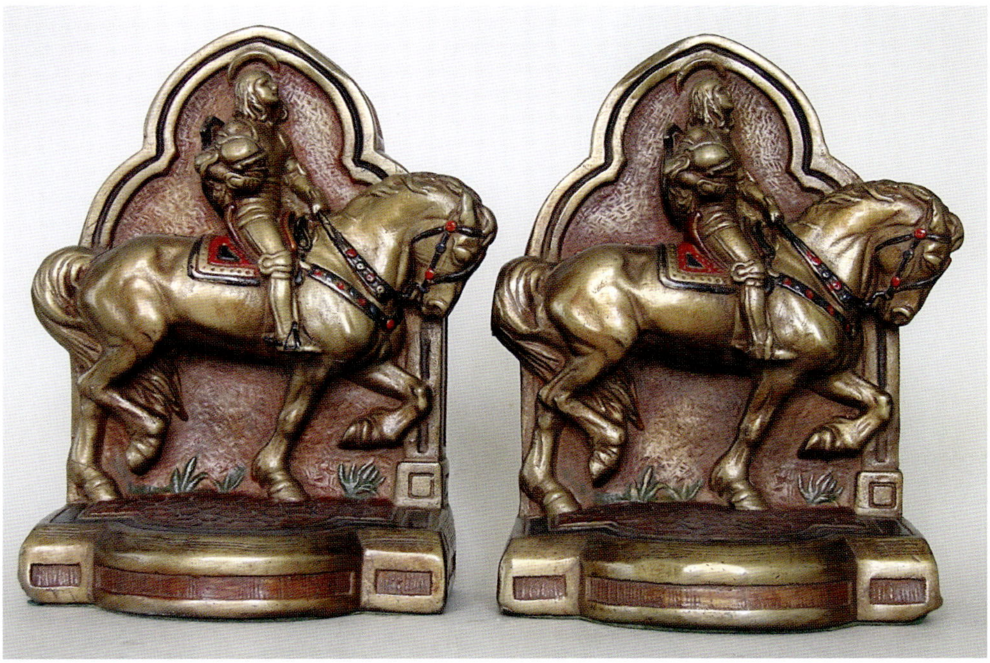

Figure 145. Joan of Arc with Halo. 8.5", electroformed bronze. Inscription: Armor Bronze company label, and signature of Gregory S. Allen. Circa 1920. Rarity 4. Arts & Crafts. $260-380.

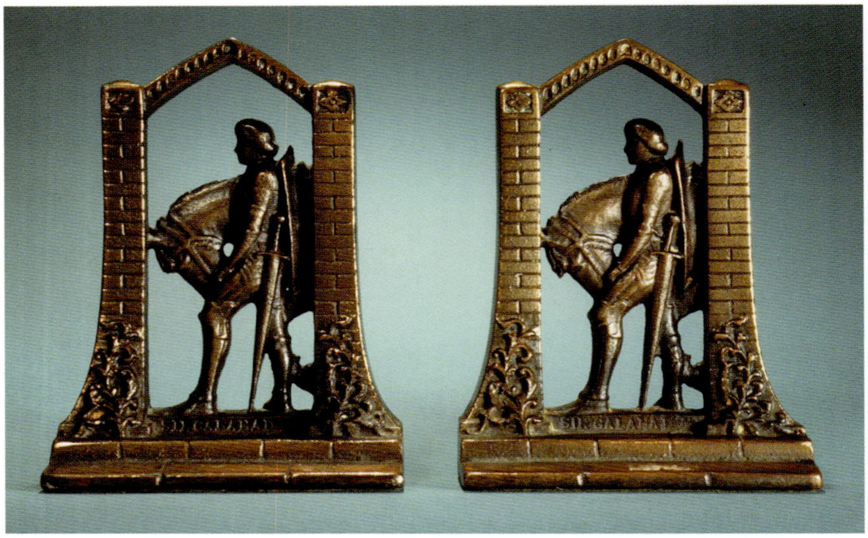

Figure 146. Sir Galahad. 6", iron. Circa 1920. Rarity 3. Arts & Crafts. $60-90.

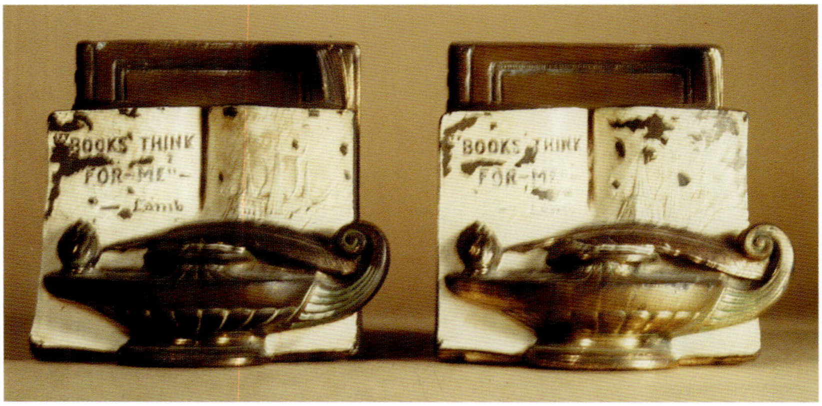

Figure 147. Lamp and Book. 5", gray metal. Inscription: LVA, 1942. The book reads "Books think for me. (Charles) Lamb" Foundry: Ronson. Rarity 3. Arts & Crafts. $120-180.

Today we celebrate this movement by building room décor in Arts & Crafts style, using furnishings that recall the preferred artwork of the English progenitors. The décor rings true, but most often it celebrates the contributions of the artists and neglects the intellectual and philosophical underpinnings of the movement. An appreciation for philosophy is difficult to build into room décor, but there is no better way to do this than to display books, preferably the writings of John Ruskin, William Morris, or Elbert Hubbard, with the books supported and highlighted with appropriate bookends.

The Arts & Crafts Movement and style reached the United States in about 1890. By that time it was associated with hand-crafted objects, simplicity of design, the use of natural, local materials, and the exposure of construction details in order to appreciate the human effort. Interestingly, the movement also became associated with philosophy, especially with literature in general, books, reflective moods, and wisdom. This was likely due to its association with Ruskin and Morris and their philosophy, or because it was the only style that was publicly associated with philosophy at all. Today we find Arts & Crafts bookends showing these philosophy-related subjects, with owls, and lamps symbolizing wisdom, and books symbolizing literature and intellectual pursuits.

Because the bookend boom, which started in about 1900, roughly coincided with the development of the Arts & Crafts Movement in America, it is not surprising that Arts & Crafts style bookends were among the earliest produced here. These bookends were made at the same time as our early Victorian-style ones but even though the styles overlap, each can usually be identified clearly, and the bookends tell us that both fashions were popular at that early time.

Metal Workshop Bookends

Early metal bookends of the Arts & Crafts style were frequently hand crafted in an L form. These were generally fashioned from commercial sheet copper in metal-working shops. A piece of the correct size was cut from the sheet, then shaped by hammering and bending. Decoration was provided by hand stamping, repoussé, cut outs, and riveting. Some were covered with leather. The finished product was L-shaped, with a flange at the base that formed a foot on which books could sit, and an upright section to hold the books from falling (Figure 148).

These bookends clearly fulfilled criteria of the Arts & Crafts Movement. Each was handcrafted, utilitarian, and showed all the details of construction. The form was clean and simple, with little or no attached ornament. Some embodied the purest Arts & Crafts ideal in being made individually by the artist, who also served as artisan. Workshop bookends designed, made, and signed by a well-known artist, such as those by Dirk Van Erp, are among the most desirable today.

Among the many metal workshops that produced copper bookends, the one best remembered is that of the Roycrofters in East Aurora, New York, which was known also for furniture, printing, and the inn which attracted prominent visitors. The enterprise was founded in 1895 by Elbert Hubbard, a philosopher and businessman who admired William Morris and hoped to bring the Arts & Crafts Movement to America. The shop still produces these bookends, but uses a recent shop mark. Roycroft shop marks are shown in the Appendix.

Although Roycroft bookends showcased Hubbard's Arts & Crafts efforts, they were usually not produced individually by the same men who designed them. One-of-a-kind products were expensive to make and, therefore, not suitable for serving a large clientele. Instead, at Roycroft, as at many other respected workshops, each bookend design was reproduced in large numbers by several craftsmen. This need to produce multiple copies was a limitation on the strict Arts & Crafts demands that haunted all manufacturers of this style of products. But the fact that an artist did not separately design and fashion each pair of bookends did not detract from their Arts & Crafts status, then or now.

Workshop bookends, especially Roycroft bookends, are well regarded today, but only by aficionados who understand and sympathize with the philosophy behind them, because they are small and generally not very showy. Frequently, the face of the bookend has no added decoration or only a small motif in repoussé, and, although the surface was usually enriched by patination, their simplicity generally cannot be appreciated at a distance.

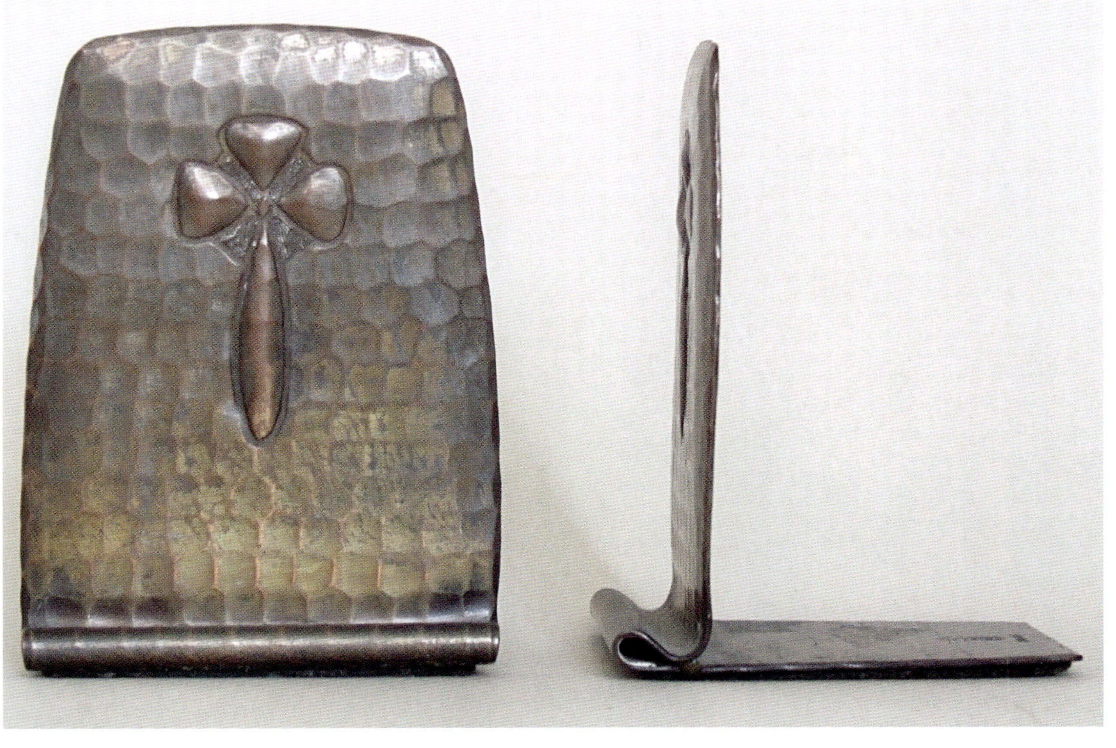

Figure 148. Roycroft Flower. 3", copper Inscription: Roycroft Late Mark. Circa 1934. Rarity 3. Arts & Crafts. Small books and small bookends were common prior to 1930. $120-180.

A few workshops did make more highly-decorated L-shaped metal bookends. For example, the Heintz Art Metal and SilverCrest shops issued patinated bronze bookends embellished with applied motifs in sterling silver. In California, Craftsman Studios (not to be confused with Gustav Stickley's New York-based Craftsman Workshops) produced L-shaped copper bookends, some faced with colorful designs in enamel. All of these are well accepted today, and collectors particularly desire bookends with well-preserved original finishes. Many simple Arts & Crafts bookends were produced at this time in woodworking shops as well, and these were often no more than blocks of polished wood, although some were made from quarter-sawn oak, the most popular wood for Arts & Crafts furniture. Metal and wood workshop bookends are shown in Figures 148-166.

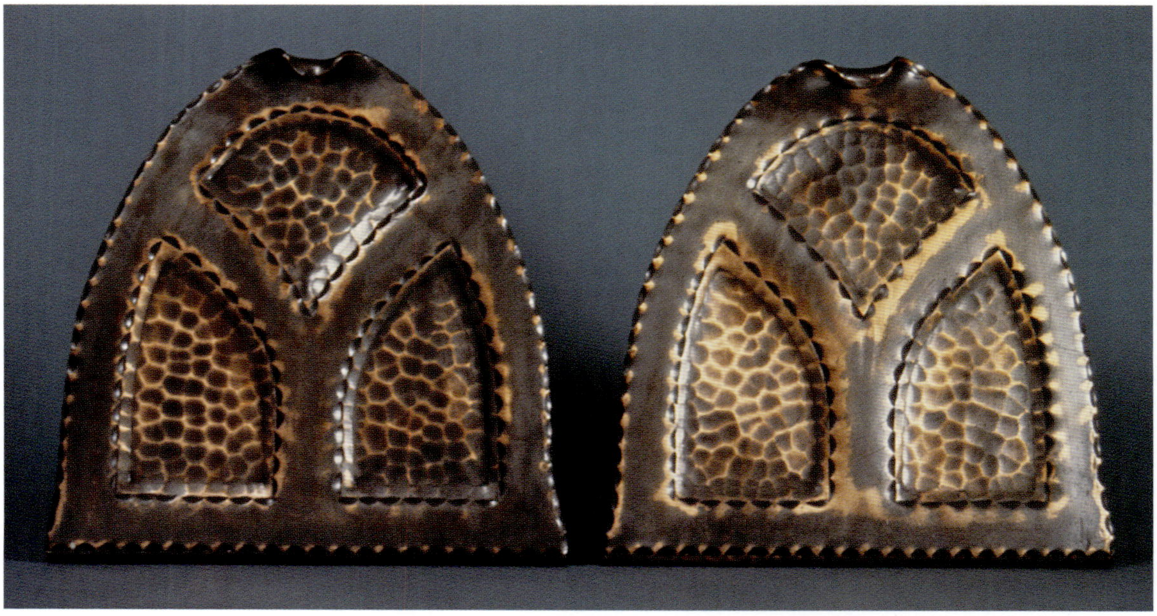

Figure 149. Tripartite. 5.25", copper. Circa 1919. Rarity 5. Arts & Crafts. $60-90.

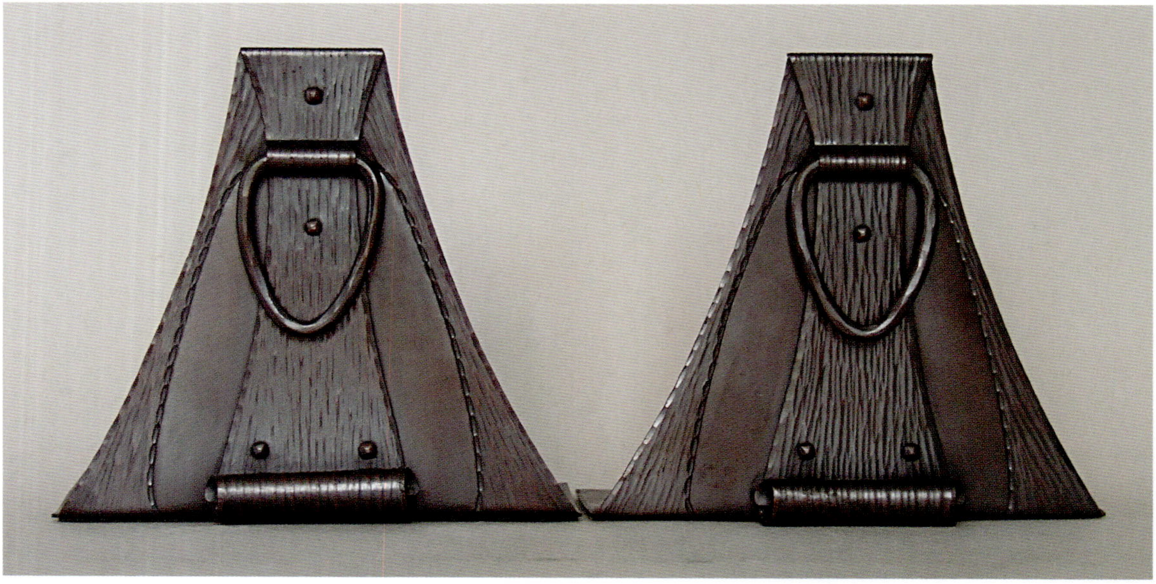

Figure 150. Triangle Upright with Attached Ring. 5", copper. Inscription: Roycroft middle mark. Circa 1924. Rarity 3. Arts & Crafts. $290-430.

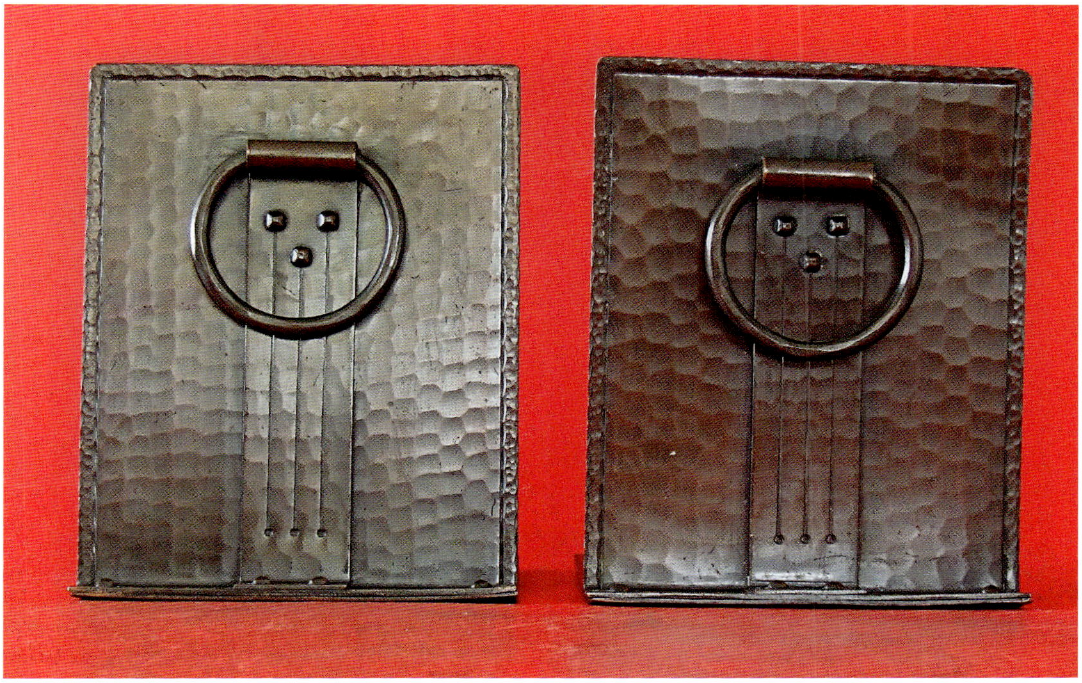

Figure 151. Rectangular Upright with Attached Ring. 5", copper. Inscription: Roycroft middle mark. Circa 1924. Rarity 3. Arts & Crafts. $290-430.

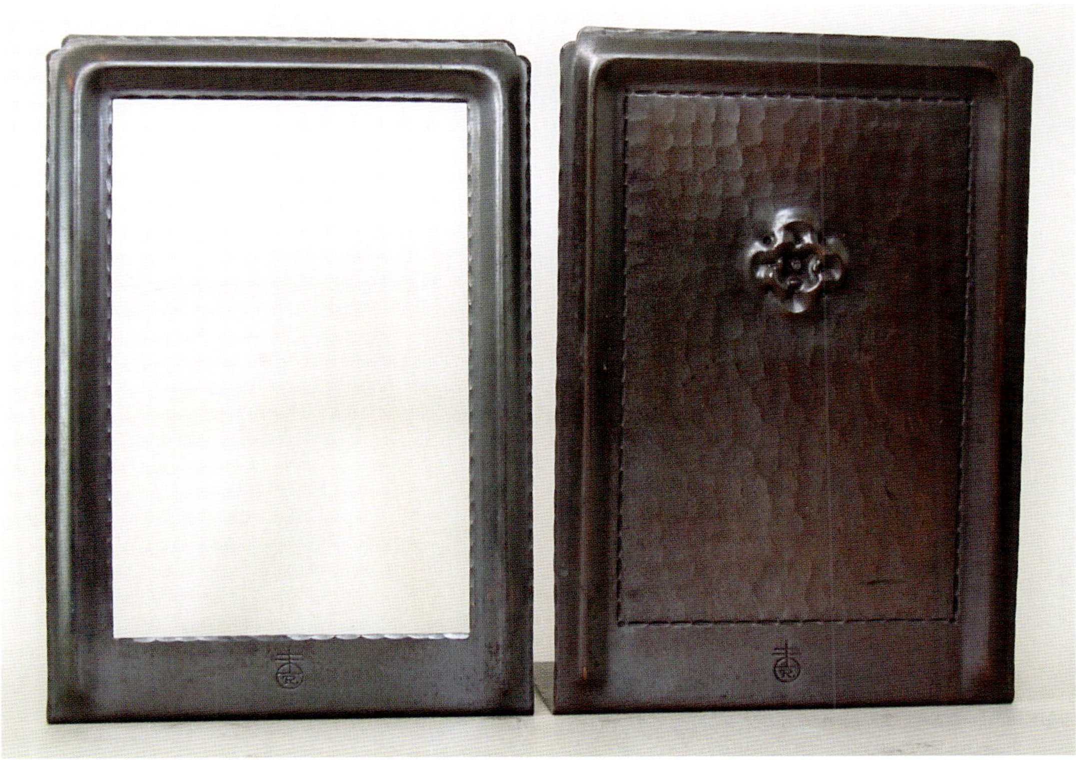

Figure 152. One Cut Out. 8.5", copper. Inscription: Roycroft early mark. Circa 1914. Rarity 3. Arts & Crafts. These bookends were sold with volumes of Hubbard's *Little Journeys*. $250-350.

Figure 153. Geometry in Copper. 5", copper. Inscription: Roycroft, late mark. Circa 1934. Rarity 4. Arts & Crafts pedigree with a Deco scroll. $180-270.

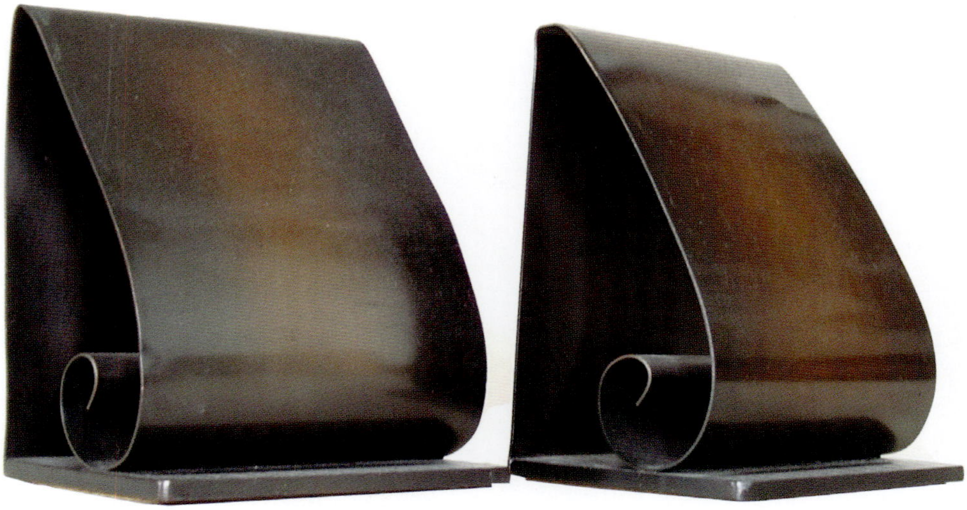

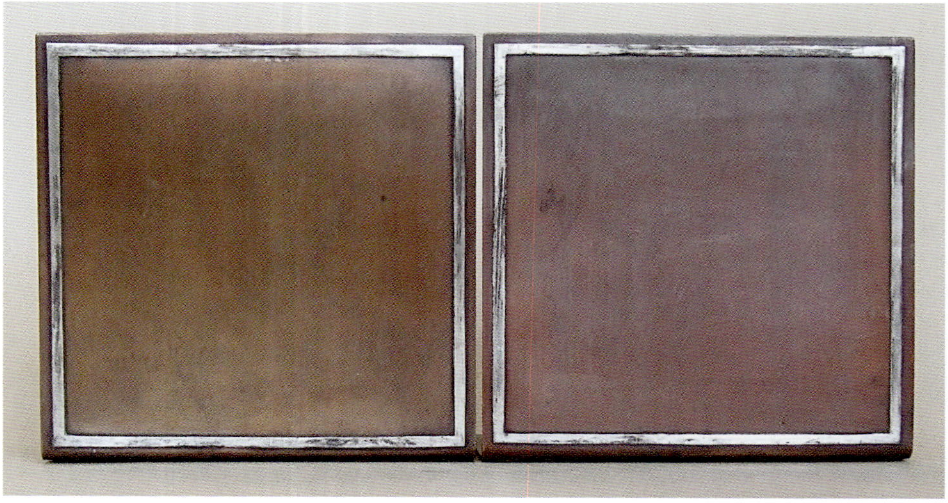

Figure 154. Silver Border. 6", bronze and silver. Inscription: Shop mark of Heintz. Circa 1912. Rarity 4. Arts & Crafts. $200-300.

Figure 155. Silver Peacock. 5", bronze and silver. Inscription: Shop mark of Heintz. Circa 1912. Rarity 3. Arts & Crafts. $250-370.

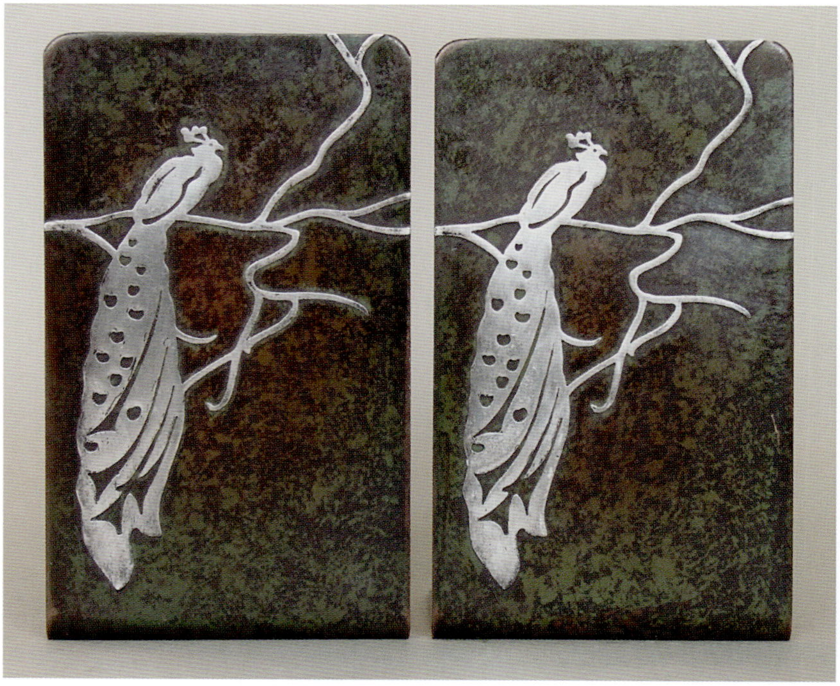

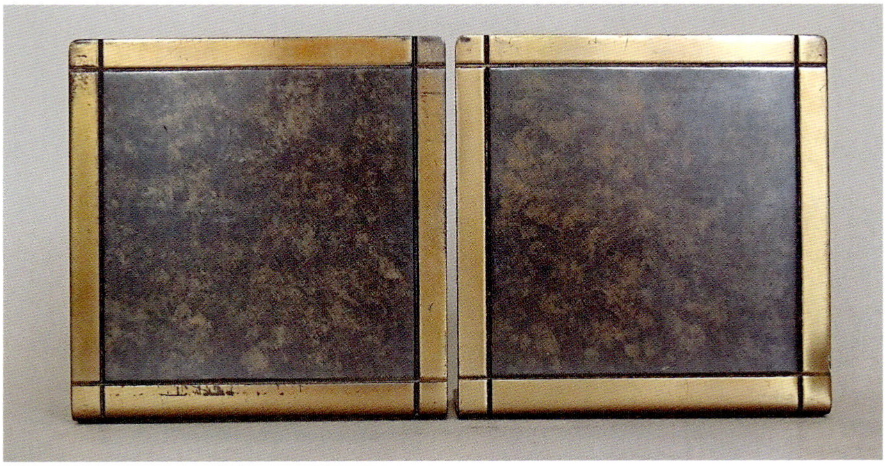

Figure 156. Bronze Only. 5", bronze. Inscription: Shop mark of SilverCrest. Circa 1924. Rarity 4. The trade-secret patina was very desirable, and did not require silver ornamentation. Arts & Crafts. $250-370.

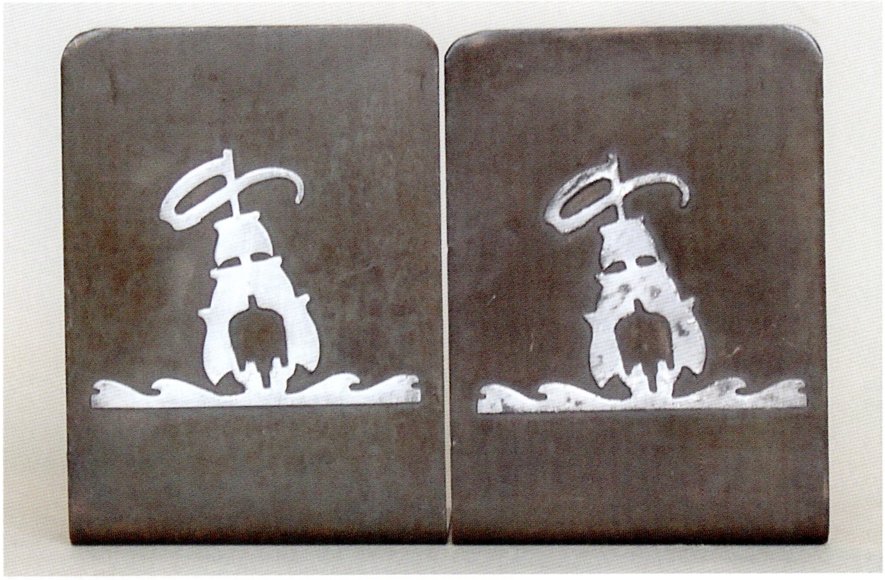

Figure 157. Edgewater Beach Hotel. 4.25", bronze and silver. Inscription: Shop mark of SilverCrest, and date 1925/26. Rarity 2. Arts & Crafts. $80-120.

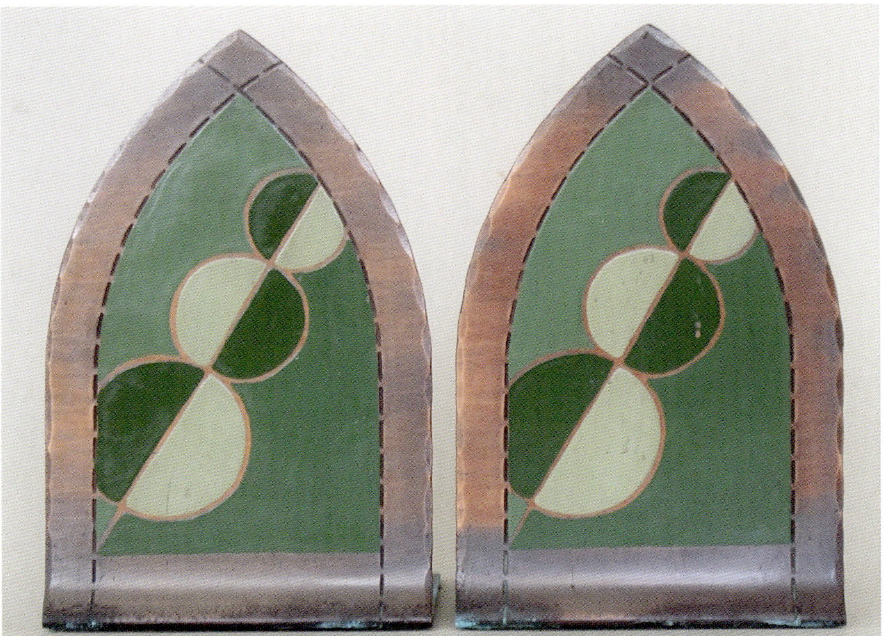

Figure 158. Three Discs. 4.75", copper and enamel. Inscription: Craftsman Studios, Laguna Beach, 230. Circa 1928. Rarity 3. Arts & Crafts. $80-120.

Figure 159. Abstract Owl. 4.75", copper and enamel. Inscription: Craftsman Studios, Laguna Beach, 268. Circa 1928. Rarity 2. Arts & Crafts. $80-120.

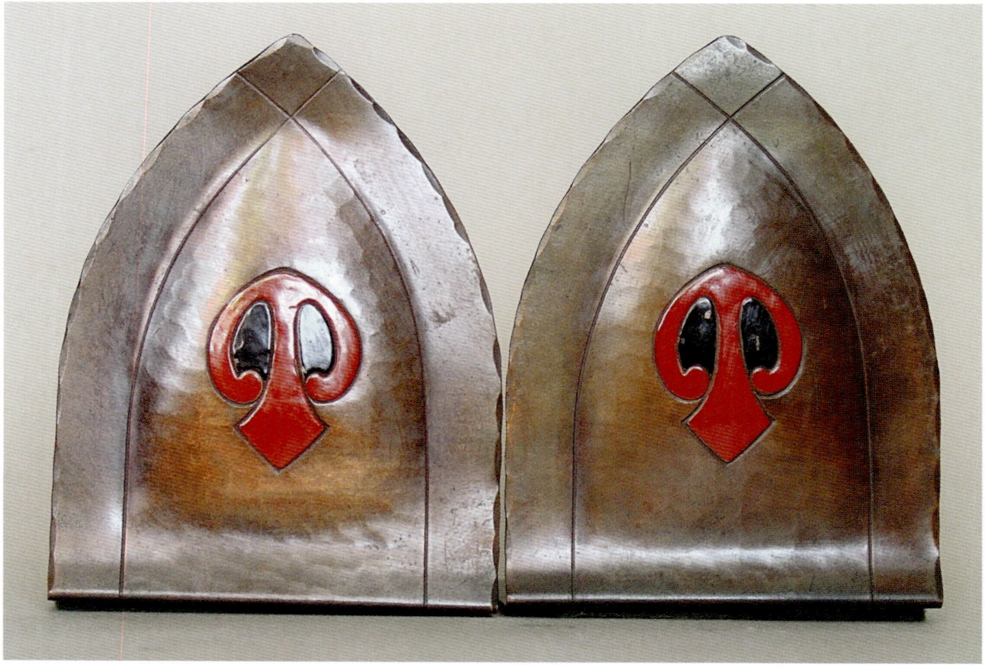

Figure 160. Nouveau Flower. 5", copper and enamel. Inscription: A shop mark of Made by Hand and a rolled-up sleeve grasping a hammer. Circa 1915. Rarity 5. Extensive handwork. Arts & Crafts.$80-120.

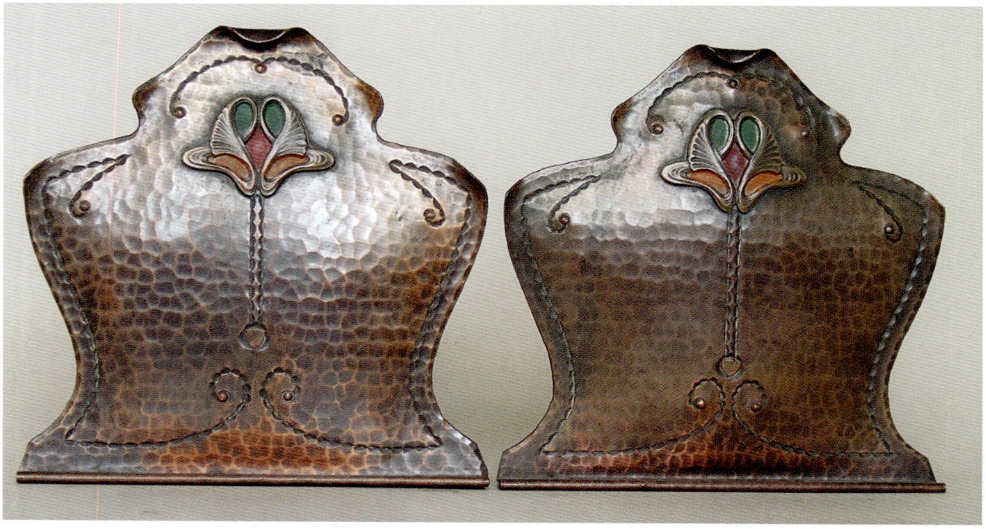

Figure 161. Abstract Butterfly. 6.25", copper with blue patina. Inscription: shop mark of Carl Sorenson. Circa 1914. Rarity 5. Unique midnight blue color on large bookends. Arts & Crafts. $290-444.

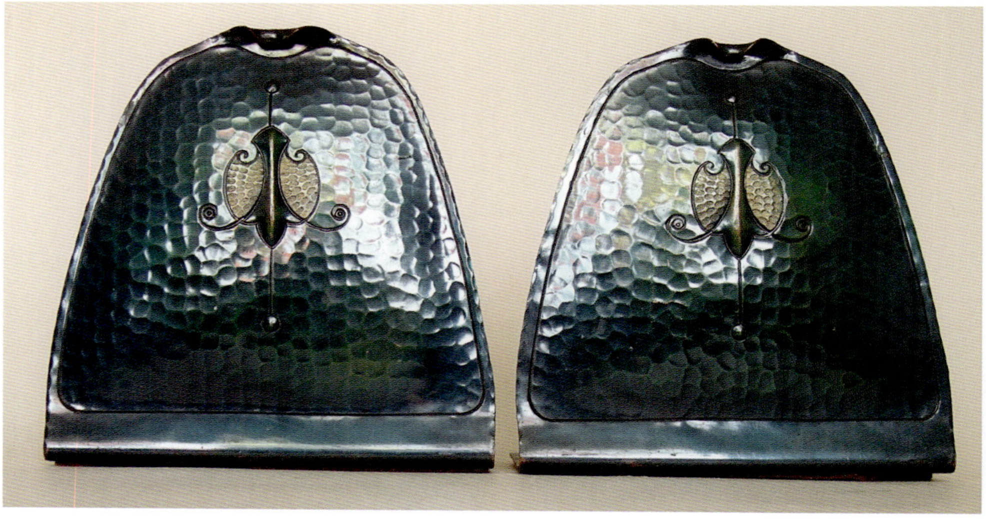

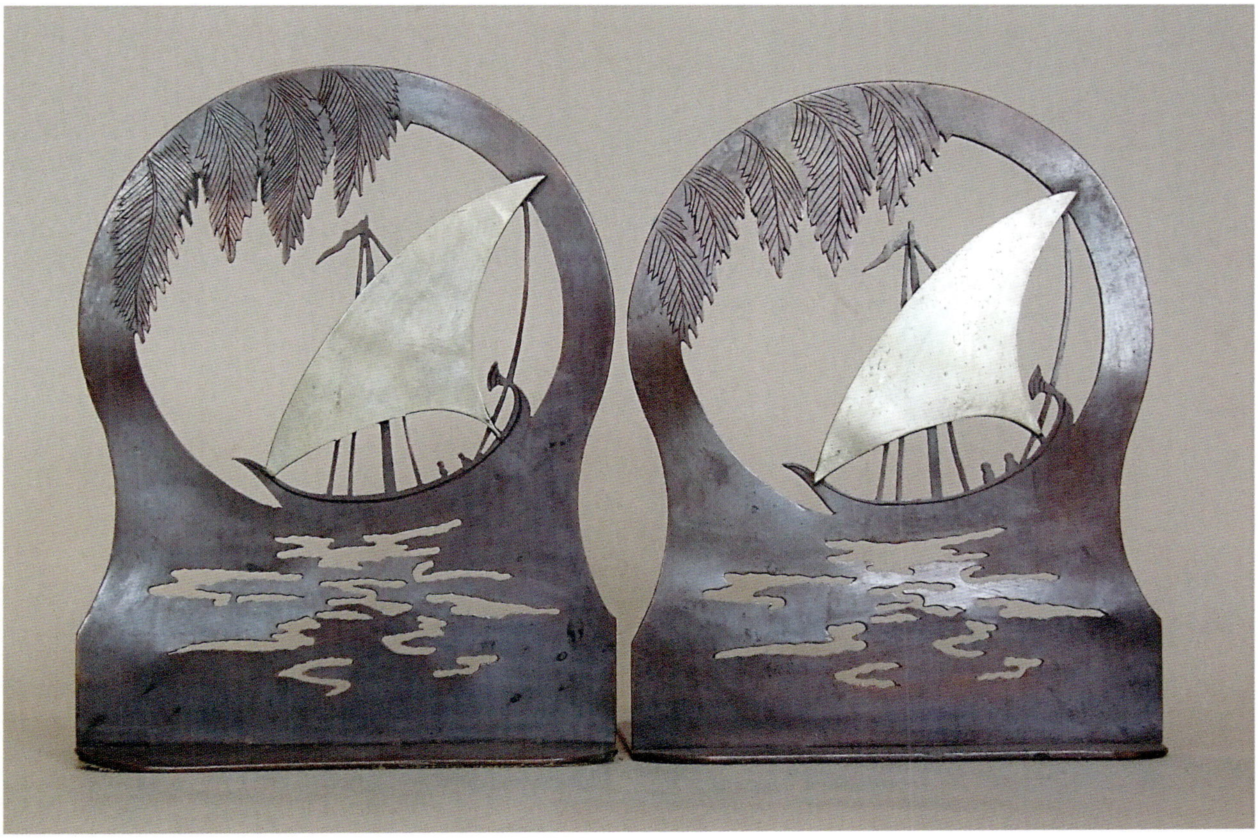

Figure 162. Tropical Cruise, 6.5", copper and brass. Circa 1915. Rarity 5. Arts & Crafts. $200-300.

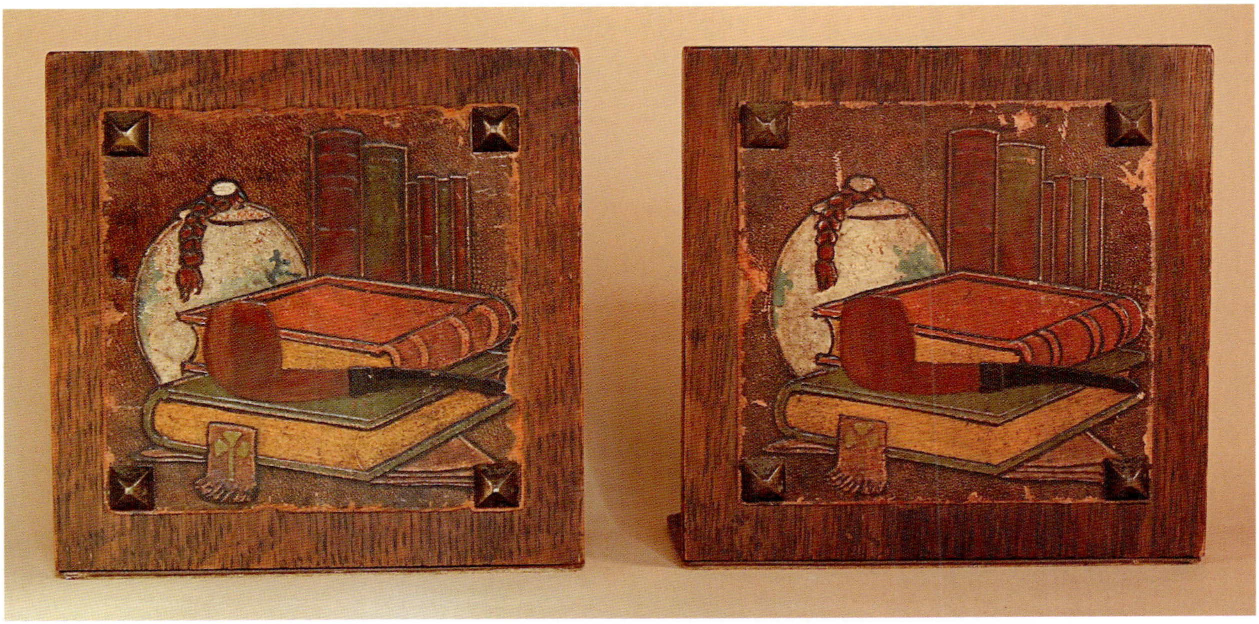

Figure 163. Pipe and Book. 5.5", quarter-sawn oak, painted leather, pyramidal tacks. Circa 1915. Rarity 5. Arts & Crafts. Suggestion of intellectual reflection. Wood-working shop. $240-360.

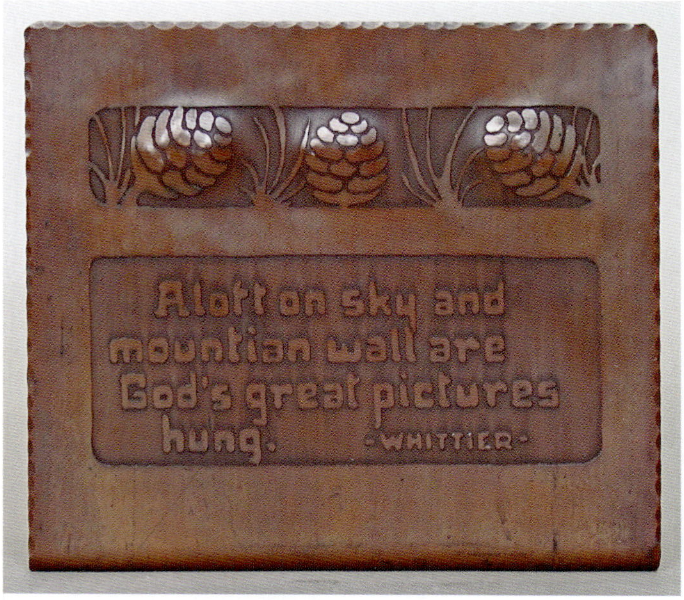

Figure 164. Pinecones and Whittier Poem. 5.25", copper. Inscription: Whittier poem. Circa 1918. Rarity 5. Arts & Crafts. $160-240.

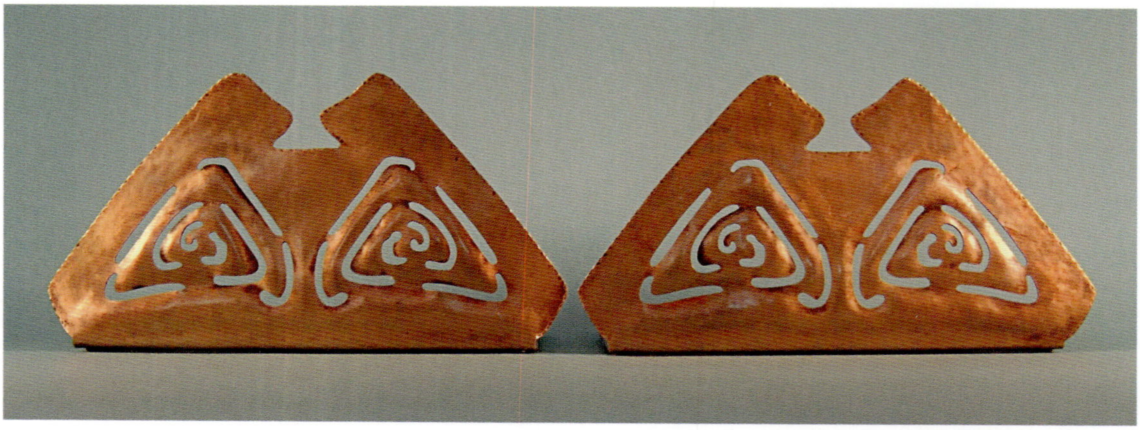

Figure 165. Cut out Pine Trees. 4.5", brass. Inscription: Forest Craft Guild. Circa 1912. Rarity 5. Arts & Crafts. *By courtesy of Marcia Reisner, From her collection.* $320-480.

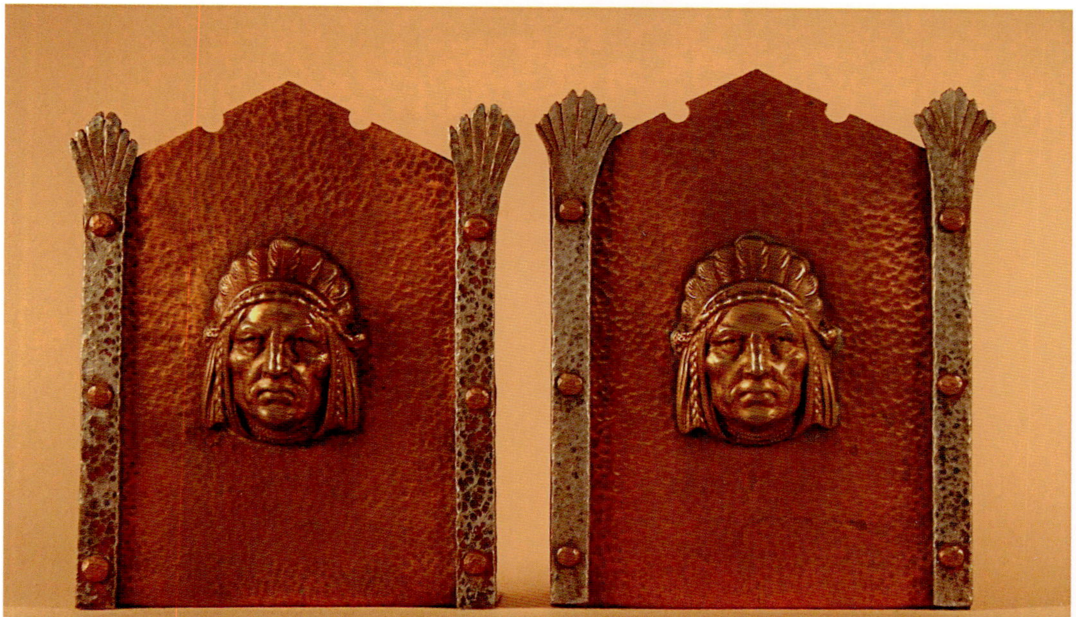

Figure 166. Workshop Indian. 5", copper, gray metal, and iron. Circa 1915. Rarity 5. Arts & Crafts. The Indian face is apparently soldered on. $275-420.

Art Pottery Bookends

Art pottery matched the time frame of the American Arts & Crafts scene and also the prescribed criteria for the style.

Some of the early pots were hand-thrown by artists, and many of these were signed by the artist and the pottery. These are the most valuable pots today. The great majority of the bookends, however, were produced by slip casting, a method that relied on molds and produced runs of identical pots. Artists designed the molds, but workmen with few artistic skills carried out the production. This was a method of mass production, related to machine production, and the resultant pots were hollow, thin walled, relatively light in weight, and fragile. Slip-cast pots clearly do not meet the demands of the Arts & Crafts Movement, but collectors today class them as Arts & Crafts objects, and they command high prices.

Slip casting was particularly unsuitable for bookends, which should be heavy and sturdy, but old, slip-cast bookends are valued today because they were made by prestigious potteries like Rookwood, Roseville, or Van Briggle.

Some of the old pottery bookends were solid-cast as tiles. These were also formed in artist-designed molds, but they were not hollow and were comparatively heavy and sturdy. The tiles were flat, like ordinary wall tiles, and set in frames, or were thick and solid and meant to stand alone. These pieces conformed better to the Arts & Crafts requirement for functionality, but not for skillful artisan workmanship for each bookend. Bookends of art pottery are shown in Figures 167-173.

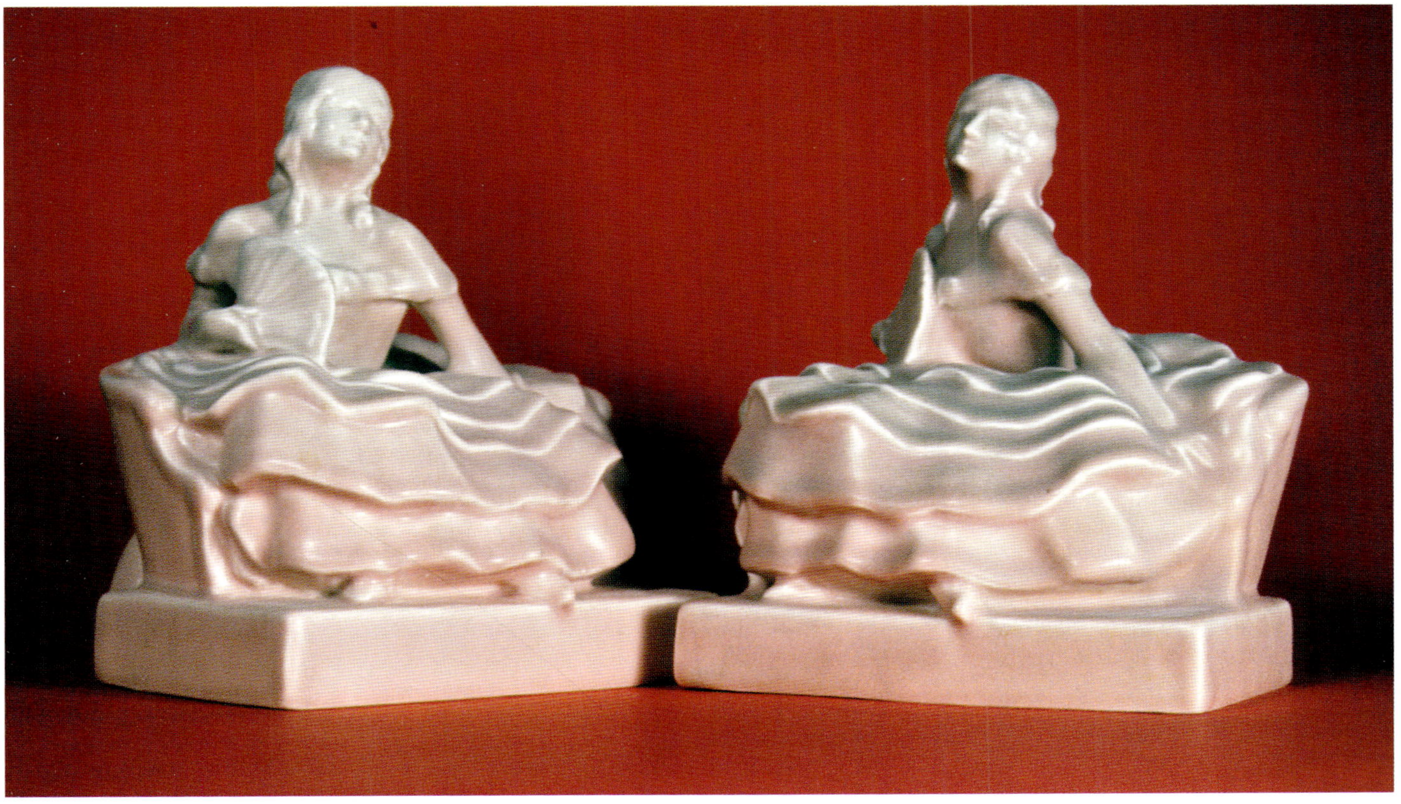

Figure 167. Lady with Fan. 6.25", earthenware. Inscription: shop mark with the word Rookwood, 1931. Rarity 2. Art pottery, slip cast. $240-360.

Figure 168. Boots and Horseshoes. 6.5", earthenware. Foundry: Frankoma Potteries, Sculptor: Joseph Frank. Circa 1952. Rarity 2. Art Pottery, slip cast. $80-120.

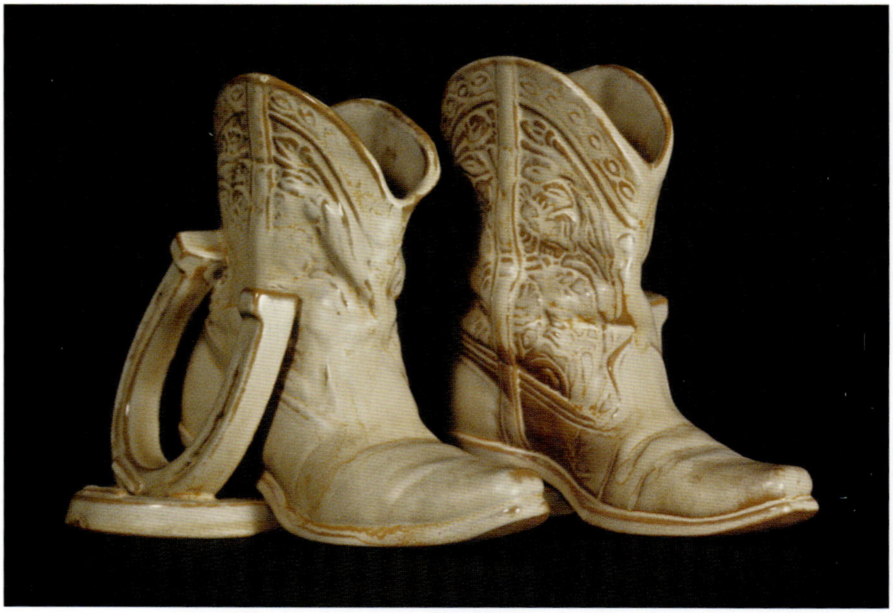

Figure 169. Nubian. 7", earthenware. Inscription: Pierce (Howard Pierce). Circa 1950. Rarity 5. Art pottery, slip cast. $200-300.

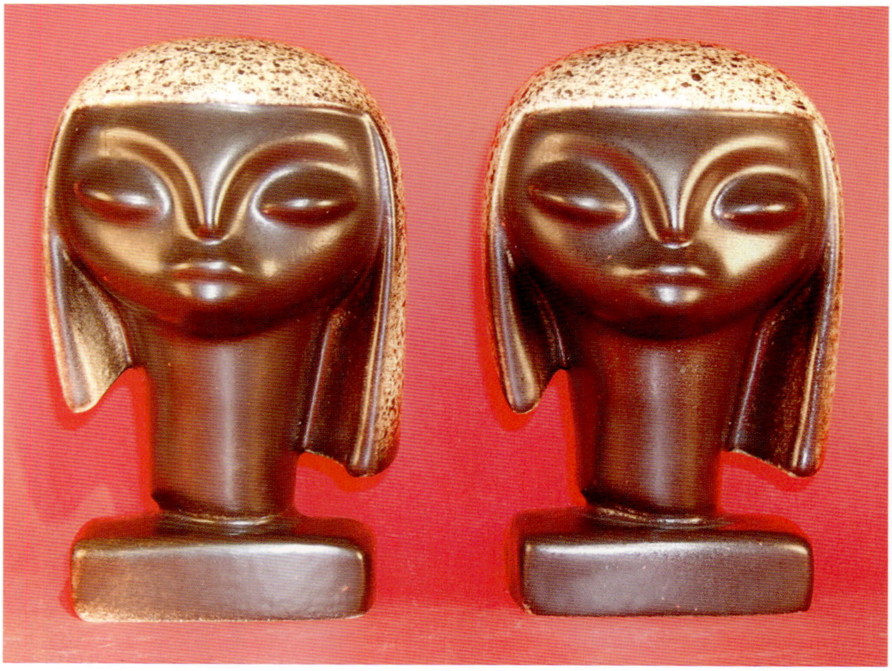

Figure 170. Adam and Eve. 6", earthenware. Inscription: CALCo. Circa 1927. Rarity 2. Art pottery. Solid cast. $200-300.

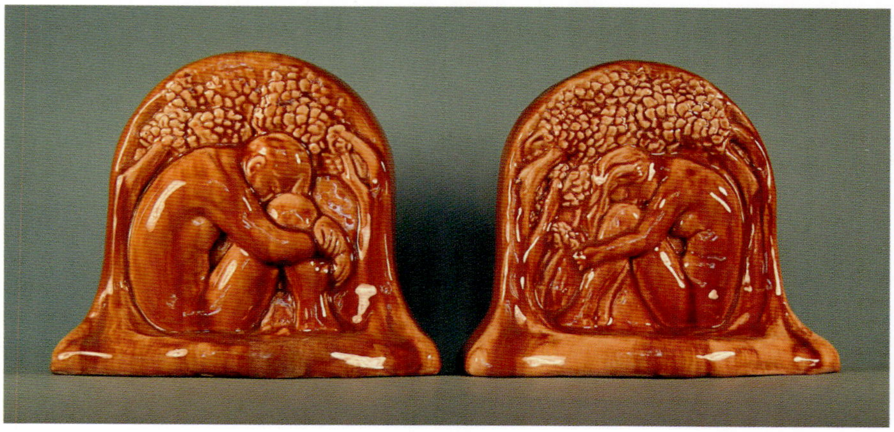

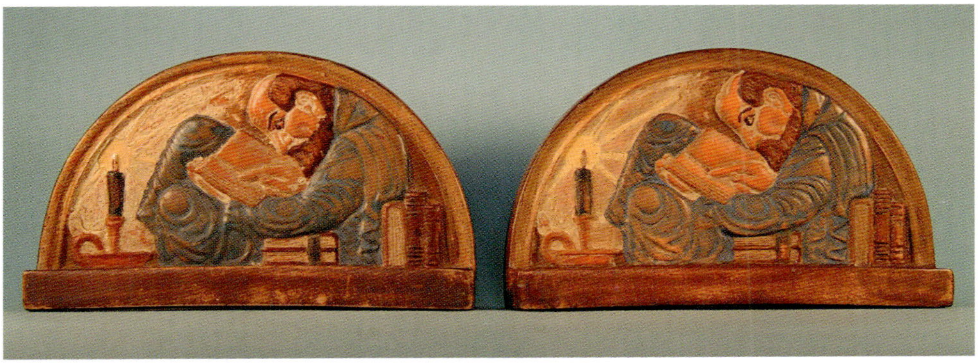

Figure 171. Padre and Candle. 5.25", earthenware. Inscription: Flint Tile Company. Foundry: Flint Faience and Tile Co. Circa 1930. Rarity 3. Art pottery. Solid cast. $520-820.

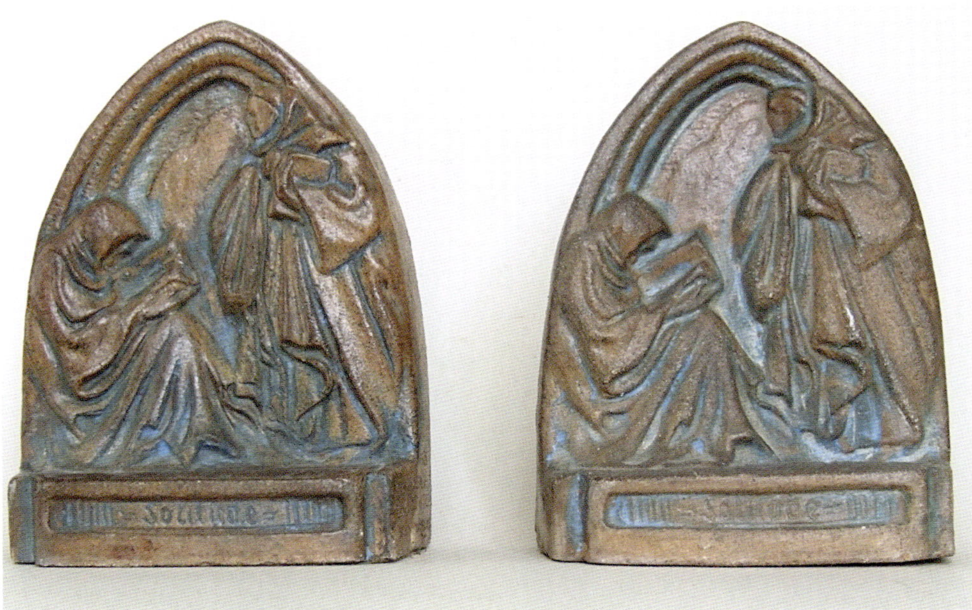

Figure 172. Solitude. 6", earthenware. Inscription: Solitude, Continental Faience and Tile, South Milwaukee, 1926. Rarity 2. Art pottery. Solid cast. $520-820.

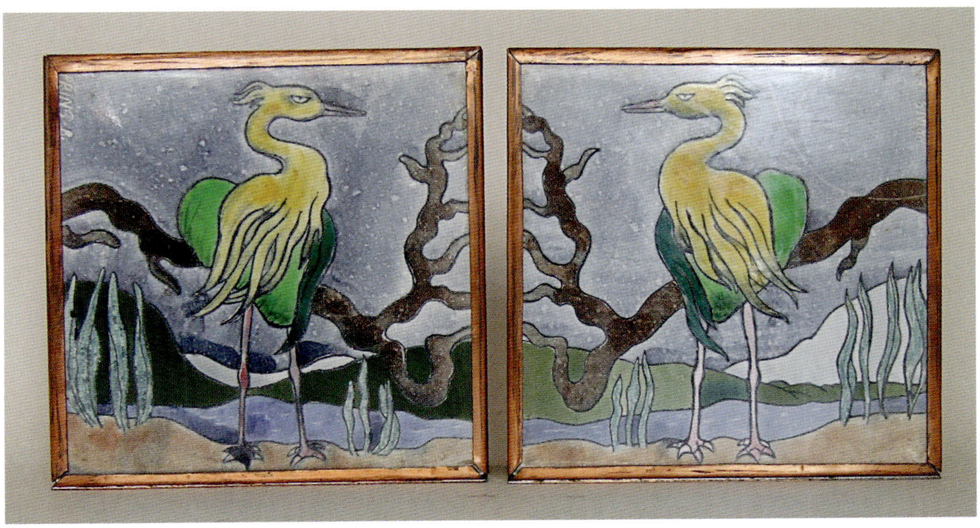

Figure 173. Stork. 6.25" Ceramic tile and copper frame. Inscription: Prins B., Sculptor: Ben Prins. Circa 1930. Rarity 5. Art pottery. $160-240.

Metal Foundry Bookends

While metal-working shops were producing L-shape metal bookends and potteries were producing chiefly earthenware bookends, metal foundries, such as Armor Bronze Inc. or the Judd Mfg. Co., began producing Arts & Crafts genre bookends by conventional techniques of sand casting, slush casting, and electroform casting. Electroform casting was very popular, but is now obsolete and these electroformed bookends, usually bronze, are now wrongly called copper clad or bronze clad. Electroform casting and other metal-casting procedures are described in the Appendix.

Metal-foundry bookends of Arts & Crafts genre were not manufactured by strict Arts & Crafts criteria because they were mass produced according to foundry procedures. They were cast from an artist's sculpture model rather than sculpted individually by the artists, although hand work was required throughout the foundry procedures. Because of their foundry origins, metal-foundry bookends are generally not accepted as Arts & Crafts items by collectors. And yet, in an analogous situation, today's art-pottery collectors accept mass-produced pots made from molds by companies like Rookwood or Van Briggle for their design value, despite the missing handmade criterion. Foundry bookends should be given the same Arts & Crafts status as given to such pottery and as given to serially-produced metal workshop bookends. Foundry bookends of arts and crafts style are recognized by the medieval motifs or by their historical associations.

Furthermore, Gustav Stickley, a father of the American Arts & Crafts Movement, believed that metal-foundry bookends belonged to Arts & Crafts décor. His shop in New York City was an exclusive outlet for Kathodion Bronze Works metal-foundry bookends, where they must have been sold as adjuncts to his classic Arts & Crafts furniture (Figures 174-175).

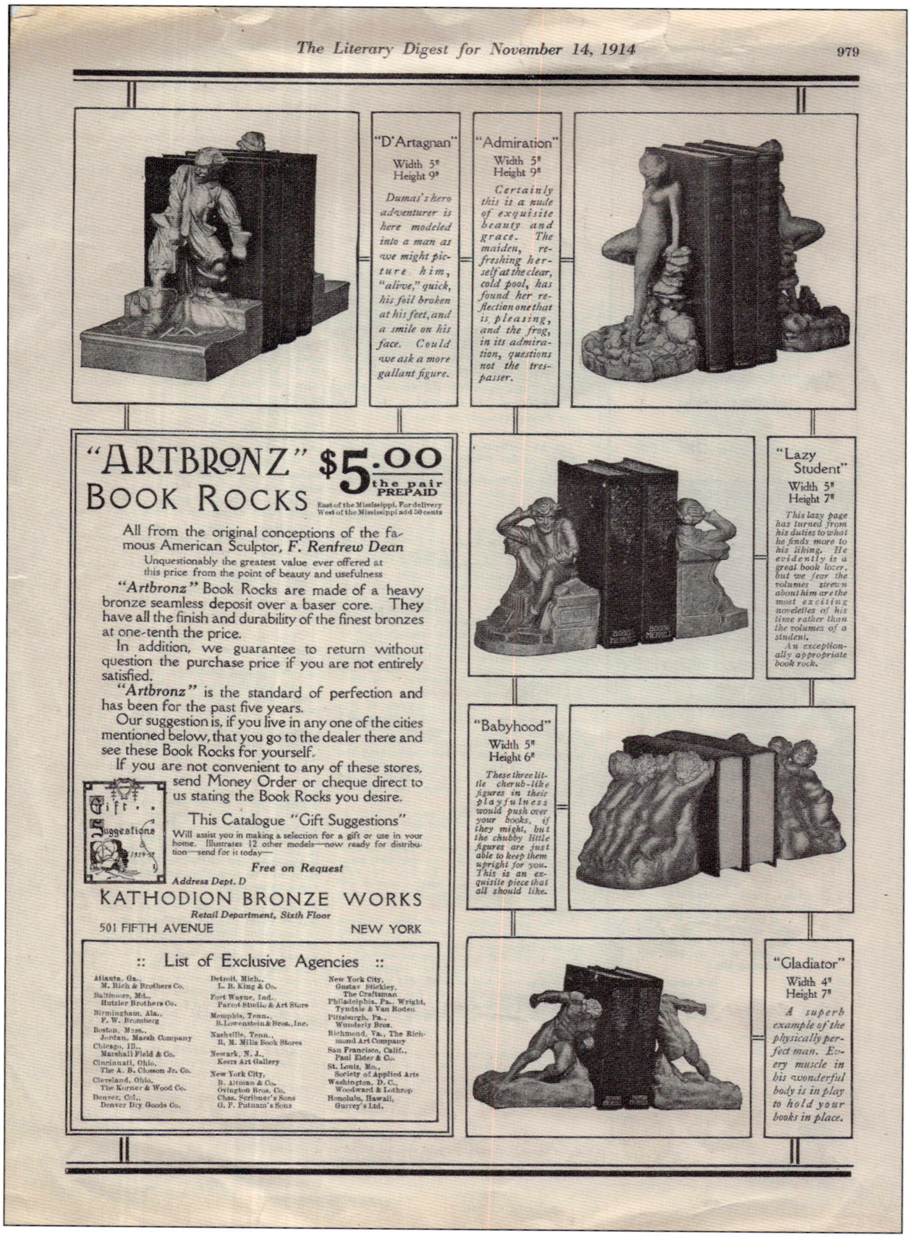

Figure 174. Advertisement from the *Literary Digest, Nov. 14, 1914,* citing Gustav Stickley's outlet, The Craftsman, as the exclusive agency in New York City for the Kathodian Bronze Works metal foundry bookends. 1914. Rarity 5.

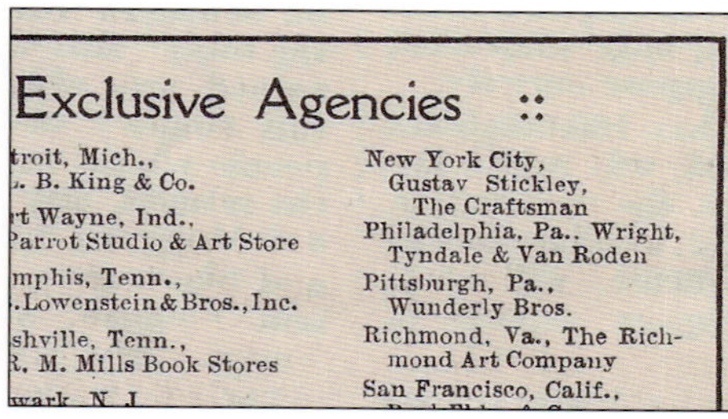

Figure 175. Enlargement from the advertisement from the *Literary Digest, Nov. 14, 1914* (Figure 119), showing that Gustav Stickley sold metal foundry bookends in his New York City outlet, The Craftsman.

Early metal-foundry bookends were generally beautiful, durable, utilitarian sculptures that were designed and often signed by the artists. Many had medieval subject material that had impeccable Arts & Crafts pedigree because it was favored by William Morris and his Pre-Raphaelite associates.

Bookends of Arts & Crafts genre became associated with other subject material as well, including oak leaves, acorns, and other objects from nature. (Figures 176-178). These associations were apparently derived from the focus on nature promoted by the romantic writings of John Ruskin in England and Henry Thoreau and Ralph Waldo Emerson in America. The influential architecture of Gustav Stickley, Frank Lloyd Wright, Greene and Greene, and others, encouraged life in harmony with nature in America, and bookends with naturalistic motifs joined the movement.

Bookends depicting American Indians were popular with the general public and fit nicely into Arts & Crafts décor. Bookend collectors have never adopted the term Native American, so we use the traditional term – Indian. Gustav Stickley suggested American Indian blankets to accompany his Craftsman furniture. Hand-crafted Indian blankets, baskets, and so on, are still regarded as part of the Arts & Crafts genre and so are the many different Indian bookends. Some foundry bookends of Arts & Crafts style are shown in Figures 176-215.

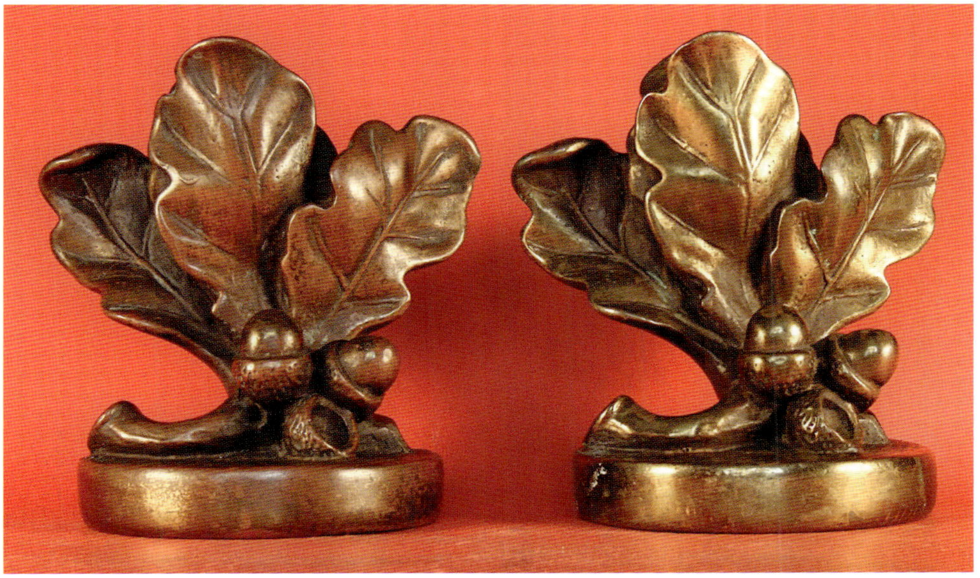

Figure 176. Acorns and Oak Leaves. 6", electroformed bronze. Attrib. Paul Mori. Circa 1915. Rarity 5. Arts & Crafts. $200-300.

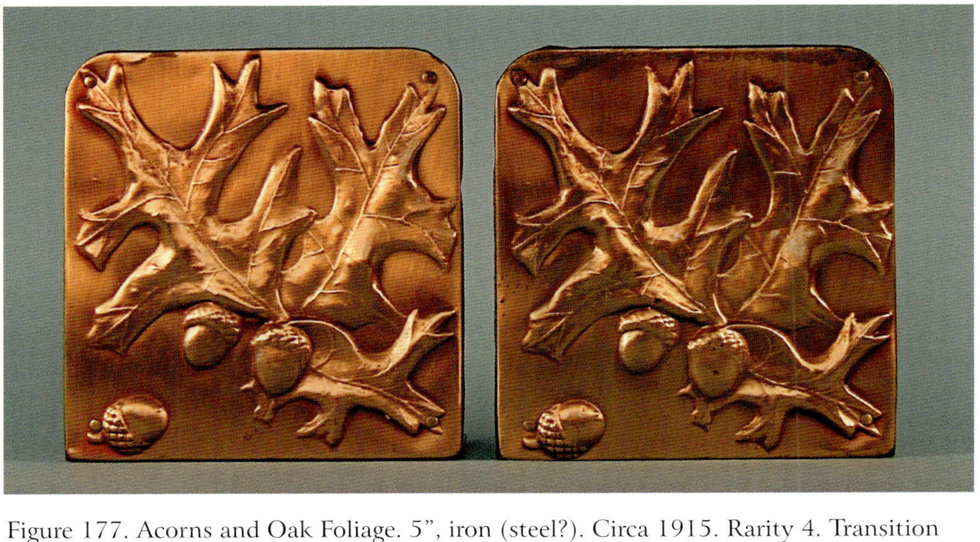

Figure 177. Acorns and Oak Foliage. 5", iron (steel?). Circa 1915. Rarity 4. Transition from Arts & Crafts to Modernist. The upright is machine-pressed iron or steel with oak leaves and acorns. $120-180.

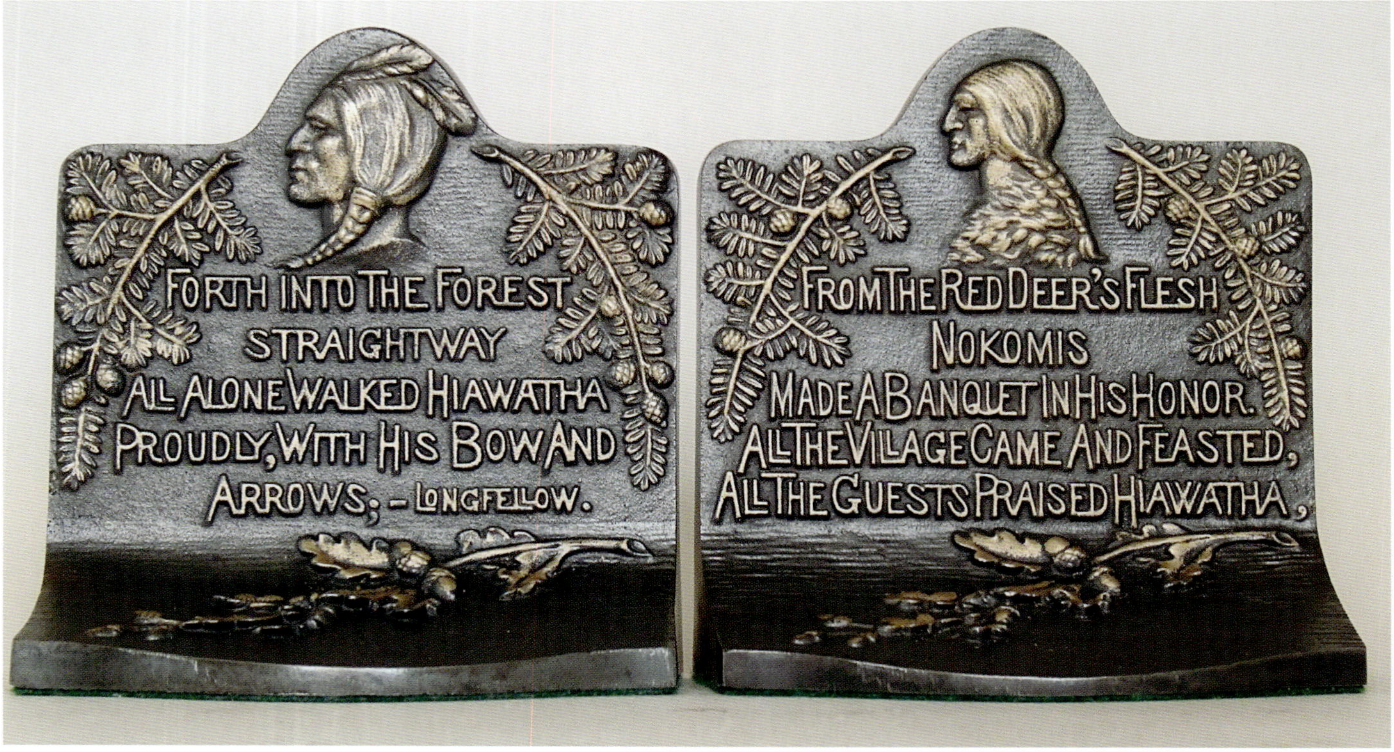

Figure 178. Hiawatha and Nokomis. 6.25", iron. Inscription: Shop mark of Bradley and Hubbard, excerpt from the poem *Song of Hiawatha* by Longfellow. Circa 1915. Rarity 2. Very Arts & Crafts. Subjects of Indians, acorns, oak leaves, pine cones, pine boughs, poem. The gold paint is uncommon. $250-370.

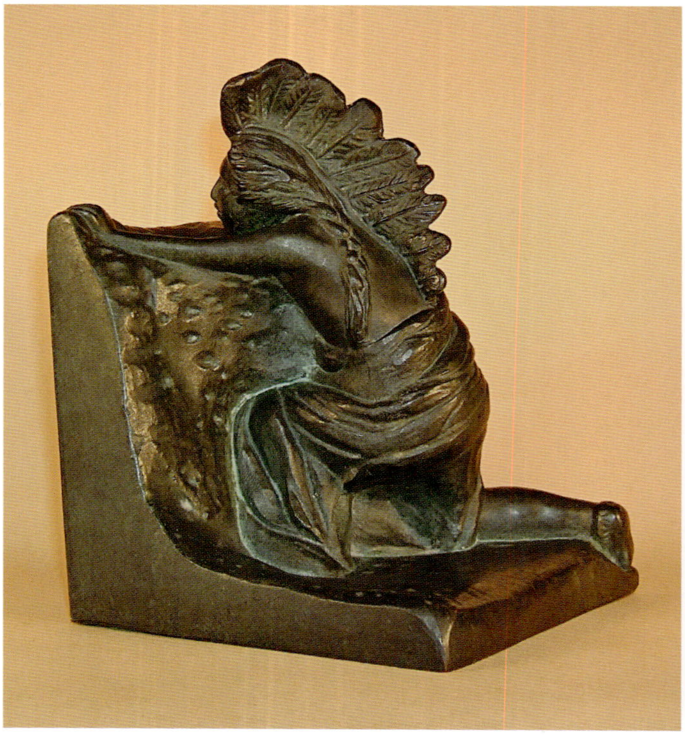

Figure 179. Indian Ambush. 7", bronze plating on gray metal. Inscription: Nellye Partridge, 1911. Foundry: Attrib. NAL Co. Rarity 3. Arts & Crafts. $400-600.

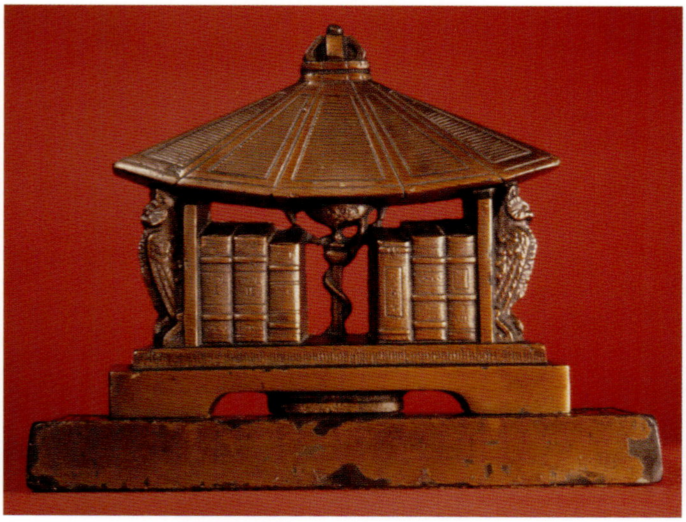

Figure 180. Lamp of Wisdom. 4.75", iron. Inscription: 9986. Foundry: Judd. Circa 1920. Rarity 3. Arts & Crafts. $200-300.

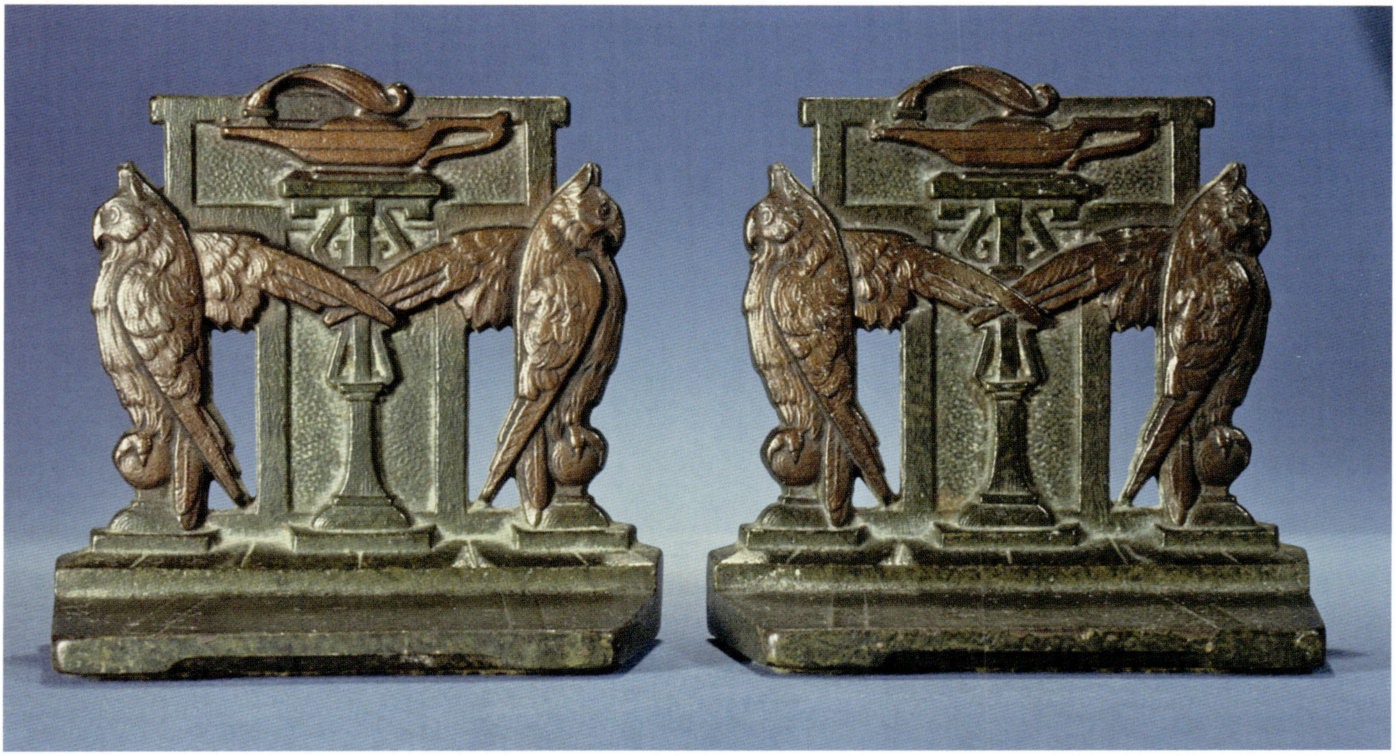

Figure 181. Lamp of Knowledge and Owls. 4.75", iron. Inscription 9886. Foundry: Judd. Circa 1920. Rarity 2. Arts & Crafts. A grouping of wisdom symbols. $200-300.

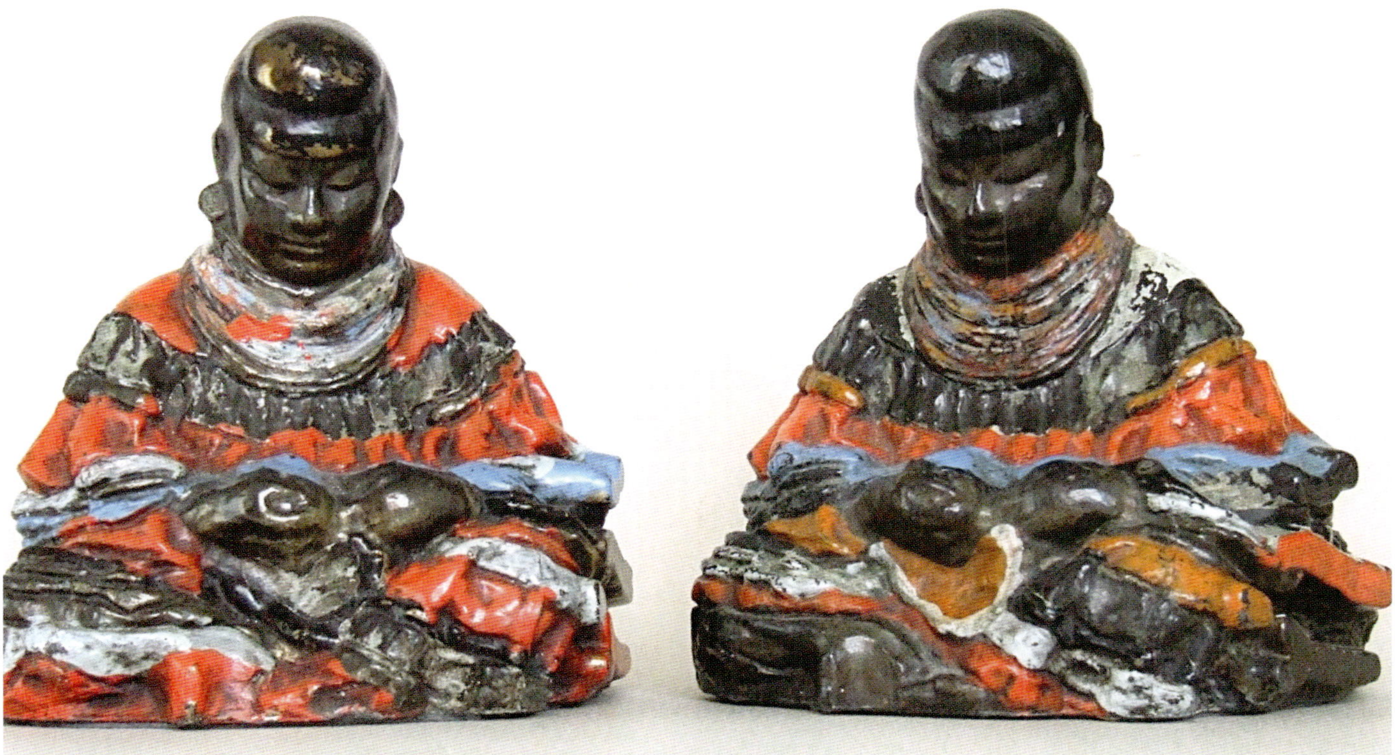

Figure 182. Seminole Lady. 4.5", gray metal. Inscription: Paper label describing Seminole Indians and listing the sculptor. Sculptor: Serena Plasikowski. Circa 1926. Rarity 5. Arts & Crafts. $240-360.

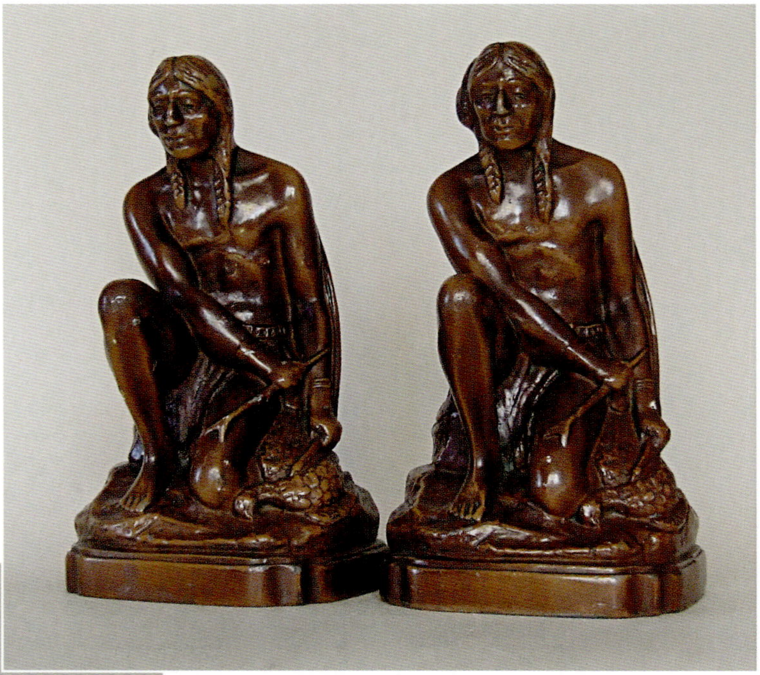

Figure 183. Indian with Turkey. 7.75", gray metal. Foundry: Nuart. Circa 1922. Rarity 2. Arts & Crafts. $240-360.

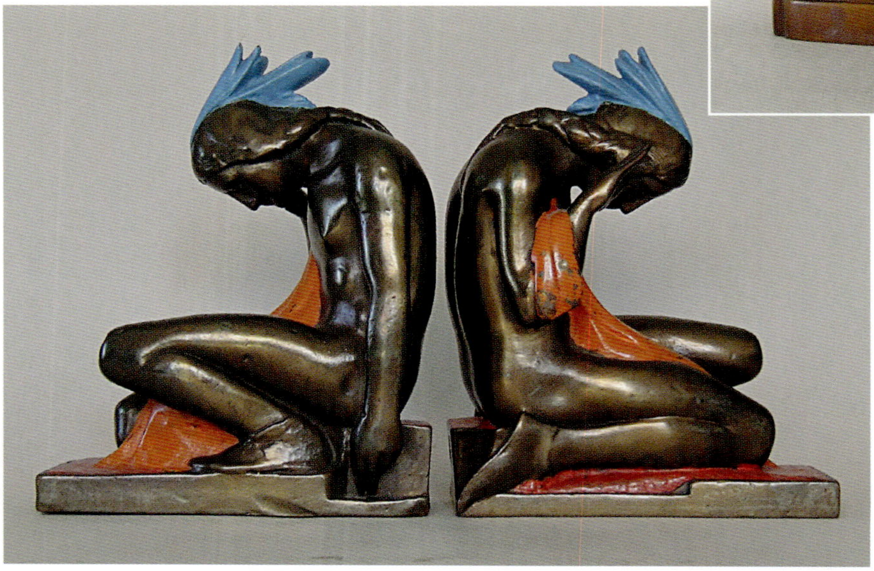

Figure 184. Sunset Devotion. 7.5", electroformed bronze. Inscription: Pompeian Bronze Co, Sunset Devotion. Circa 1918. Rarity 2. Arts & Crafts. $200-300.

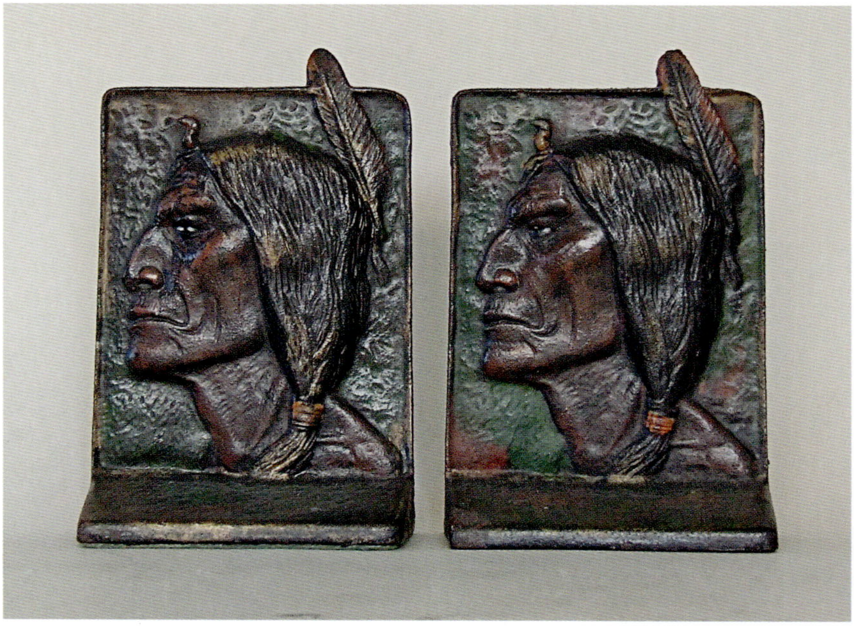

Figure 185. Solemn Indian. 8.5", iron. Inscription: Z-R 44 Sculptor: Attrib. Francis West. Circa 1916. Rarity 2. Arts & Crafts. $180-280.

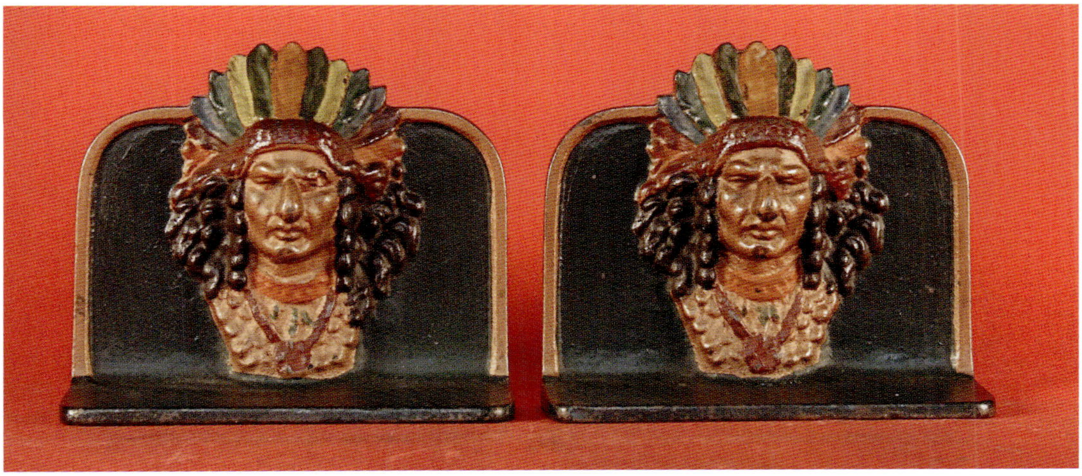

Figure 186. Small Indian. 3.5", iron. Circa 1920. Rarity 1. Arts & Crafts. $20-30.

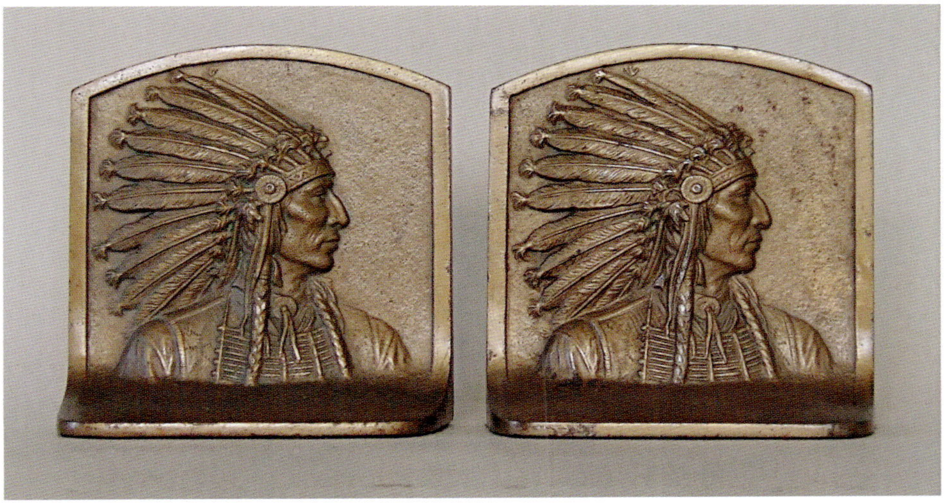

Figure 187. Indian Chief Profile. 5", iron. Inscription: Gregory S. Allen, 174. Foundry: Hubley. Circa 1924. Rarity 2. Arts & Crafts. $200-300.

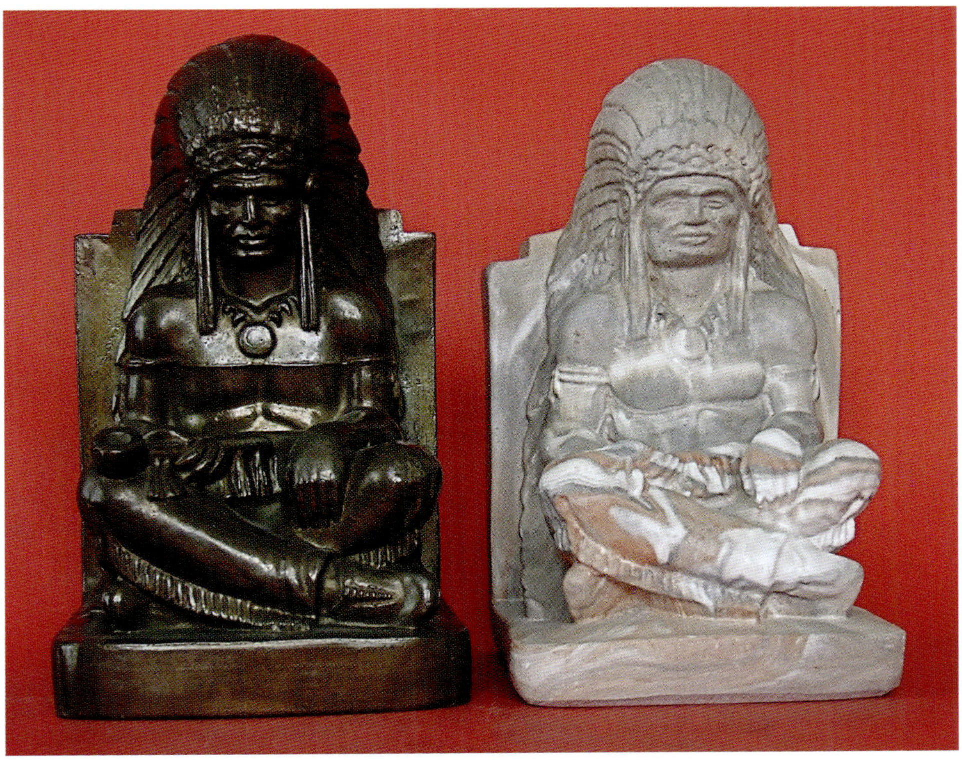

Figure 188. Indian with Pipe and Leggings. 7.75", gray metal (on the left). Circa 1938. Rarity 3. Arts & Crafts. $240-360. Pottery (on the right) 7" Foundry: Attrib. Nemadji. Circa 1938. Rarity 2. Arts & Crafts. $80-120.

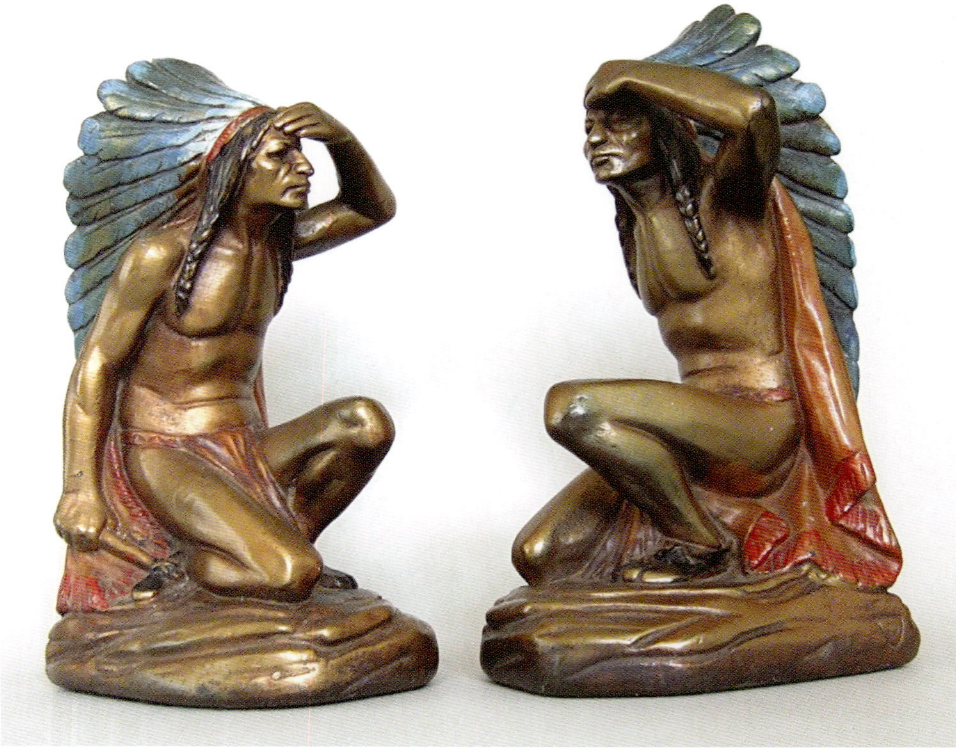

Figure 189. Indian with War Bonnet and Tomahawk. 9.25", electroformed bronze. Inscription: Armor Bronze shop mark, signed Ruhl. Circa 1923. Rarity 3. Arts & Crafts. $640-960.

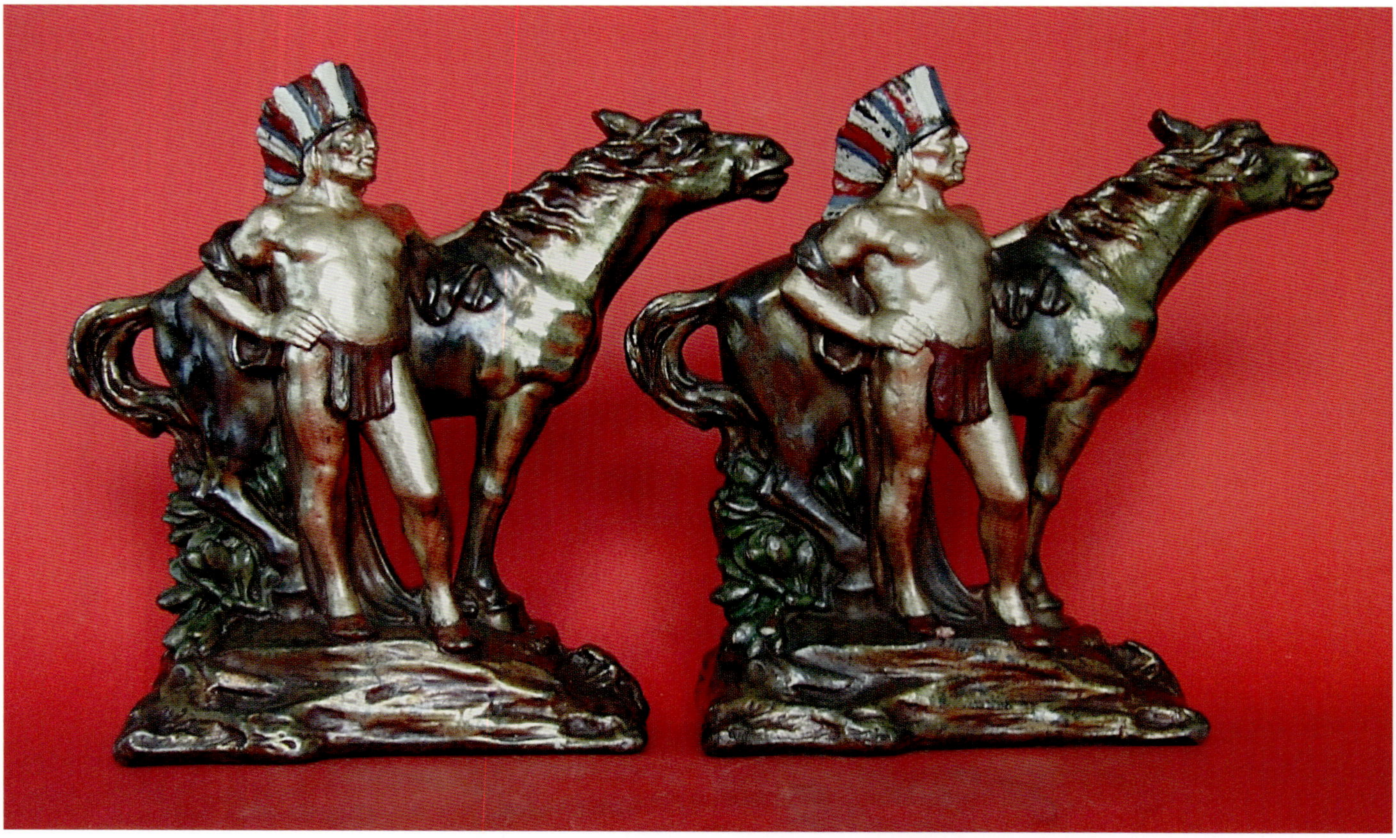

Figure 190. Indian Standing with Horse. 8.25", electroformed bronze. Inscription: Armor Bronze, 1928. Rarity 3. Arts & Crafts. These are large bookends. $580-870.

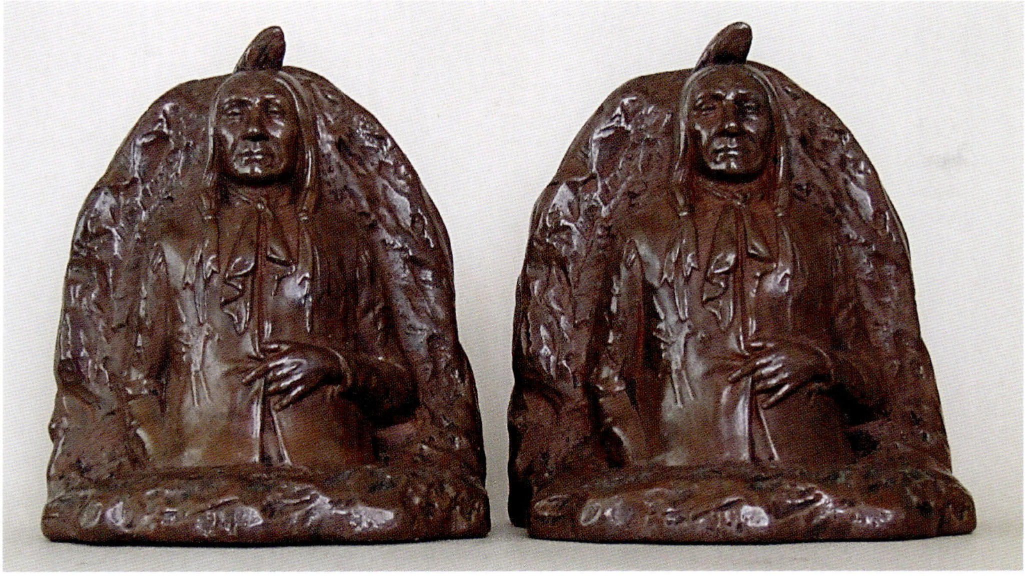

Figure 191. Indian Emissary. 6", electrofomed bronze. Foundry: Attrib. Armor Bronze. Circa 1915. Rarity 5. Arts & Crafts. Indian in white man's garb, ready to visit Europe or the American president. $270-420.

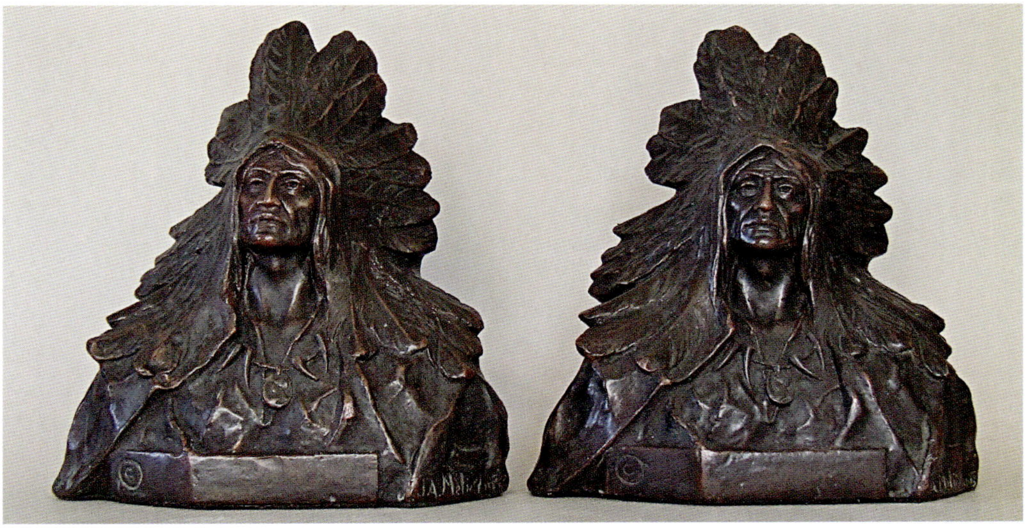

Figure 192. Indian and Feathers. 8", electroformed bronze. Inscription: Signed Meliodon. Foundry: Attrib. Armor Bronze Inc. Circa 1920. Rarity 3. Arts & Crafts. These are large, heavy bookends, 12 lbs./pair. $270-420.

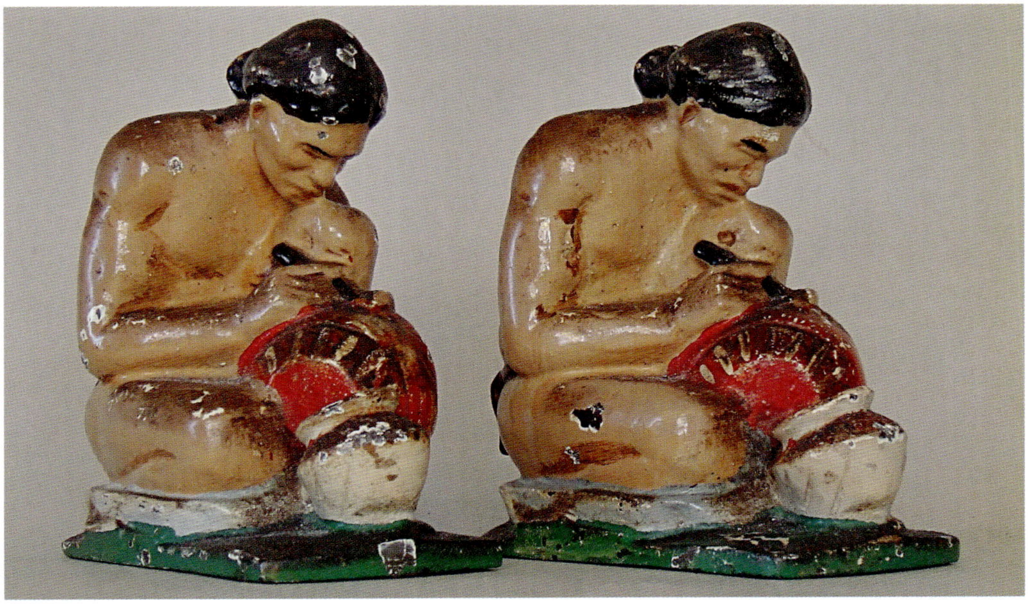

Figure 193. Indian Potter. 4.5", iron. Circa 1925. Rarity 2. Foundry Attrib. Littlestown. Arts & Crafts. Indian potters were frequently men. $120-180.

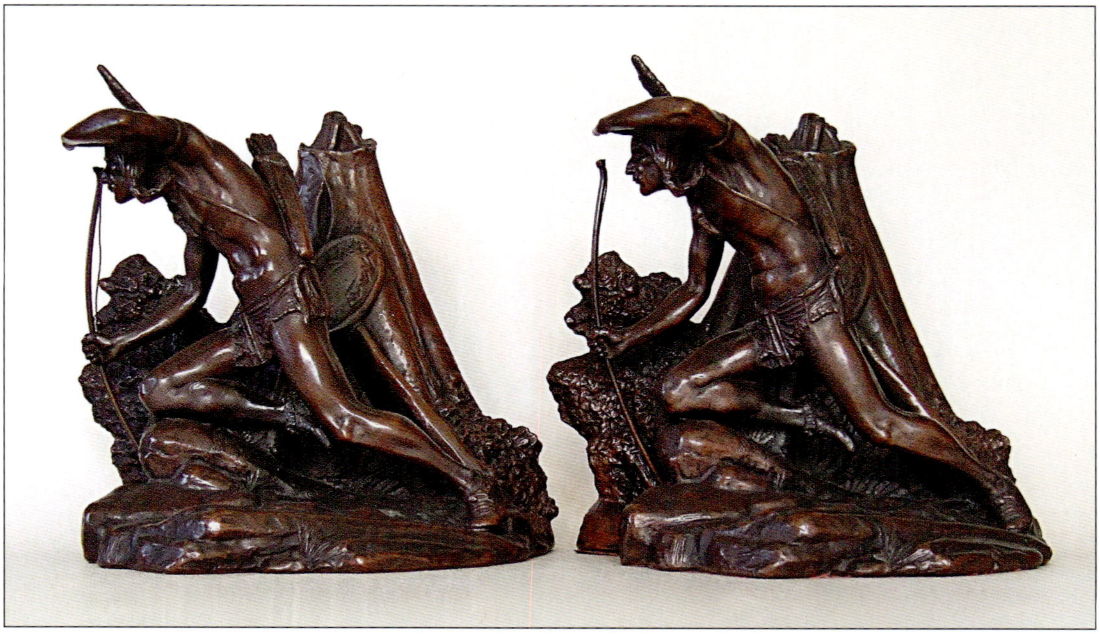

Figure 194. Indian and Teepee. 7.75", bronze plating on gray metal. Foundry: Attrib. Weidlich Brothers. Circa 1915. Rarity 3. Arts & Crafts. These are large, complex, heavy bookends, 11 lbs./pair. $800-1,200.

Figure 195. Indian with Hand on Breast. 8.25", electroformed bronze. Inscription: Armor Bronze shop mark, signed J. Lambert. Circa 1915. Rarity 2. Arts & Crafts. These are large, heavy bookends, 10.bs./pair. $340-520.

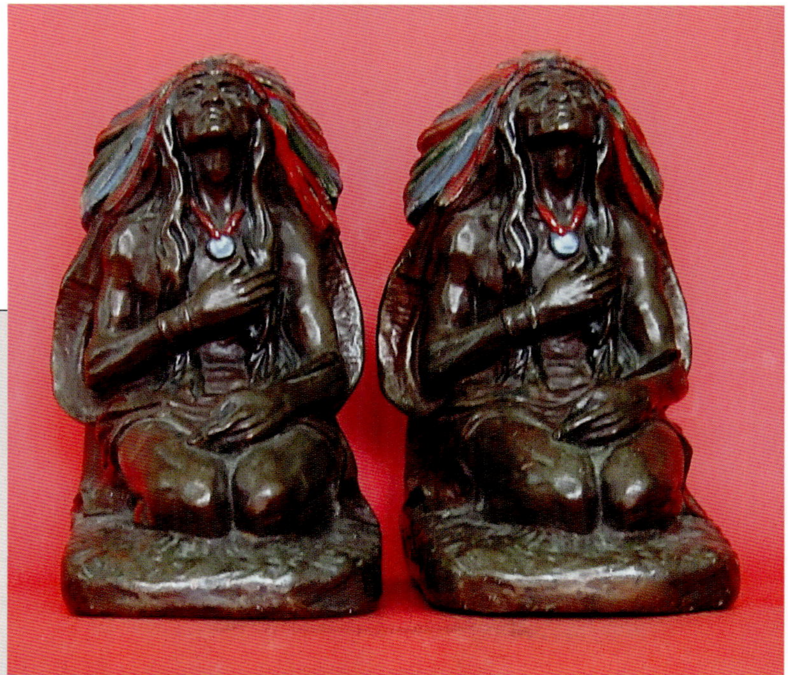

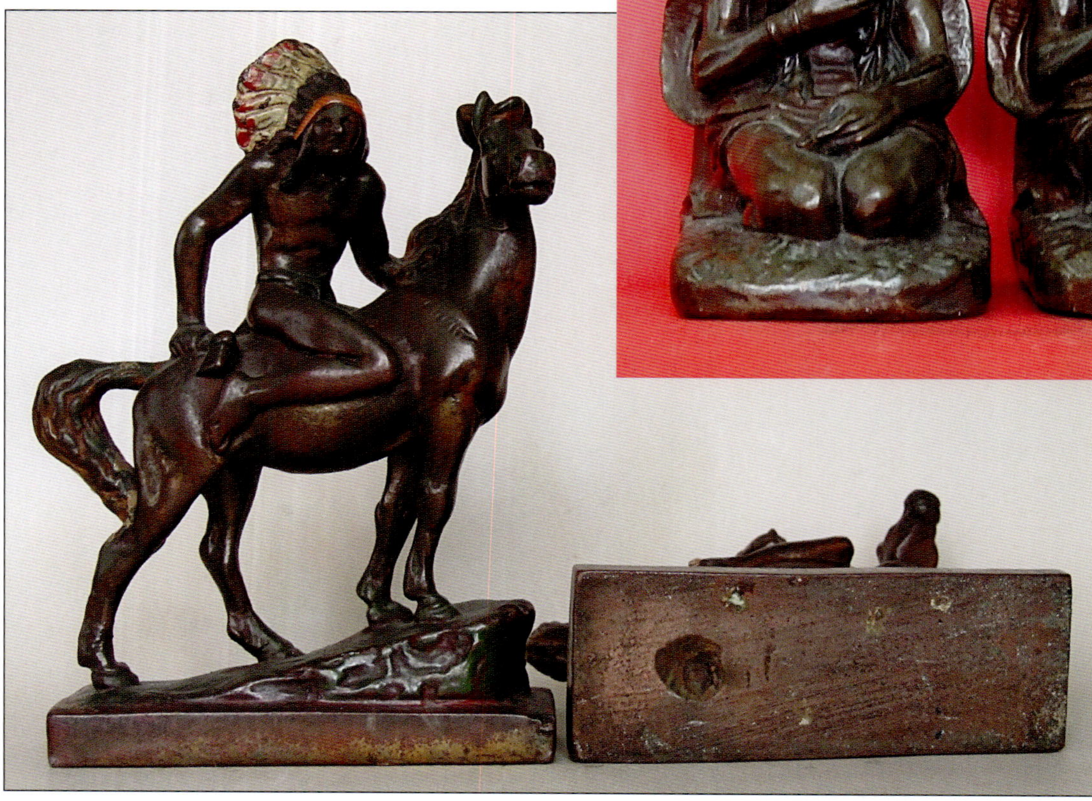

Figure 196. Mounted Indian. 9", electroformed bronze. Armor Bronze Inc. Circa 1923. Rarity 2. Arts & Crafts. The scar on the bottom from the electroform process is shown. $240-360.

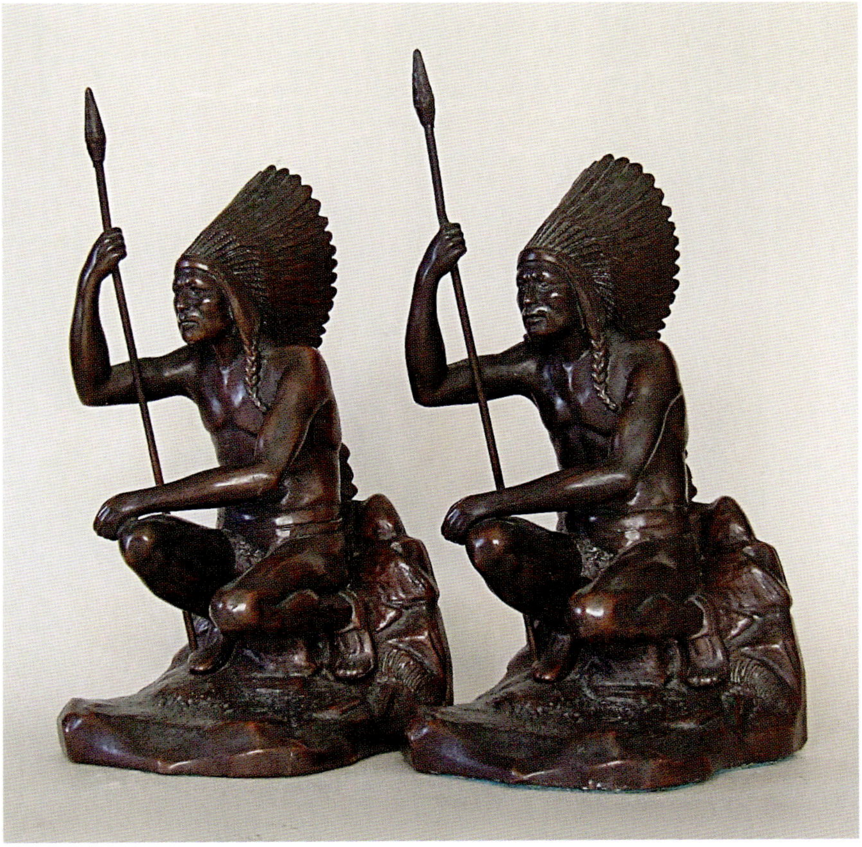

Figure 197. Indian Holding Lance. 8", bronze plating on gray metal. Inscription: Shop mark of Jennings Brothers, 1996. Circa 1923. Rarity 4. Arts & Crafts. $340-520.

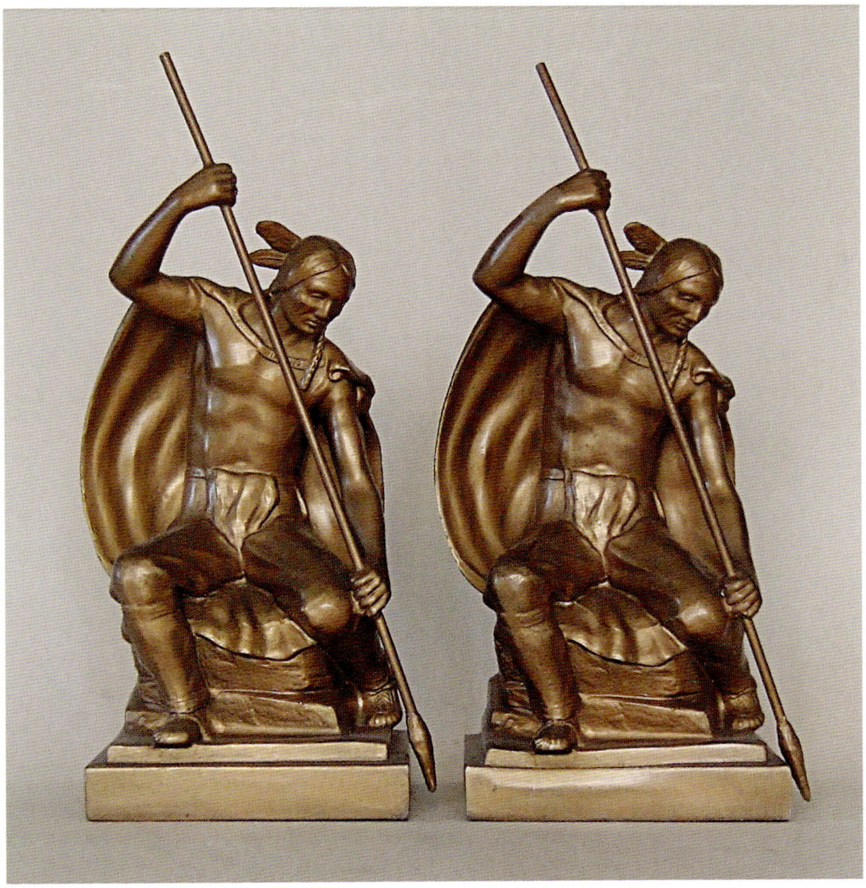

Figure 198. Indian with Cape and Spear. 9.25", bronze plating on gray metal. Inscription; Shop mark of Jennings Brothers, 1699. Circa 1923. Rarity 3. Arts & Crafts. Rare gold finish. $320-480.

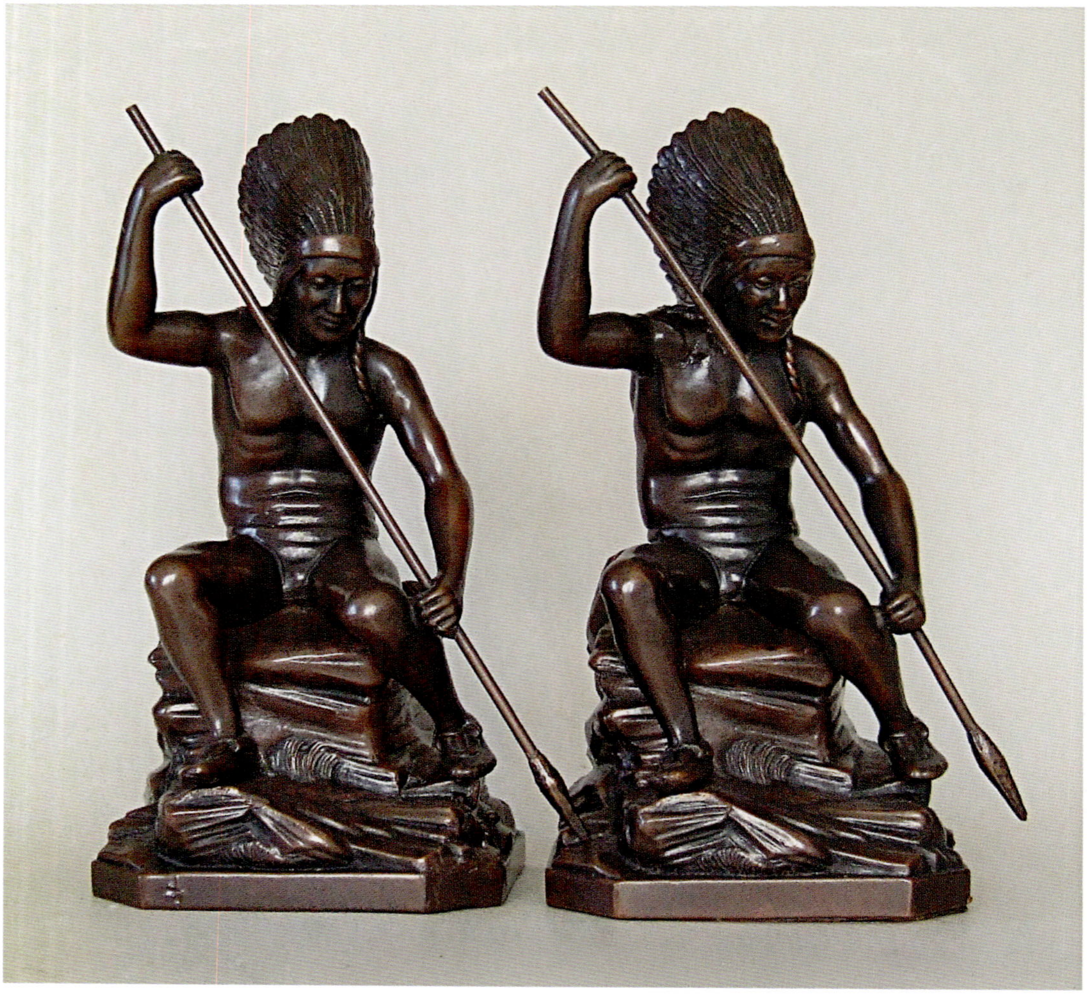

Figure 199. Indian Spear Fishing. 8" Bronze plating on gray metal. Inscription: Shop mark of Jennings Brothers, 2245. Circa 1923. Rarity 2. Arts & Crafts. $270-400.

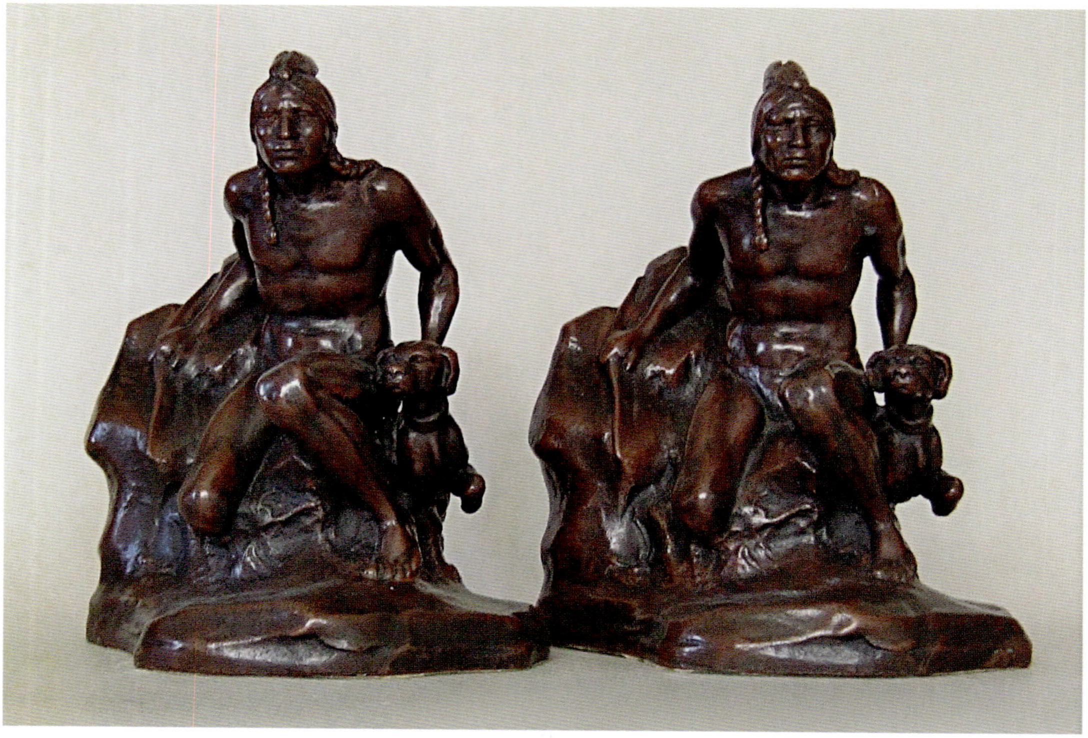

Figure 200. Indian and Dog. 6.5", bronze plating on gray metal. Inscription: Shop mark of Jennings Brothers, 1524. Circa 1923. Rarity 2. Arts & Crafts. A K&O copy without the dog is frequently seen. $240-360.

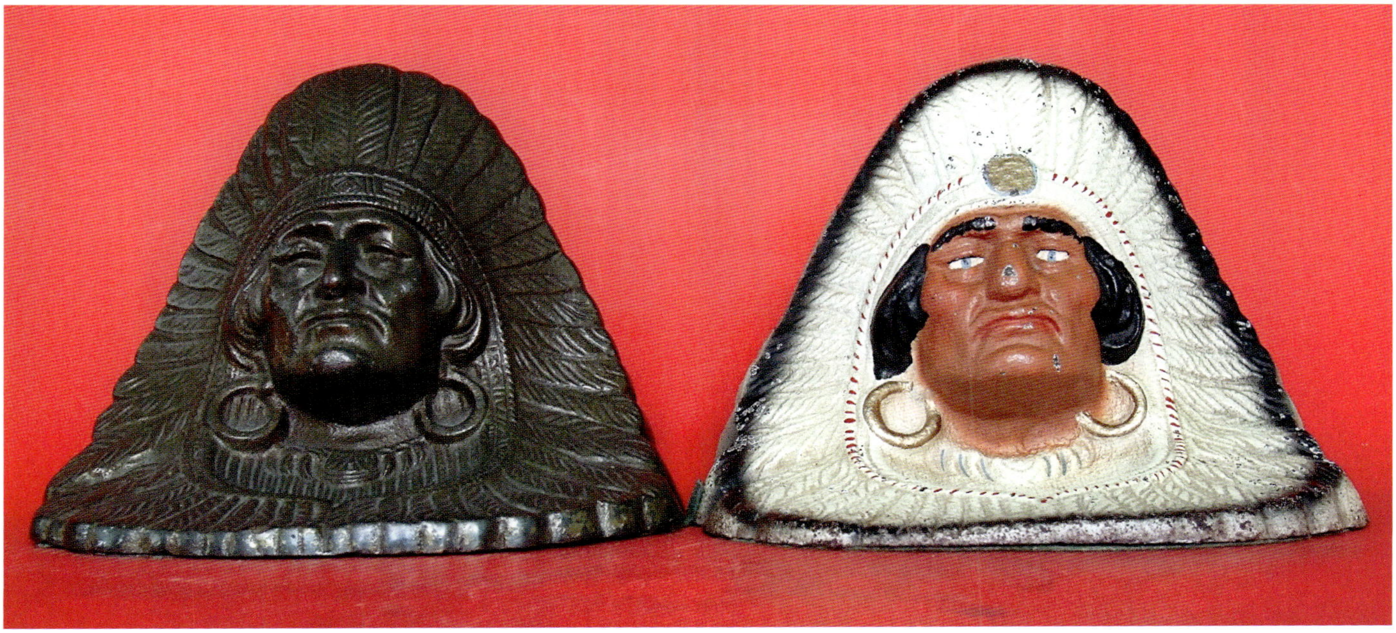

Figure 201. Indian with Ear Rings. 5", iron. Foundry: Attrib. Littlestown. Copper-flashed shown on the left. Circa 1923. Rarity 2. Arts & Crafts. Polychrome shown on the right. Circa 1923. Rarity 3. Arts & Crafts. $270-400. These are large, heavy bookends, 9 lbs./pair. $260-380.

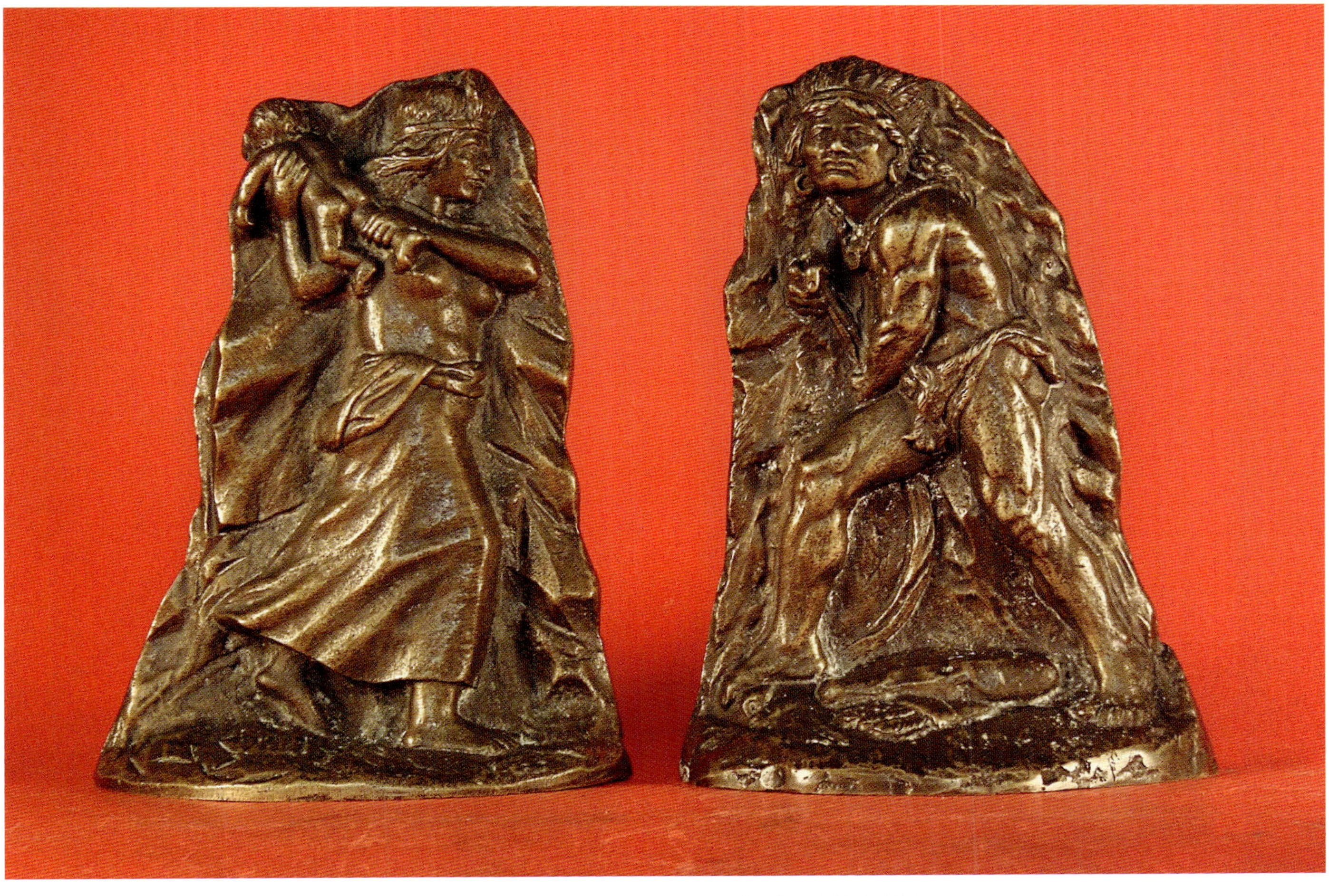

Figure 202. Indian Family. 6.25", bronze. Circa 1915. Rarity 5. Arts & Crafts. $320-480.

Figure 203. Indian on Bench. 5.75", gray metal. Inscription: K&O shop mark. Circa 1920. Rarity 4. Arts & Crafts. $220-330.

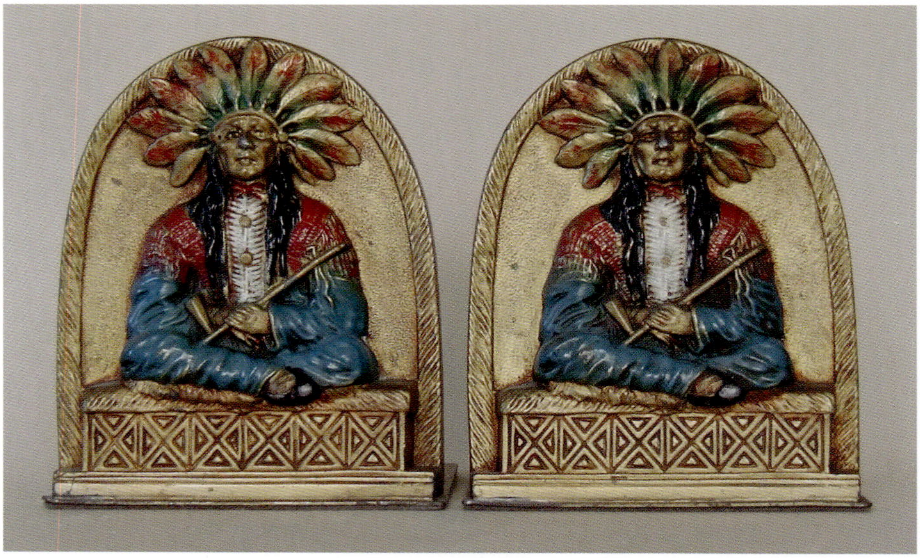

Figure 204. Indian Chief. 6.5", solid bronze. Inscription: Griffoul Newark, signed Peinlich. Sculptor. Circa 1917. Rarity 4. Arts & Crafts. These are finely-cast, large, heavy bookends, weight 17 lbs./pair. $960-1,400.

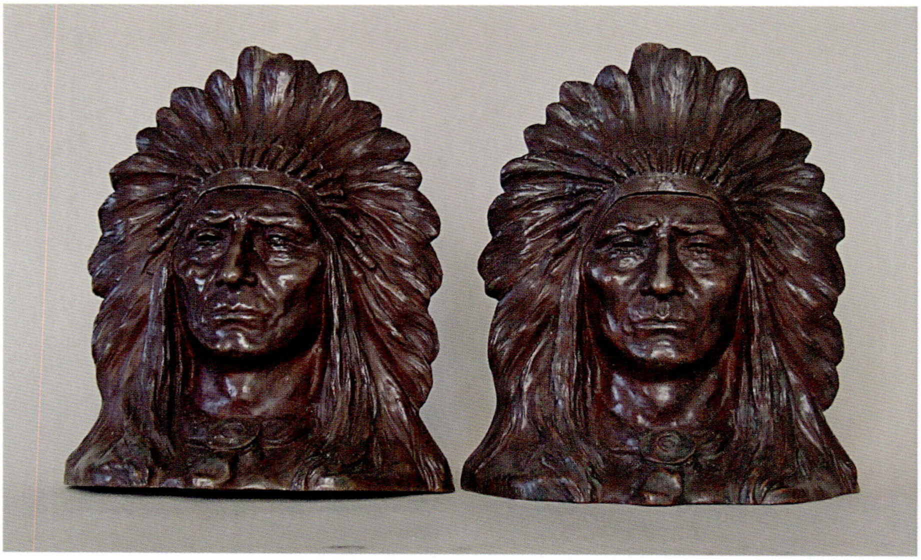

Figure 205. Sitting Bull. 7", iron. Inscription: Sitting Bull. Foundry: Attrib. Griffoul. Circa 1917. Rarity 3. Arts & Crafts. These are large, heavy bookends, 13 lbs./pair, but they do not resemble portraits of Sitting Bull. $600-900.

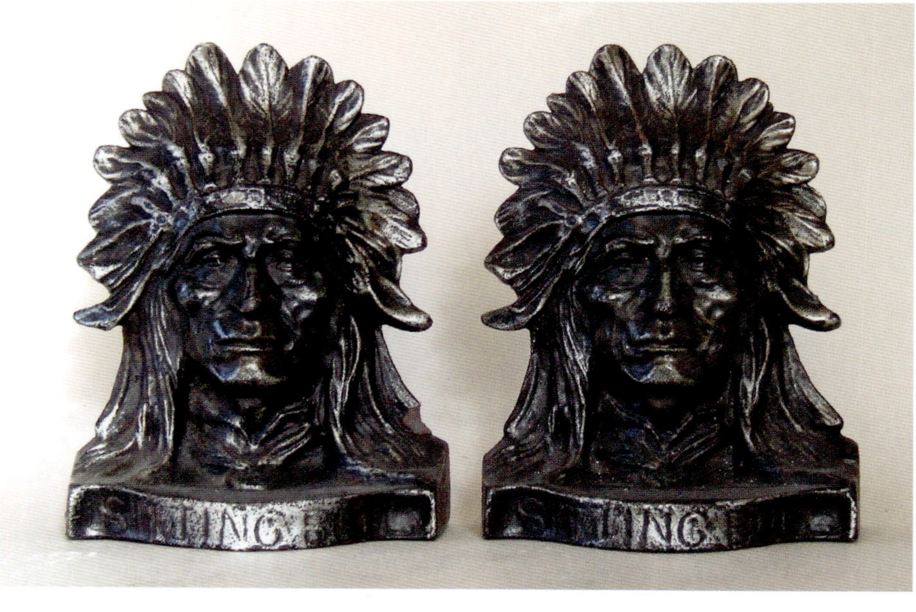

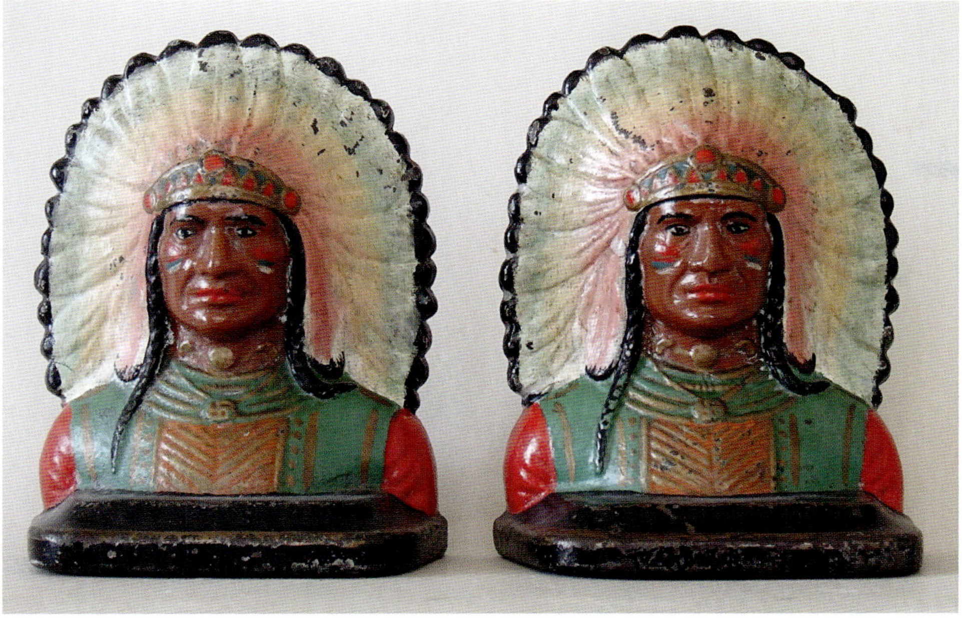

Figure 206. Sachem. 6.25" Iron. Apparently, Sachem image bookends were made by several different foundries, including W D Allen Co. and probably Judd. Circa 1929. Rarity 1. Arts & Crafts. Copper-flashed iron is most common, and it was pictured in the Sears catalog of 1929. Some are polychrome iron; least common are bronze. $70-90.

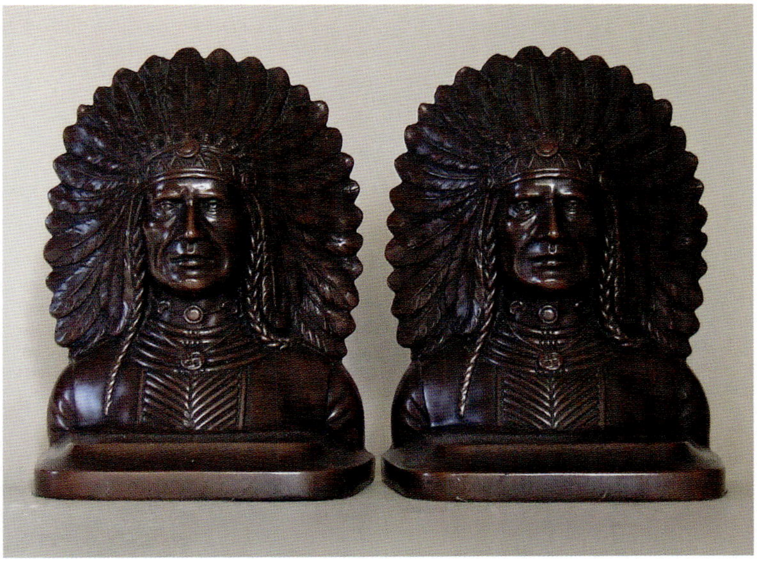

Figure 207. Sachem. 6", bronze plating on gray metal. Inscription: Shop mark of Jennings Brothers. 2061. Circa 1923. Rarity 3. Arts & Crafts. This image is seen on many iron bookends. $200-300.

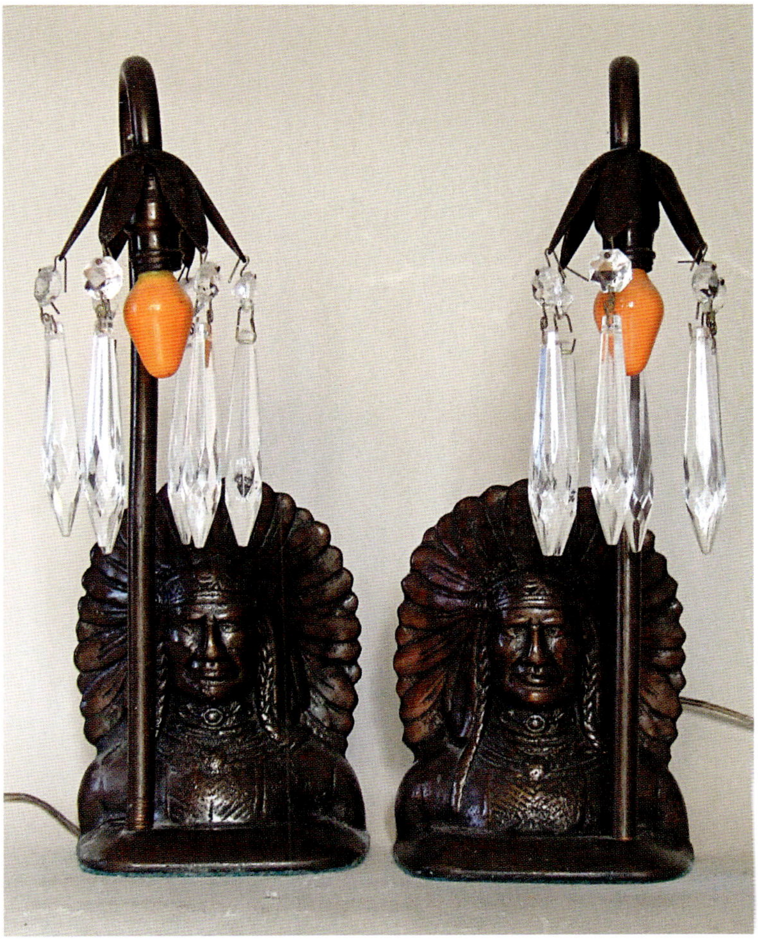

Figure 208. Sachem Lamp. 11.75", bronze and crystal. Circa 1929. Rarity 5. Arts & Crafts. This pair is functional as bookends and lamps. $900-1,400.

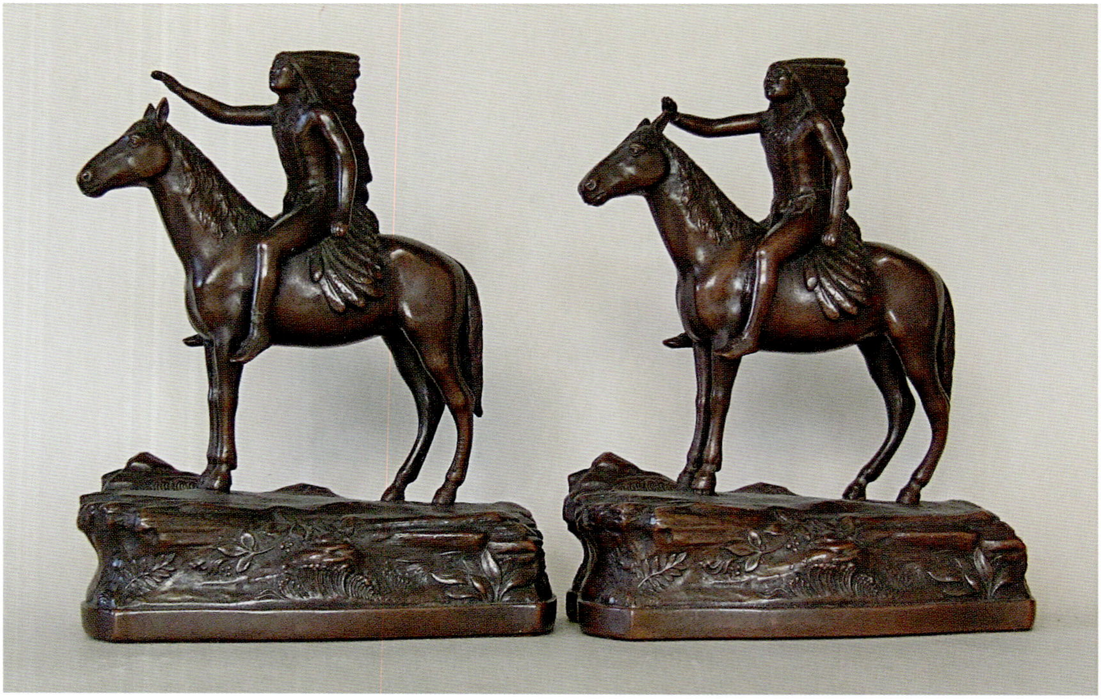

Figure 209. Indian Gesture. 7.5", bronze plating on gray metal. Inscription: Shop mark of Jennings Brothers. Circa 1923. Rarity 3. Arts & Crafts. $256-384.

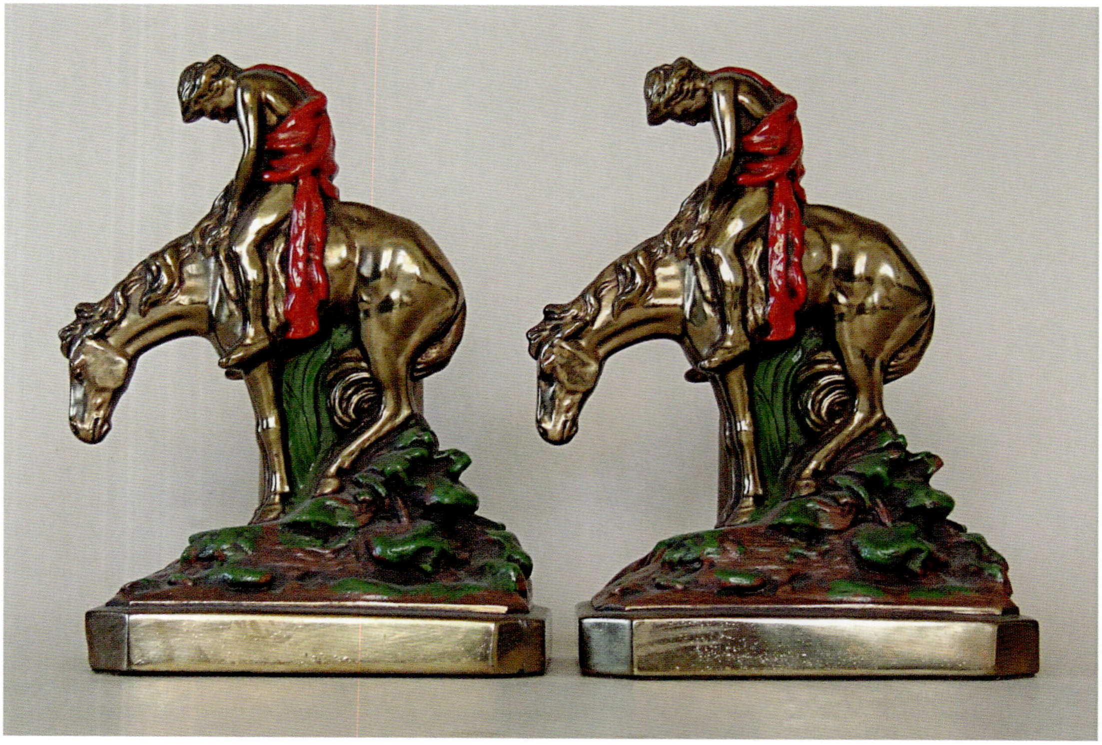

Figure 210. The End of the Trail. 6", gray metal. Inscription: Label citing Ronson. Sculptor: Modeled after a statue by James Earl Fraser. Circa 1925. Rarity 2. Arts & Crafts. Bookends with this subject were produced by many companies. $100-150.

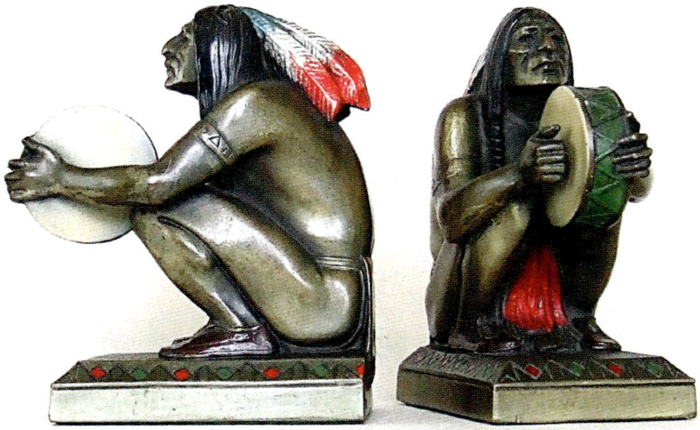

Figure 211. Indian with Drum. 5", gray metal. Inscription: K&O. Circa 1920. Rarity 5. Arts & Crafts. The gold color of the skin has tarnished to dark gray. $200-300.

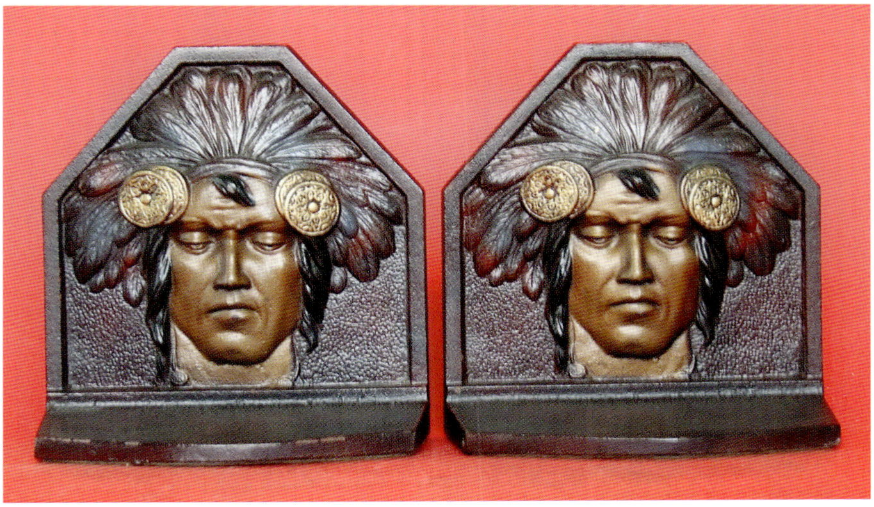

Figure 212. Handsome Indian. 5.25" iron. Inscription: 6868. Foundry Judd. Circa 1923. Rarity 2. Arts & Crafts. $200-300.

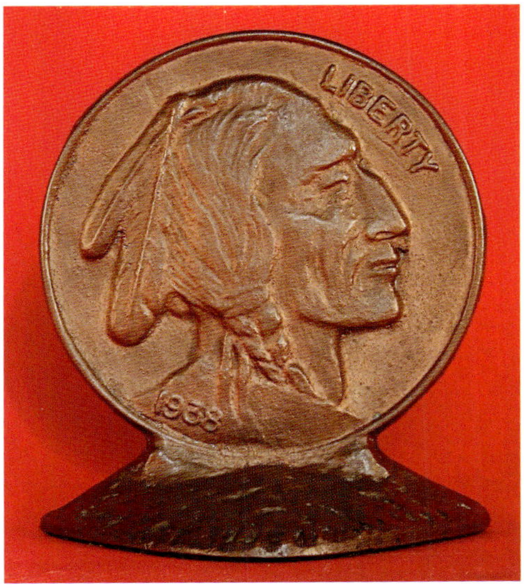

Figure 213. Buffalo Nickel Indian. Ht. 6", gray metal. Inscription: Liberty, 1938. Sculptor: Modeled after a coin designed by James Earle Fraser. Circa 1939. Rarity 5. Arts & Crafts. The Indian head / buffalo nickel was produced from 1913 to 1938. Only one bookend was available to photograph. The other member of this pair of bookends shows a buffalo. $275-420.

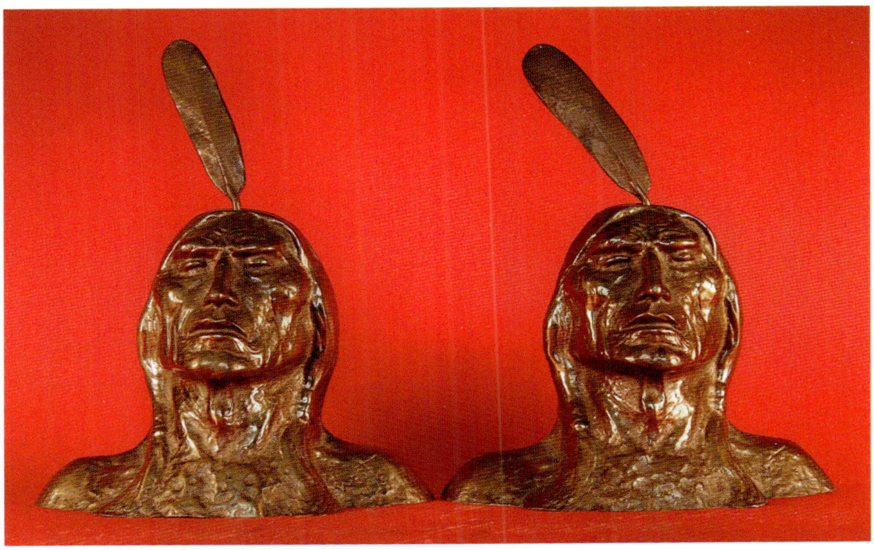

Figure 214. Indian with Removable Feather. 8.25", bronze. Inscription: Signature of West. Circa 1922. Rarity 4. Arts & Crafts. The quill of each feather fits into a hole in the top of the Indian's head and can be removed. Bookends missing the feather and the signature are seen frequently. $400-600.

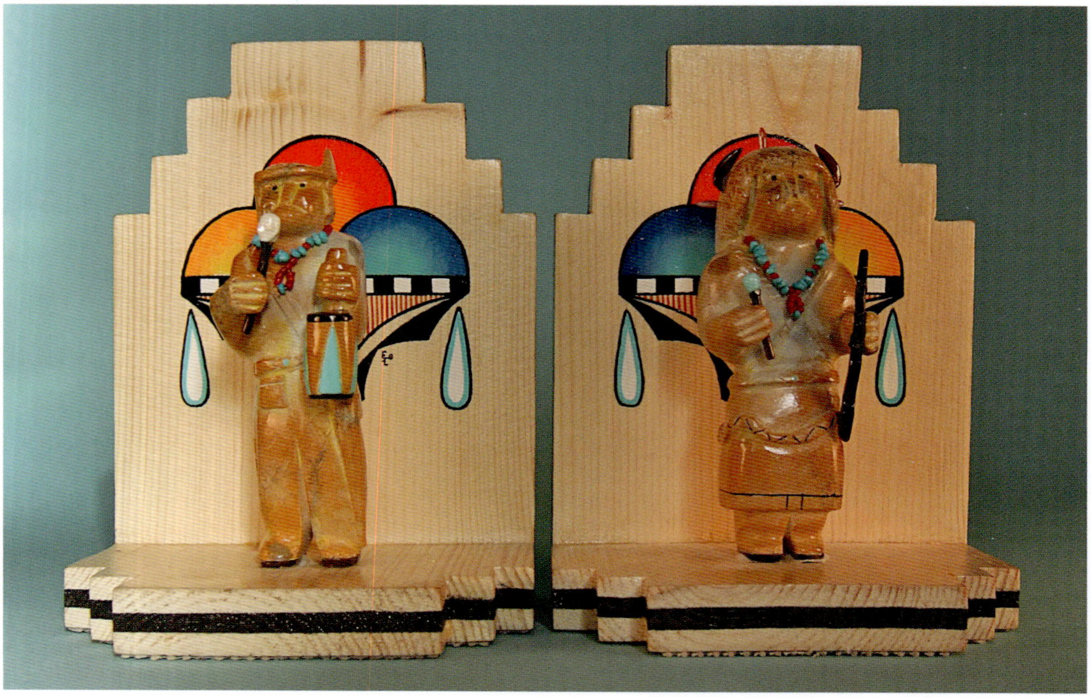

Figure 215. Zuni Buffalo Dancer and Drummer. 7.5", local carved rock figures, wood base and upright. Sculptor: Freddie Leekya, painting by Edward Lewis. 2011. Rarity 5. Arts & Crafts. Folk art. $660-990.

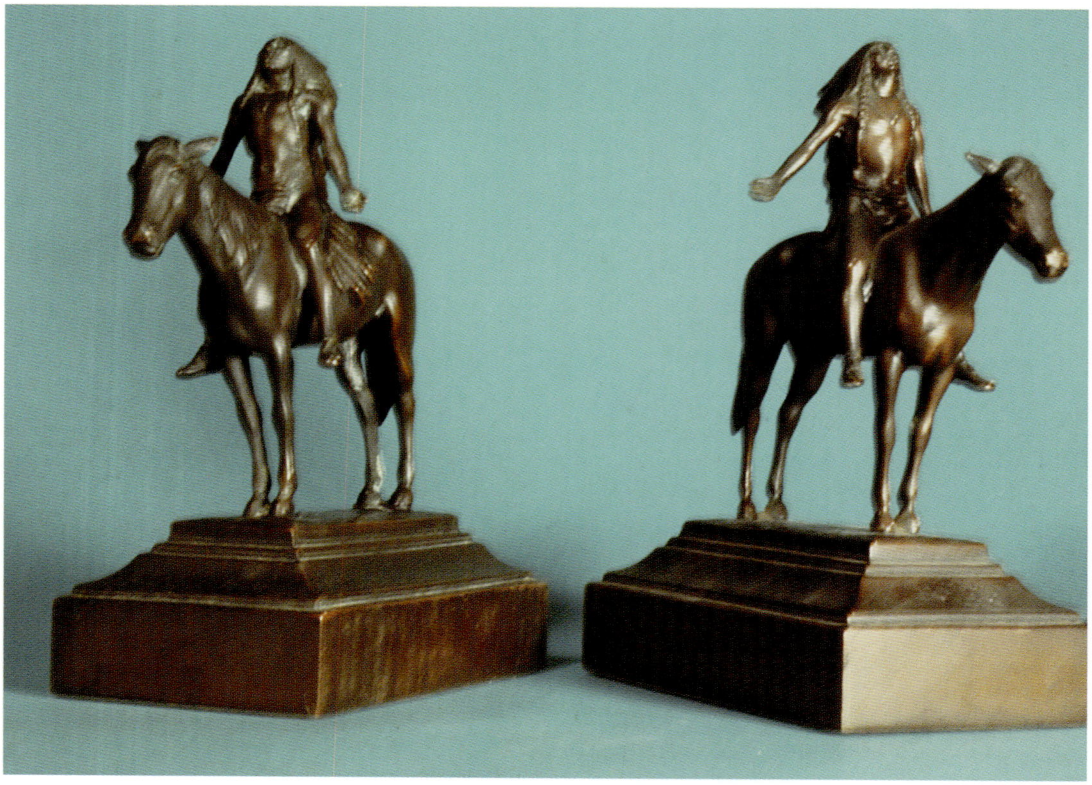

Figure 216. Appeal to the Great Spirit. 7.25", gray metal. Circa 1925. Rarity 2. Arts & Crafts. Modeled after a statue by Cyrus Edwin Dallin. These are sold as bookends, but do not hold books vertically so they are garnitures.

Mission Bookends

In 1895, Joseph McHugh, a New York furniture manufacturer and retailer, obtained a chair from San Francisco that reflected California Mission design. He then produced a line of rustic furniture based on this chair and named it "Mission" furniture. The California missions were self-sufficient settlements founded in the 18th and 19th centuries by Catholic priests from Spain, by way of Mexico. The missions were churches and outbuildings surrounded by ranch lands. The name "Mission style" was adopted then by Gustav Stickley and other manufacturers to describe their Arts & Crafts-style furniture. The name Mission was appropriate because the Catholic missions of early California, and their rustic contents, the buildings, furniture, and religious artwork, were hand crafted from local materials by local Indian artisans. The furnishings met the criteria of the Arts & Crafts movement, although the workers were unaware of the connection. The Mission architecture was based on Mexican architecture of the time, which itself was based on architecture carried over from Spain by the Spanish padres.

Although appropriate, the term Mission brought a disconnect to the fashion world because the parent Arts & Crafts style became known as the Mission style in California and in other places, and this is still largely true today. Many people now admire Mission-style furniture and accessories without understanding the relationship to Arts & Crafts philosophy or style.

More confusion was added when Spanish revival became popular in California and the Southwest from about 1920 to 1940, and very popular again in the last decade. Spanish Revival meant a return to the Spanish-derived Mexican buildings and furnishings of the Missions and especially to the haciendas of early California and the Southwest. Revival furniture and accessories of iron, tile, wood, rope, and leather, were produced by companies like Mason (Monterey) or Imperial. Matching bookends depicting California missions, padres, Mexican peasants, other Mexicana, and Spanish flamenco dancers were produced from about 1915 through about 1950. (Figures 216-231). Today furniture and bookends like these are sold as Spanish-revival style at premium prices.

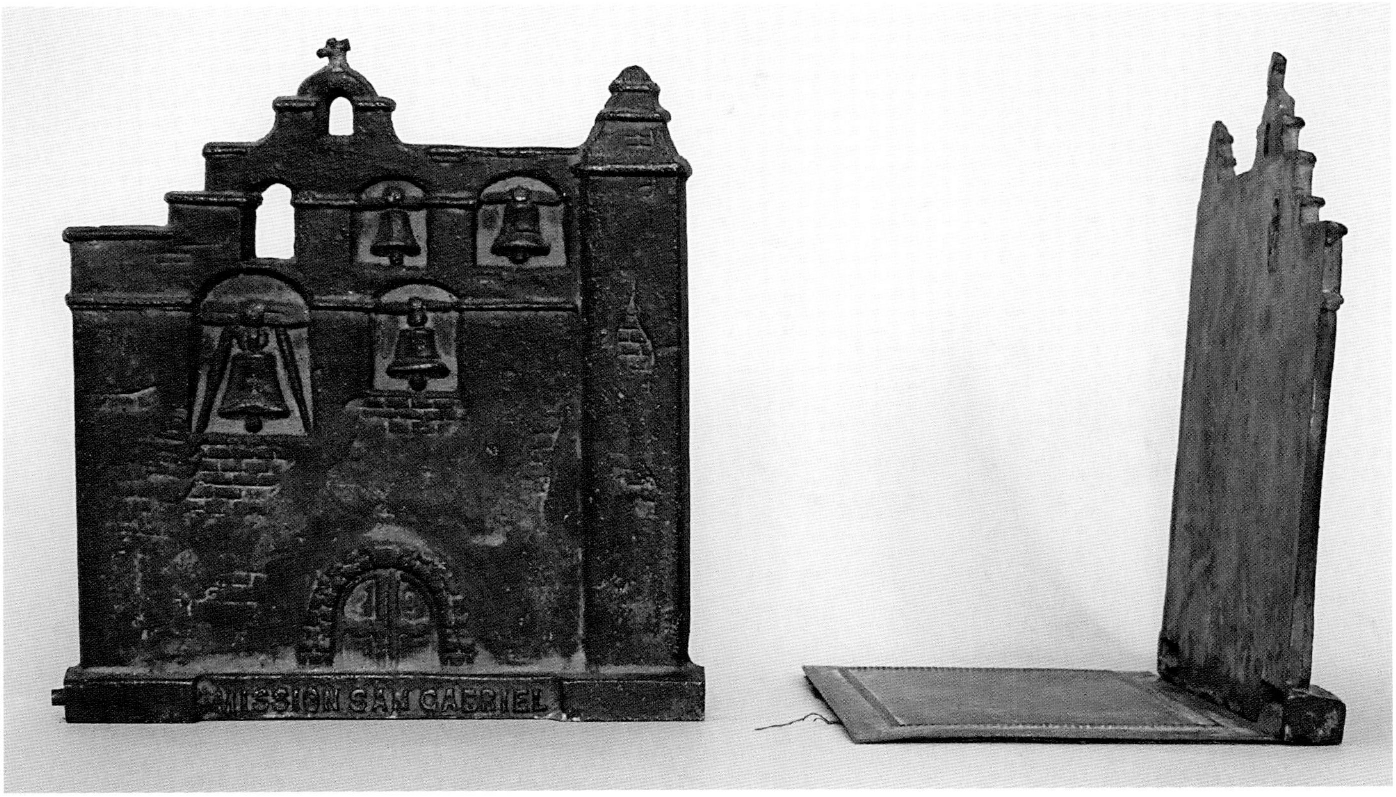

Figure 217. Mission San Gabriel with Foot. 5", bronze. Foundry: California Bell Co. Circa 1911. Rarity 5. Arts & Crafts, Spanish Revival. Each bookend is hinged so the upright can be folded down. $400-600.

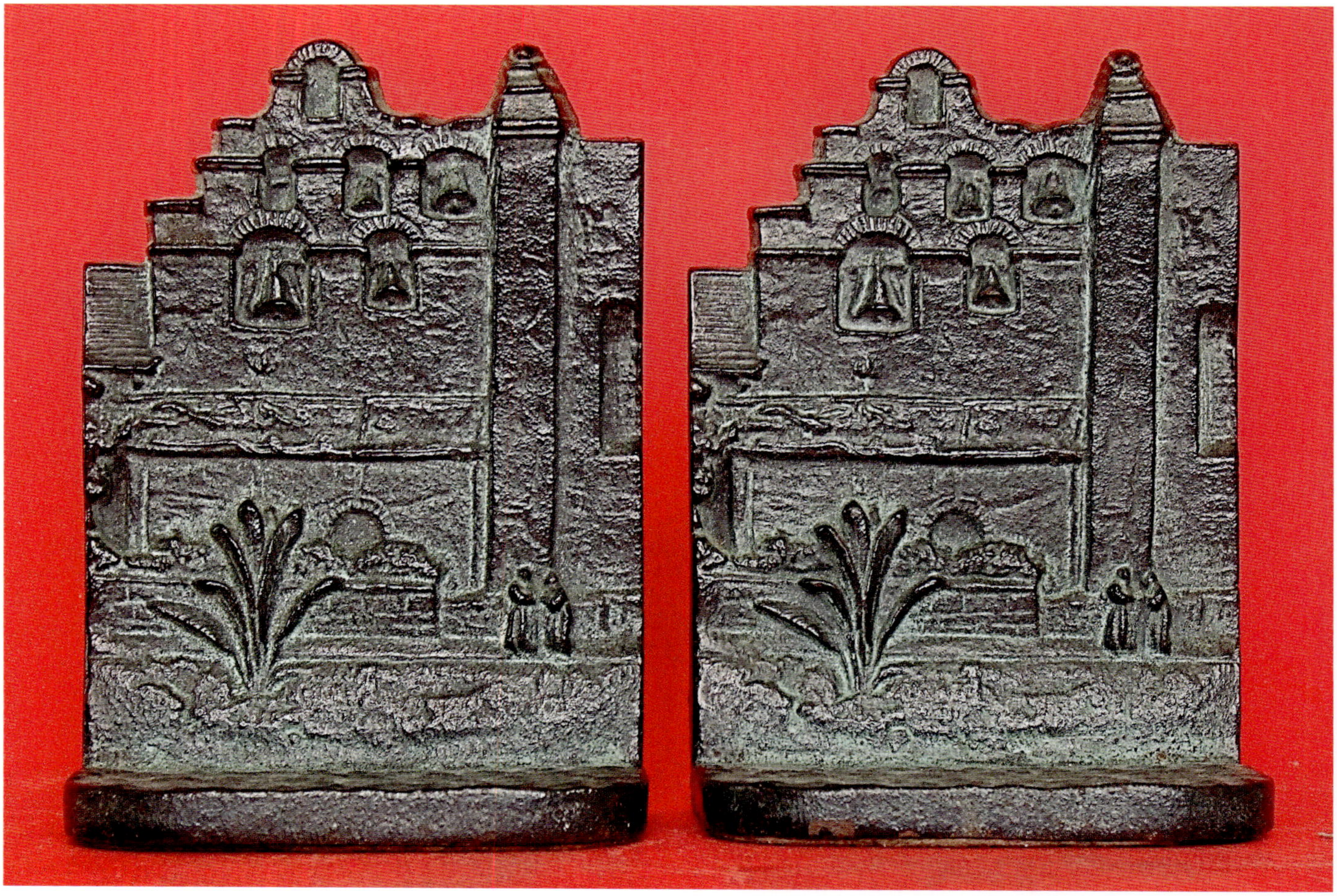

Figure 218. Mission San Gabriel. 5", iron. Inscription: A history of the San Gabriel Mission is inscribed on the back. Foundry: California Bell Co. Circa 1911. Rarity 4. Arts & Crafts. Spanish Revival. $240-360.

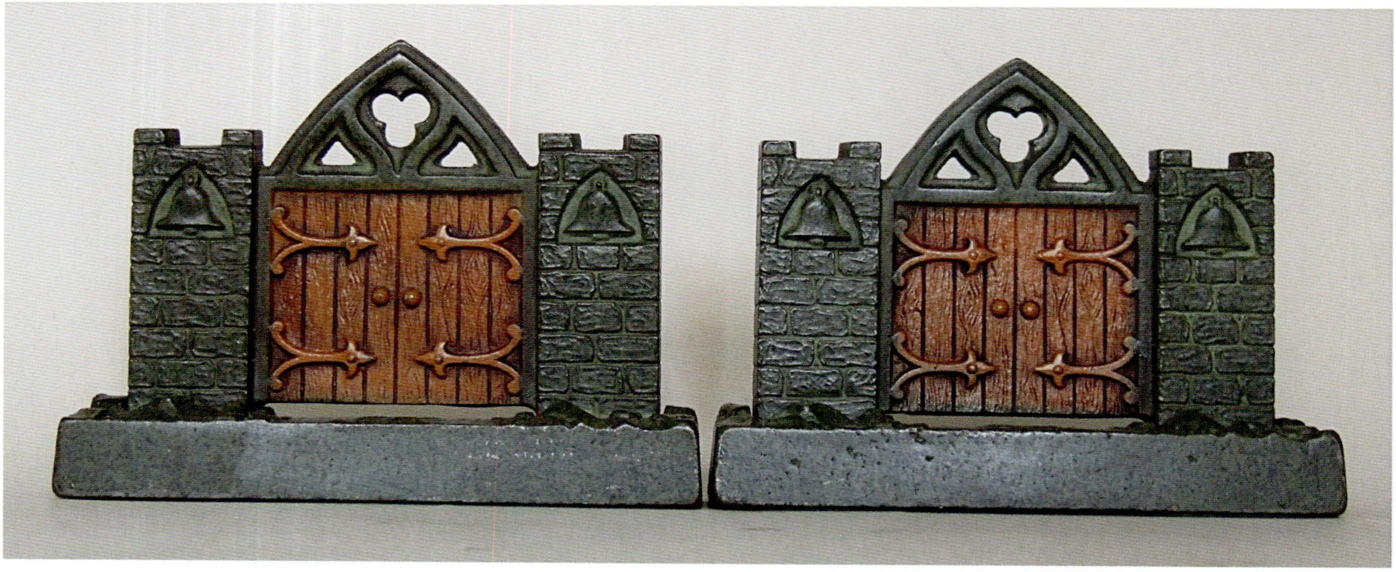

Figure 219. Mission Gate. Ht. 5.5", iron. Inscription: 9737. Foundry: Judd. Circa 1917. Rarity 2. Arts & Crafts. Spanish Revival. $160-240.

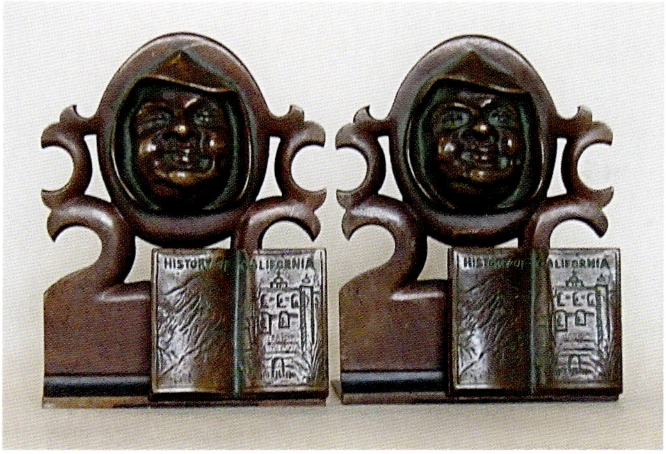

Figure 220. Mission Padre. 6.5", bronze. Inscription: History of California. Circa 1917. Rarity 4. Arts & Crafts, Spanish Revival. $275-420.

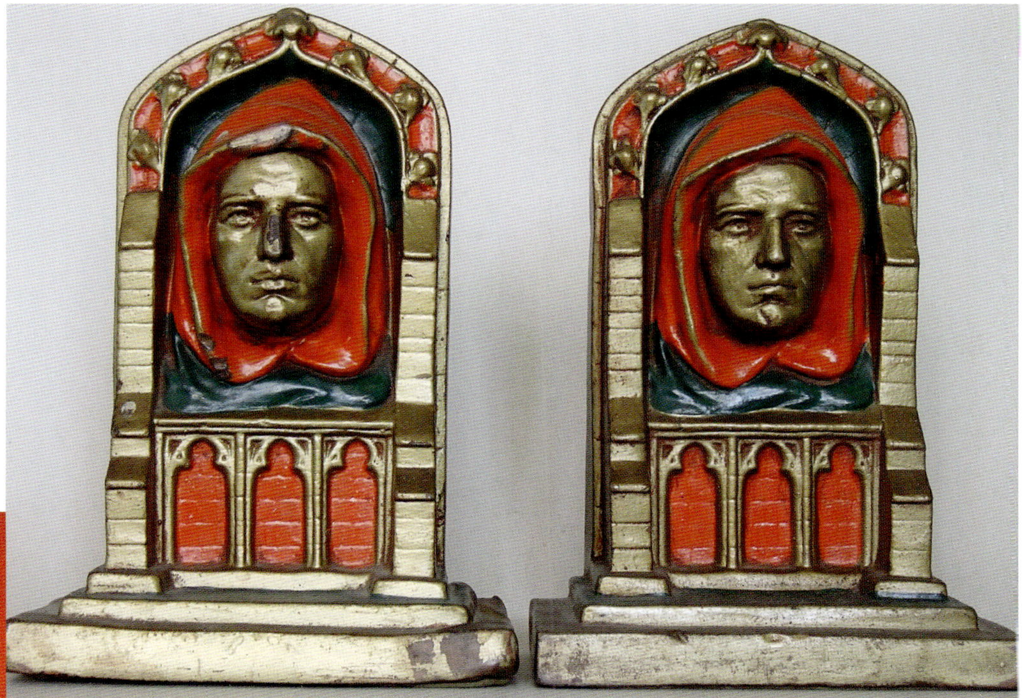

Figure 221. Friar in Cathedral. Ht. 8.5", electroformed bronze. Inscription: Hirsch. Circa 1920. Rarity 3. Arts & Crafts, Spanish Revival. Hirsch is either the foundry or the artist. $240-360.

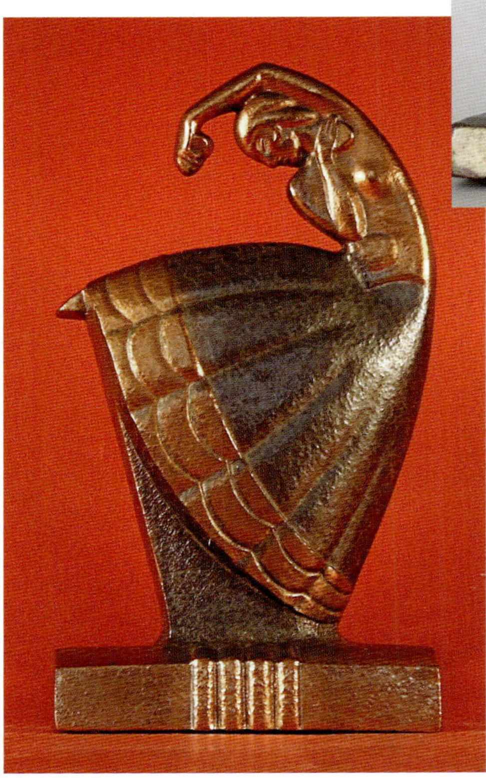

Figure 222. Spanish Dancer. 7", gray metal. Attrib. Dodge Inc. Circa 1940. Rarity 2. Arts & Crafts, Spanish Revival. $140-210.

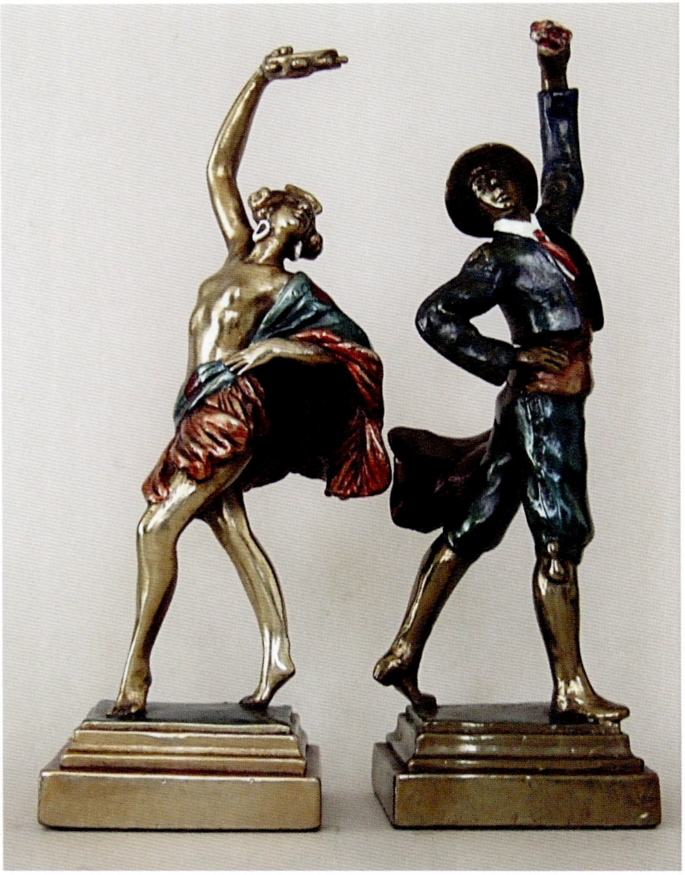

Figure 223. Flamenco Dancers. 11", electroformed bronze. Inscription: signed P. Herzel. Foundry: Pompeian Bronze. Circa 1923. Rarity 2. Arts & Crafts, Spanish Revival. $275-420.

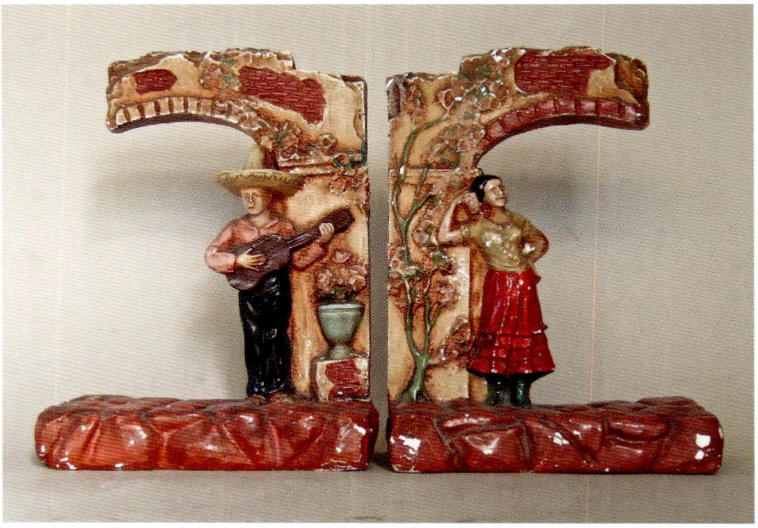

Figure 224. Old Mexico. 7", chalkware. Circa 1940. Rarity 5. $60-90. Arts & Crafts, Spanish Revival. $60-90.

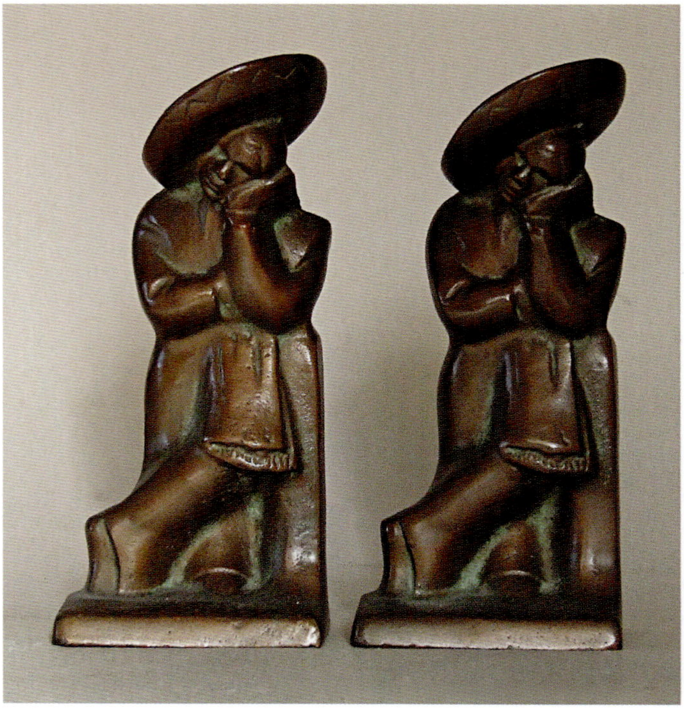

Figure 225. Sleeping Pedro. 6", iron. Inscription: 498. Foundry: Hubley Mfg. Co. Circa 1929. Rarity 3. Arts & Crafts, Spanish Revival. $160-240.

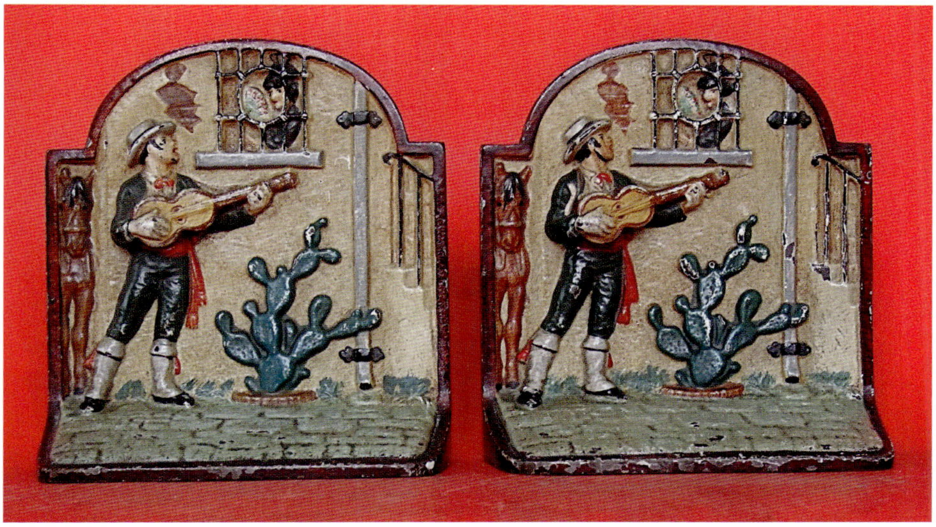

Figure 226. Mexican Serenade. 5.5", iron. Inscription: 233. Foundry: Hubley Mfg. Co. Circa 1929. Rarity 4. Arts & Crafts, Spanish Revival. Usually seen copper flashed. $240-360.

Figure 227. Mayan Indians. 5.5", onyx. Tijuana, Mexico. Circa 1950. Rarity 4. Arts & Crafts, Spanish Revival. A variety of crude onyx bookends from Tijuana are frequently seen. $12-18.

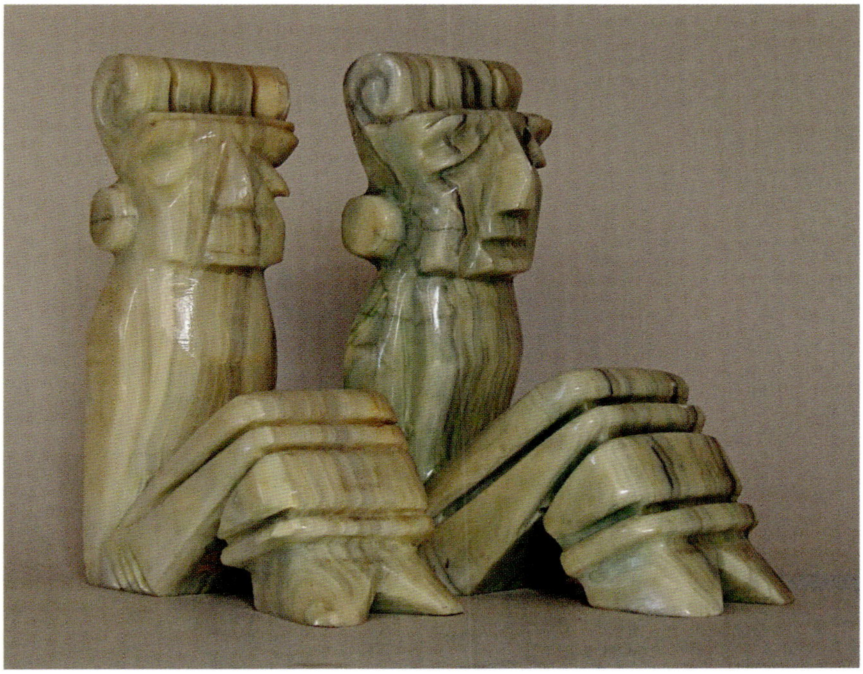

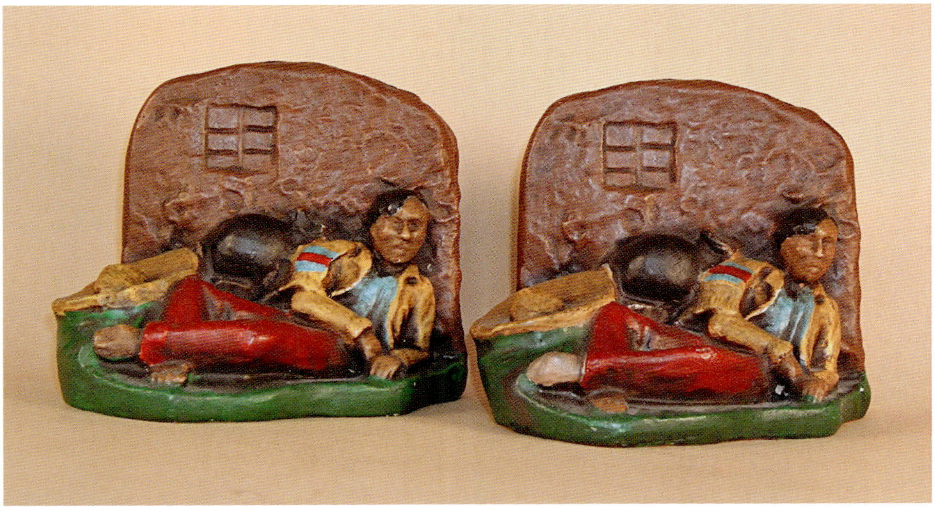

Figure 228. Sleeping Mexican. Ht. 4.25", chalkware. Circa 1940. Rarity 5. Arts & Crafts, Spanish Revival. $40-60.

Figure 229. Cart and Oxen 5.5", chalkware. Circa 1940. Rarity 5. Arts & Crafts, Spanish Revival. $40-60.

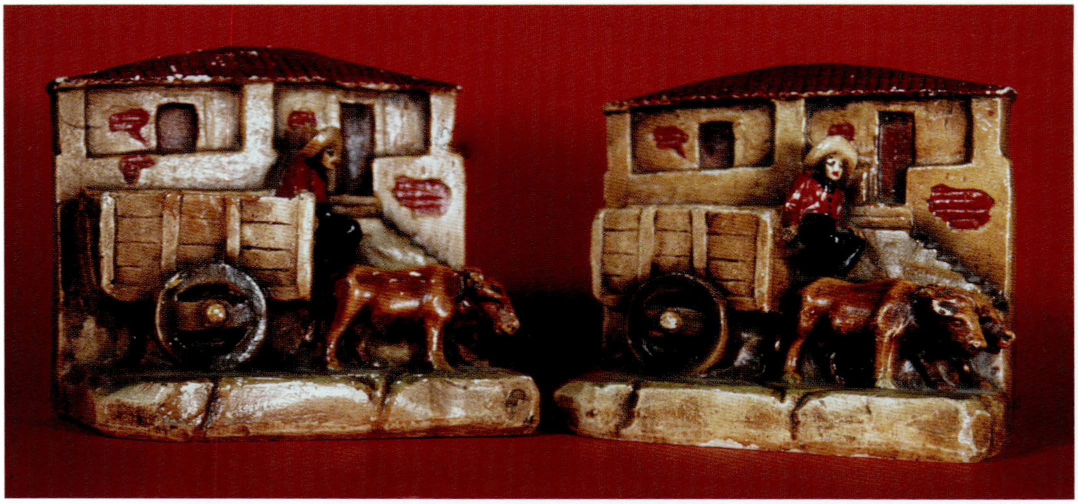

Figure 230. Siesta. 6.5". chalkware. Circa 1940. Rarity 5. Arts & Crafts, Spanish Revival. $40-60.

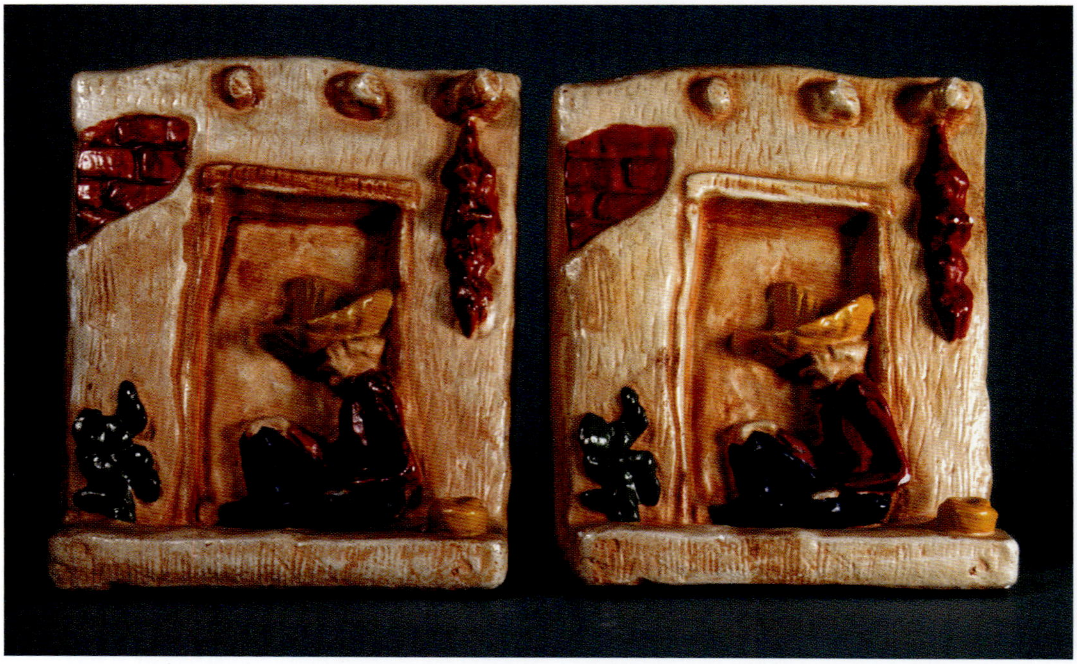

Figure 231. Mexican and Palm Tree. 6" Painted wood, crackle finish, iron foot, rope finial. Attrib. Mason (Monterey). Circa 1930. Rarity 5. Arts & Crafts, Spanish Revival. $200-300.

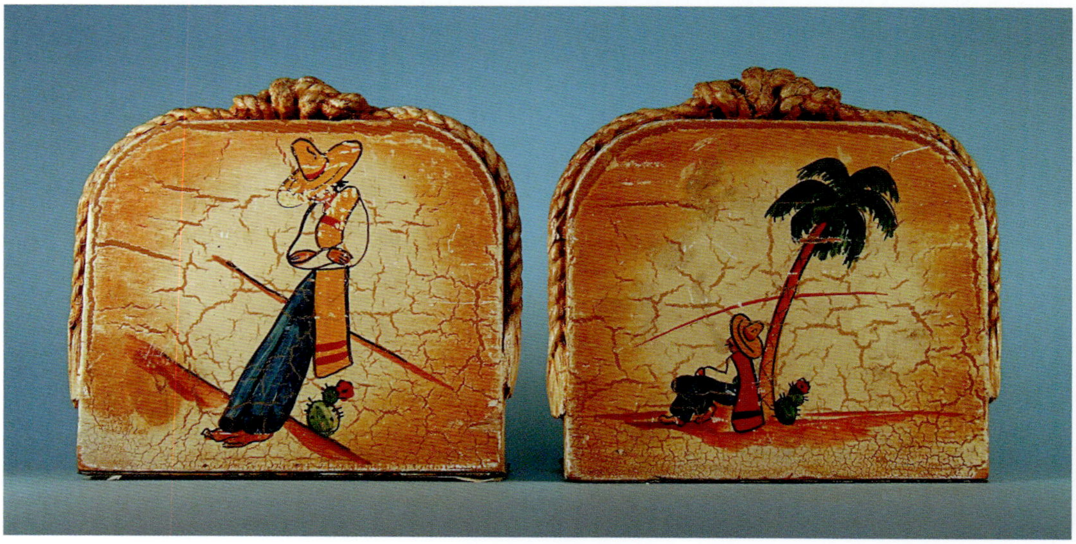

Chapter 5

Art Nouveau Style Bookends

During the 19th century, artwork in England, France, and other European nations was controlled by art academies staffed by eminent artists. The academies promoted classical art standards, including a hierarchy of genres for painters in England. Painting of history was top-ranked, and then came portraiture, still life, and lastly, landscape. There was little room for creativity, so it was not surprising that a new art style, now called by the French term, *Art Nouveau* (new art), appeared in about 1890, and swept England and Europe as a reaction against the classical, formal art of the period. The style was very popular but only lasted in Europe until about 1914, when World War I took everyone's attention.

Art Nouveau was a curvilinear style used in architecture and art work in general, and it attempted to make objects of beauty, including mundane objects of everyday use, thus eliminating the distinction between fine art and decorative art. In this respect it was honoring the stances of Ruskin and Morris in England, and the foundations of Art Nouveau are usually attributed to the Arts & Crafts Movement. The interpretation of the style and the name differed from one country to another, but many lay people embraced the style in their daily lives.

Art Nouveau came to the United States around 1900. It appeared in art pottery and in the output of Louis Comfort Tiffany and others. Art Nouveau-style bookends emerged to take their place alongside these fashionable objects. Bookends utilized the typical decorative elements that characterized Art Nouveau creations. Because the details of the style differed from nation to nation, the list of decorative elements is a long one. These elements included lion fountains and intertwined organic forms, especially leaf, tendril, and vine motifs. The motifs also depicted lavish peacocks, peacock feathers, other birds, flowers, insects, and other natural forms. The luxurious hair and curvaceous bodies of beautiful women were prominent, especially as portrayed in posters by Alphonse Mucha, a Czech artist. The style frequently utilized so-called "whiplash curves" which were sinuous and graceful rather than geometric. Additional subjects were wings, winged ladies, bats, or other winged creatures. Ladies were shown in shifts or other scanty dress on the one hand, or in dresses with luxurious folds on the other. The interest in Art Nouveau fashion apparently lasted somewhat longer in the United States than in Europe because some American bookends in this style date from the 1920s. Art Nouveau style bookends are shown in Figures 232 to 240.

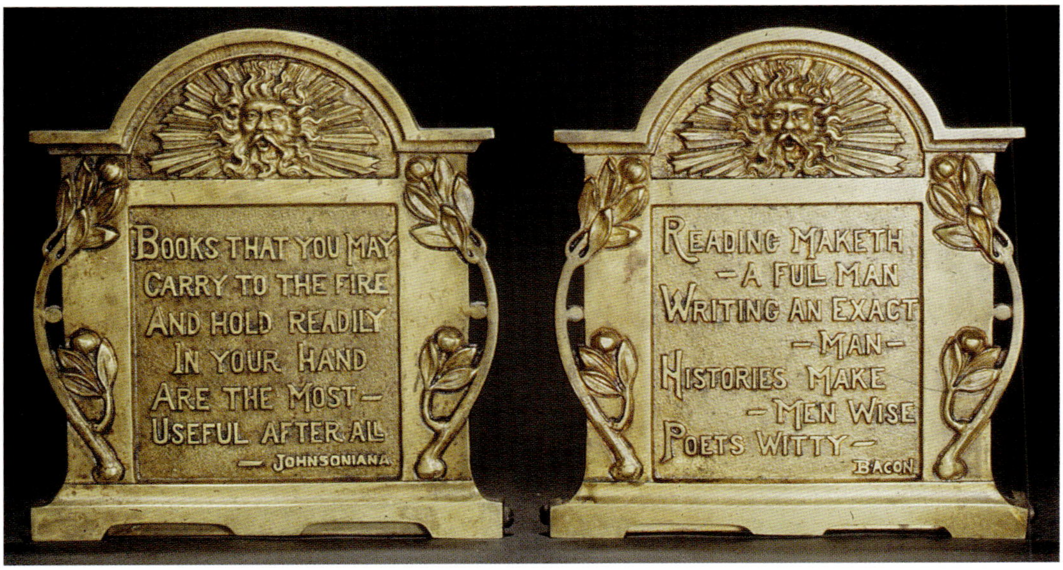

Figure 232. Bacon and Johnson. 6.75", iron. Circa 1920. rarity 3. Transition from Arts & Crafts to Art Nouveau. $80-120.

Figure 233. Britannia Rules the Waves. 6.25", bronze. Foundry: Attrib. England. Circa 1913. Rarity 5. Transition, Victorian to Art Nouveau. Nude lady with helmet stands with one foot on the detached head of Neptune. Sinuous British lions to either side. $200-300.

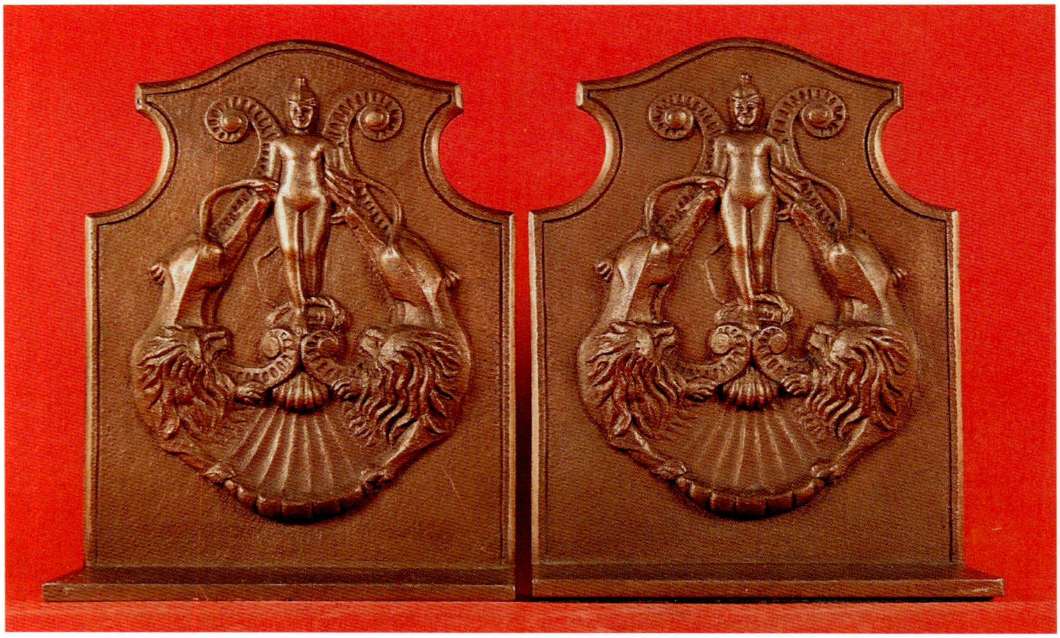

Figure 234. Butterfly Girl. 6", gray metal. Circa 1923. Foundry: Attrib. Ronson. Rarity 2. Art Nouveau. Girl in a revealing shift, wings with whiplash markings. Many reproductions available, showing prominent, uplifted breasts. Modified from a poster by F. X. Leyendecker, 1922. Art Nouveau. $200-300.

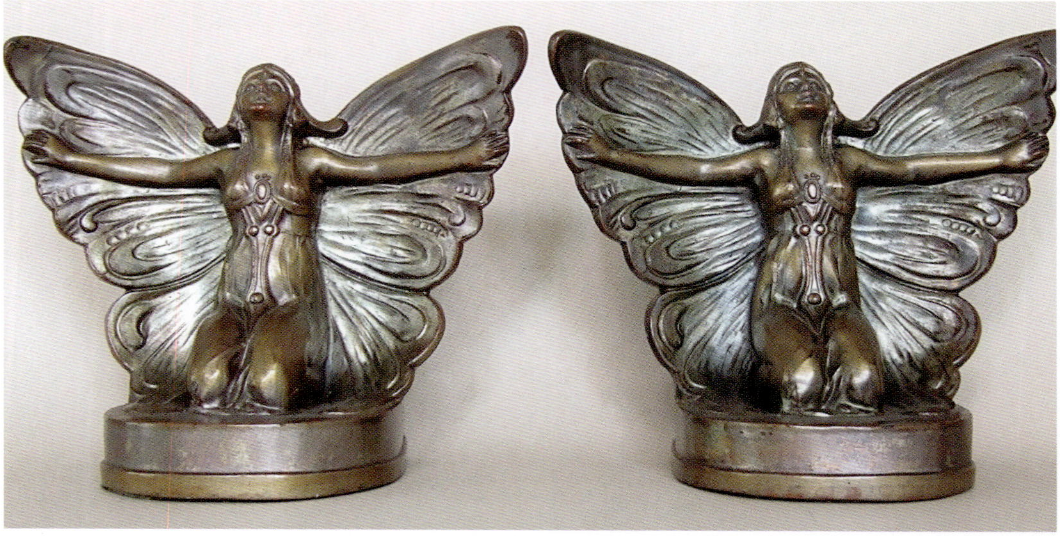

Figure 235. Mucha Maiden. 5.5", gray metal. Circa 1919. Rarity 3. Art Nouveau. Beautiful girl with masses of whiplash hair. $160-240.

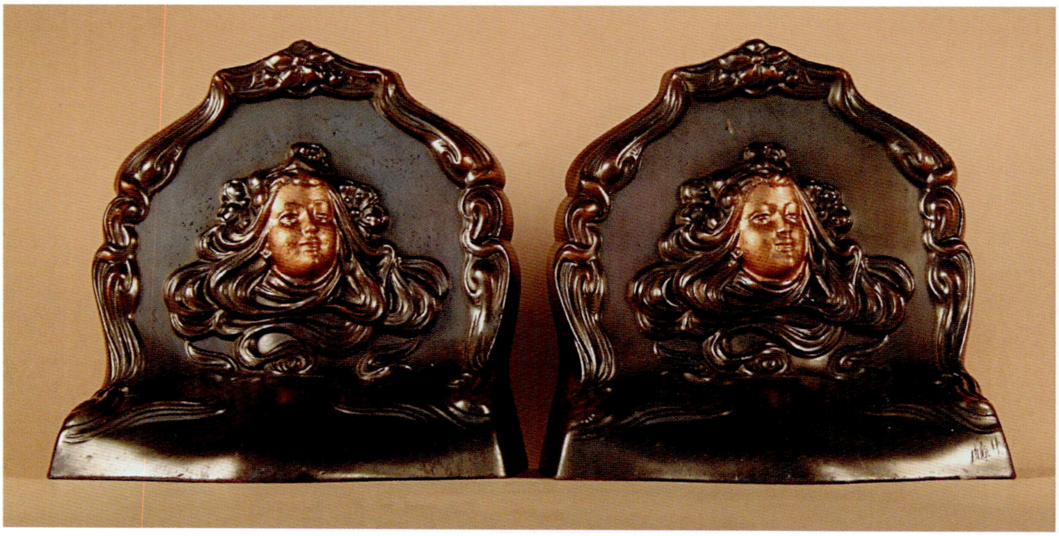

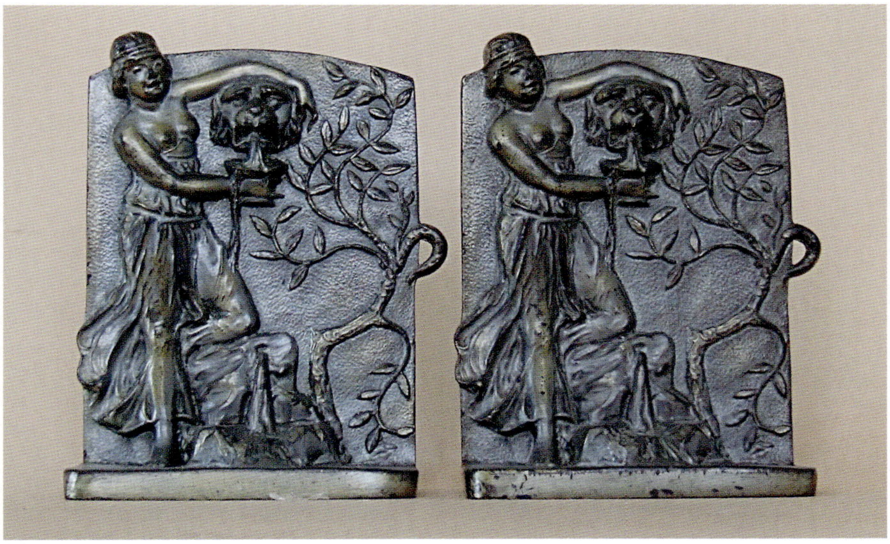

Figure 236. Lady at lion Fountain. 5", gray metal. Circa 1919. Rarity 2. Very Art Nouveau. Lady in a shift, lion fountain, winding vine. $200-300.

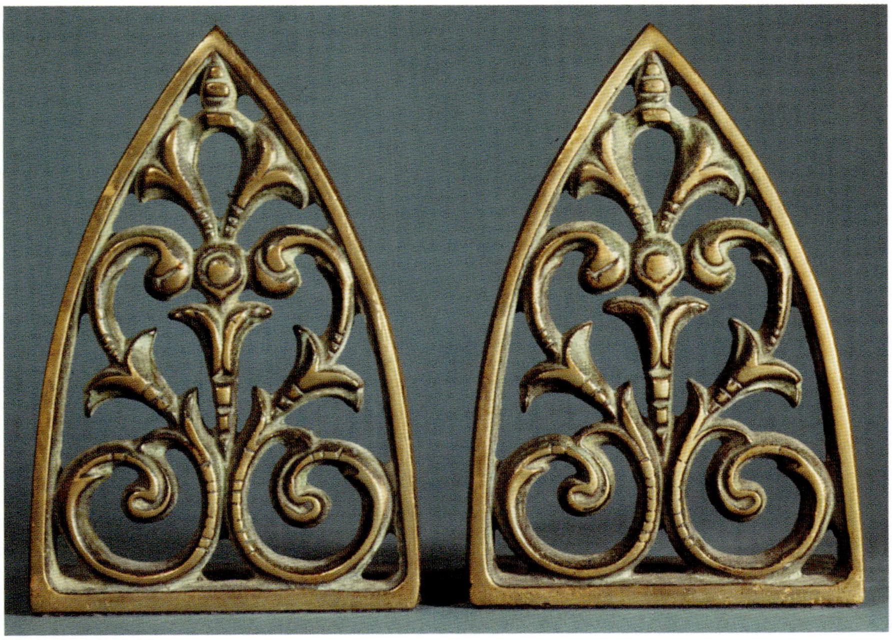

Figure 237. Floral Design. 6", brass. Circa 1920. Rarity 4. Art Nouveau. $60-90.

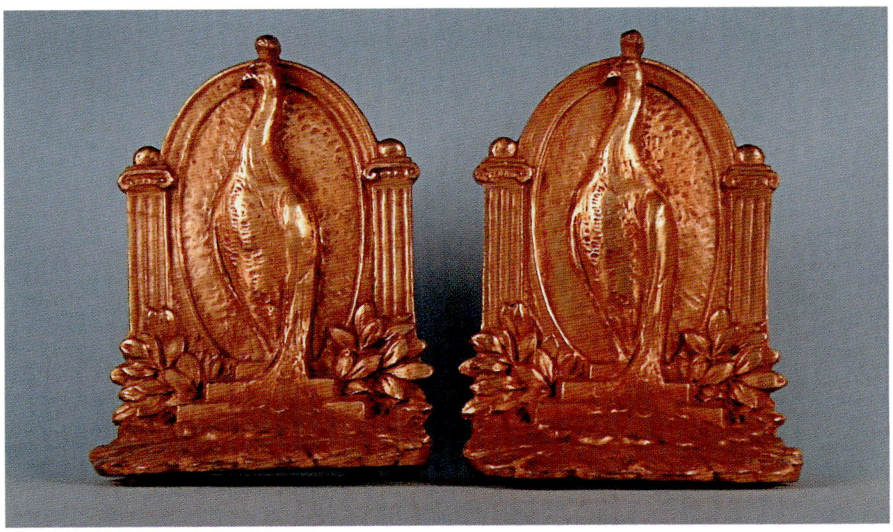

Figure 238. Peacock. 6", bronze plating on gray metal. Inscription: Shop mark of Weidlich Brothers. Circa 1915. Rarity 2. Peacocks and peacock feathers were important Art Nouveau and Aesthetic art motifs. $140-210.

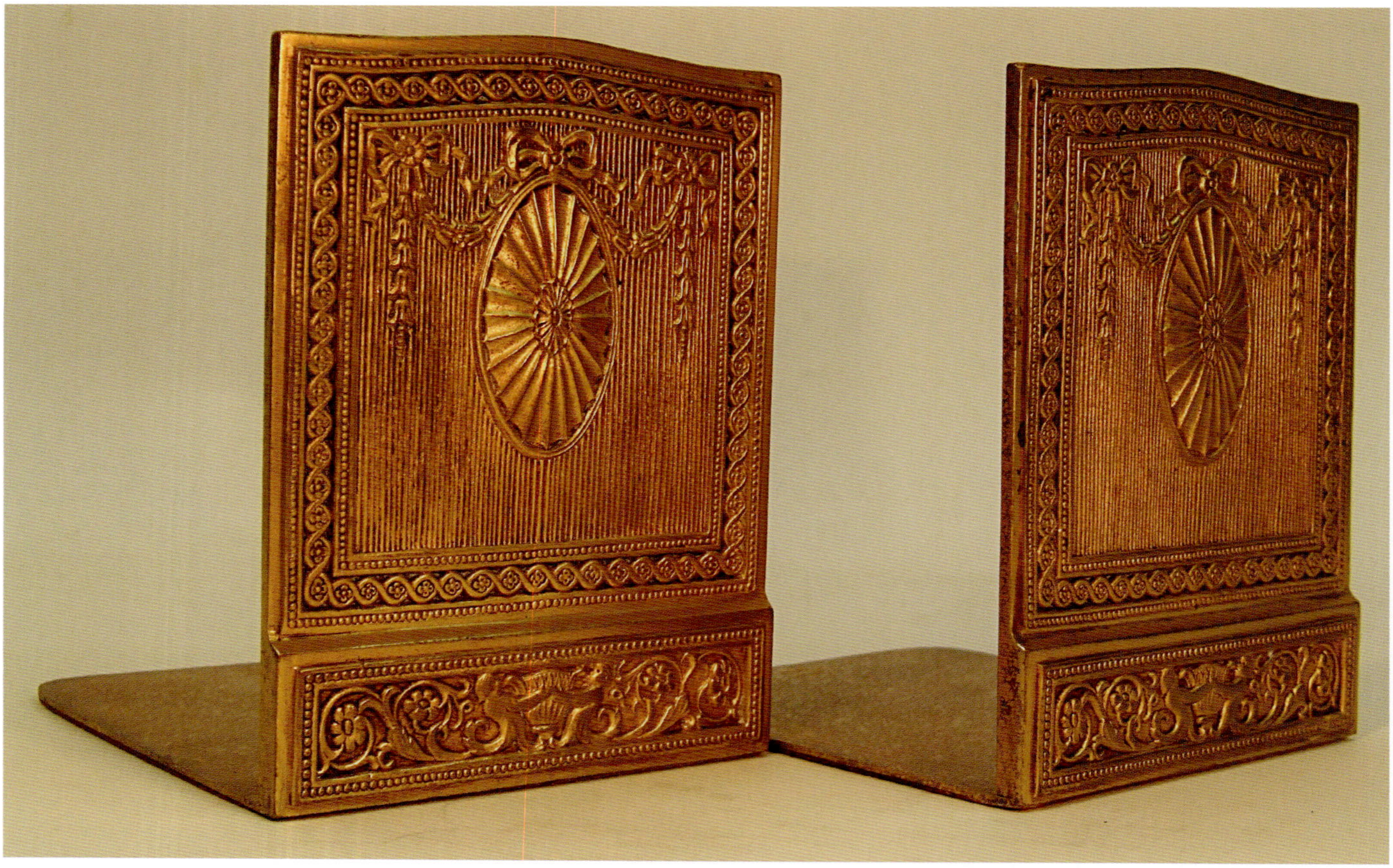

Figure 239. Book Mark Pattern. 6", solid bronze, gold plated. Inscription: Tiffany Studios, New York, 1853. Circa 1916. Rarity 5. Art Nouveau. *By courtesy of Charles DeCosta, from his collection.* $1,800-2,200.

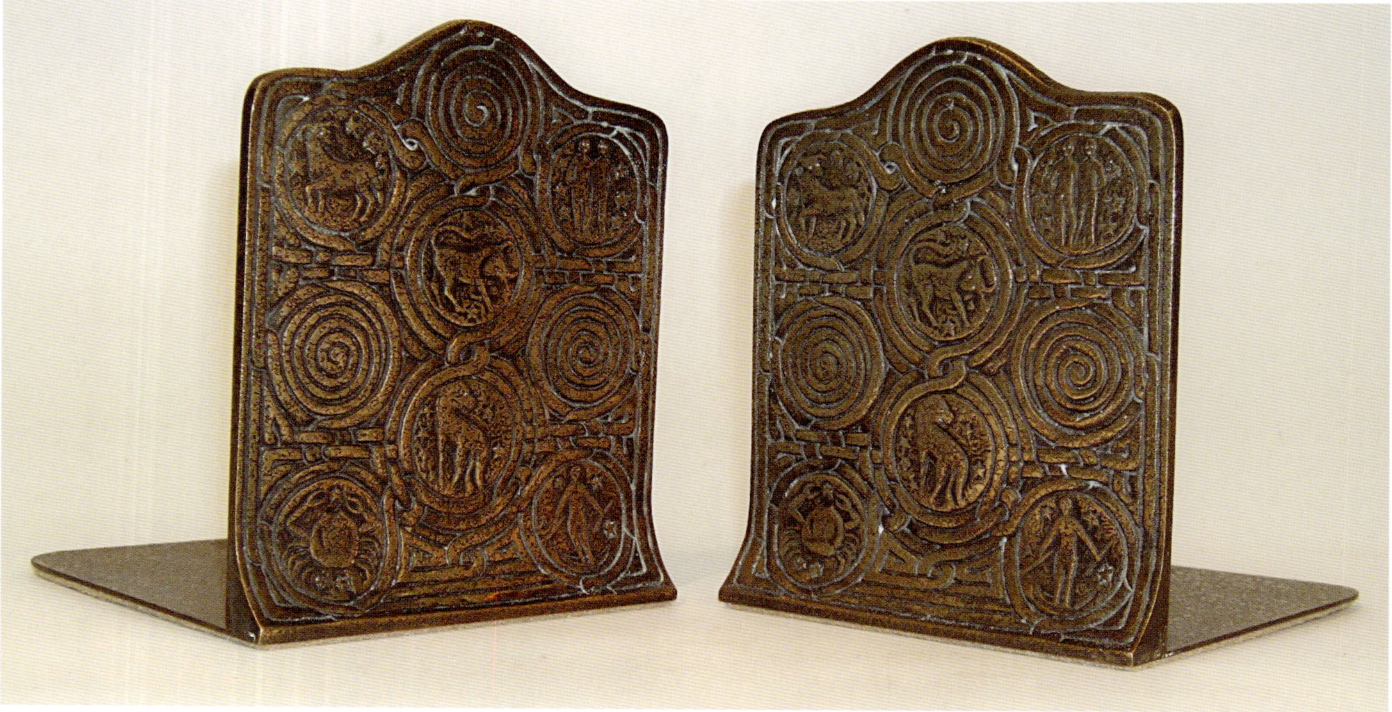

Figure 240. Signs of the Zodiac Pattern. 6", solid bronze. Inscription: Tiffany Studios, New York 1091. Circa 1918. Rarity 4. Art Nouveau. *By courtesy of Charles De Costa, from his collection.* $600-800.

Chapter 6

Art Deco Style Bookends

Before we deal with Art Deco style, we will address the "Vortices" style which was initiated in 1913 by Wyndham Lewis, a British artist, and lasted in England until the beginning of World War I in 1915. The name of the style referred to the vortices of life which were seen as overpowering at that time. This style promoted geometrical figures surrounding a central figure in order to draw attention to the central figure. We have found only two pairs of bookends in this style (Figures 241 and 242); apparently the style was not very fashionable. It was a style that invoked Cubism and Futurism. Cubism, originating in about 1907, was grounded in geometry. Futurism, dating from 1909, celebrated the dawning mechanistic world, and more about this style is presented below.

Cubist figures referred, of course, to the cubist style. Cubist compositions portrayed geometric structures and showed subjects from several points of view. In analytical Cubism, the subject was rendered as a set of discrete planes. Cubist forms appear later in American modern bookends, as we will see.

In the United States during the period from 1900 through 1920 there were three concurrent popular art fashions, Victorian, Arts & Crafts, and Art Nouveau, each with its devotees. These fashions did not disappear by 1920, but they were reduced to boutique status by the onrush of Art Moderne, which gathered huge popularity in the Western world beginning in about 1915. Art Moderne evolved into a style that was popularly called Art Deco which was destined to last until about 1941, when we entered World War II.

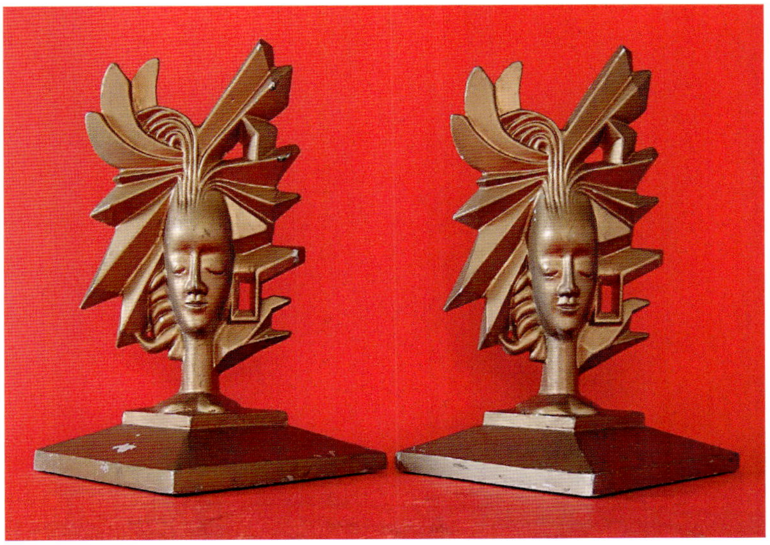

Figure 241. Cubist Surround. 9.5", gray metal. Foundry: Attrib. England. Circa 1913. Rarity 5. Vortices style. $200-300.

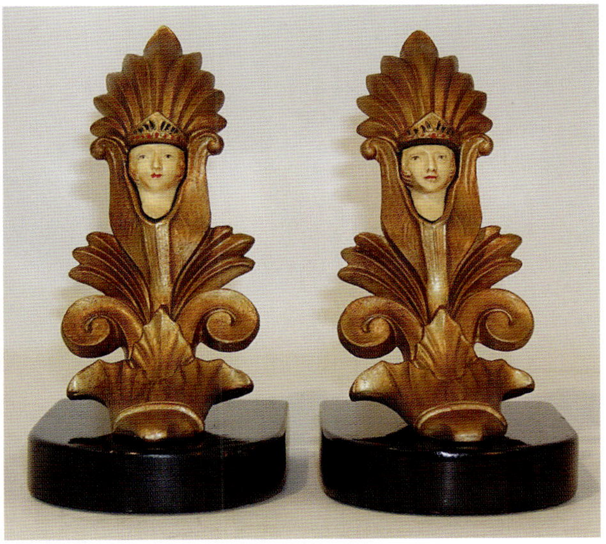

Figure 242. Fancy Lady. 5.75", gray metal, celluloid, Bakelite. Attrib. Hirsch. Circa 1913. Rarity 5. Vortices style. *By courtesy of Charles DeCosta, from his collection.* $250-350.

Modernist and Art Moderne Styles

The term Art Deco describes the art that was produced in the 1920s and 1930s, although we have seen that art during this period was fragmented into several styles. The dominant Art Deco style originated in France and Germany at the turn of the 20th century. In France it was called Art Moderne, and it was primarily decorative. The new art of Germany was different. This art was simplified, austere, deliberately lacking in applied decoration, standardized, functional, and intended to be suitable for machine production. It can be traced at least as far back as the Deutscher Werkbund in 1907 in Munich, and it became known as Modernist art. Early Modernist bookends are shown in Figures 243-244. Modernist art reappears later in the American modern style, as we will see.

In the early 1900s French artists set about inventing a new style, but they wanted it to be recognizably French, so they used traditional French styling and modified it to their new requirements. They used rare and expensive materials like ivory and ebony, and created handmade objects that were frequently decorated with traditional French motifs such as sunbursts, baskets of flowers, leaping gazelles, and lyre forms, and later used zigzags, chevrons and other geometric markings. This was the pure, high-style French Art Moderne of the 1910s and 1920s, and it was sumptuous and very expensive.

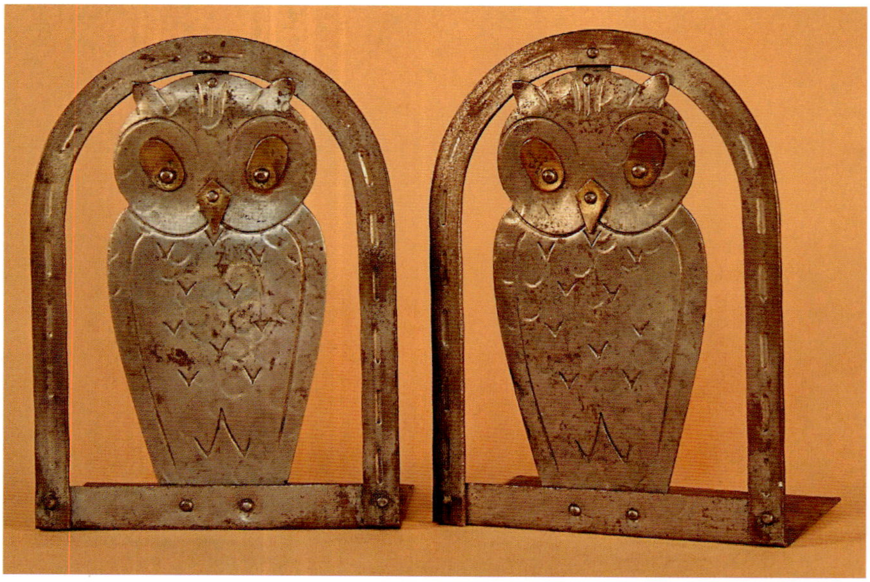

Figure 243. Flat Owl. 5.75", pressed iron, brass eyes and beak. Inscription: Austria. Foundry: Goberg Metallwarenfabrik. Sculptor: Hugo Berger. Circa 1910. Rarity 5. Modernist style. Simple machine construction with pressed iron and brass parts, and assembled with only nine rivets. This owl was also used in box lids, candlesticks, and other items. $264-396.

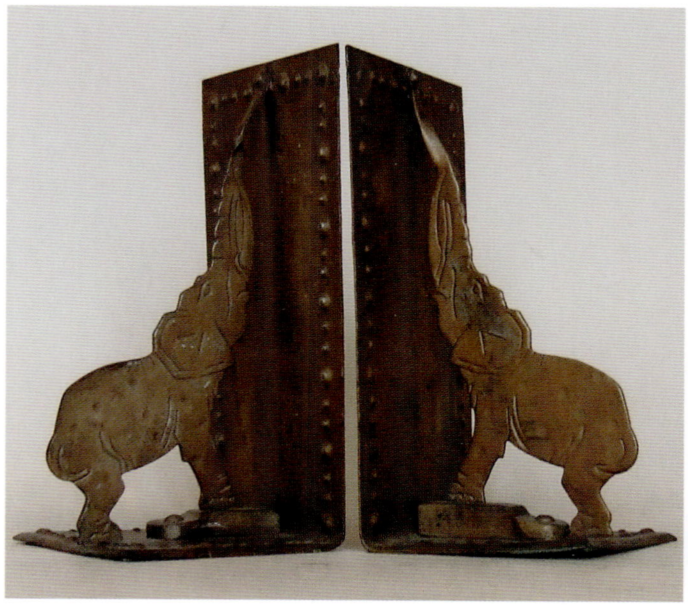

Figure 244. Flat Elephant. Ht. 7.25", pressed iron. Inscription: Made in Germany. Foundry: Goberg Metallwarenfabrik. Sculptor Hugo Berger. Circa 1910. Rarity 4. Modernist style. Simple but rigid. Only three iron parts and two rivets. $264-396.

Art Moderne quickly reached America. Early in the twentieth century, foundries responded to the new fashion, and bookends appeared that included the traditional French motifs (Figures 245-249). Baskets of flowers became popular. This motif has been traced all the way back to rustic decoration chosen by Marie Antoinette for the Trianon. The sunburst signified the moment of dawn. It was a metaphor for the future. In the United States, it was also compatible with fetishes for fresh air, unprocessed food, and healthy life style early in the century. Not surprisingly, lyre forms were associated with music. The leaping gazelle proved very enduring here. It appeared on bookends from the 1920s through the 1930s and persisted on household objects, including TV lamps into the 1950s. Geometric markings appeared on bookends by the 1920s and afterwards.

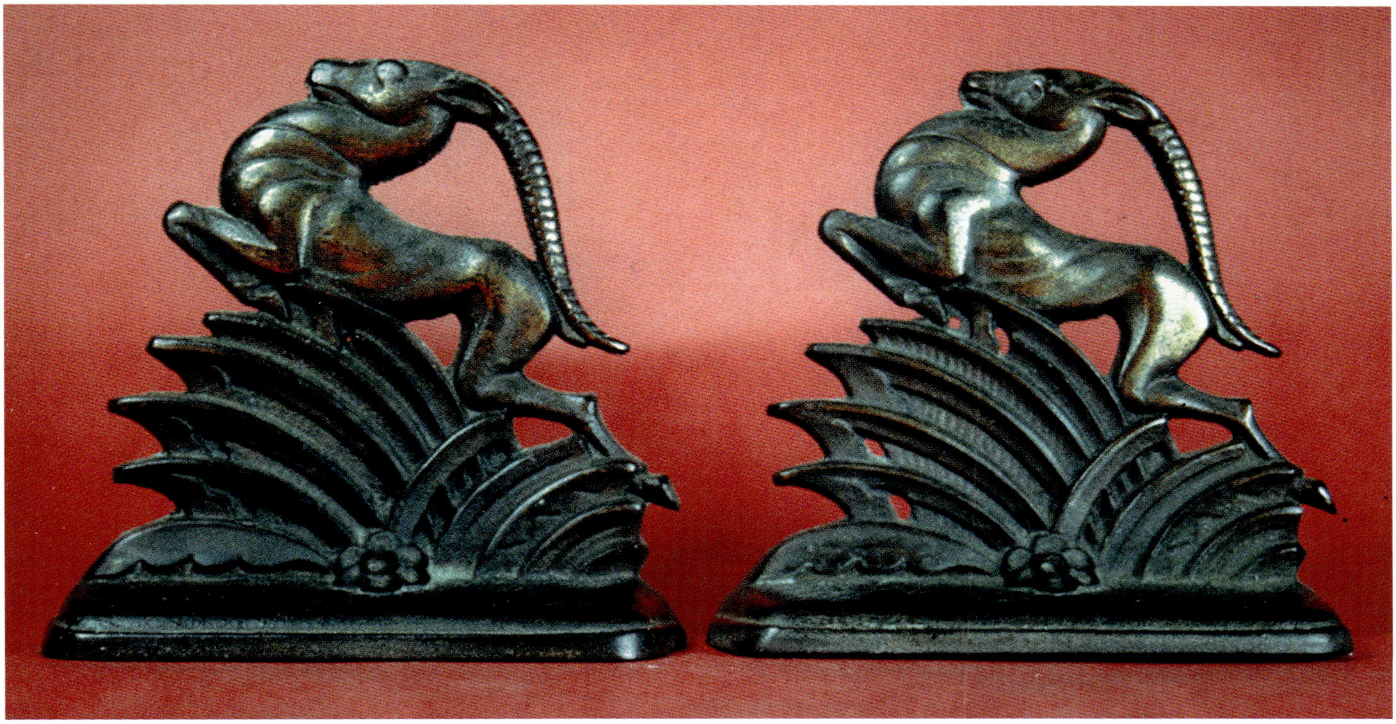

Figure 245. Leaping Gazelle and Vegetation. 5", iron. Inscription: W. H. Howell Co. Circa 1910. Rarity 3. Art Moderne. Early French motif. $160-240.

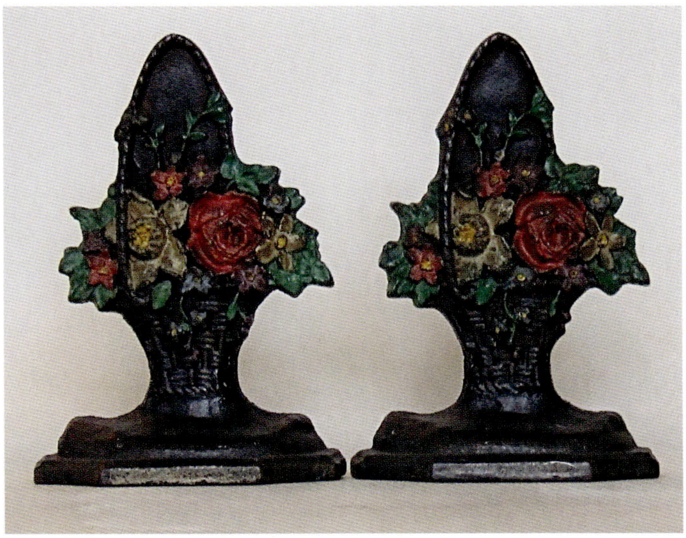

Figure 246. Basket of Flowers. 6", iron. Inscription: Jersey. Circa 1915. Rarity 5. Art Moderne. Early French motif. $100-150.

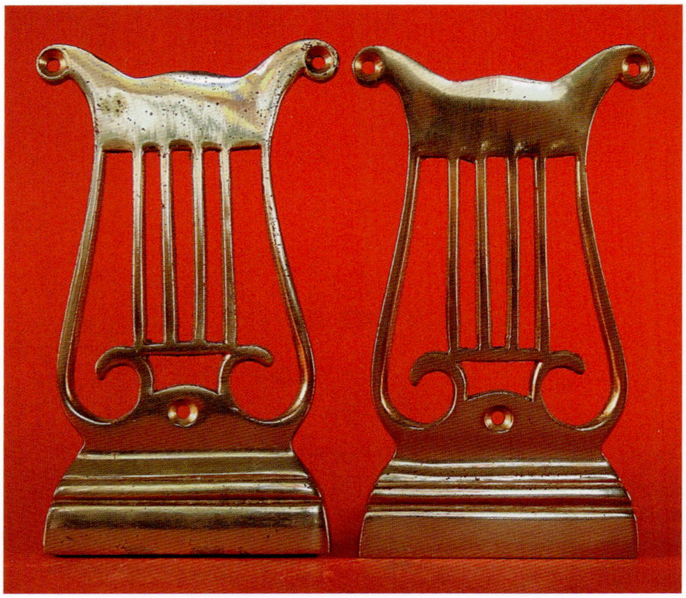

Figure 247. Lyre. 6.25", gray metal. Circa 1915. Rarity 2. Art Moderne. Early French motif. $80-120.

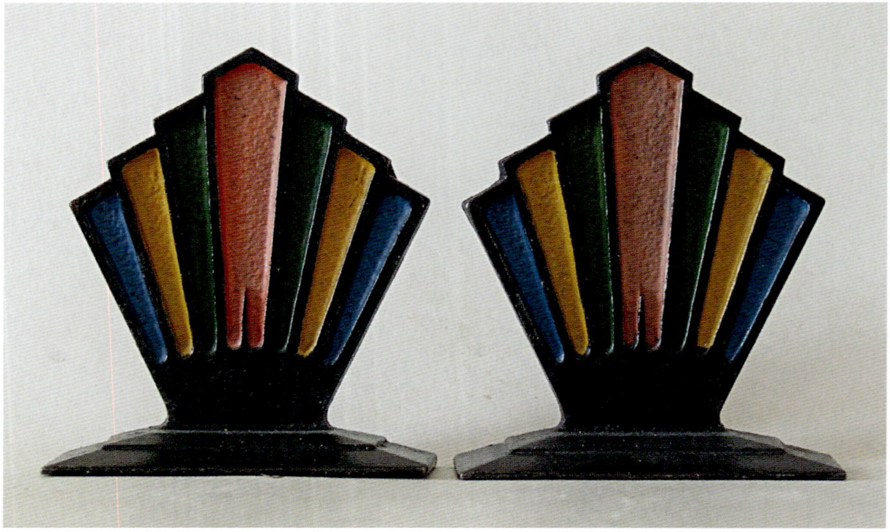

Figure 248. Colorful Sunburst. 4.5" iron. Inscription: 589. Foundry: Hubley Mfg. Co. Circa 1915. Rarity 4. Art Moderne. Early French motif. $120-180.

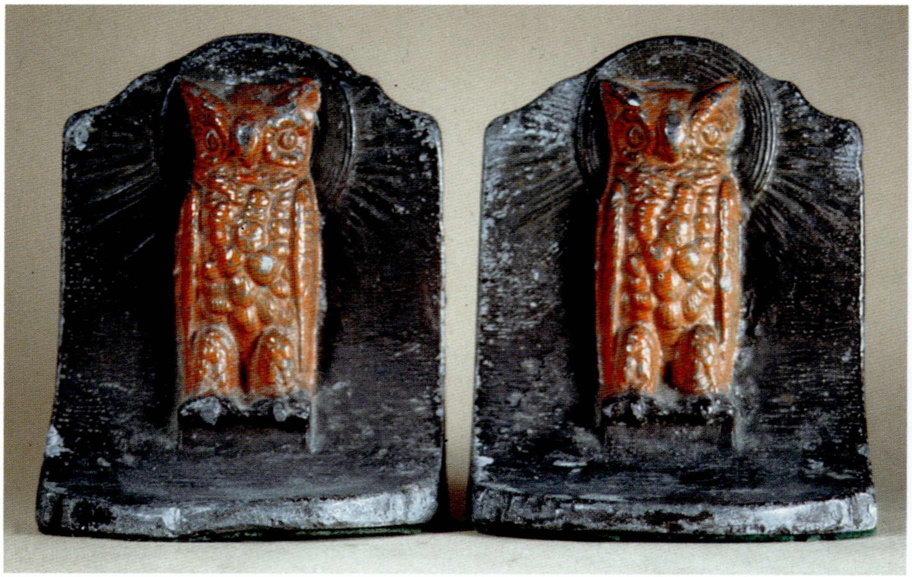

Figure 249. Owl and Sunburst. 5.5", lead. Circa 1912. Rarity 5. Art Moderne. Early French motif. $320-480.

French Art Moderne continued to evolve with new subjects through the 1910s and into the 1920s, and steadily filtered into the U.S. and other parts of Europe. European artists drew inspiration from many other European countries in addition to France, and from Africa, China, Japan, India, Mexico, and other far-away places. Europeans found the art from other continents to be fascinating and invigorating. Foreign artists were considered primitive, but were romantically believed to create art that was innocent, unspoiled by civilization, and, therefore, more interesting than jaded European art. In this way, exotic subjects from distant lands became part of Art Moderne and appeared on bookends as well (Figures 250-255). Art Moderne picked up some exotic names along the way as well, such as Art Decoratif, Zigzag Moderne and Jazz Moderne, but the term Art Moderne covers all of these.

Products from East Asia were already familiar to America and Europe, and interest in Japanese and Chinese art increased steadily after 1900. Chinese rounded necklines, tubular sleeves, and decorative dragons became part of Moderne couture after World War I. Chinese and Japanese lacquer work was admired and lacquer appeared on Deco furniture and bookends in the 1920s and 1930s.

Bookends took their lead from these European fashionable interests, both in Europe and America. Beginning in about 1915, bookends exhibited Buddhas, temples, and elephants from India. Chinese figures in native dress and Japanese Geishas appeared. The exotic bookends were still in a minority compared to those of Victorian or Arts & Crafts styles, but they showed that Americans developed a gradual appreciation of Art Moderne as it evolved through the 1910s and 1920s.

France hosted the Exposition Internationale des Arts Décoratifs et Industriels Modernes in 1925. French Art Moderne was showcased and related art from many other foreign lands was shown as well, although U.S. and German exhibits were missing. The show gave Art Moderne great international impetus and created a pulse of demand and production in the United States that lasted until the stock-market crash of 1929. This disaster distracted Americans from expensive articles with foreign associations.

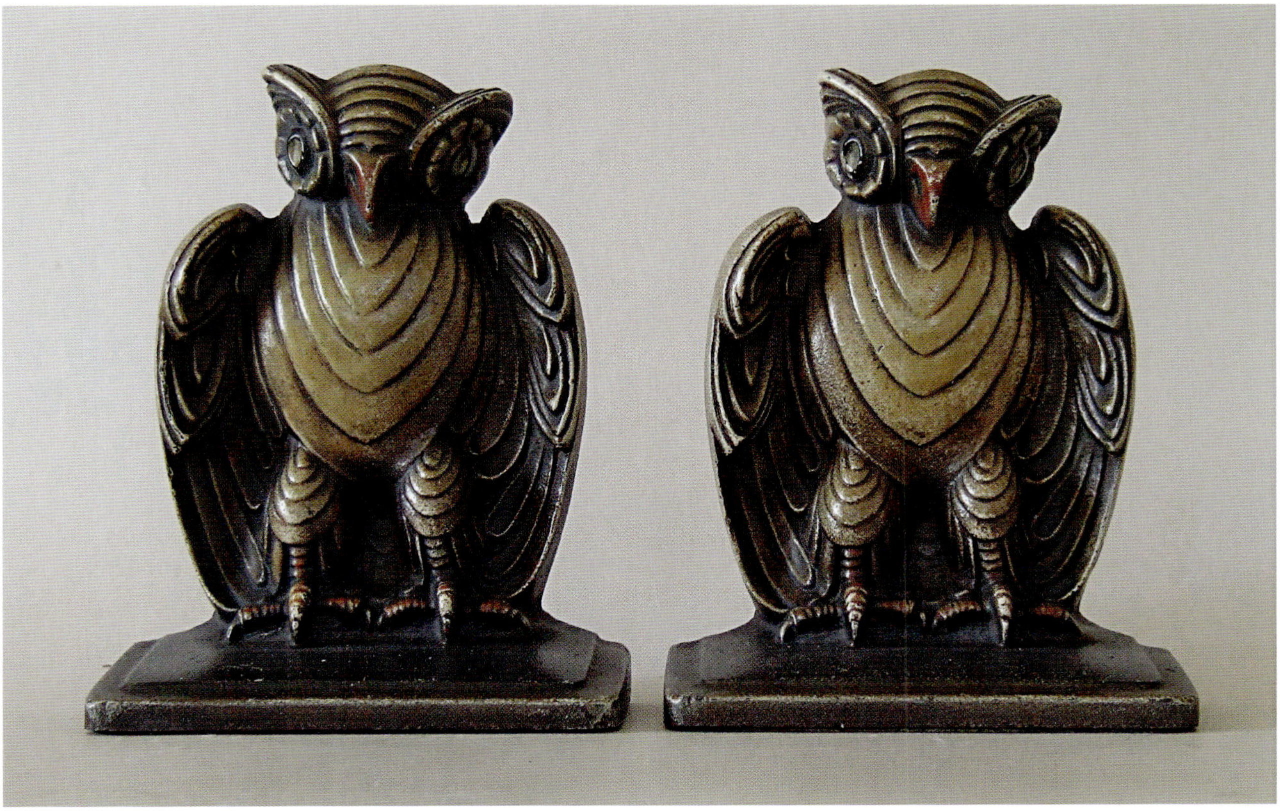

Figure 250. Predator Owl. 6", iron. Foundry: Shop mark of Bradley and Hubbard. Circa 1915. Rarity 4. Art Moderne. Notice the chevron pattern of the feathers. $260-400.

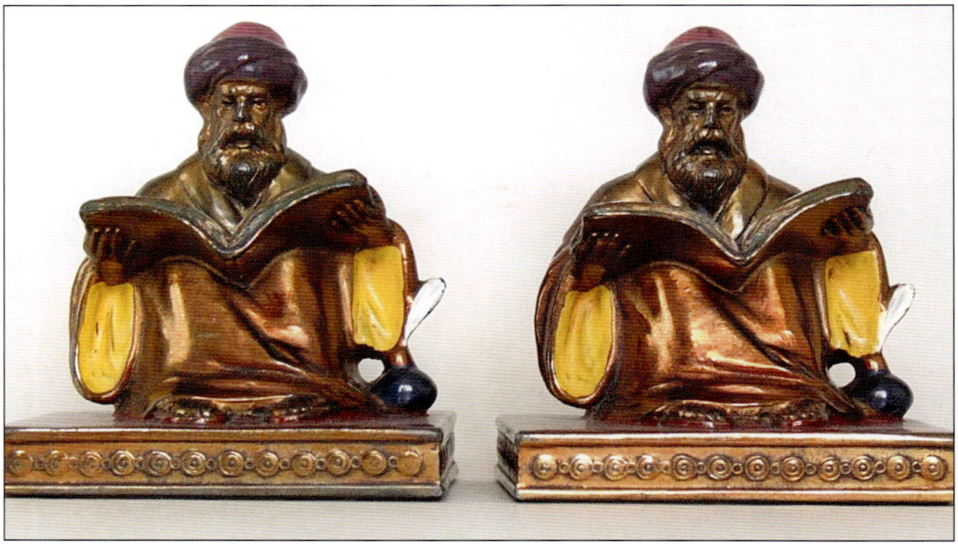

Figure 251. Scribe. 3.75", gray metal. Inscription: L. V. Ronson, 1923. Rarity 2. Art Moderne. Exotic foreign lands. $160-240.

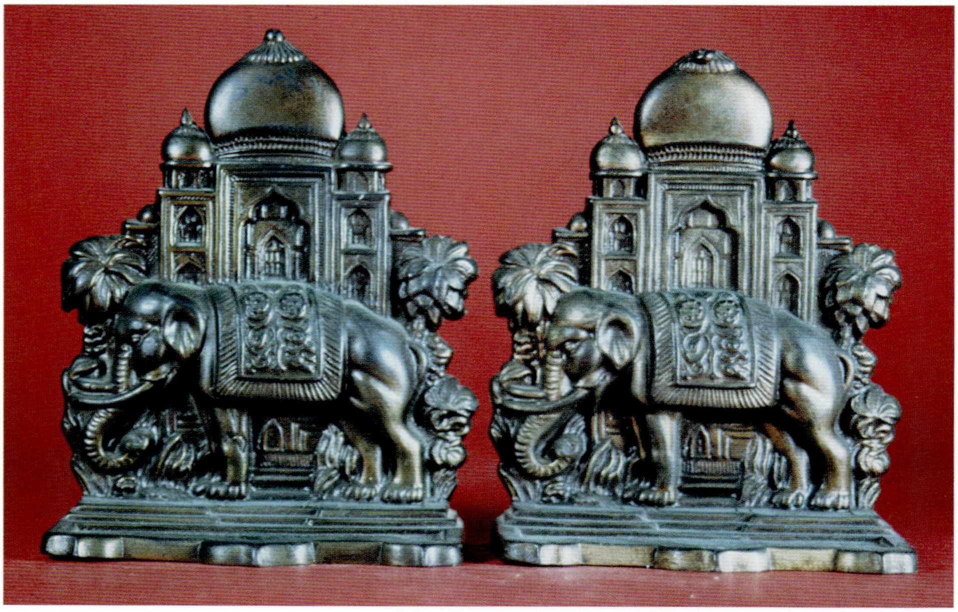

Figure 252. Elephant and Temple. 5.5", bronze. Circa 1923. Rarity 5. Art Moderne. Exotic foreign lands. Outstanding detail in the casting. $160-240.

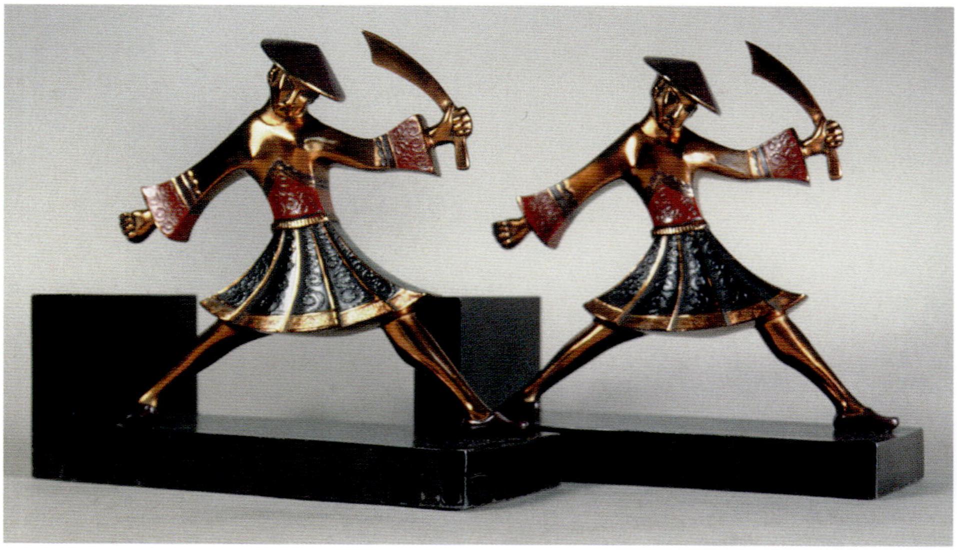

Figure 253. Asian Fighters. 6.75", gray metal. Inscription: Ronson company label. Circa 1924. Rarity 2. Art Moderne. Exotic foreign lands. These are large, heavy bookends, 9 lbs./pair. $400-600.

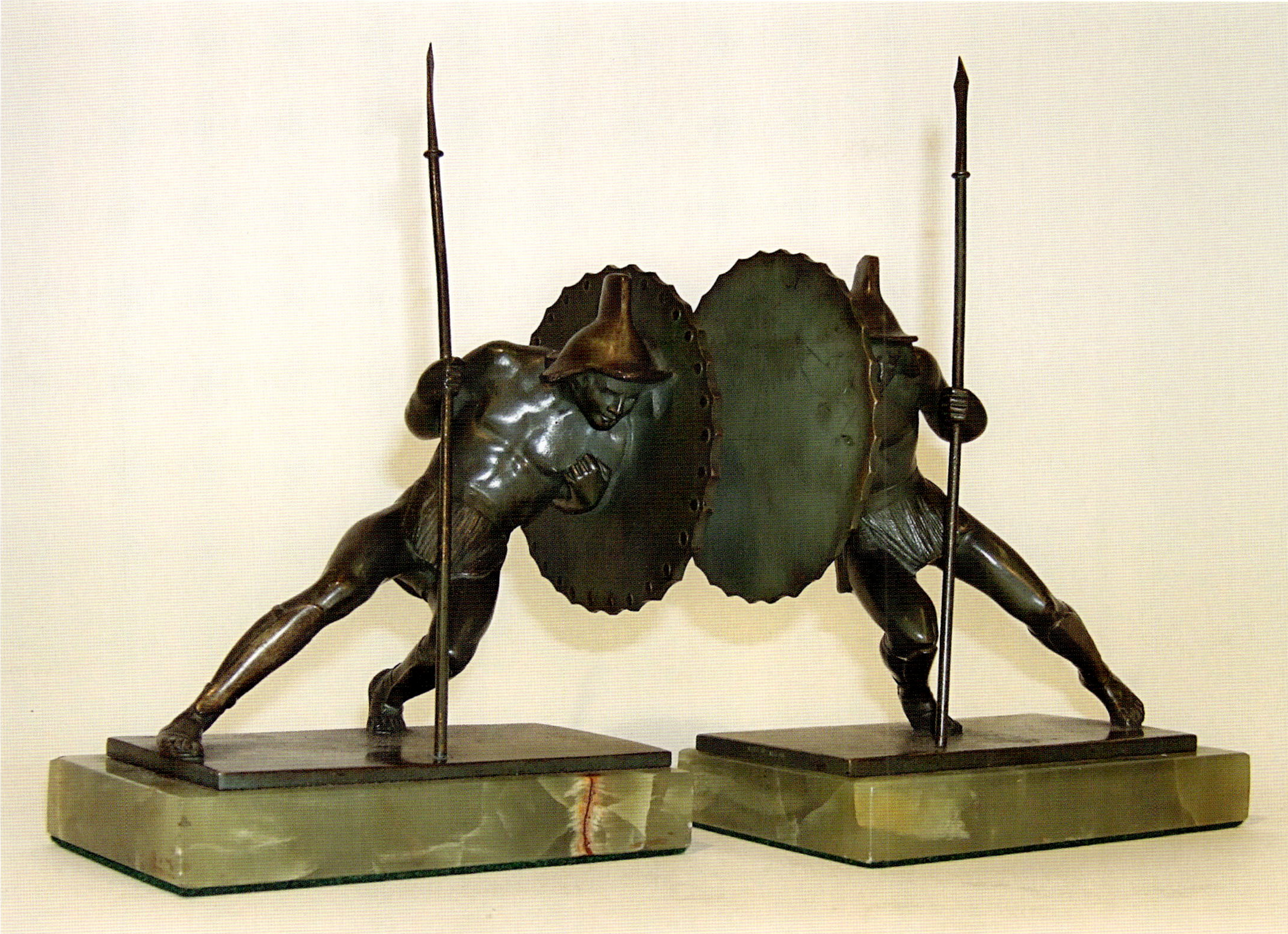

Figure 254. Asian Warriors. 8.5", solid bronze, marble. Inscription: Made in Austria, signed Zach. Circa 1925. Rarity 4. Art Moderne. Exotic foreign lands. *By courtesy of Charles DeCosta, from his collection. $1,800-2000.*

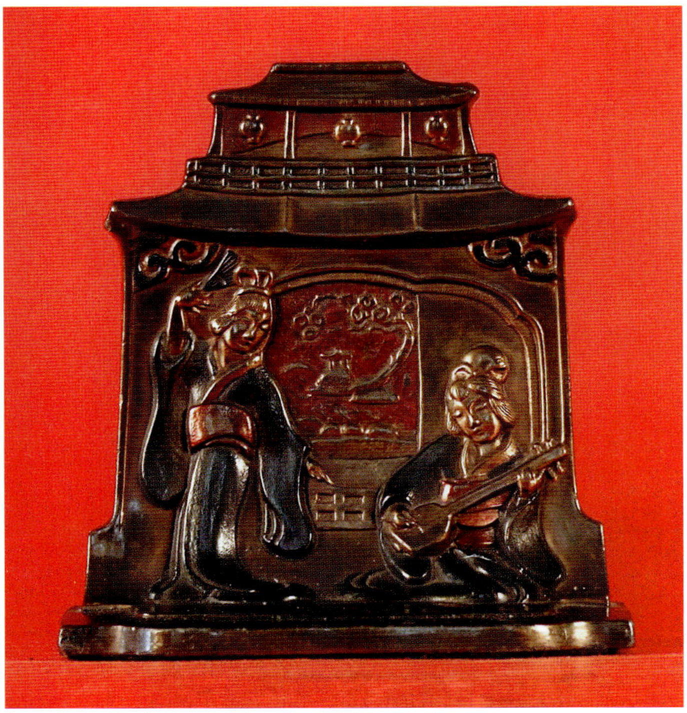

Figure 255. The Geisha Girl. 4.5", gray metal. Circa 1924. Inscription: The Geisha Girl, Shop mark of Pompeian Bronze Co. Rarity 3. Art Moderne. Exotic foreign lands. $200-300.

Early American Modern Bookends

More important, Americans were already on their way to building their own popular Art Deco style, a style that had been building through the 1920s mixed with Art Moderne, which we can call Early American Modern, and eventually became full-fledged American Modern in the 1930s. During the 1920s, bookends tell us that Americans had their own Deco-era interests and that they were not limited to the very rich. Wealthy Americans could buy expensive one-of-a-kind Art Moderne objects, but mass-produced items became fashionable too.

American romance with machinery was already evident in the early 1920s, and bookends showing machinery began to appear. Egyptiana blossomed after King Tutankhamens's tomb was opened in 1923, and bookends showed pharaohs, tomb entrances, tomb jewelry, and so on (Figures 256-258). The vogue for ancient Egypt was Deco exotica shared with Europe, but pirates and clowns appeared on bookends, and these were exotic subjects of American fashion. A fascination with speed was already detectable. Horse racing bookends were popular. Irish wolfhounds and greyhounds were admired for elegance and speed, both in high fashion and on bookends. Golf and physical culture became important. European designers had focused on their native traditions to produce Art Moderne, but American designers played on current lifestyle rather than tradition. American interests from the 1920s, like pirates, speed, liberated women, and machinery, became subjects of early American Modern and of bookends. Early American Modern bookends are shown in Figures 259-279.

Again, bookends documented the development of fashion in the U.S., this time the development of American Modern. Bookends were works of art in themselves, but they continuously reflected the changing American fashions and helped cement fashions by their appearances.

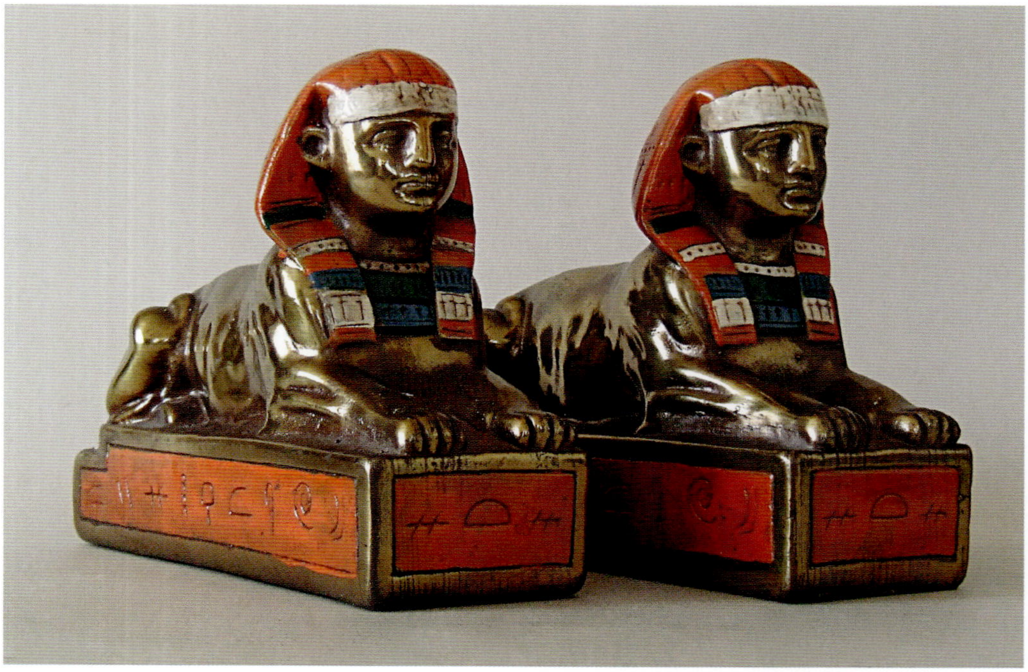

Figure 256. Sphinx in Pharaoh Head Dress. 6", electroformed bronze. Inscription: Several Egyptian-like hieroglyphics. Attrib. Marion Bronze. Circa 1958. Rarity 3. Art Deco. Egyptian revival. Probably a reproduction of earlier bookends. $320-480.

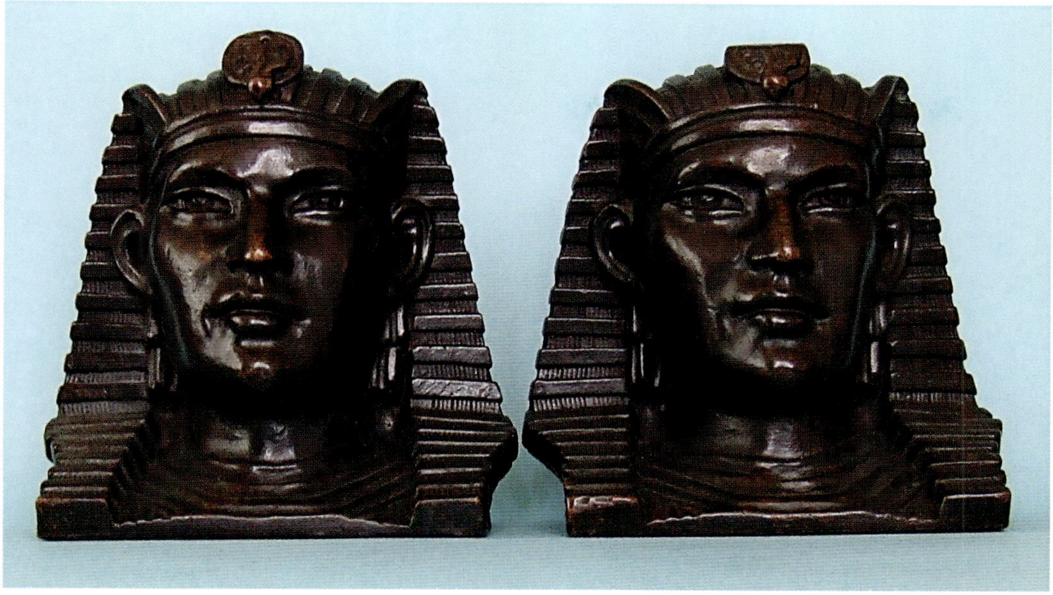

Figure 257. Pharaoh Head. 7", electroformed bronze. Attrib. Paul Mori. Circa 1924. Rarity 4. Art Deco. Egyptian revival. These are large, heavy bookends. 11 lbs/pair. A polychrome version is available. $320-480.

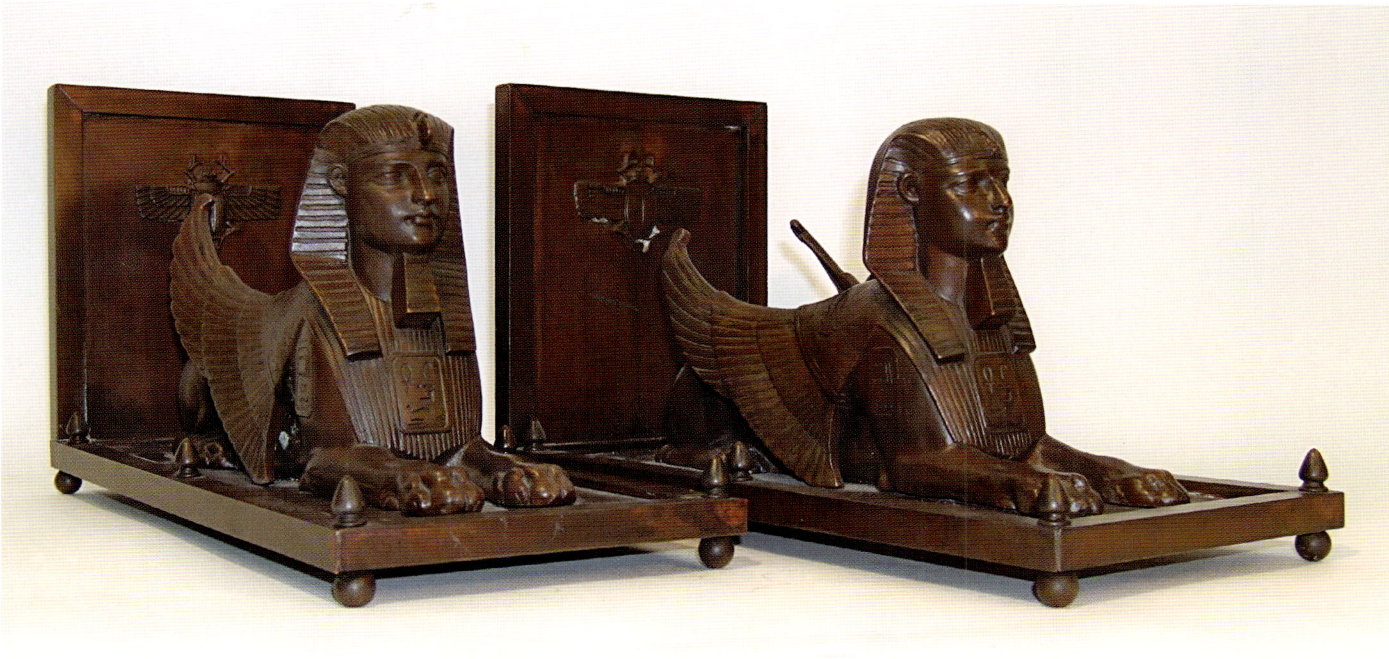

Figure 258. Sphinx. 7.25" solid bronze. Inscription: Handel Lamps company label. Circa 1924. Rarity 5. Art Deco. Egyptian revival. Massive bookends, 35 lbs./pair. *By courtesy of Charles DeCosta, from his collection.* $5,000-6,000.

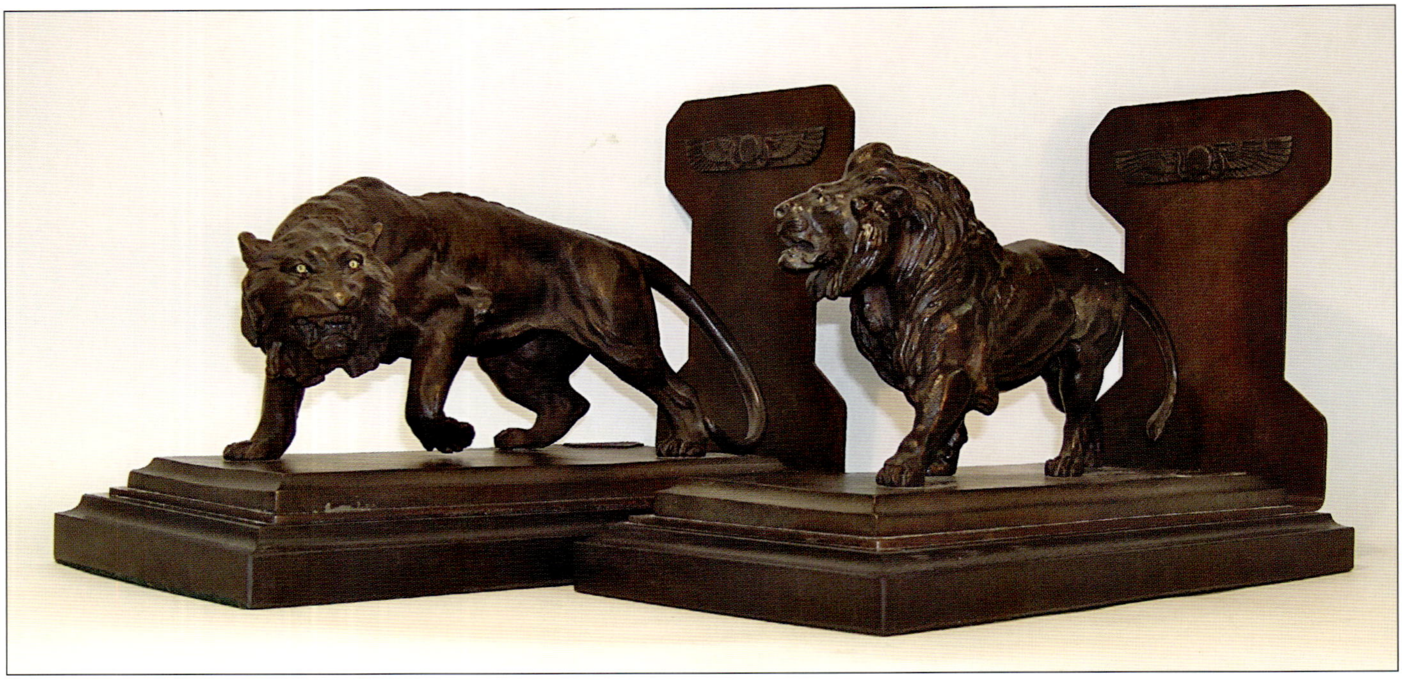

Figure 259. Lion and Tiger. 10.25", bronze, stone, glass eyes. Inscription: Bradley and Hubbard Mfg. Co., 1924. Rarity 5. Art Deco. The eye of Horus on the upright signifies Egyptian revival. Massive bookends, 52 lbs./pair. *By courtesy of Charles DeCosta, from his collection.* Art Deco. $14,000-16,000.

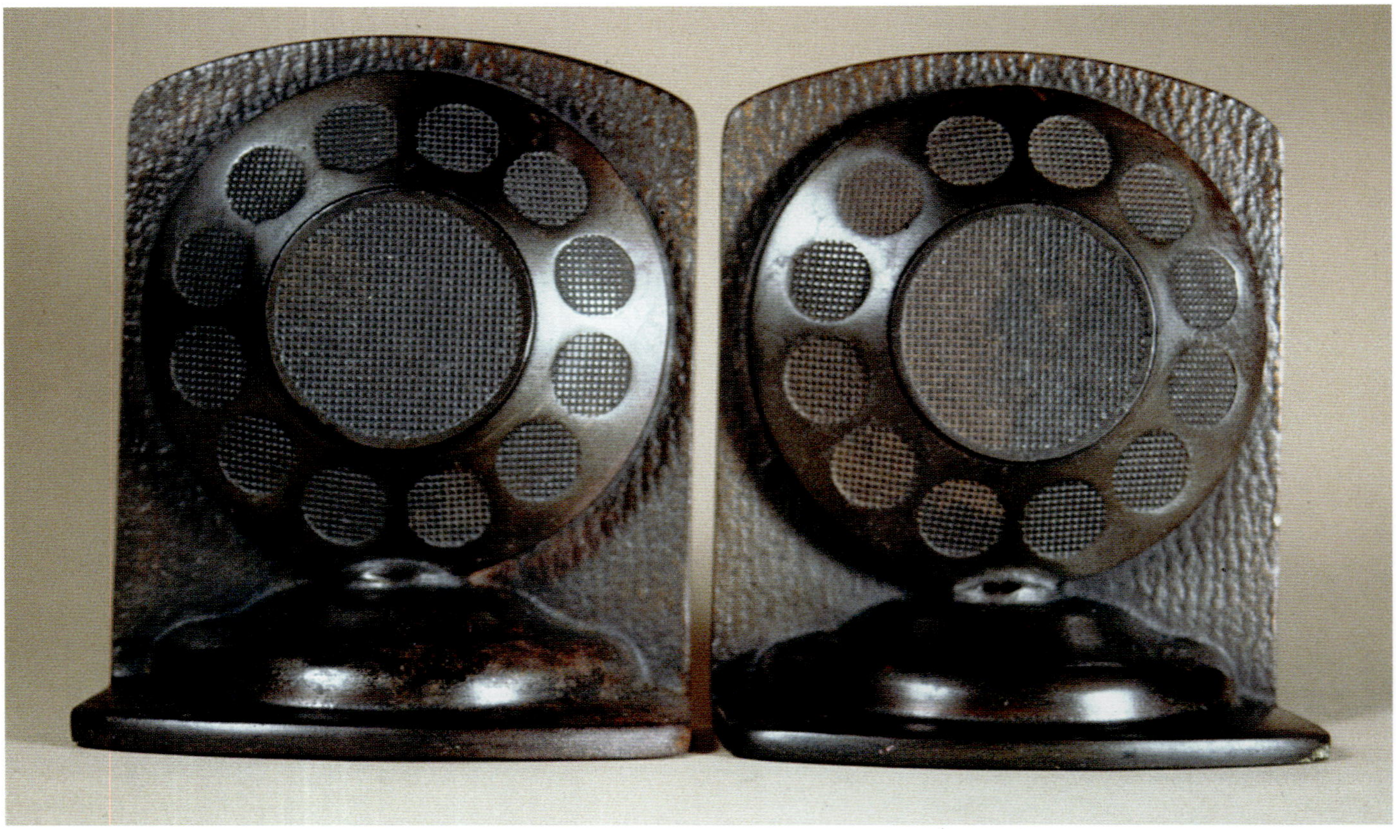

Figure 260. Westinghouse Carbon Microphone. 6", iron. 1922. Rarity 5. Art Deco. Machine age interest. Early American Modern. $160-240.

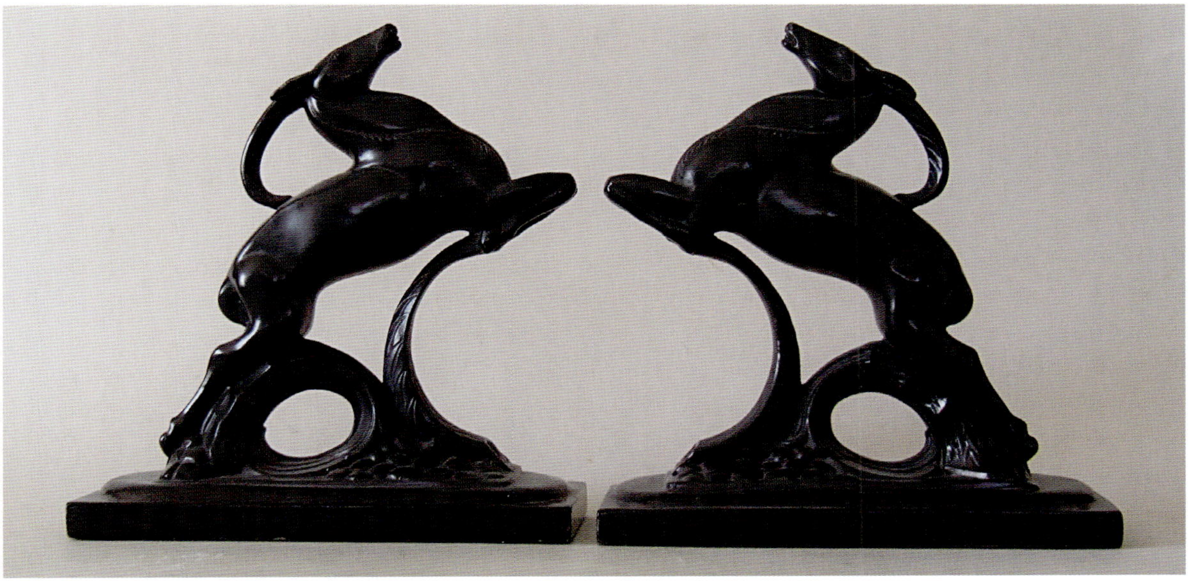

Figure 261. Late Time Leaping Gazelle. 7.25", gray metal. Circa 1922. Rarity 2. Art Moderne. Early motif. The image was still popular. Beautiful silhouette. $100-150.

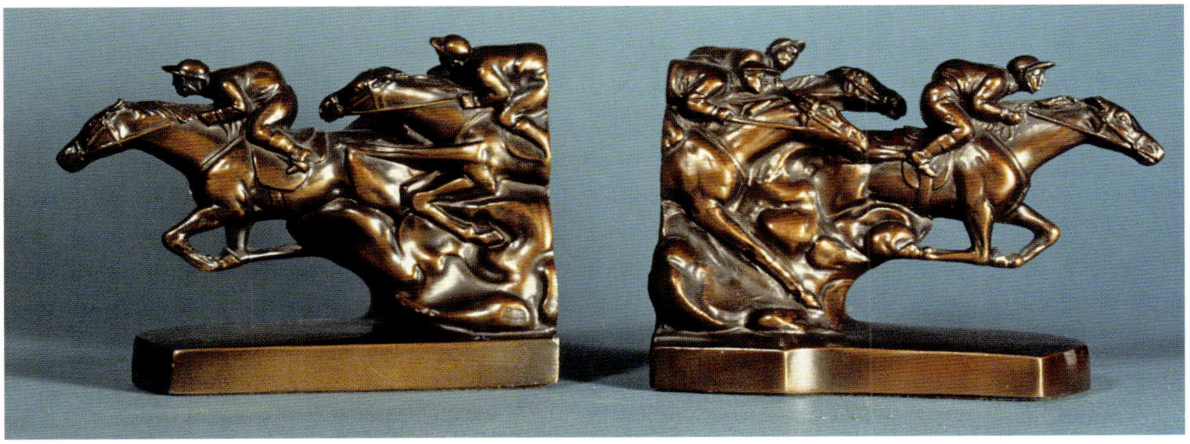

Figure 262. Horse Race 4.75", gray metal. Inscription: Shop mark of Nuart. Circa 1924. Rarity 3. Early American Modern. $200-300.

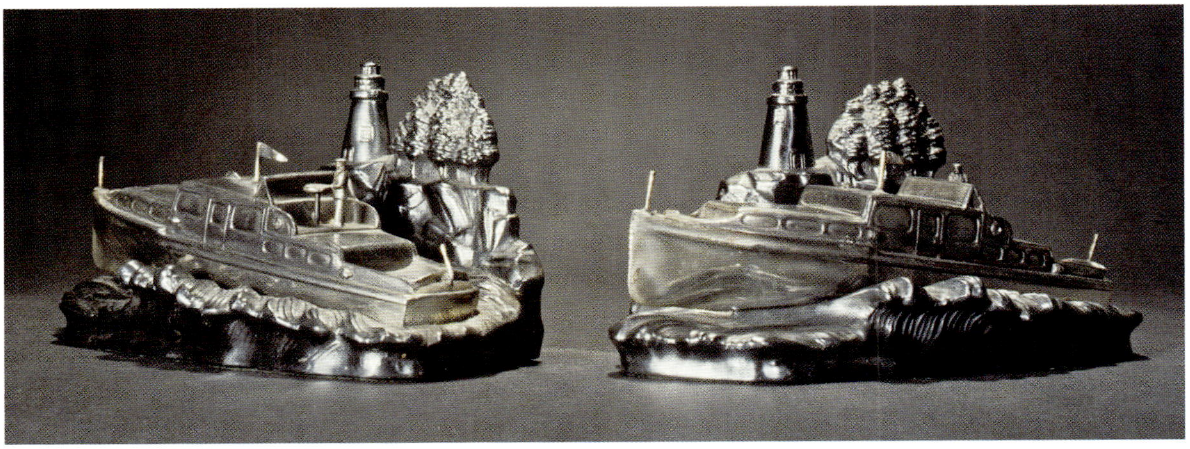

Figure 263. Speed Boat. 3.5 ", gray metal, chrome or silver plating. Inscription: Shop mark of Jennings Brothers. Rarity 4. Circa 1926. Art Deco era. Early American Modern. $200-300.

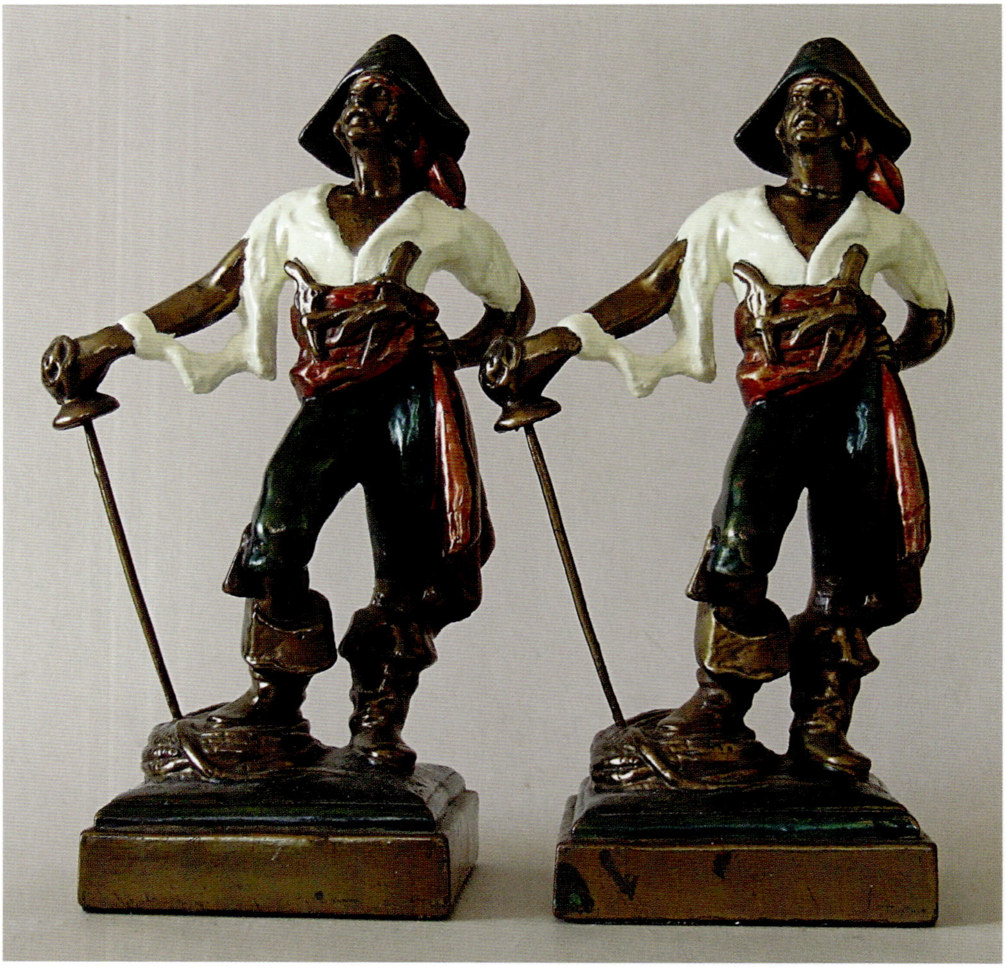

Figure 264. Pirate Standing on Rope. 9.5", electroformed bronze. Inscription: Signed by Paul Herzel. Foundry: Attrib. Pompeian Bronze Co., 1928. Rarity 2. Art Deco. Early American Modern. $260-390.

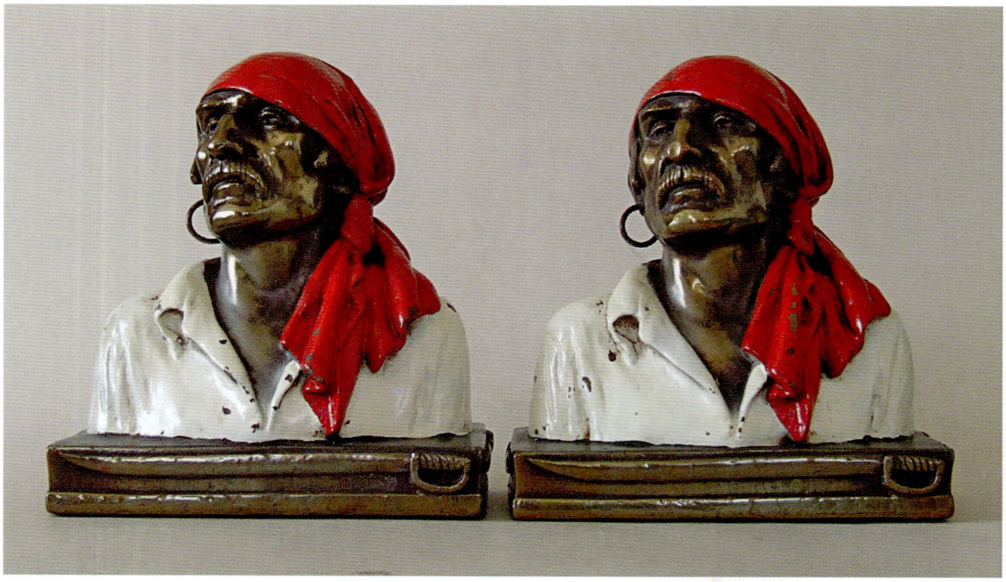

Figure 265. Pirate Bust. 7", gray metal. Inscription: signed by Paul Herzel. Attrib. Armor Bronze Inc. Circa 1927. Rarity 2. Art Deco. Early American Modern. $240-360.

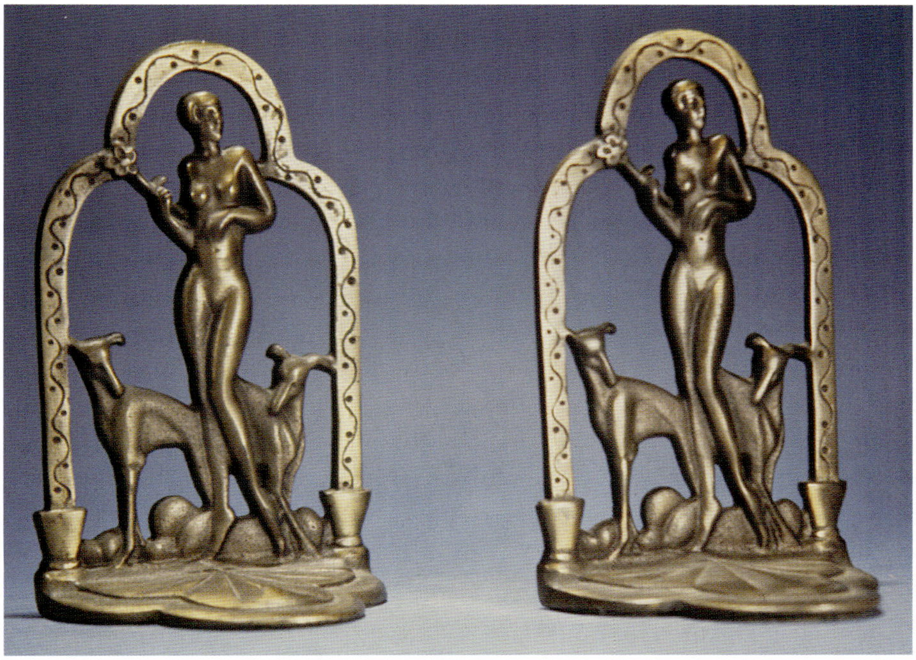

Figure 266. Nude with Hounds. 7", iron. Circa 1925. Rarity 2. Art Deco. Early American Modern. $120-180.

Figure 267. Polo Player. 5.5", iron. Foundry Attrib. Littlestown. Circa 1925. Rarity 3. Art Deco. Early American Modern. $100-150.

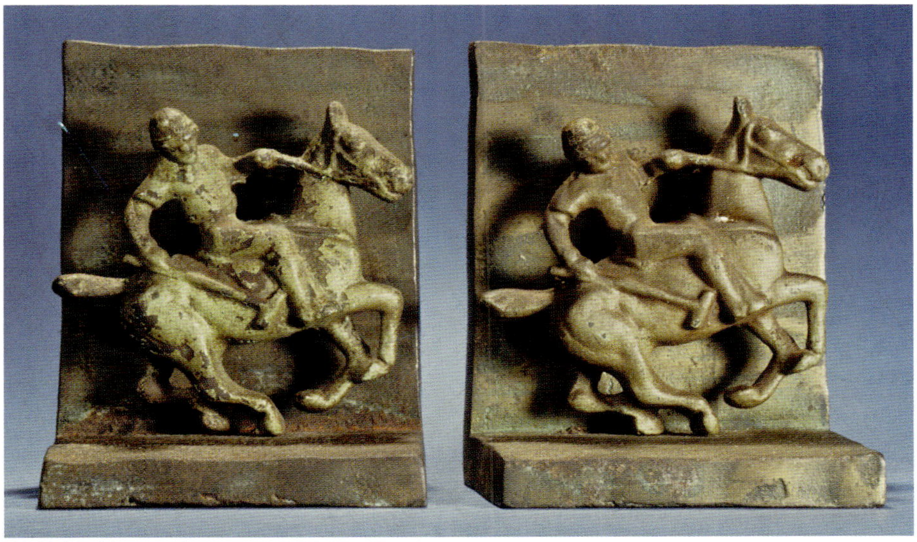

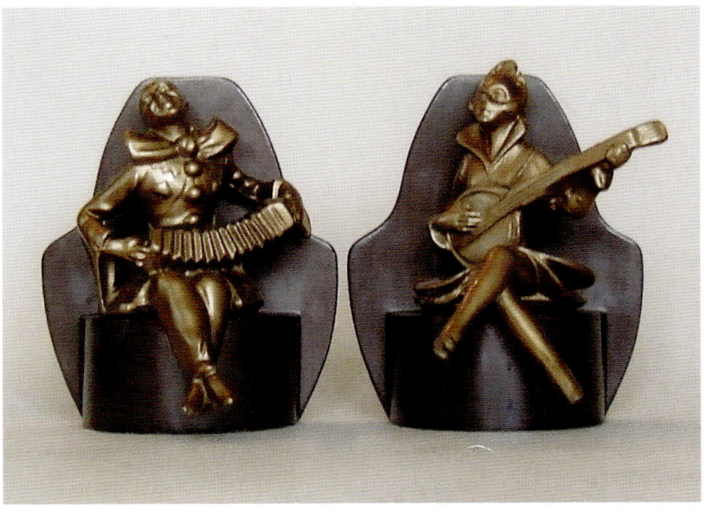

Figure 268. Clown Couple. 5" gray metal. Inscription: Shop mark of Nuart. Circa 1928. Rarity 3. Art Deco. Early American Modern. $240-360.

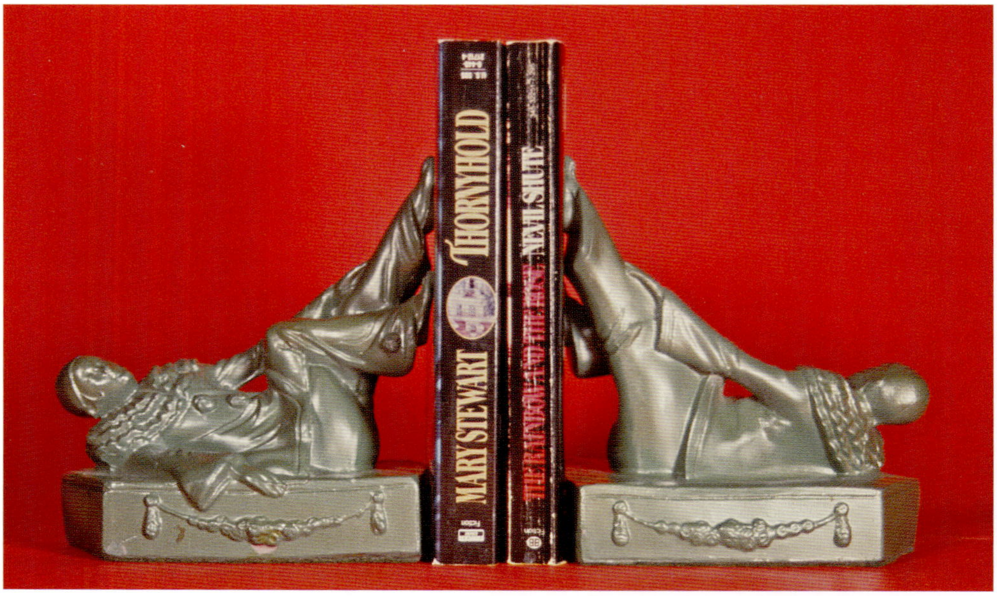

Figure 269. Supine Clown. 5.75", gray metal. Circa 1928. Rarity 2. Art Deco. Early American Modern. $160-240.

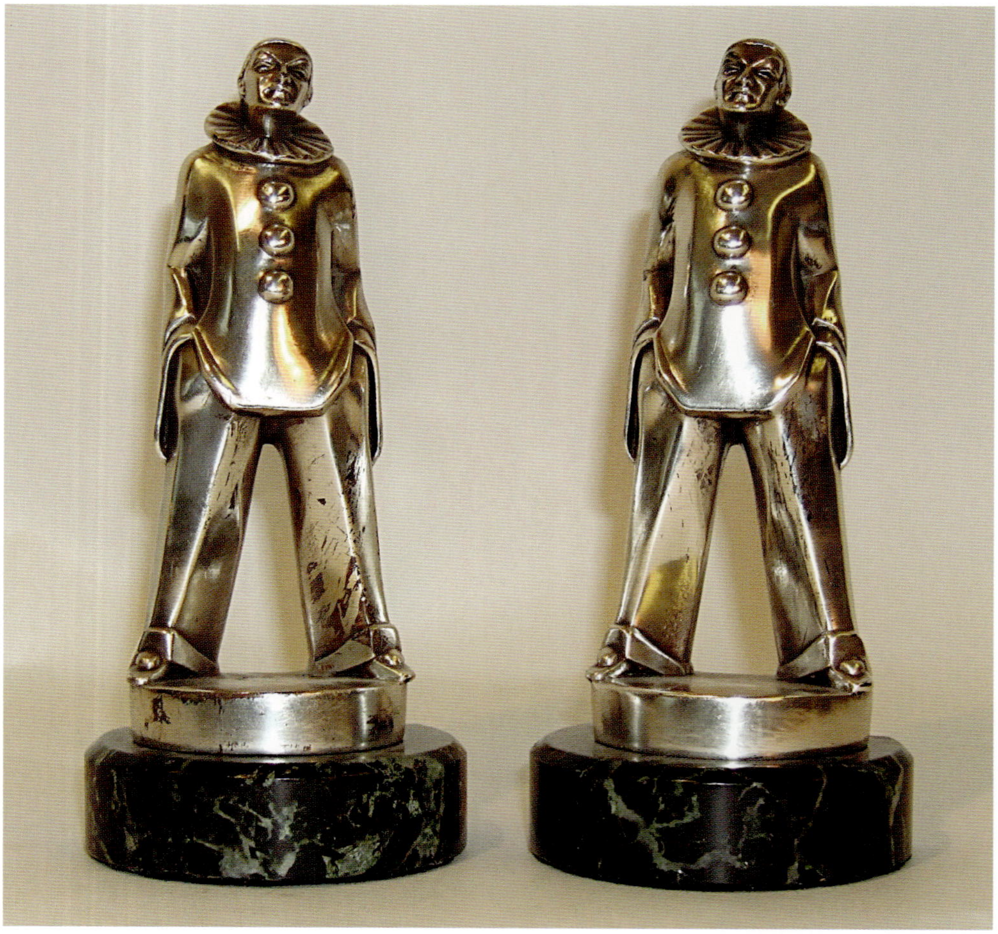

Figure 270. Pierrot. 7.25", gray metal, silver plated, marble. Inscription: signed M. Le Verrier (sculptor). Circa 1930. Rarity 5. Art Deco. Early American Modern *By courtesy of Charles DeCosta, from his collection.* $1,800-2000.

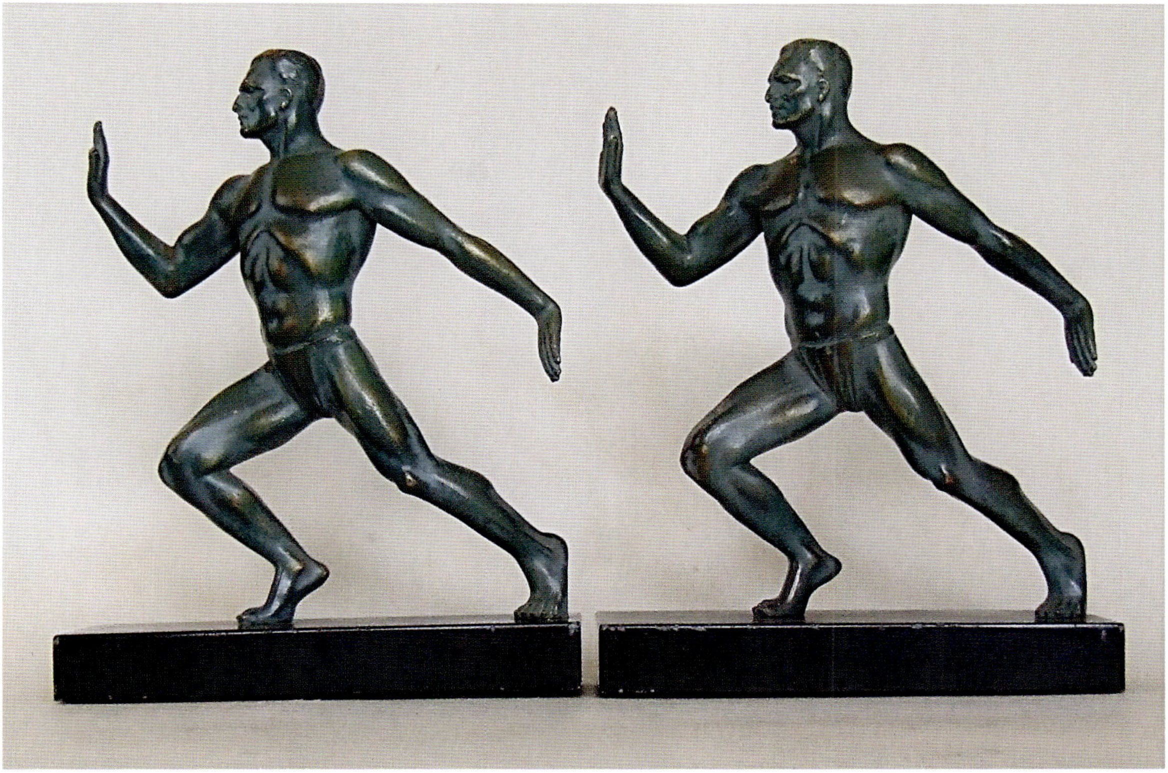

Figure 271. Athlete 8.5", gray metal. Foundry: Attrib. Hirsch Foundry. Circa 1934 Rarity 3. Art Deco. Physical culture. $240-360.

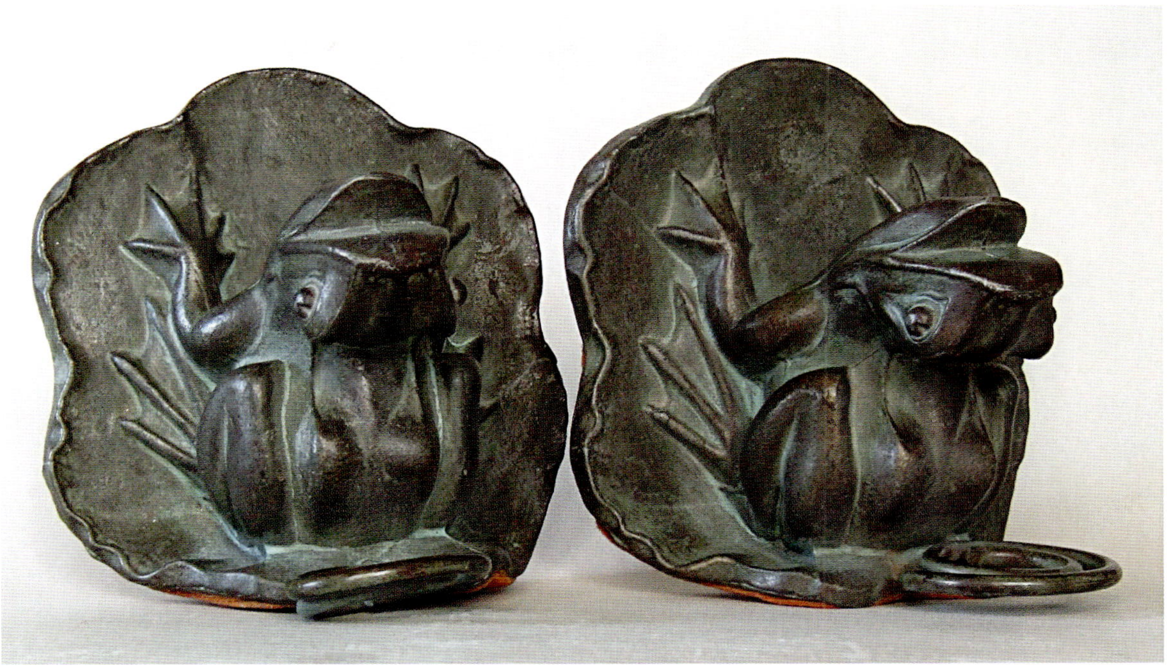

Figure 272. Frog on Lily Pad. 4", gray metal. 1931. Rarity 5. Art Deco. Early American Modern. $140-210.

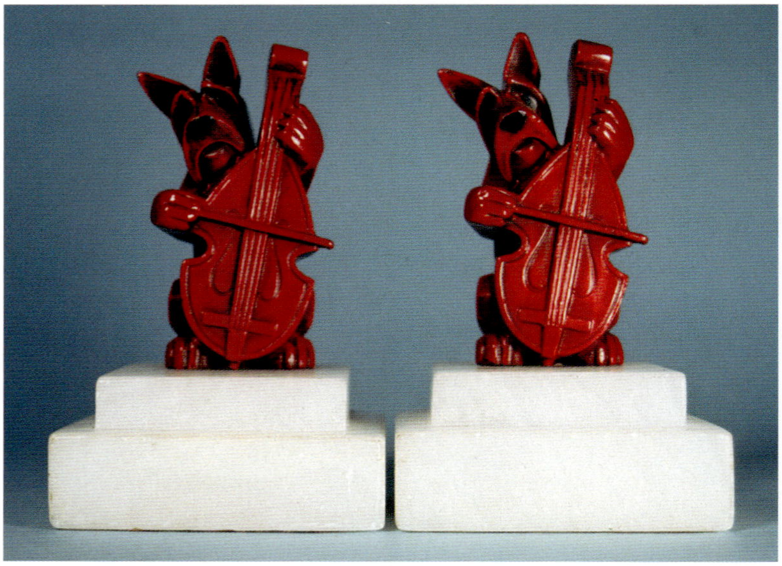

Figure 273. Fala with Fiddle. 6", gray metal and marble. Foundry: Attrib. Hirsch Foundry. c, 1934. Rarity 4. Art Deco. Early American Modern. Jazz age and F.D.R.'s Scottish terrier Fala. $240-360

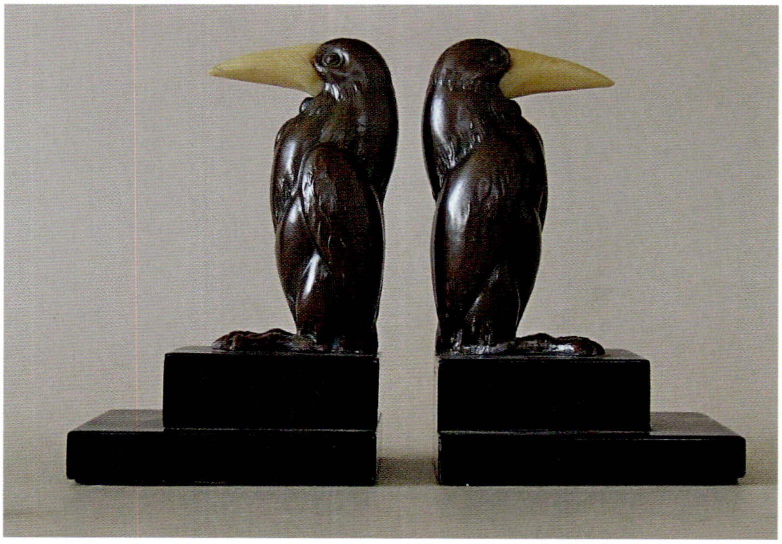

Figure 274. Mystery Bird. 5.75", gray metal and celluloid. Foundry: Attrib. Hirsch Foundry. Circa 1934. Rarity 3. Art Deco, American Modern. $275-420.

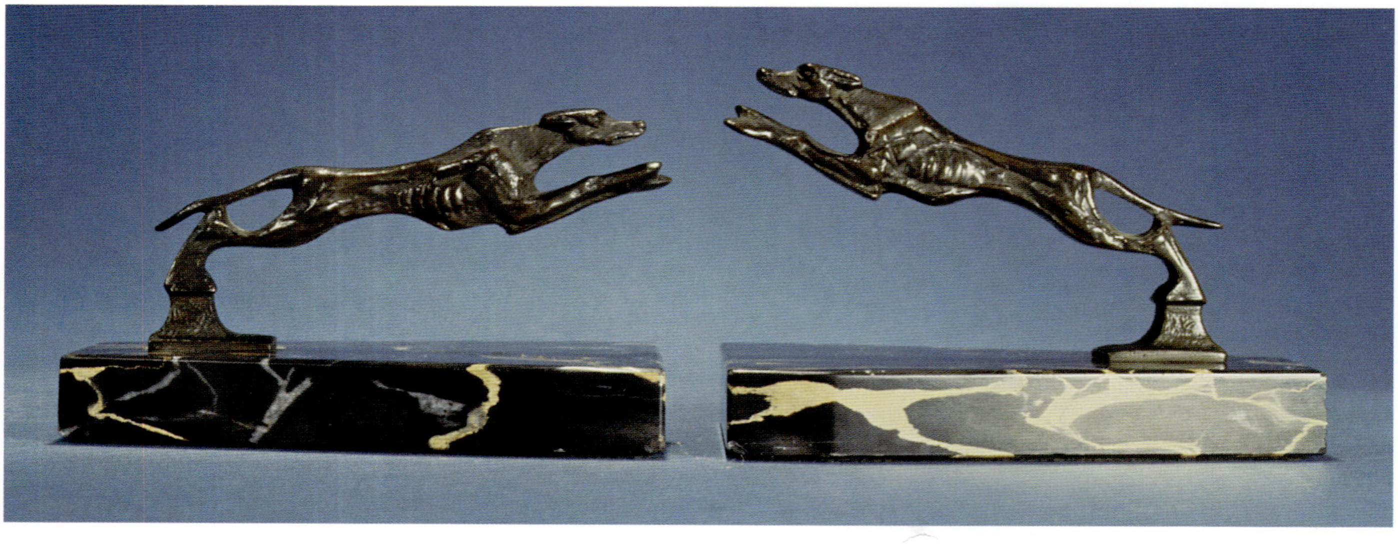

Figure 275. Greyhounds. 3", iron, marble. Foundry: Attrib. LITTCO. Circa 1934. Rarity 3. These are Ford hood ornaments or copies thereof. Art Deco. American Modern. $120-180.

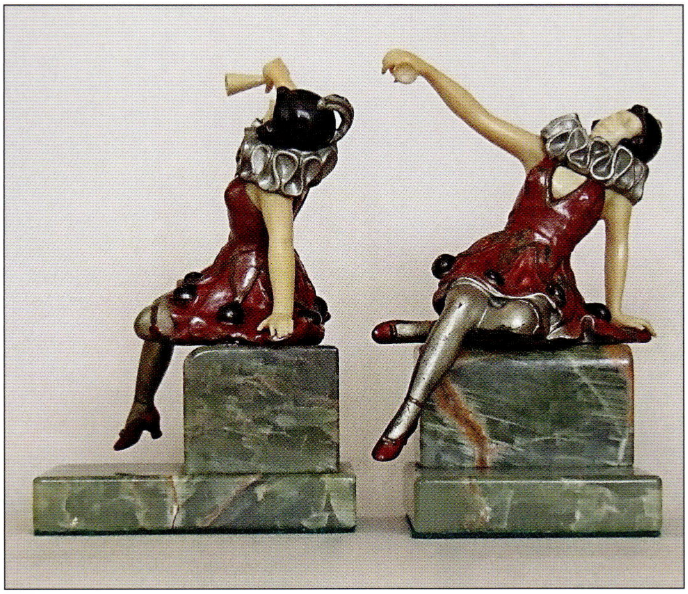

Figure 276. Party Girl 6", gray metal and celluloid. Inscription: Made in Germany. Circa 1935. Rarity 3. Art Deco. $240-360.

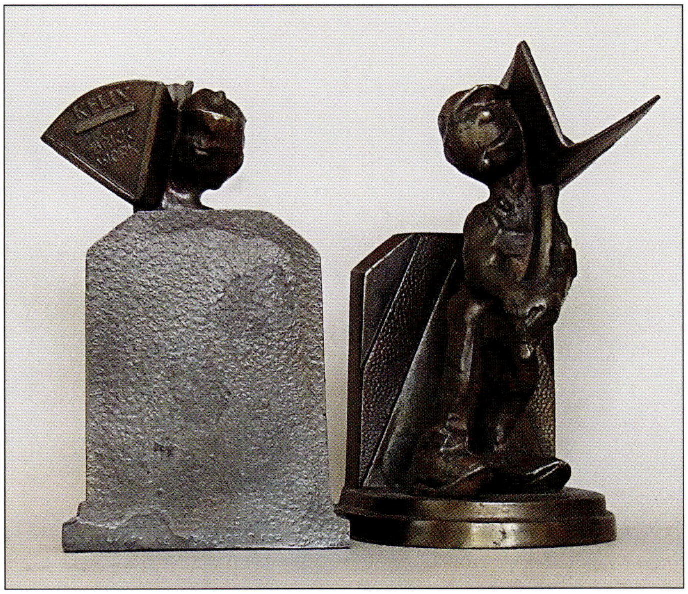

Figure 278. Hod Carrier. 7.25", gray metal. Inscription: Frankart Inc. and Kelly Brickwork. Circa 1935. Rarity 4. Art Deco. American Modern. The bookends are believed to be promotional for actress Grace Kelly's family brick works. $275-420.

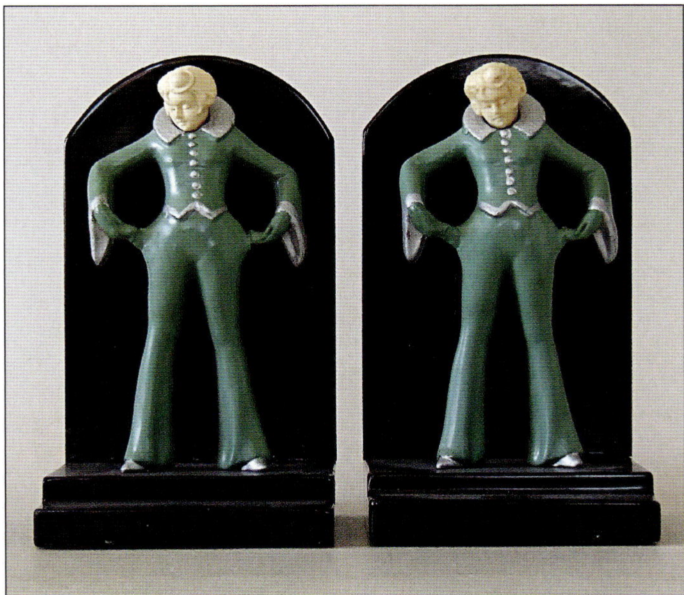

Figure 277. Pauvre. 6.5", gray metal and celluloid. Foundry: Attrib. Hirsch foundry. Circa 1931. Rarity 3. Art Deco. Copied from a French sculpture entitled Pauvre (Poor Girl). $264-396.

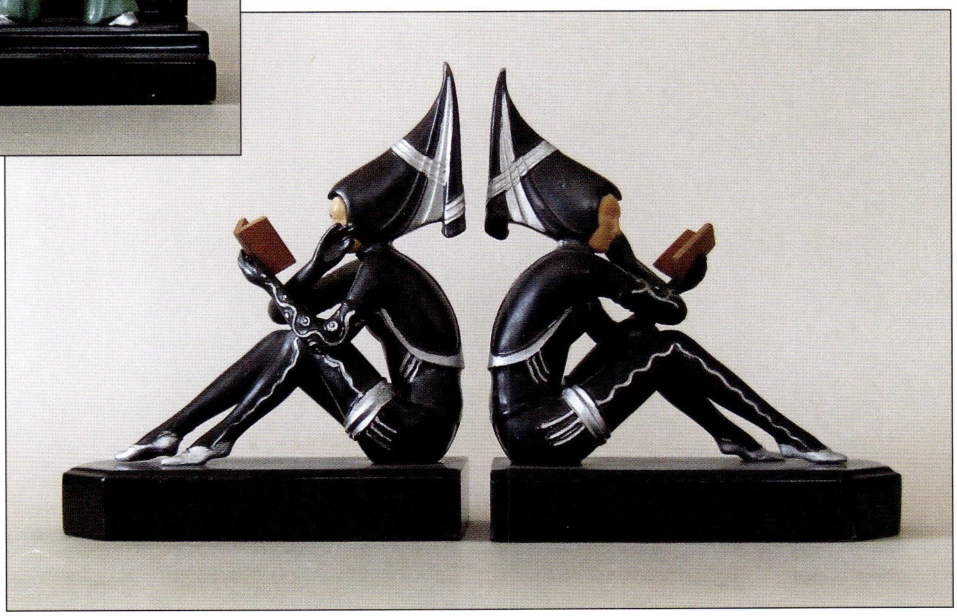

Figure 279. Gerdago Girl. 7.25", gray metal. Foundry: Hirsch Foundry. Sculptor: Attrib. Gerda Gerdago. Circa 1923. Rarity 5. Art Deco. This is a reproduction of Gerdago's work. A rare version with wood books and composition face is shown here. Most issues were all metal or metal with celluloid faces. Art Deco. American Modern. $460-690.

Flapper Era and Bookend Nudes

The 1920s were a time of prosperity in the U.S., and it generated the legendary era of flappers, women's liberation, speak-easies, jazz, the Charleston, wolfhounds and greyhounds, and so on. The flapper era peaked in 1924, 1925, and 1926. Women's liberation was very prominent here in the 1920s. Women received the vote in 1920, and showed their zest for life with parties, booze, and sex. Bobbed hair and dresses with low waistlines were produced by American designers for a new, boyish look. This was part of the Early American Modern. Bookend nudes became popular and documented the changes in the ideal female figure that took place in the early twentieth century.

For at least two centuries before the Victorian era, the idealized female figure was Rubensesque, full and fleshy. During the last half of the nineteenth century the hourglass figure became the ideal female figure. Women with bust and hips several inches wider than waists were considered beautiful. A woman's figure did not need to be fleshy; correct measurement ratios would do, and waists could be diminished by corsets. The hourglass figure frequently became exaggerated to full bosoms, wasp waists, and prominent derriers. The wasp waist was generated by very tight corsets, and this was a serious matter because many women suffered damage to their internal organs from the corset pressure. Bustles supplied heavy bottoms.

With the advent of the twentieth century, hourglass figures were still fashionable and early American bookends showed nudes with busts and hips wider than waists. These hourglass figures remained popular until the 1920s, when the flapper's boyish figure came into fashion. Now the ideal figure had small or flat breasts and narrow hips, and bookend nudes showed this changing ideal. (Figures 280-282).

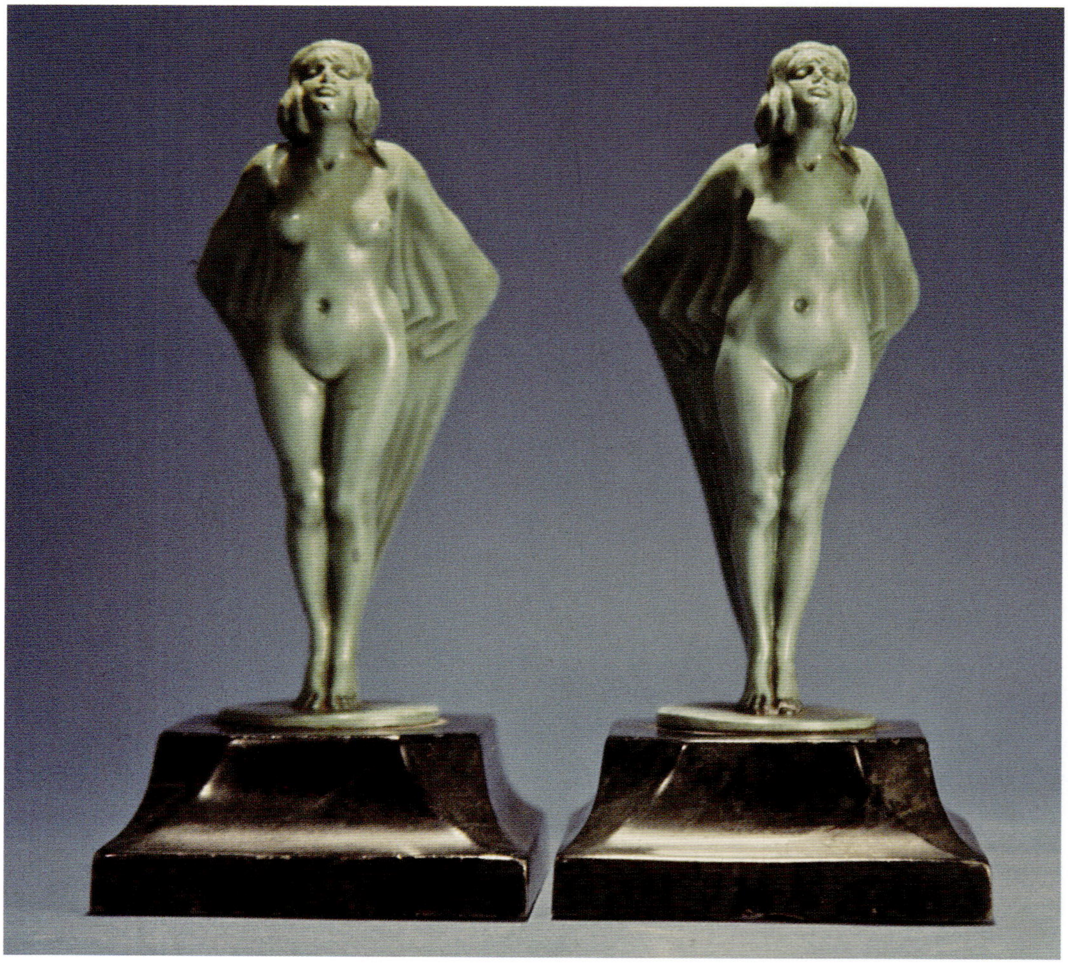

Figure 280. Rubensesque Nude. 7", gray metal. Inscription: L V Aronson (Ronson). 1920. Rarity 4. Art Deco. Early American Modern. This is a fleshy full figure desirable in the seventeenth and eighteenth centuries. $400-600.

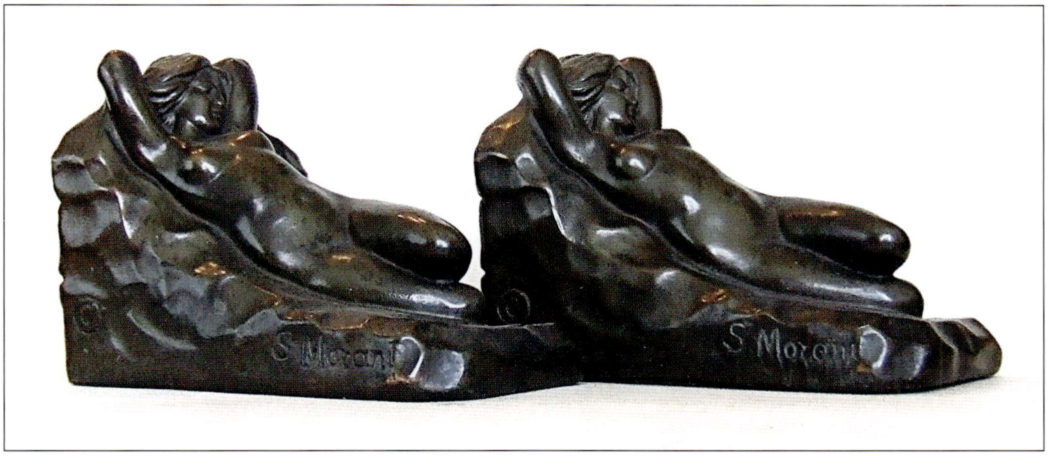

Figure 281. Hourglass Nude. 5.5", electroformed bronze. Inscription: S. Morani, shop mark of Armor Bronze. Sculptor: Salvatore Morani. Circa 1914. Rarity 3. Victorian style. Her hourglass figure would be improved by a corset around the waist. $240-360.

Figure 282. Victorian Couple. 6", iron. Inscription: Shop mark of Judd, 09662. Circa 1915. Rarity 2. Victorian style. Hourglass figure. Her clothing accentuates her small waist and hourglass shape. $100-150.

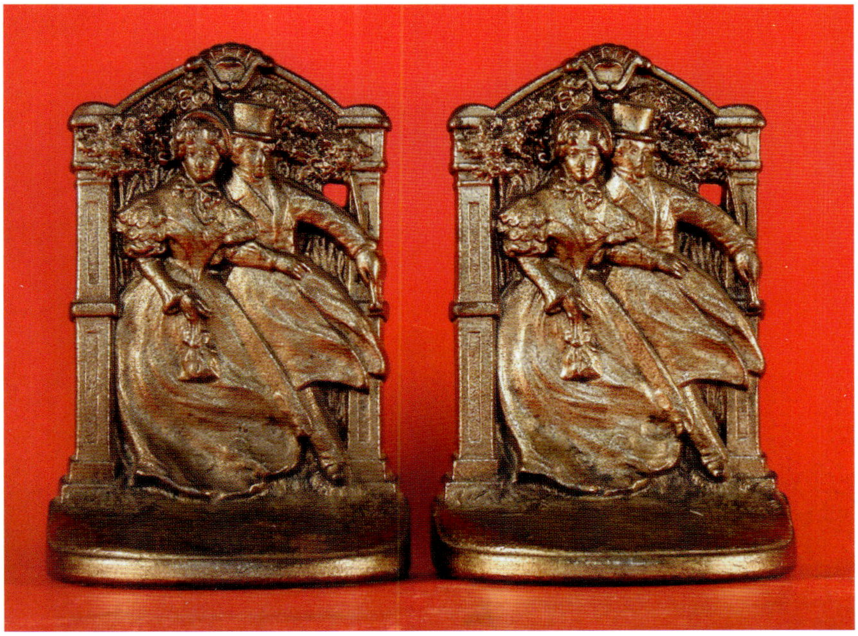

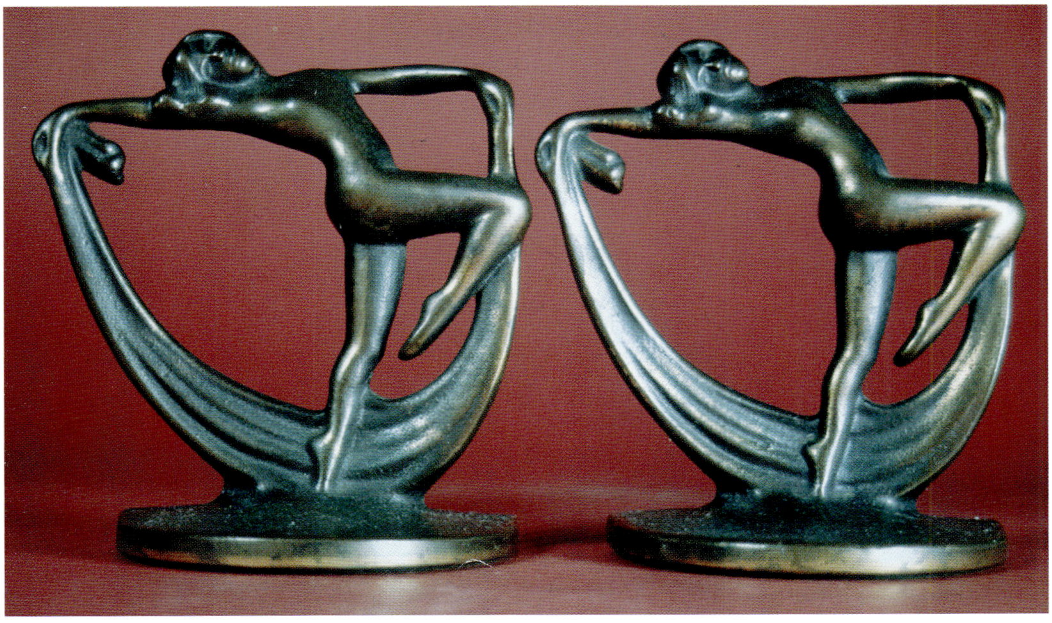

Figure 283. Nude Dancing with Drape. 5.5", iron. Foundry: G.C. Kindt & Co. Sculptor: Guy Cowan. Circa 1927. Rarity 1. Art Deco. Classical flapper figure. $120-180.

Flappers were liberated and so were sculptors and bookend ladies in the 1920s. Nudes on Victorian-style bookends were usually shown as goddesses or nymphs, so their exposure could be regarded as classical and not prurient, or they were sometimes given very demure poses. The 1920s gave us a variety of Deco bookend nudes (Figures 280-309). Many were active and unabashed. Josephine Baker danced nude on stage in Paris, and nudes danced on bookends. They danced, they walked their hounds, and they perched on books and platforms. Commonly, Deco nudes were shown with heads thrown back as if defiantly reveling in their new-found liberty. Some of the bookends showed nudes performing in quite exaggerated positions; these were spoofs, meant for fun and for ridiculing women's aspirations (Figures 300-301). Later, in the 1930s, bookend nudes with prominent breasts struck still poses, presaging the more voluptuous pin-up girls of the coming World War II era (Figure 307, for example).

Certain bookends showed both Victorian and Deco characteristics, and these are regarded as transitional. For example, in Figure 293, a Nude and Frog from Frankart Inc. from 1922, the girl's figure is slender like a flapper or a pixie, but the frog places her outdoors, like a Victorian-style nymph. This is the original Frankart version of the Nude and Frog. It has the copyright sign and buttressing around the foot. There are numerous later copies and Frankart issues of these bookends available, but they lack the copyright sign and the buttressing.

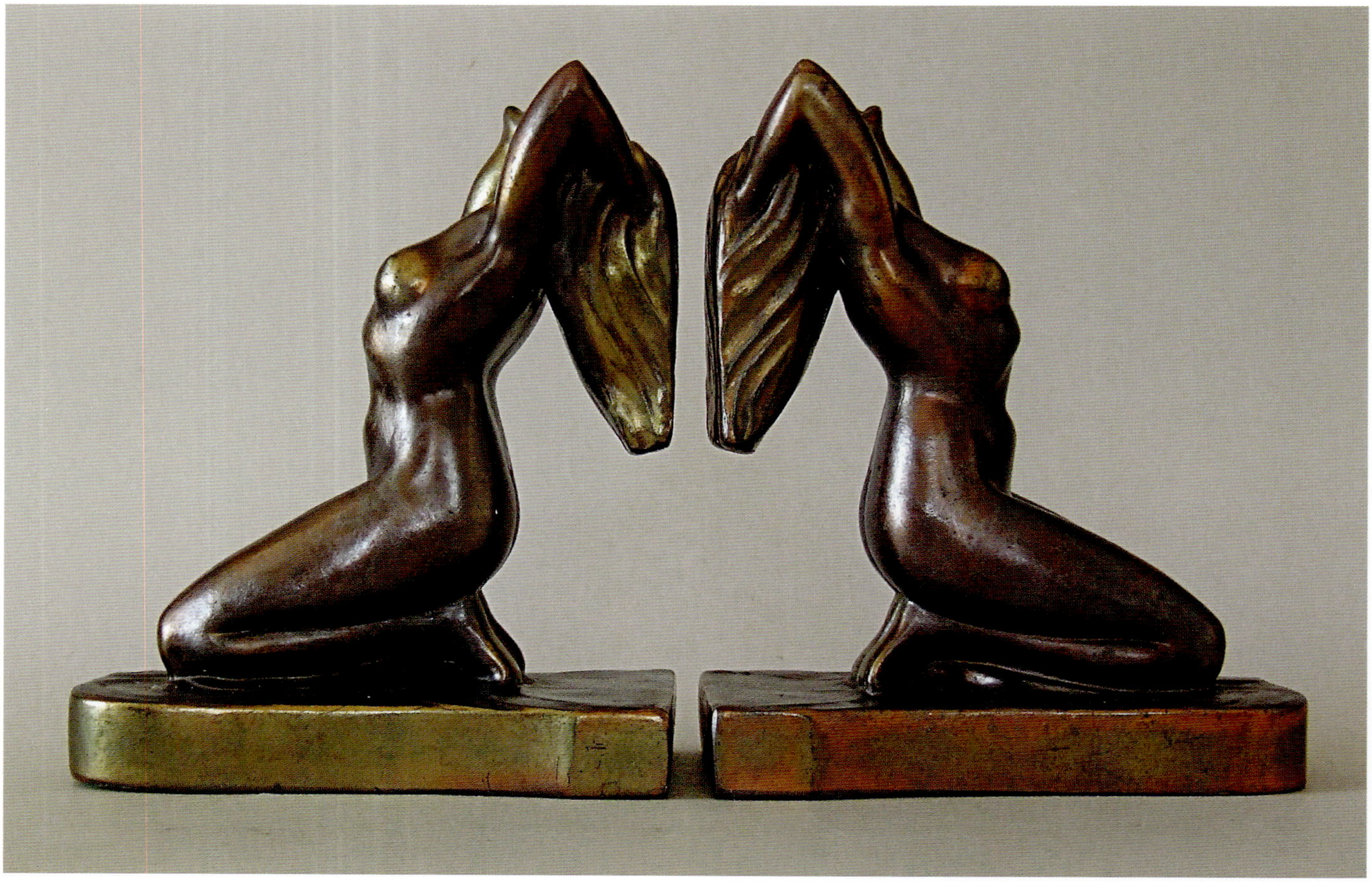

Figure 284. Nude with Long Hair. 7", gray metal. Foundry: Attrib. Dodge Inc. Circa 1937. Rarity. 2. Art Deco. Pin-up pose, American Modern. $240-360.

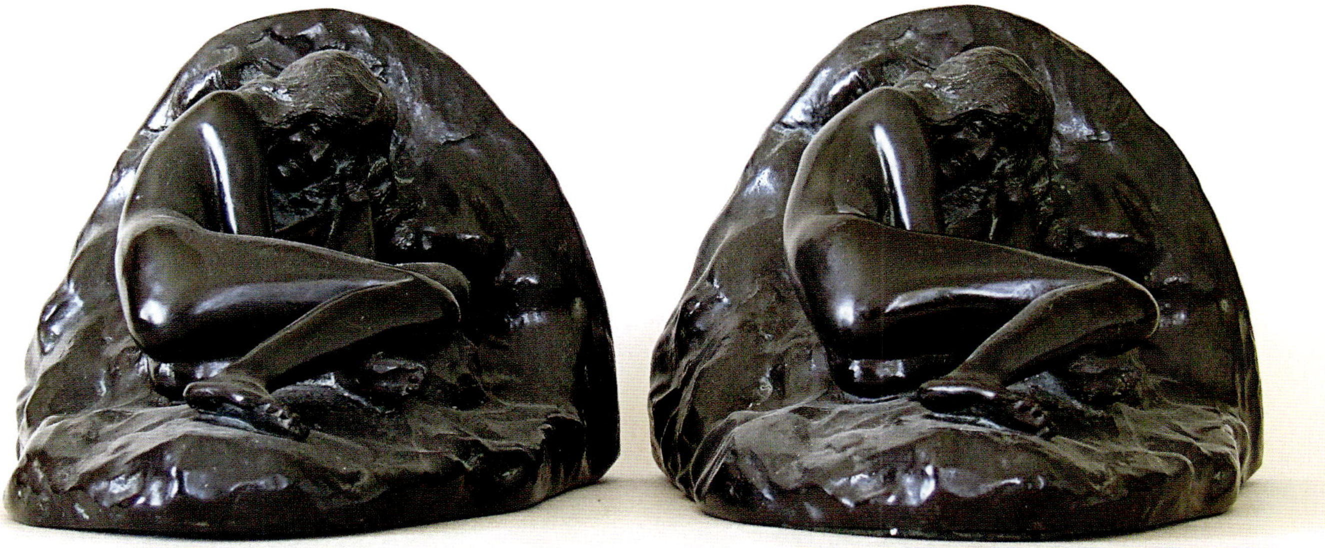

Figure 285. Sleeping Nude. 5.25", gray metal. Inscription: Ronson company label. Circa 1915. Rarity 2. Victorian style. The pose nearly conceals her nudity and she sleeps on rocks like an outdoor creature. These are large, heavy bookends, 10.bs./pair. $200-300.

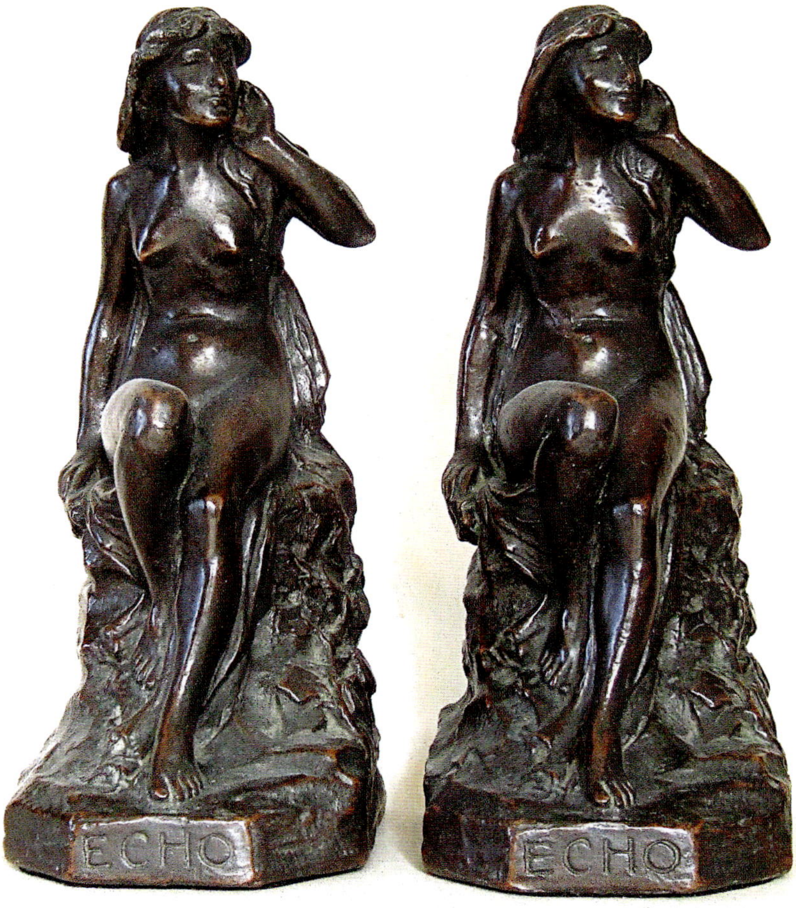

Figure 286. Echo. 9.5", electroformed bronze. Inscription: Echo. Foundry: Attrib. Armor Bronze. Signed by Ruhl, 1915. Rarity 3. Victorian style. Echo is nude here, but she is a classical figure, and, therefore, not lewd. The artist shows her cupping her ear, but Echo's problem was not with hearing. She was punished for careless talk. $275-420.

Figure 287. Nude on Meadow. Ht. 9.5", electroformed bronze. Inscription: KBW and Art Bronz. Foundry: Kathodian Bronze Works. Sculptor: Attrib. F. Renfrew Dean. Circa 1915. Rarity 4. Victorian style. There are flowers in the hair and on the base so she is sitting outdoors like a nymph, a spirit of nature. These are large, heavy bookends, 10 lbs./pair. $500-750.

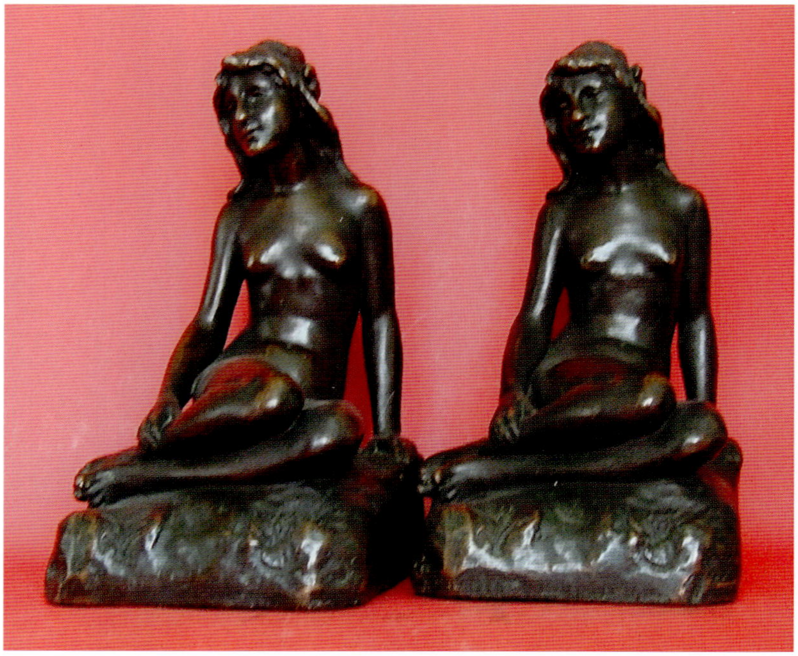

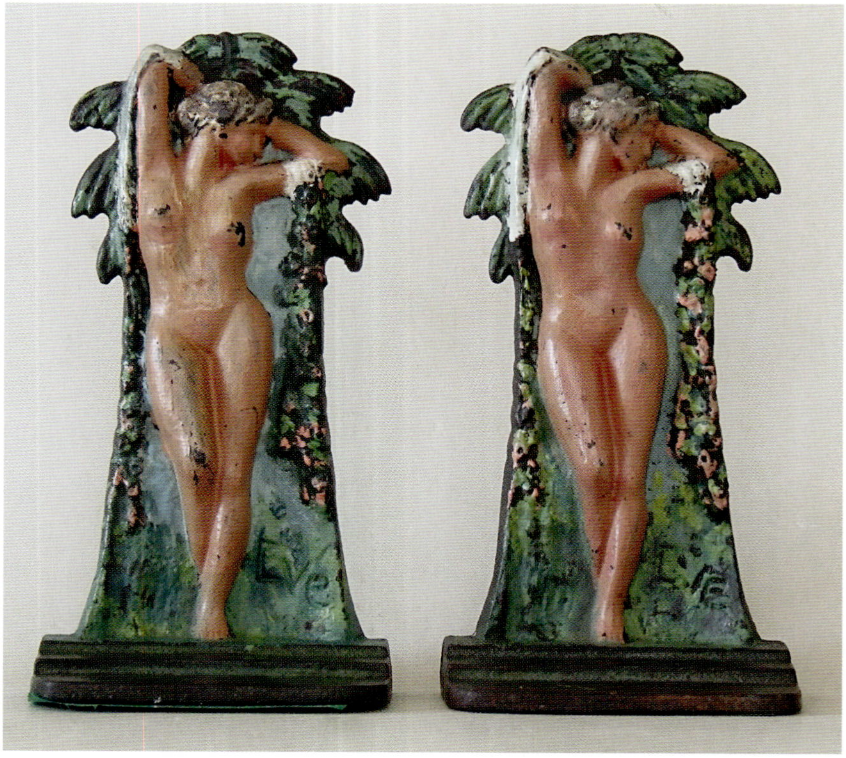

Figure 288. Eve. 7", iron. Inscription: Eve, Verona 988. Circa 1920. Rarity 5. Victorian style. Eve is an unattainable biblical figure. Any polychrome version of these bookends is very rare. $240-360.

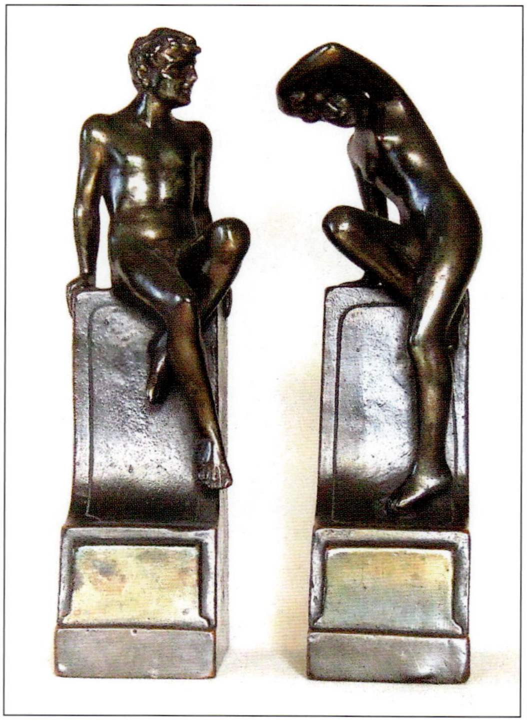

Figure 289. Classic Art. 9.5", electroformed bronze. Inscription: Classic Art. Attrib. Paul Mori. Circa 1915. Rarity 2. Victorian style. These nudes seem too risqué to be Victorian style, but the inscription assures us that the figures are classical and, therefore, acceptable. $380-570.

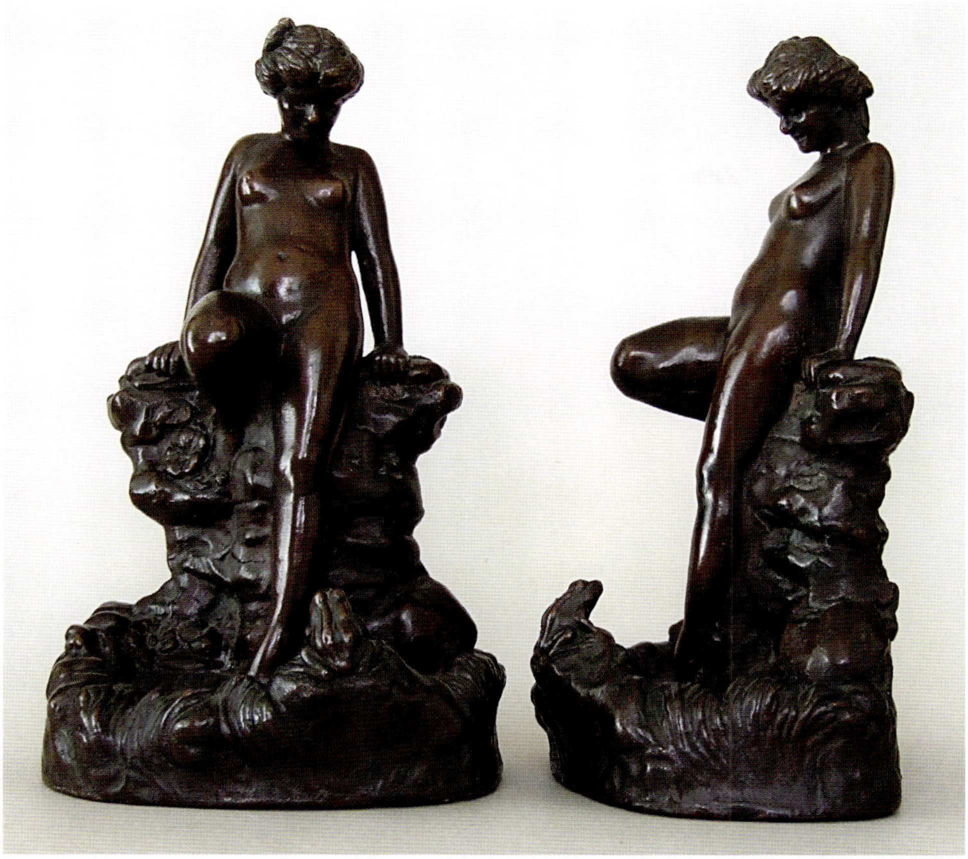

Figure 290. Nude in Fountain. 9.75", electroformed bronze. Inscription: KBW and Art Bronz. Foundry: Kathodian Bronze Works. Sculptor: F. Renfrew Dean. Circa 1915. Rarity 3. Transition from Victorian style to Art Deco. She is a mythical creature. The frog confirms she is outdoors, like a nymph. These are large bookends. $400-600.

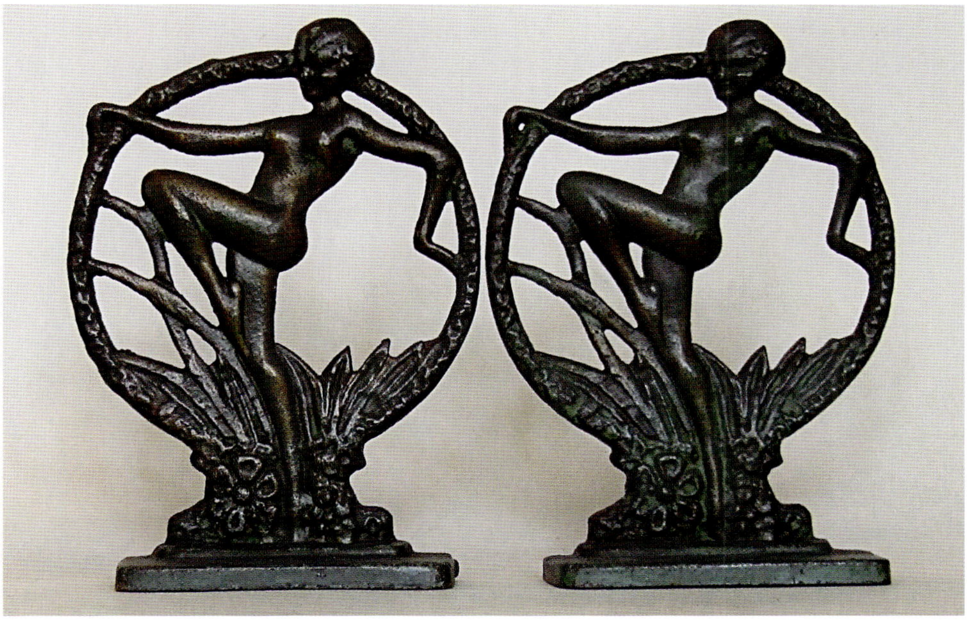

Figure 291. Nude in a Circle with Foliage. 8.25", iron. Circa 1924. Rarity 2.Transition from Victorian to Art Deco. The girl has a bobbed-style haircut (1923-1927) but the foliage places her outdoors like a dancing nymph. $208-312.

Figure 292. Bathing Beauty. 8.25", gray metal. Circa 1922. Rarity 2. Transition from Victorian to Art Deco. Her figure is too full for a flapper. Her hair is in a bun, not in a flapper bobbed cut. The daring swimsuit is c. 1922. The bookends are possibly related to the Miss America contest which began in 1921. $240-360.

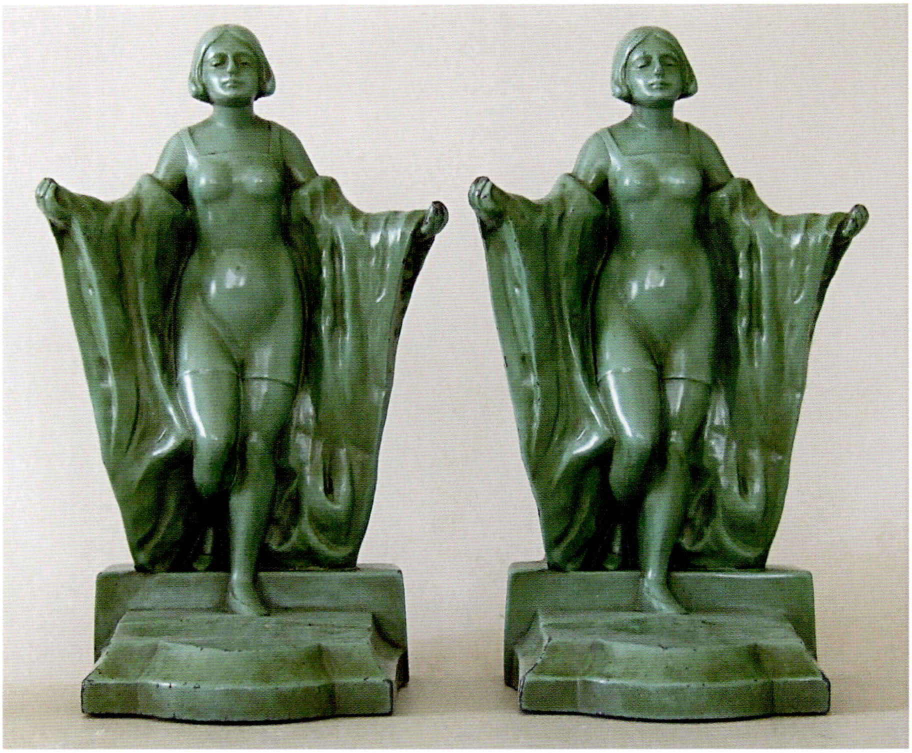

Figure 293. Nude and Frog. 10.25" gray metal. Inscription: Frankart Inc. and 1922 with a copyright symbol. Rarity 5. Transition from Victorian style to Art Deco, as explained in the text. This is the original Frankart version of the Nude and Frog, with the copyright sign and the buttressing around the foot. $500-750.

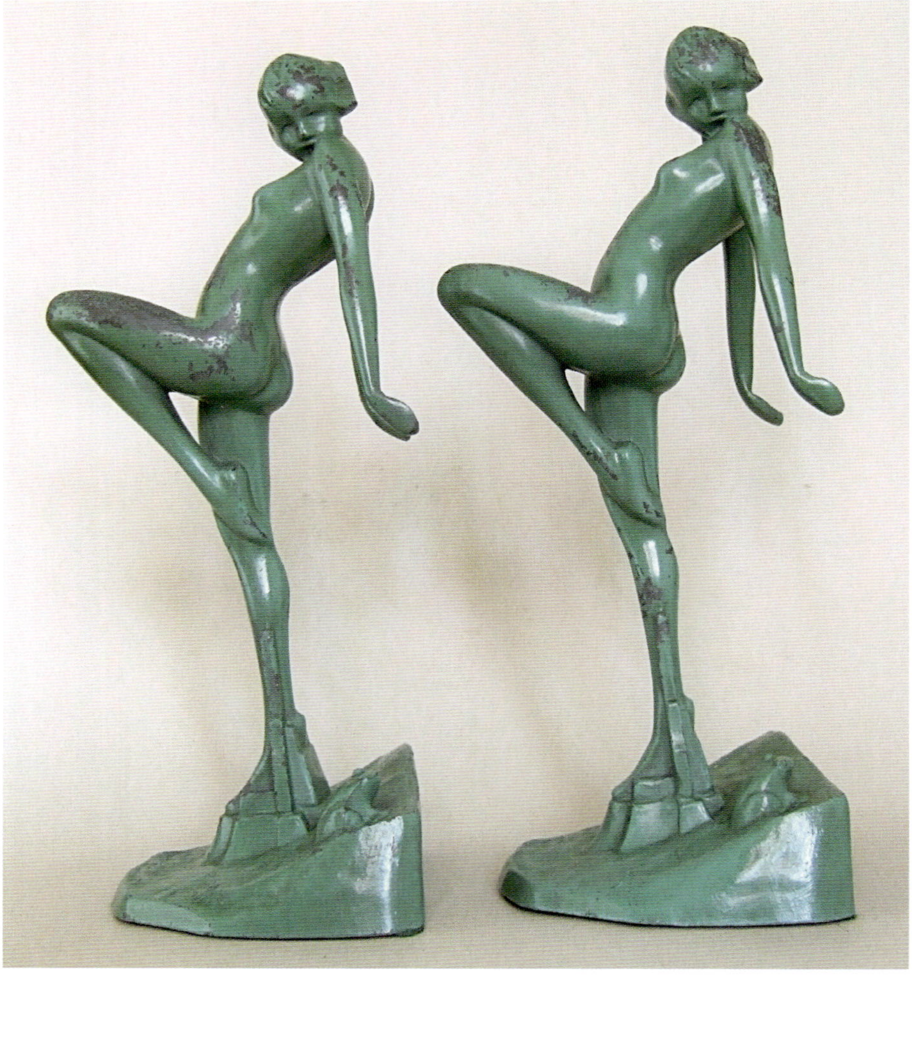

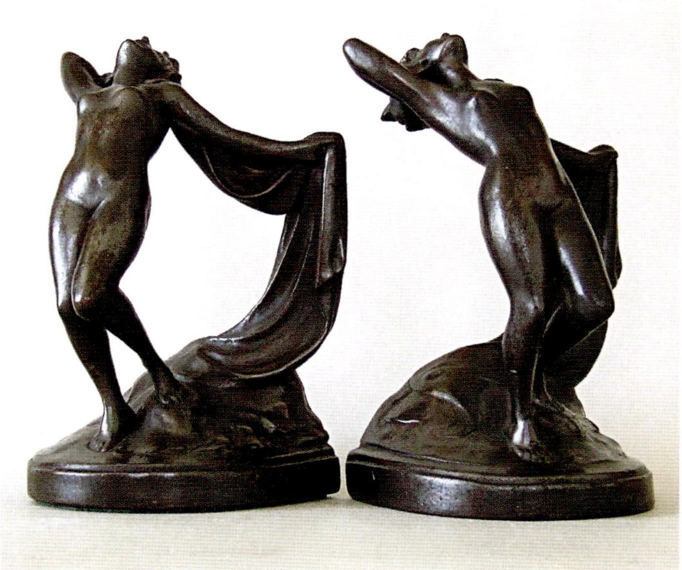

Figure 294. Nude & Drape. 7", gray metal. Foundry: Attrib. Paul Mori. Circa 1922. Rarity 2. Art Deco. $264-396.

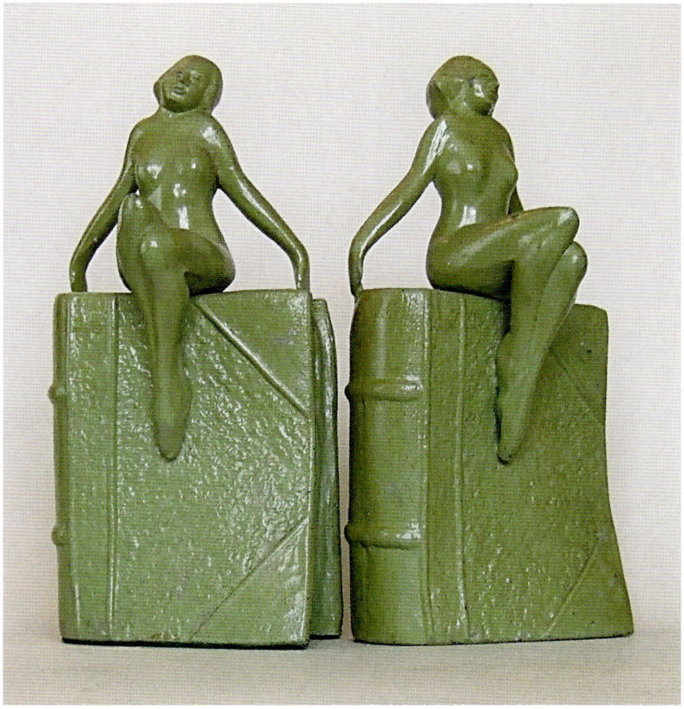

Figure 295. Nude on Book with Head Tilted. 9.75", gray metal. Foundry: Frankart. Circa 1925. Rarity 2. Art Deco. $275-420.

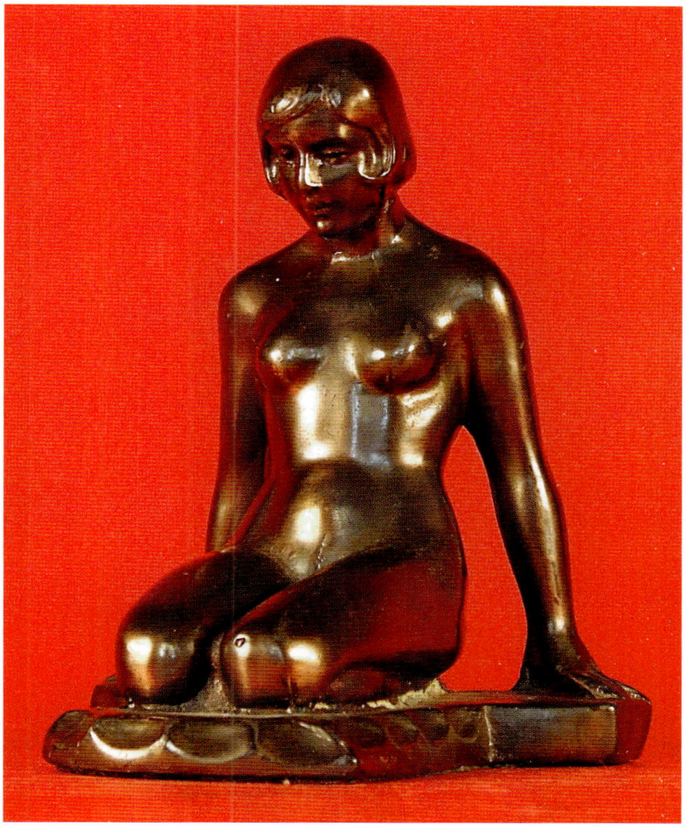

Figure 296. Leaning Nude. 5", gray metal. Attrib. Nuart. Circa 1933. Rarity 2. Art Deco. $160-240.

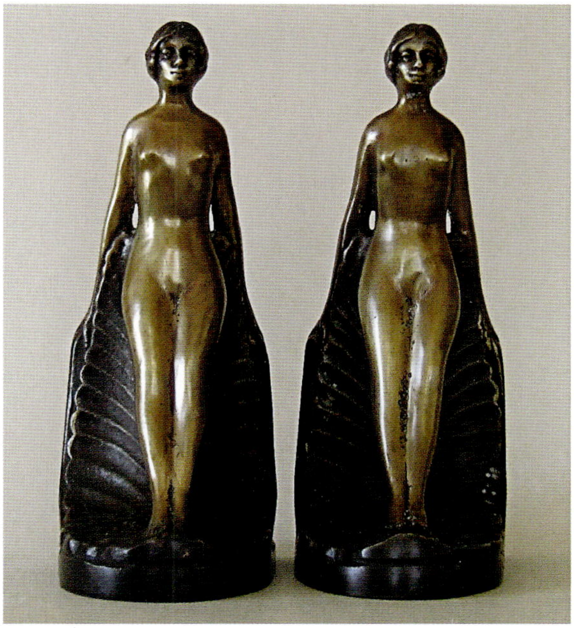

Figure 297. Art Deco Nu. 8.25", bronze. Foundry: Attrib. Hirsch foundry. Circa 1928. Rarity. 3. Art Deco. This is a copy of a French sculpture by the artist Giroud-Rivier entitled *Art Deco Nu*, c. 1925. Bronze issues are unusual; recent copies with enlarged breasts are frequent. $200-300.

Figure 298. Nude Against Chevrons. 8", gray metal. Inscription: Crescent Metal Works. Circa 1929. Rarity 4. Art Deco. American Modern, geometry. $400-600.

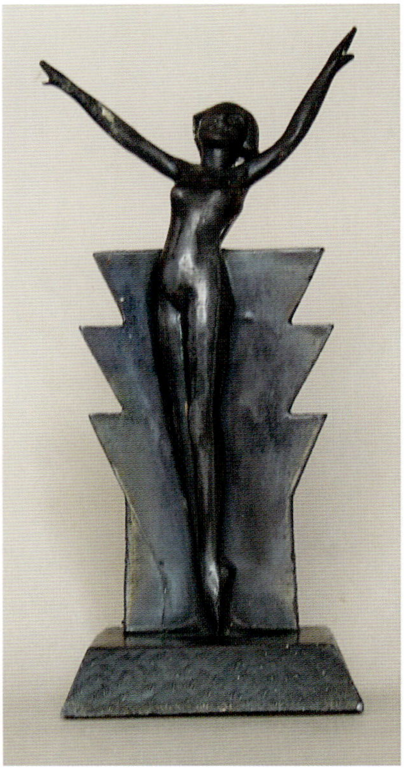

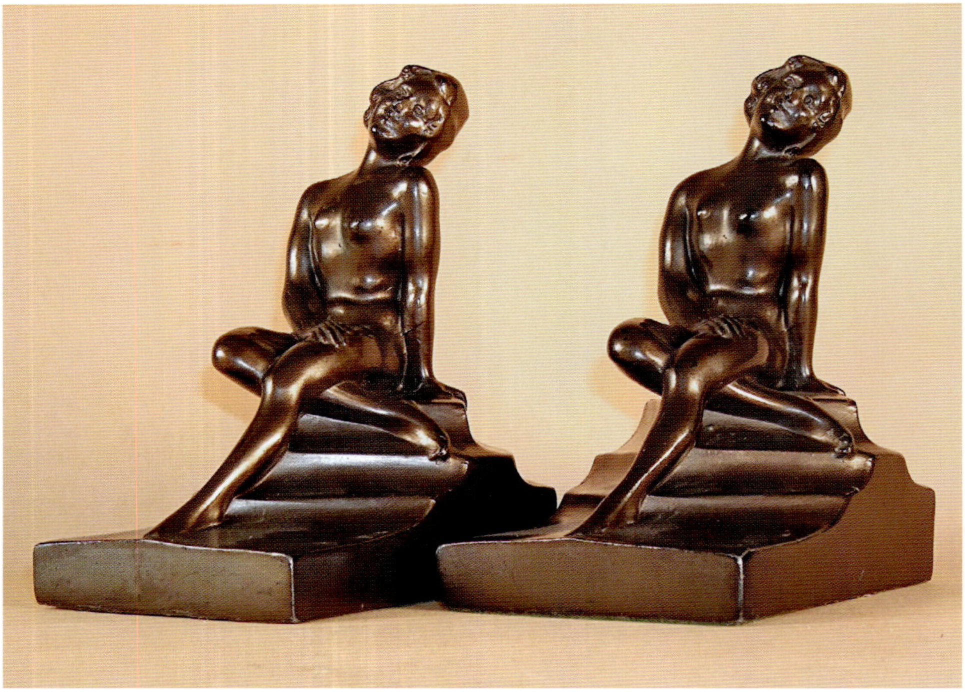

Figure 299. Nude on Geometric Pedestal. 5", gray metal. Inscription: Shop mark stating Nuart and Co. Circa 1925. Rarity 2. Art Deco. flapper figure, geometry. $200-300.

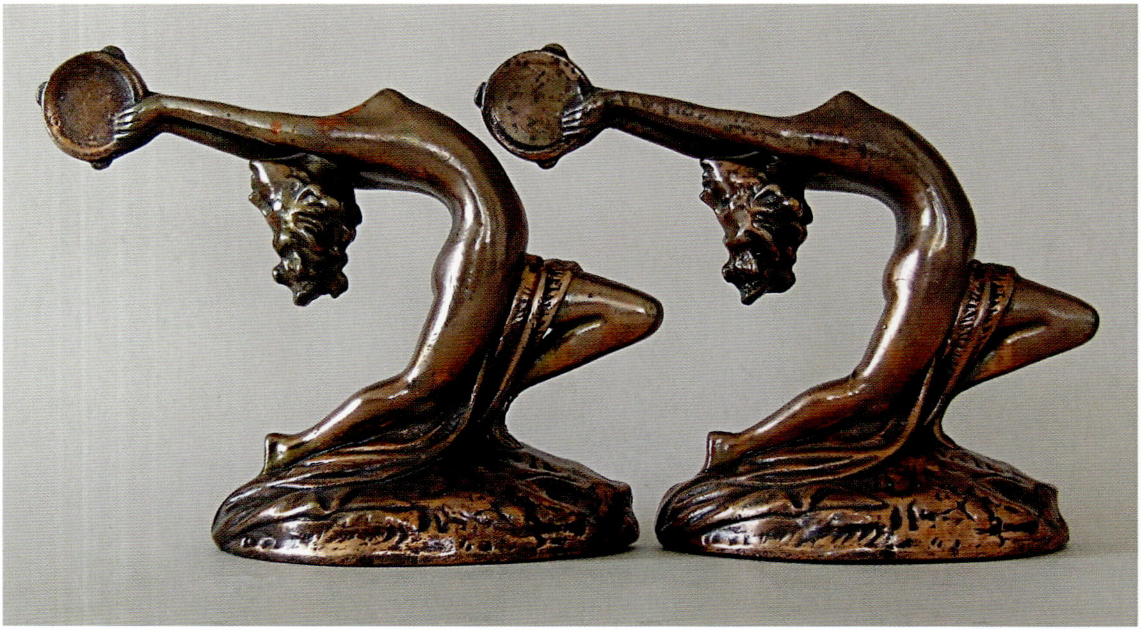

Figure 300. Nude With Tambourine 6.75", electroformed bronze. Foundry: Attrib. Armor Bronze Inc. Circa 1925. Rarity 2. Art Deco. $360-540.

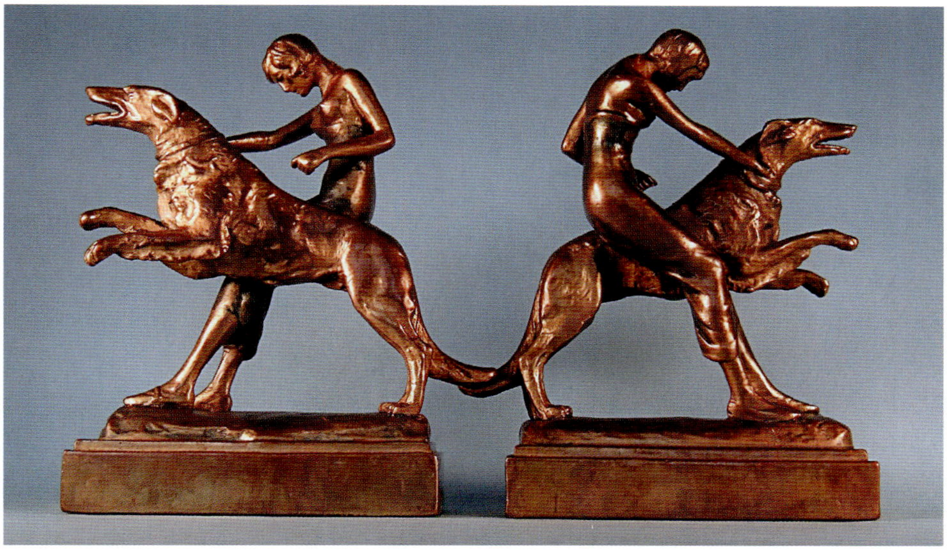

Figure 301. Flapper with Wolfhound. 9", electroformed bronze. Inscription: Pompeian Bronze. Circa 1925. Rarity 3. Art Deco. This flapper purchased a huge, fashionable wolfhound to show her liberation. Her gown is slipping down as she attempts to restrain her animal. These are large, heavy bookends, 9 lbs/pair. $720-1080.

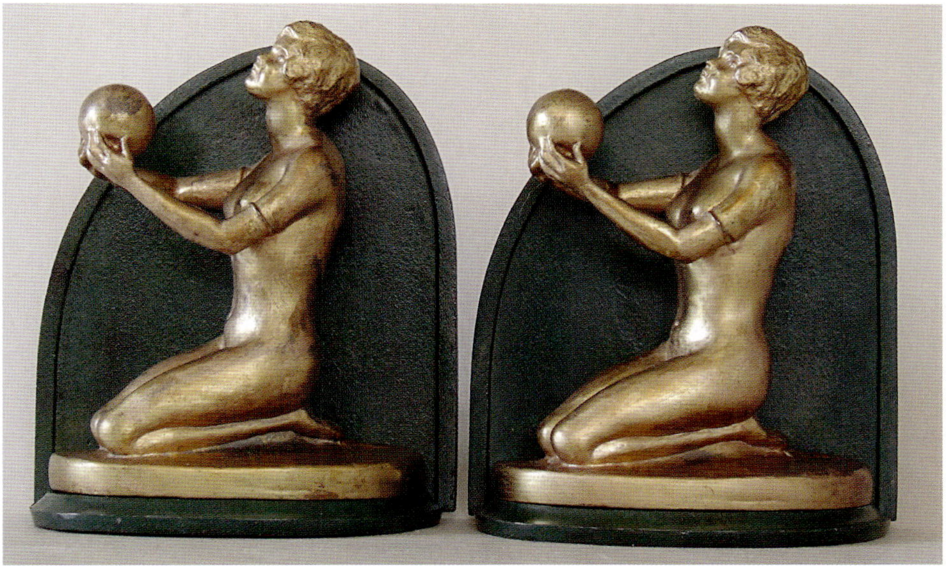

Figure 302. Nude and Sphere with Upright. 6.25", iron. Inscription: shop mark of Bradley and Hubbard Mfg. Co. Circa 1925. Rarity 4. Art Deco. $600-900.

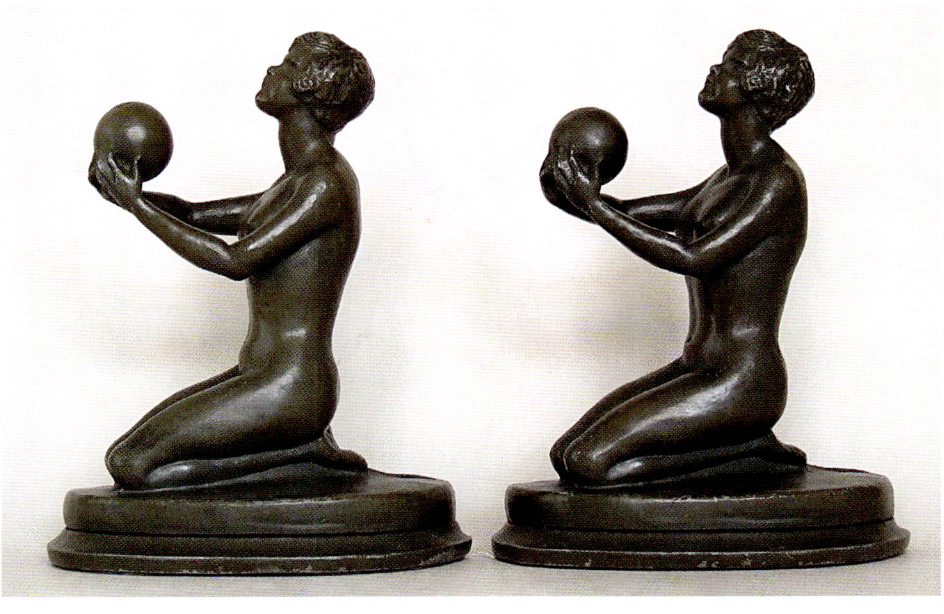

Figure 303. Nude and Sphere. 6.5", iron. Inscription: shop mark of Bradley and Hubbard Mfg. Co. Circa 1925. Rarity 4. Art Deco. This version was issued without the upright seen in Figure 302. $600-900.

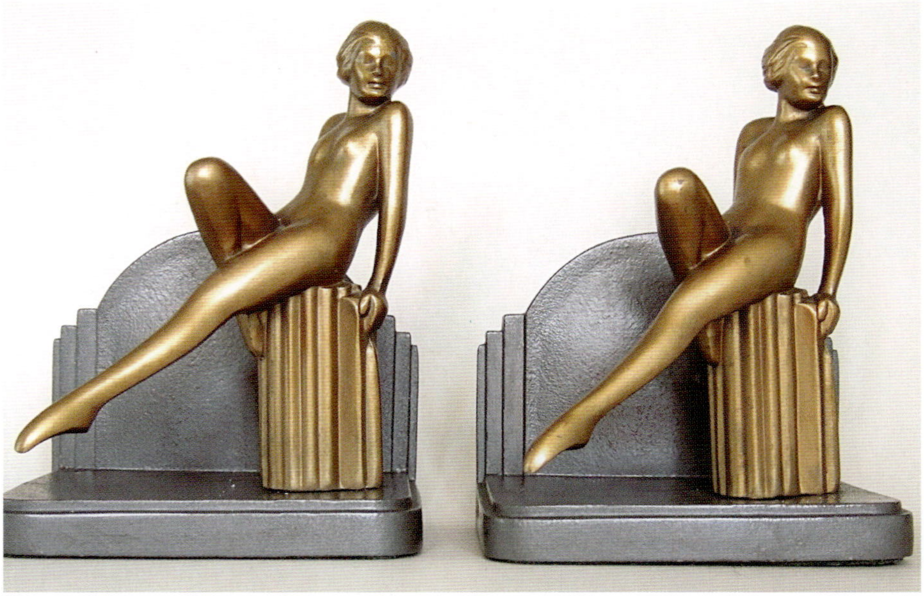

Figure 304. Nude on Fluted Pedestal. 7", gray metal. Inscription: shop mark stating Nuart Inc. Circa 1930. Rarity 3. Art Deco. A streamlined flapper body with a bobbed hair style, and a fluted column pedestal. Very American Modern. $400-600.

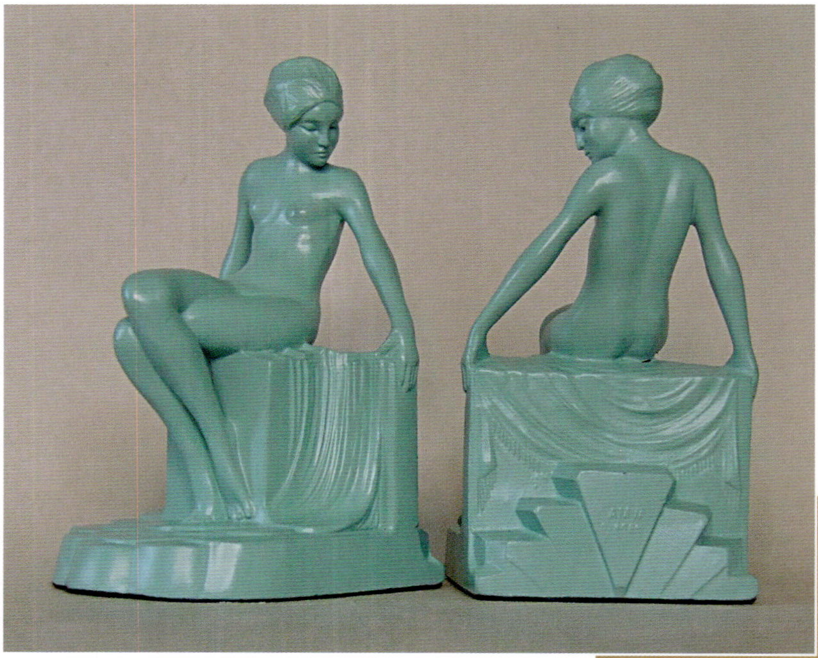

Figure 305. Nude on Draped Pedestal. 7.25", gray metal. Inscription: A.M.W. Foundry: Art Metal Works (Ronson). Circa 1933. Rarity 5. Art Deco. American Modern, streamlined flapper figure. Copies are common. $440-652.

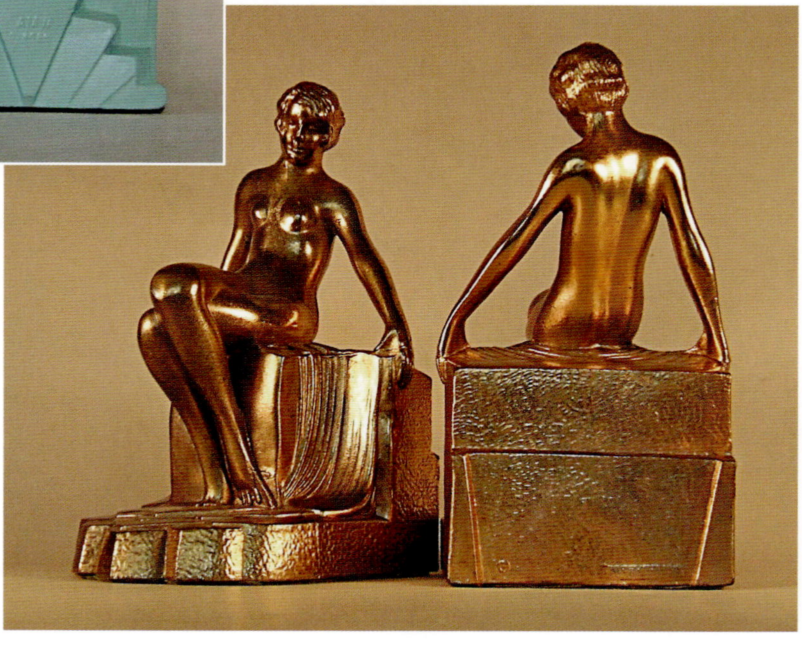

Figure 306. Nude on Draped Pedestal. 7.25", gray metal. Circa 1935. Rarity 1. Art Deco. American Modern. This is similar to the nude shown in Figure 305, but missing the Deco markings on the rear of the base. $140-210.

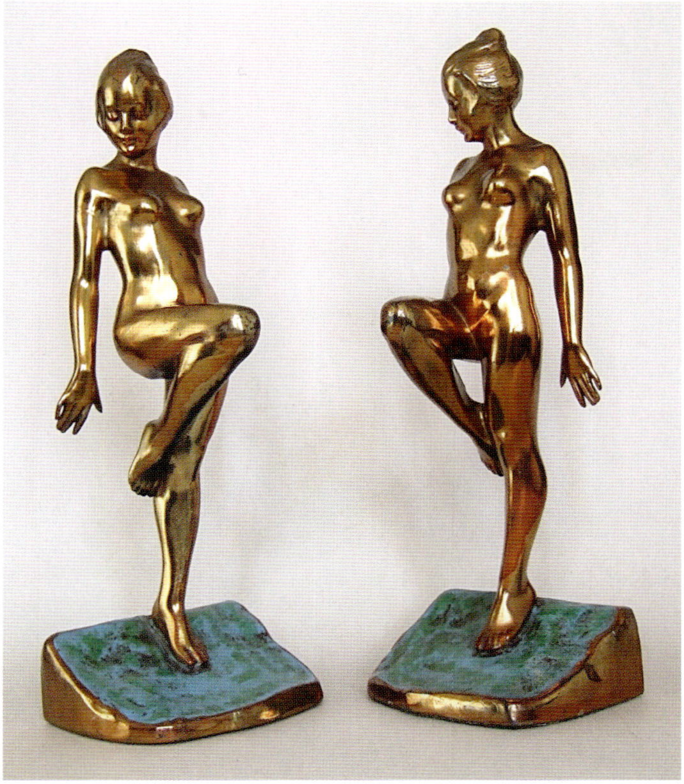

Figure 307. Free Standing Nude. 10.75", gray metal. Foundry: Ronson. Circa 1934. Rarity 3. Art Deco. American Modern. Tall bookends, pin-up pose. $640-960.

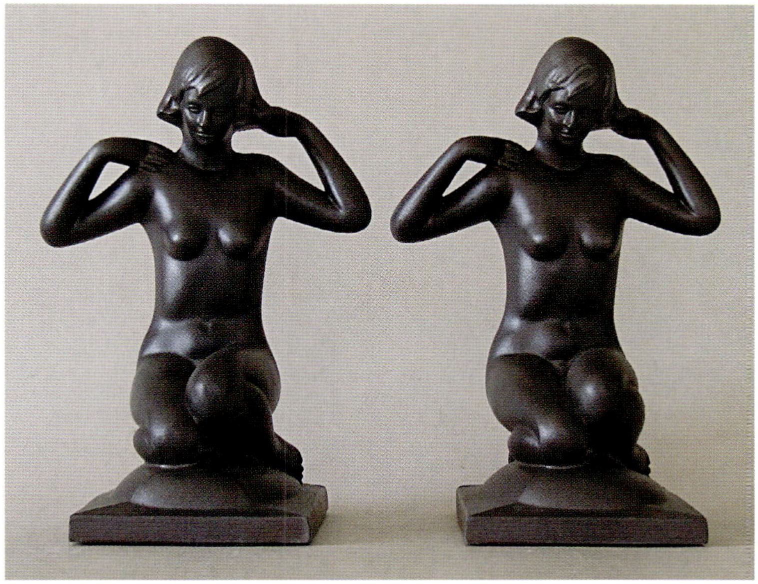

Figure 308. Nude Kneeling on Pedestal. 7", gray metal. Inscription: Bronzart. Foundry: Gifthouse. Circa 1935. Rarity 2. Art Deco. American Modern, pin-up pose. $240-360.

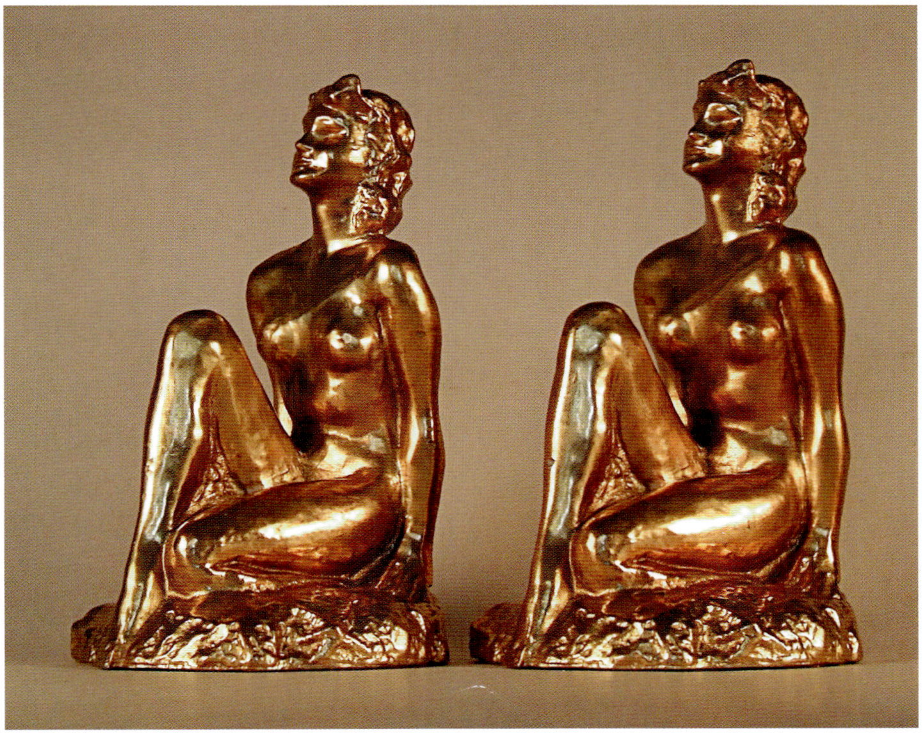

Figure 309. Sitting Nude. 6", gray metal. Inscription: signed by McClelland Barclay. Foundry: McClelland Barclay. Circa 1939. Rarity 4. Art Deco, American Modern. Pin-up pose. $500-750.

American Modern Bookends

By the 1930s, American Art Deco crystalized into an independent style we know as American Modern, which was a combination of Modernist art, Art Moderne, and Early American Modern.

What had happened to Modernist art with its emphasis on simple design suitable for machine production? It was retarded in Germany by World War I and then by the war's aftermath, so its influence was still comparatively small in 1920. However, America was introduced to Modernist art gradually in the 1920s with input from the Bauhaus in Germany, and by émigré designers from Germany and Austria who organized societies here. At the same time, machines were becoming more important in American life. Automobiles, airplanes, and radios were improving. Moving pictures became talkies and skyscrapers appeared. Our so-called machine age, from about 1920 to about 1940, had begun with an accompanying public fascination with technological progress. Bookends celebrating machinery made their appearance showing whole machines like airplanes and cars as well as machine parts like gears (Figures 310-312), and all of this fit under the American Modern umbrella. The increasing need for attractive machined goods of all kinds brought the designers to the Modernist values, and Modernist art became important to American Modern in the 1930s.

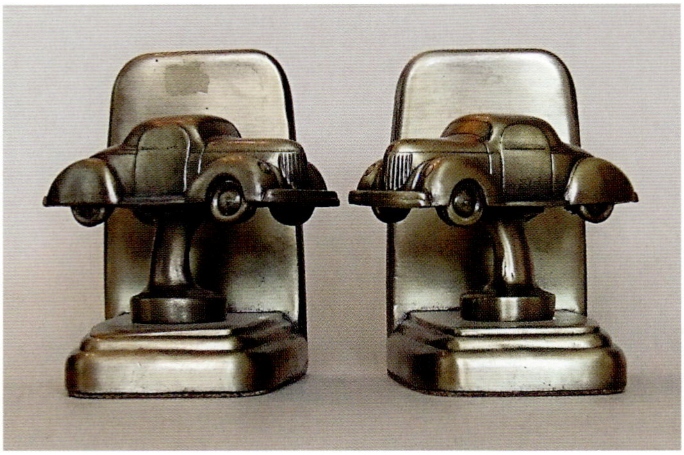

Figure 310. Classy Auto. 8", gray metal. Inscription: Sarsaparilla, Deco Designs. Circa 1955. Rarity 4. Art Deco. Machine age interest. The auto design is about 1940, but we cannot identify the make and model. Probably a reproduction bookend. $140-210.

American industry adopted Modernist criteria because they yielded attractive goods of simple design that were relatively inexpensive to produce. An object needed to be attractive without the cost of applied decoration, so they used relatively new, elegant material like chrome-plated metal or polished stainless steel, Bakelite, glass, and neon bulbs. Bakelite and celluloid parts were incorporated into bookends.

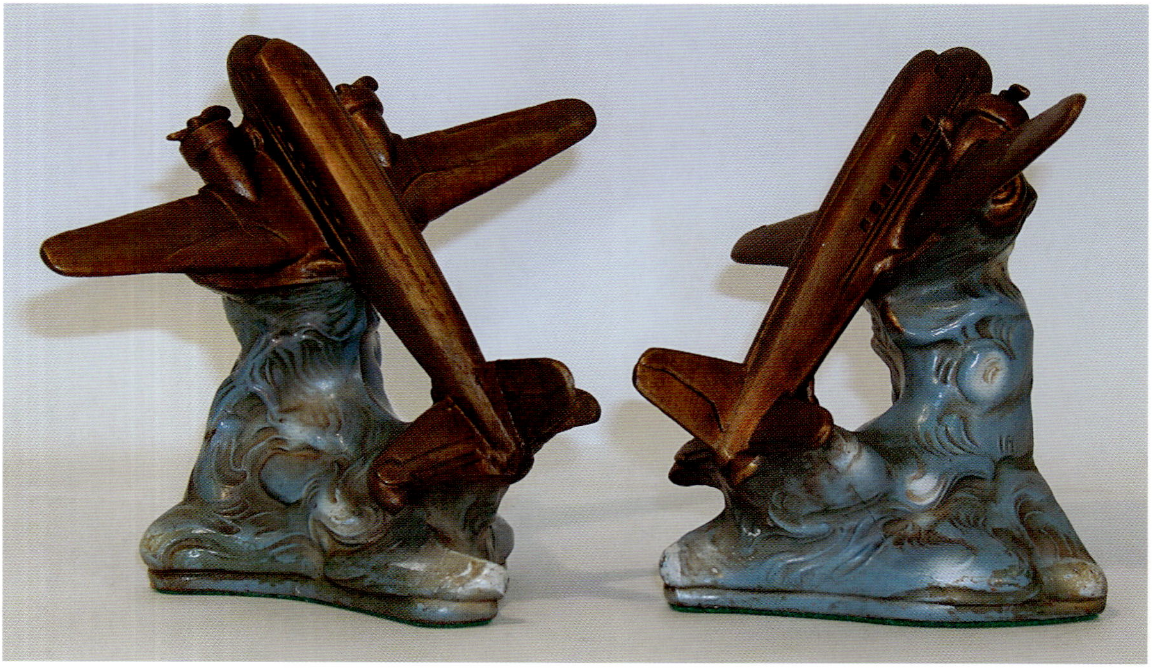

Figure 311. Airplane. 5.75", gray metal. Inscription: Shop mark of K&O. Circa 1935. Rarity 3. Art Deco. This appears to be a Douglas DC 3. The first flight of the DC 3 was in 1935. Machine age interest. *By courtesy of Charles DeCosta, from his collection.* $275-300.

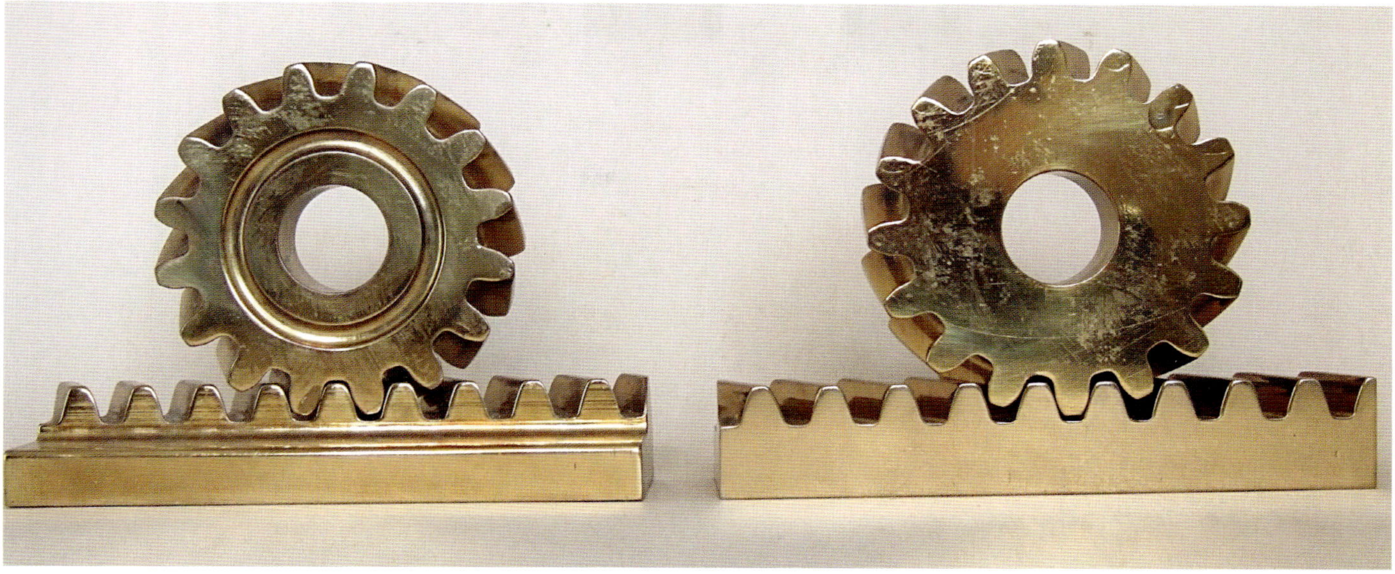

Figure 312. Gears 4", brass. Circa 1935. Rarity 3. Art Deco. Machine age interest. $200-300.

In the 1930s, commercial designs featuring flat, abstract, and geometric styling became commonplace and bookends with these designs appeared. Bookend animals with flat planes instead of rounded contours and bookends with exclusively geometric parts, like spheres and rings, recalled the geometry of earlier cubist sculptures and paintings, and American Modern became identified with geometrical styling. (Figures 313-327).

In the 1930s, everyone wanted to be modern, and geometric styling qualified as very modern indeed. It is difficult to give names to articles that were not pure Modernist or Art Moderne. The terms modern, modernist, modernistic and moderne were used interchangeably in the 1920s, and have given us confusion in terminology ever since.

Skyscrapers became icons of American Art Deco in the 1930s and they were erected with steel and glass in stark Modernist design, since called the "international style." The stepped-back construction inspired the stair-step design motif that meant skyscraper, a ubiquitous American Modern image. The stair step or skyscraper motif can be found on numerous bookends from that era, as well as the fluted column, another popular motif.

The admiration for speed that began in the 1920s rose to prominence in the 1930s. Streamline design meant aerodynamic, fast, and modern, and it appeared everywhere, on airplanes and cars, where it increased speed, and on household goods, like refrigerators, that would never move.

Streamlining became the most important design characteristic of Deco that made it American. It became a fashion statement. Horizontal lines, rounded corners, smooth, sleek, and shiny shapes joined geometric, flattened surfaces and spheres on buildings and smaller objects, including bookends again. Streamlined objects were special. Their smooth surfaces were emotion-free Modernist, but their shapes and overall appearances were highly decorative, recalling Art Moderne. American Modern managed to incorporate both the French and the German streams and gave us memorable objects that carried the promise of modern living.

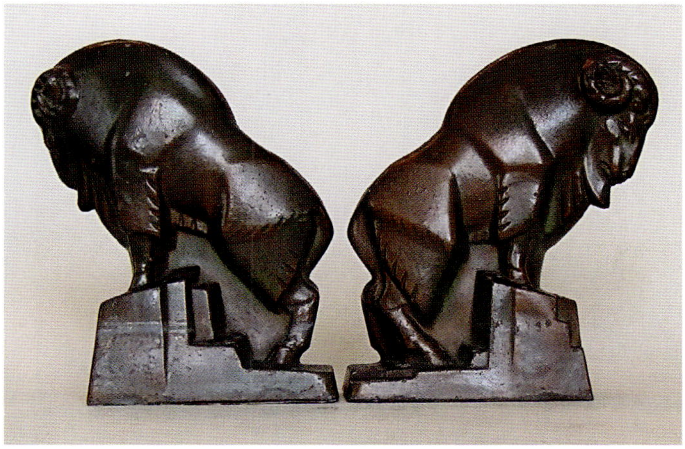

Figure 313. Geometric Ram. 7", gray metal. Inscription: McClelland Barclay. Circa 1938. Rarity 4. Art Deco, American Modern. The rounded areas flattened into planes are a cubist touch. $248-372.

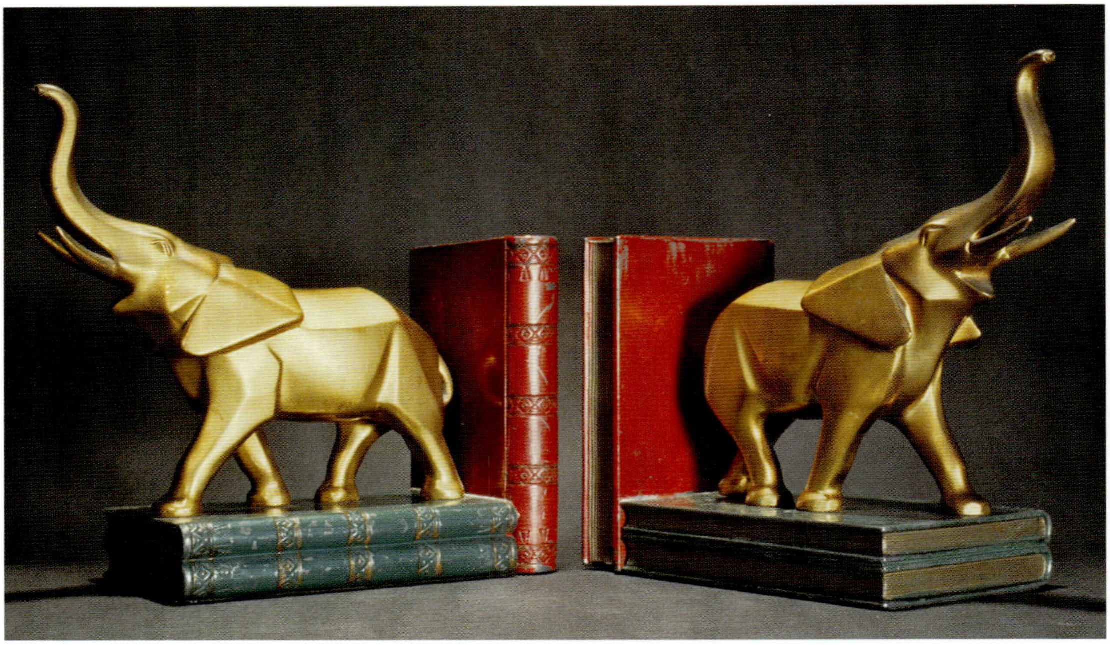

Figure 314. Geometric Elephant. 8.5", gray metal. Inscription: Shop mark of Jennings Brothers. Circa 1934. Rarity 4. Art Deco. American Modern. The rounded areas flattened into planes are a cubist touch. $200-300.

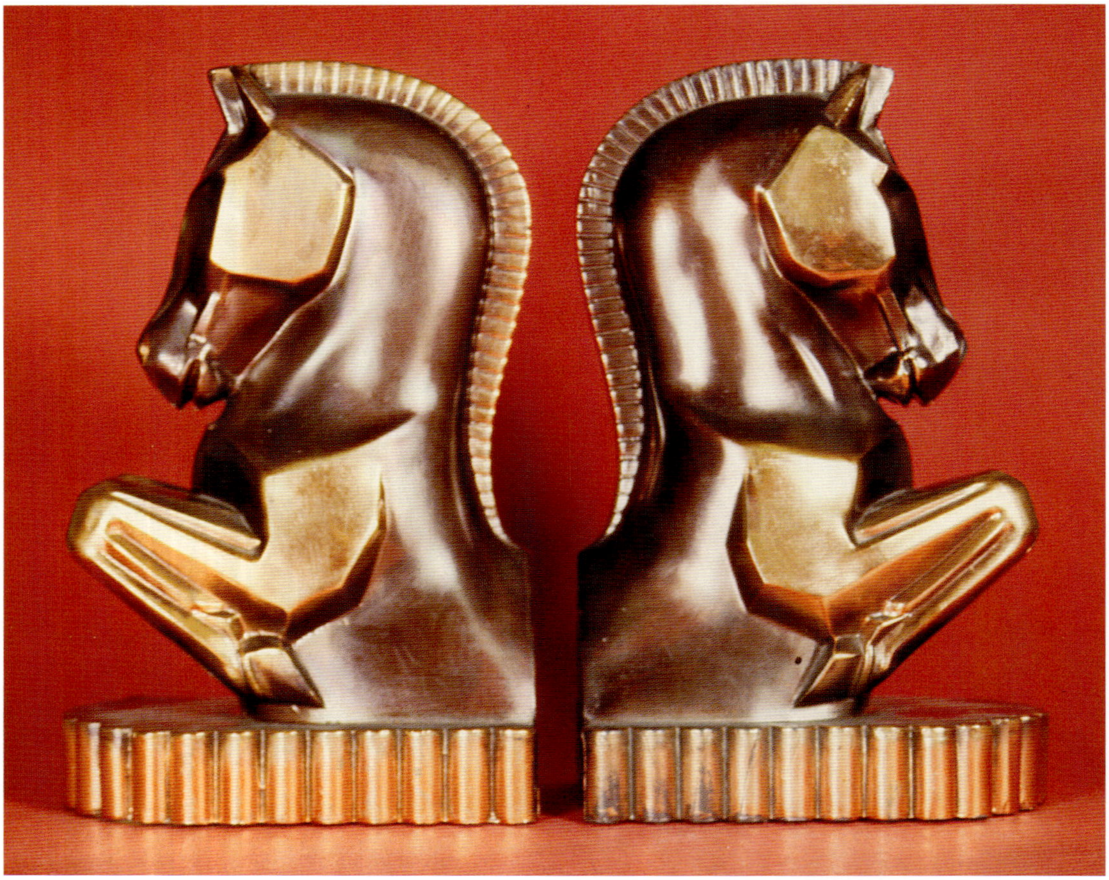

Figure 315. Geometric Horse. 8.5", gray metal. Inscription: Champion Prod's and signed by Phillip diNapoli. Circa 1934. Rarity 2. Art Deco. American Modern. The rounded areas flattened into planes are a cubist touch. $224-334.

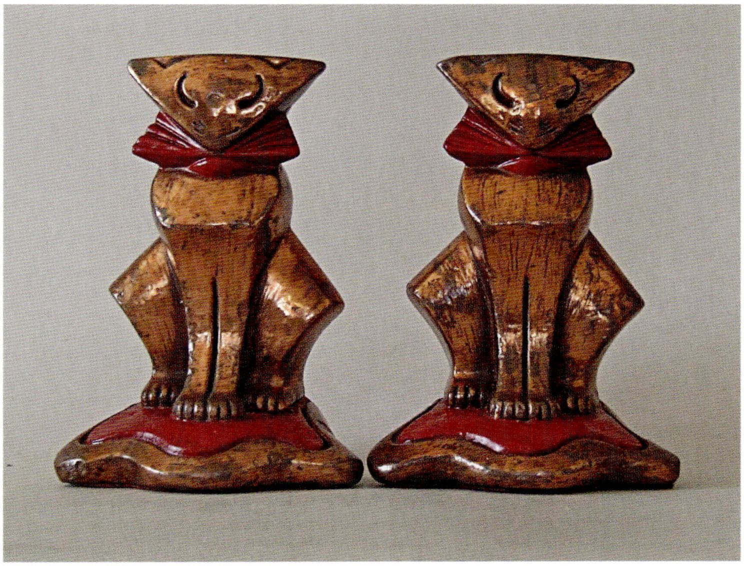

Figure 316. Geometric Cat. 6.25", electroformed bronze. Foundry: Attrib. Armor Bronze. Circa 1934. Rarity 3. Art Deco. American Modern. The rounded areas flattened into planes are a cubist touch. $224-334.

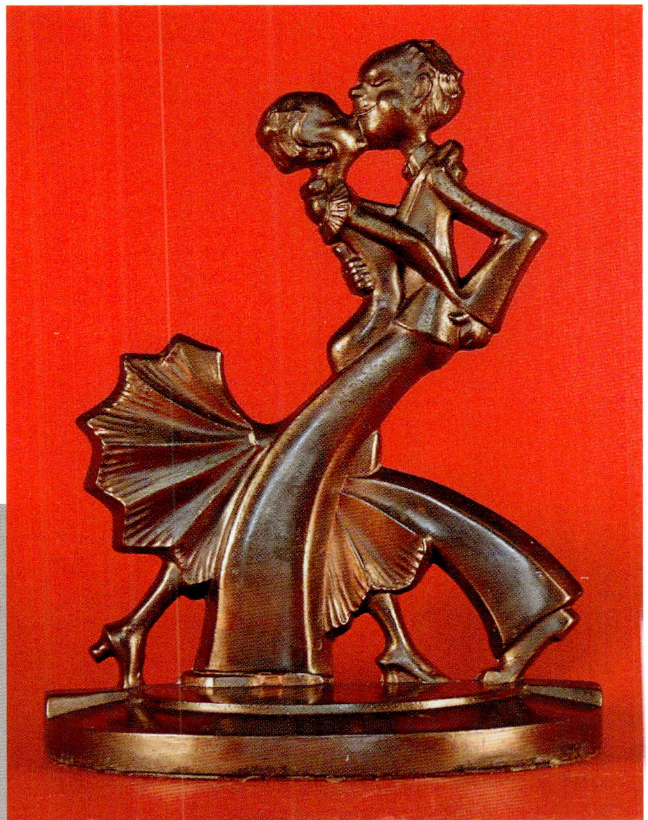

Figure 317. Geometric Dancers. 6.25", iron. Inscription: Shop mark of an acorn and no. 605. Circa 1935. Rarity 5. $240-360. Art Deco. American Modern. $240-360.

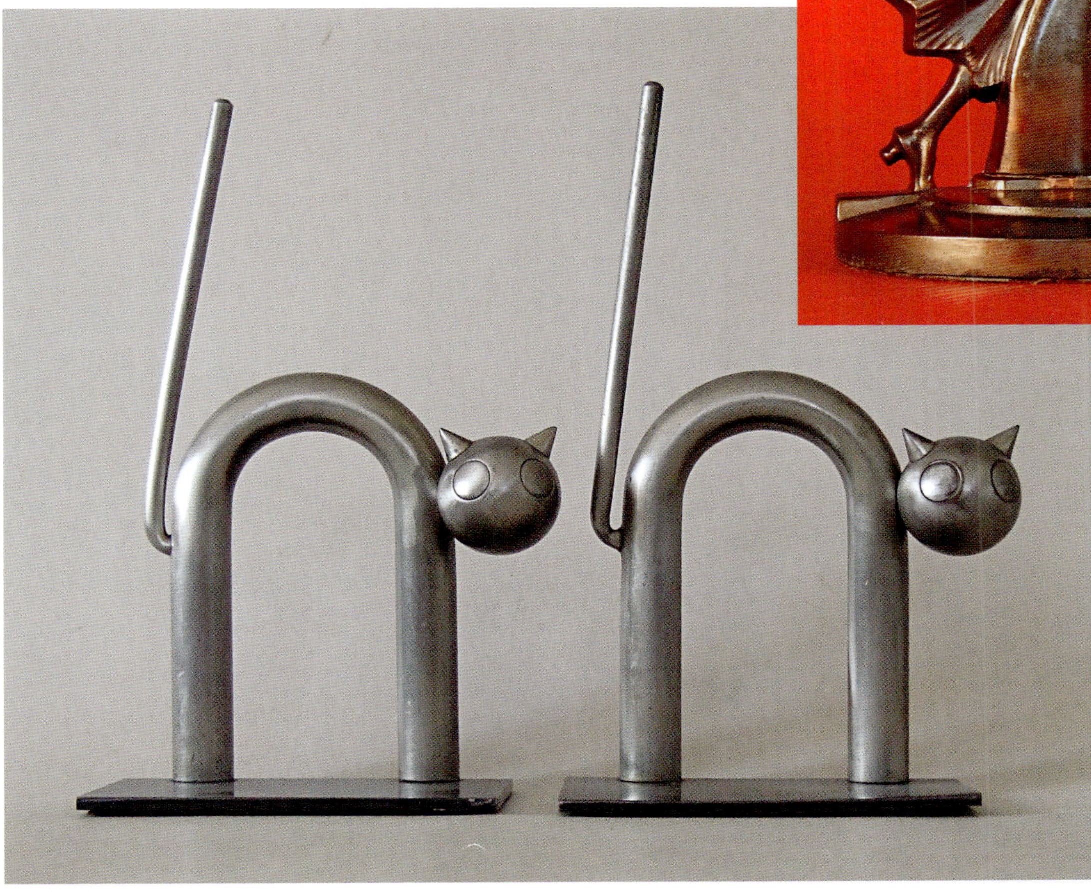

Figure 318. Tubular Cat. 7.25", copper. Inscription: Shop mark of Chase. Sculptor: Walter Von Nessen. Circa 1935. Rarity 2. Art Deco. American Modern. $660-990.

Figure 319. Hoops and Balls. 5.25", copper or brass? Inscription: Shop mark of Chase. Sculptor: Walter Von Nessen. Circa 1936. Rarity 2. Art Deco. American Modern. Very Geometric. There are many reproductions on the market and some with the shop mark. $240-360.

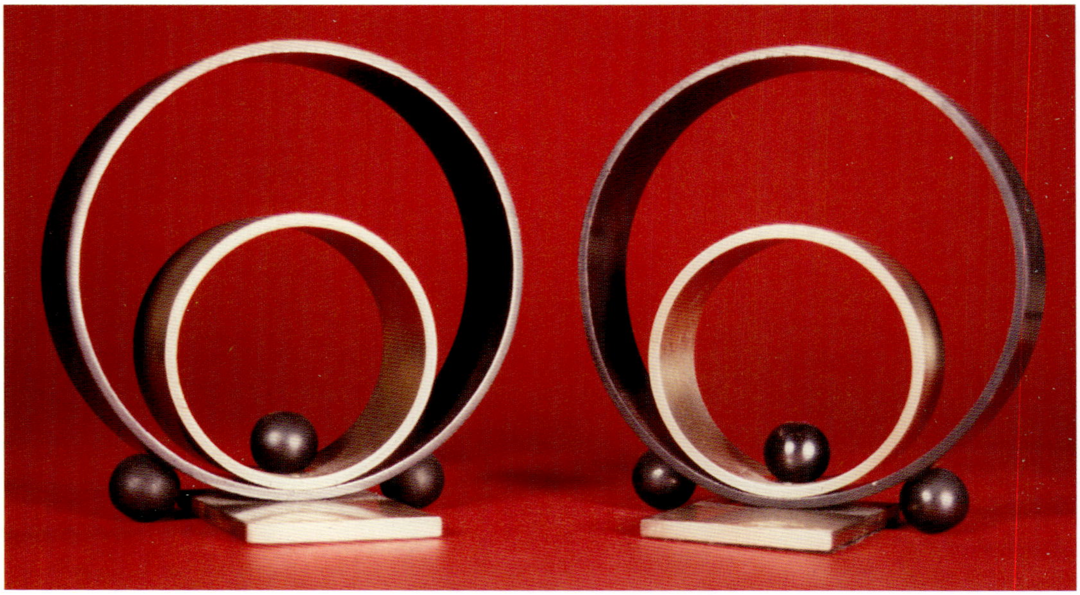

Figure 320. Rings. 5", gray metal. Circa 1936. Rarity 5. Art Deco. American Modern. Geometric. $120-180.

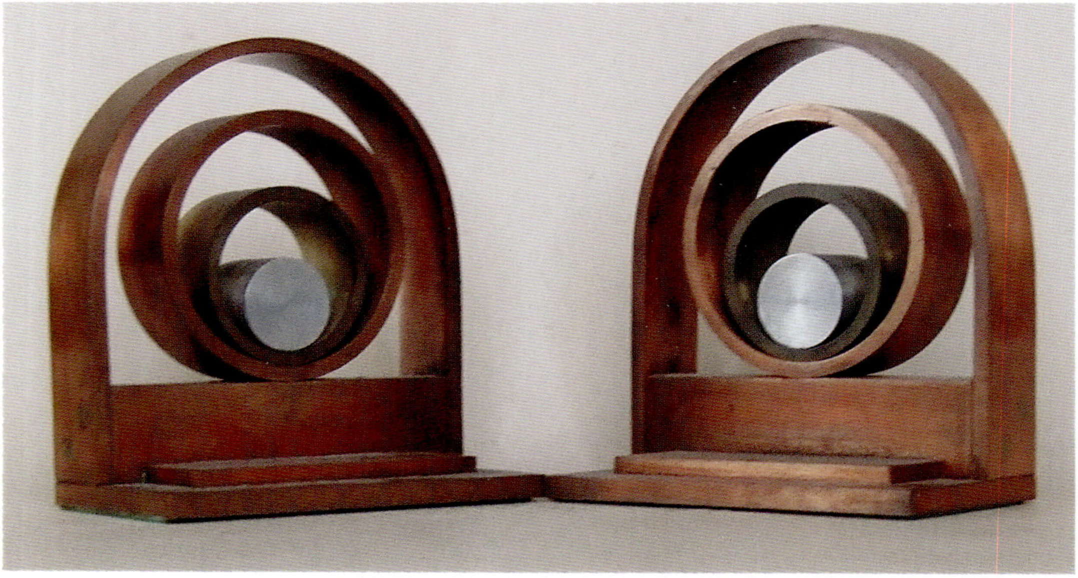

Figure 321. Tubular Elephant. 4.5", copper and Bakelite. Inscription: Shop mark of Chase Sculptor: Walter Von Nessen. Circa 1938. Rarity 2. Art Deco. American Modern. $400-600.

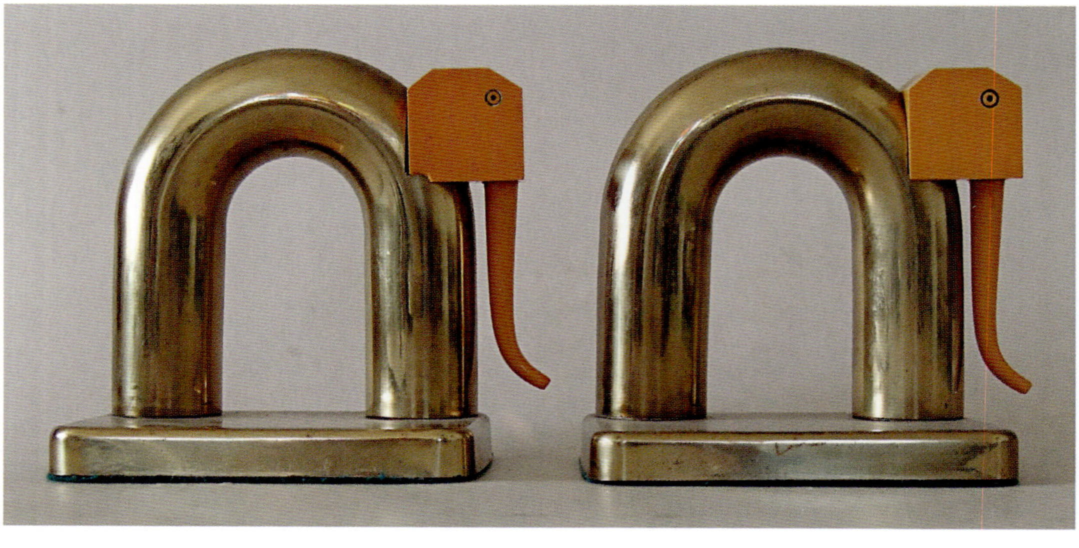

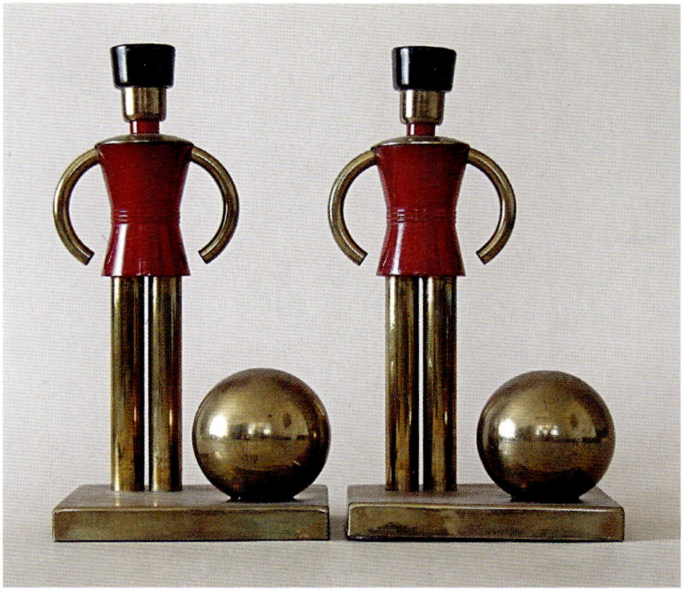

Figure 322. Tubular Sentinel. 7", copper and Bakelite. Inscription: Shop mark of Chase. Sculptor: Walter Von Nessen. Circa 1938. Rarity 2. Art Deco. American Modern. Very geometric. $440-652.

Figure 323. Hemisphere and Scroll. 4.75", wood and steel. Inscription: Revere, Rome, N.Y. Foundry: Revere Copper and Brass Co. Circa 1936. Rarity 3. Art Deco. American Modern. Very geometric. $80-120.

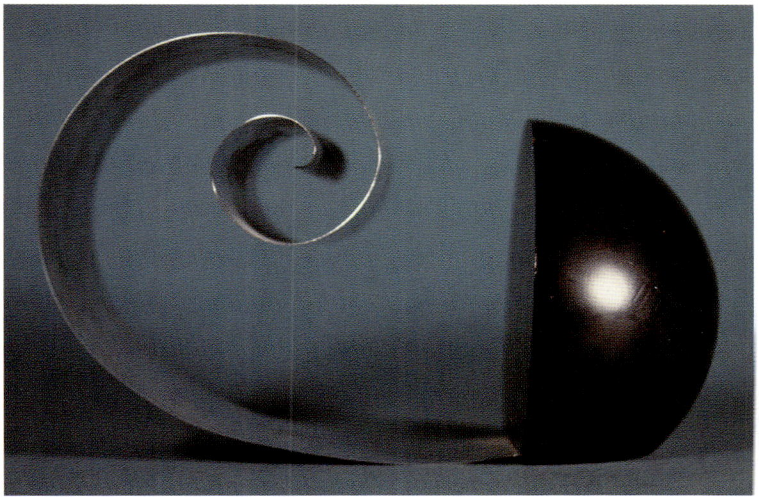

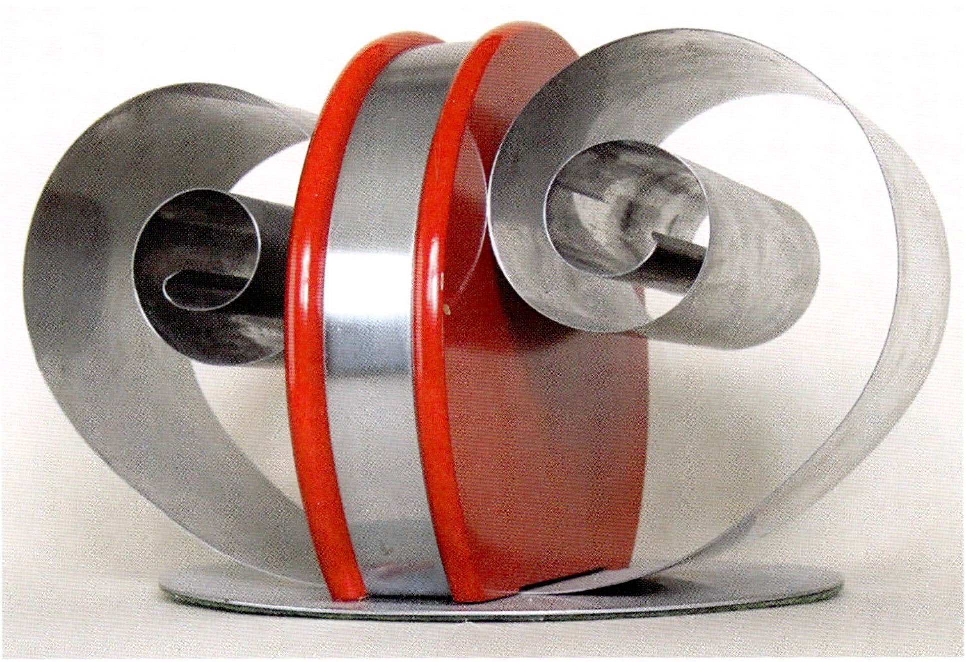

Figure 324. Double Scroll. 5", wood and steel. Inscription: Revere, Rome N.Y. Foundry: Revere Copper and Brass Co. Circa 1936. Rarity 2. $80-120. Art Deco. American Modern. Very geometric. $80-120.

Figure 325. Scroll and Barometer. 6.75", wood, gray metal, steel and barometer. Circa 1937. Rarity 5. Art Deco. American Modern. Very Geometric. $100-150.

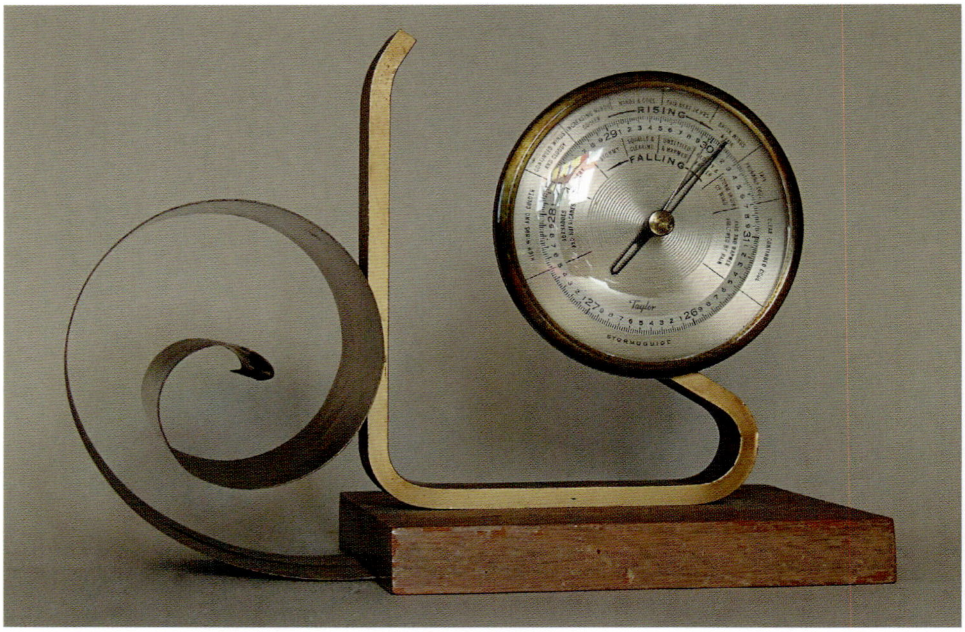

Figure 326. Abstract Skyscraper. 5.75", iron. Inscription: Shop mark of Bradley and Hubbard. Circa 1930. Rarity 2. Art Deco. American Modern. $240-360.

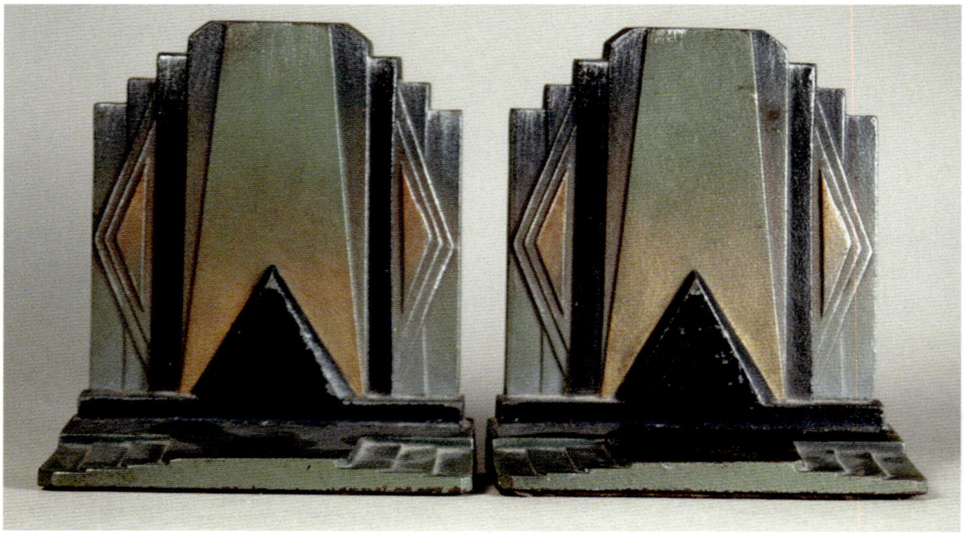

Figure 327. Skyscrapers. 4", brass and copper. Circa 1931. Rarity 5. Art Deco. American Modern. $80-120.

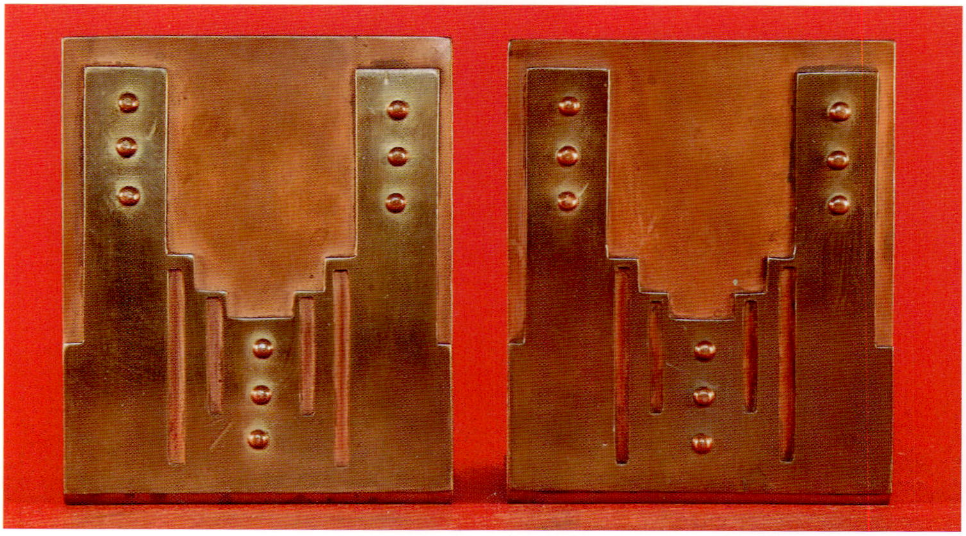

The Art Deco variants that dominated the United States in the 1930s were called "Hollywood Deco," "skyscraper Deco," "streamlined Moderne," "Moderne Deco," "streamlined Deco," and more, but the term American Modern covers them best. American Modern became a rage in the 1930s, and the intensity was promoted by advertising from manufacturers. Movies were very influential, and movie sets and costumes became very Deco. For example, from about 1931 to 1933, movies promoted an all-white room décor and put Jean Harlow with her platinum hair into movie scenes. White bookends appeared too. Hotels, diners, restaurants, theaters, and bookends became models for Deco. All of it worked together, and American Modern dominated fashion (Figures 328-338).

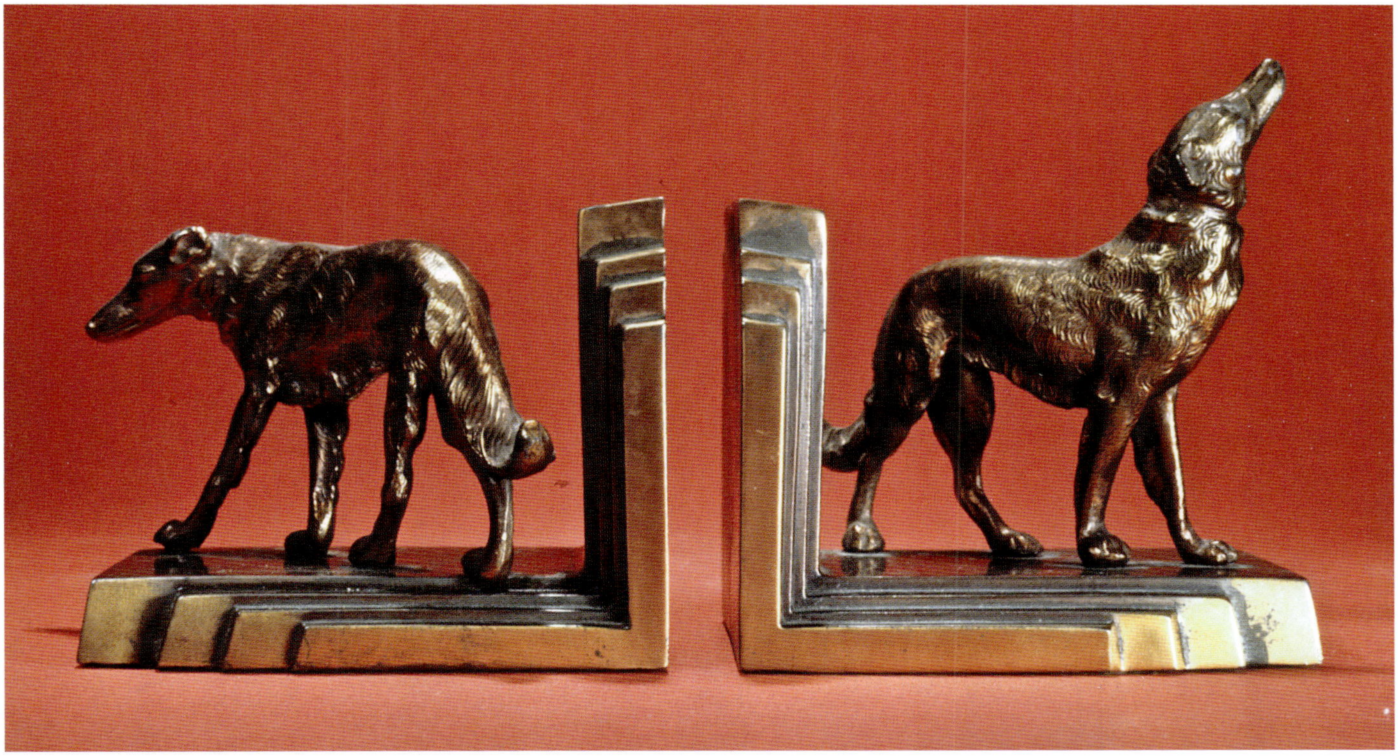

Figure 328. Afghan Hounds. 3.75", gray metal. Foundry: Ronson. Circa 1934. Rarity 3. Art Deco. American Modern. Available in chrome plating. $140-180.

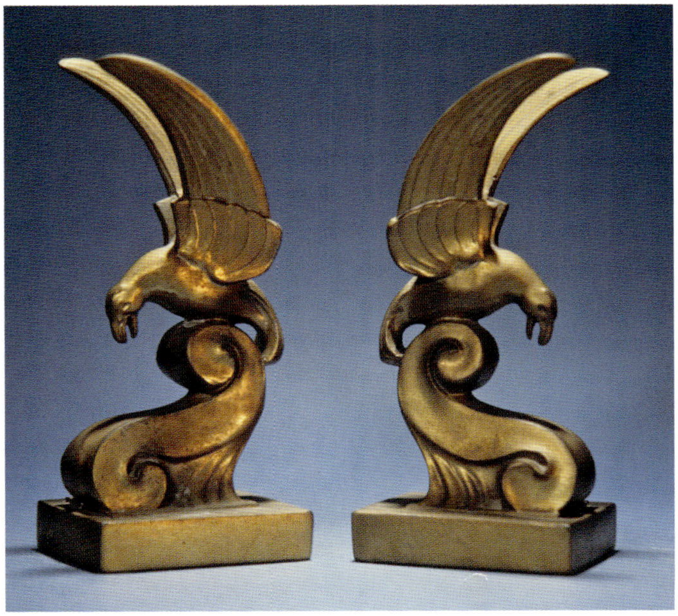

Figure 329. Perched Eagle. 7.5", gray metal. Circa 1934. Rarity 3. Art Deco. American Modern. $100-150.

Figure 330. Bright Greyhound. 5.75", gray metal. Inscription: Frankart Inc. Circa 1935. Rarity 4. Art Deco. Very American Modern. The greyhound is a symbol of speed. Note the stairstep base and support, the circular see-through, and the decorative shining surface. The turned head is a cubist touch. $440-652.

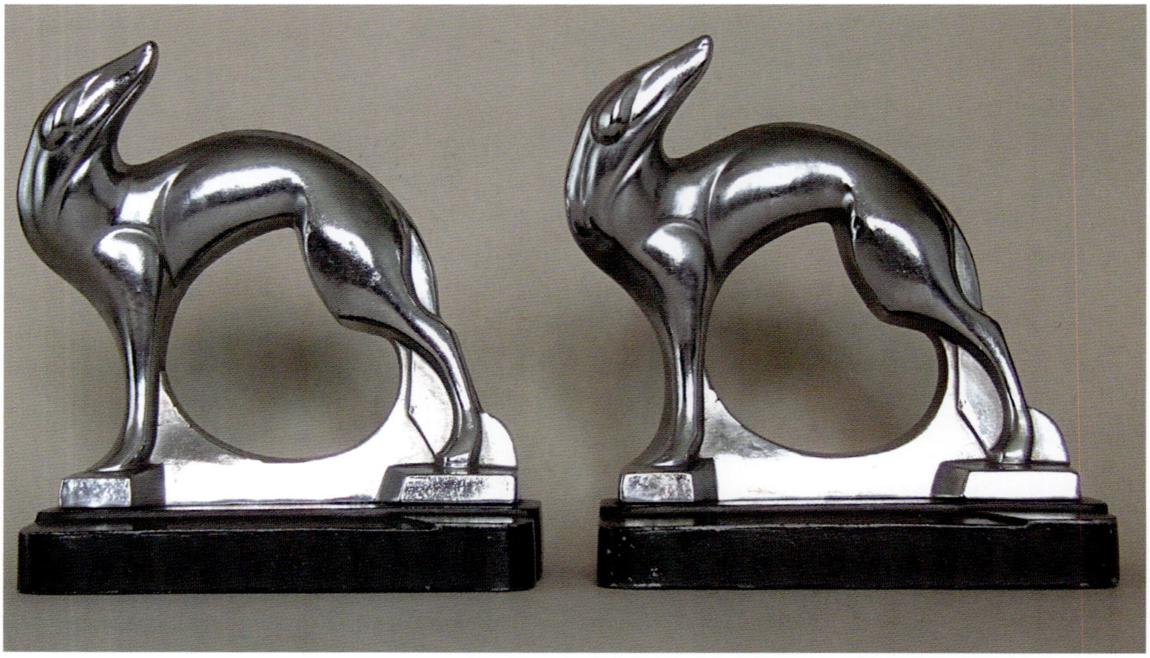

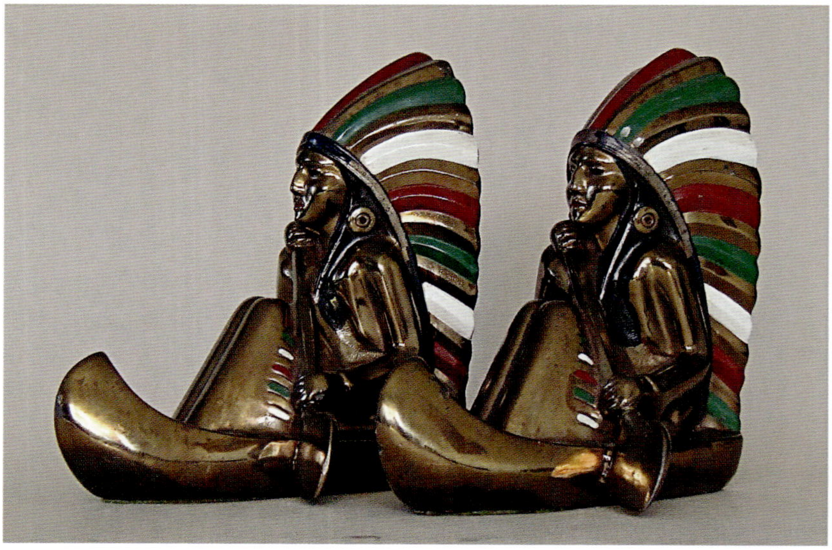

Figure 331. Birchbark Trip. 6.5", gray metal. Inscription: Ronson company label. Circa 1936. Rarity 2. Art Deco. Streamlining. American Modern. $240-370.

Figure 332. Neck and Neck. 5", gray metal. Inscription: Frankart Inc. Circa 1934. Rarity 2. $120-180. Art Deco. American Modern. $160-240.

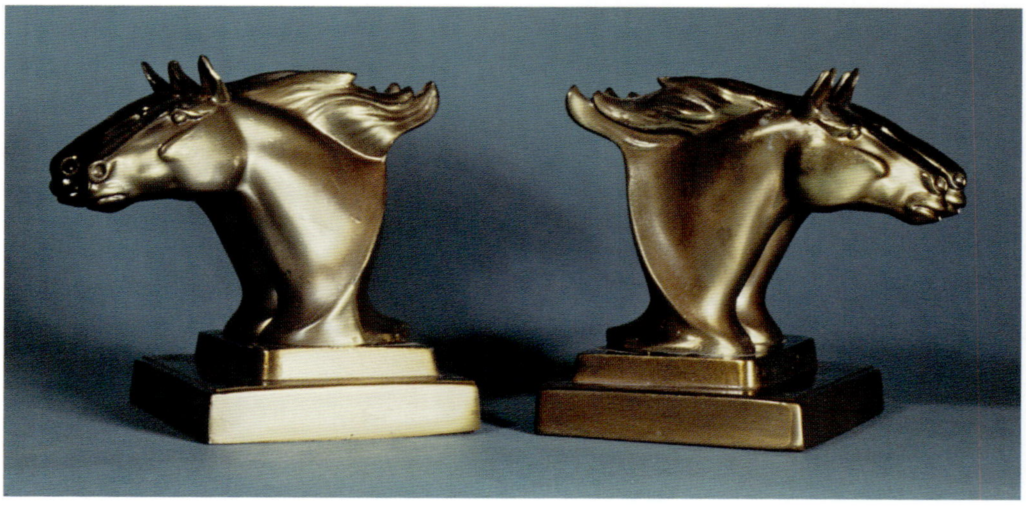

Figure 333. Party Girl. 4.5", gray metal, chrome plating. Circa 1930. Rarity 5. Art Deco. American Modern. $120-180.

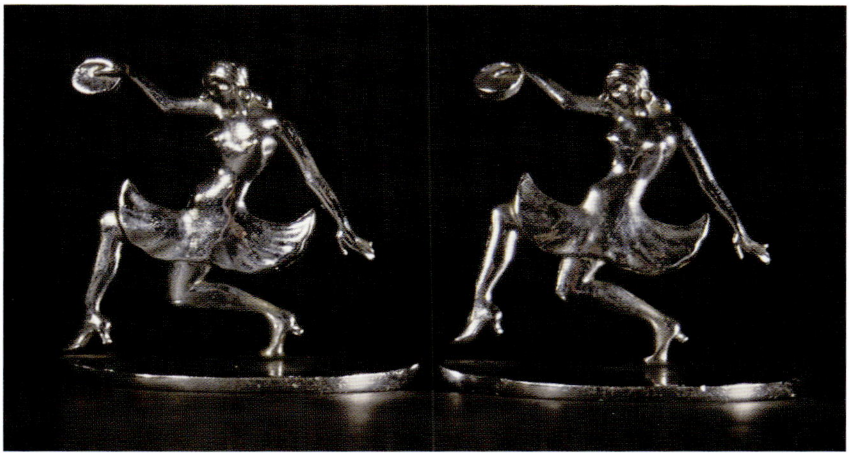

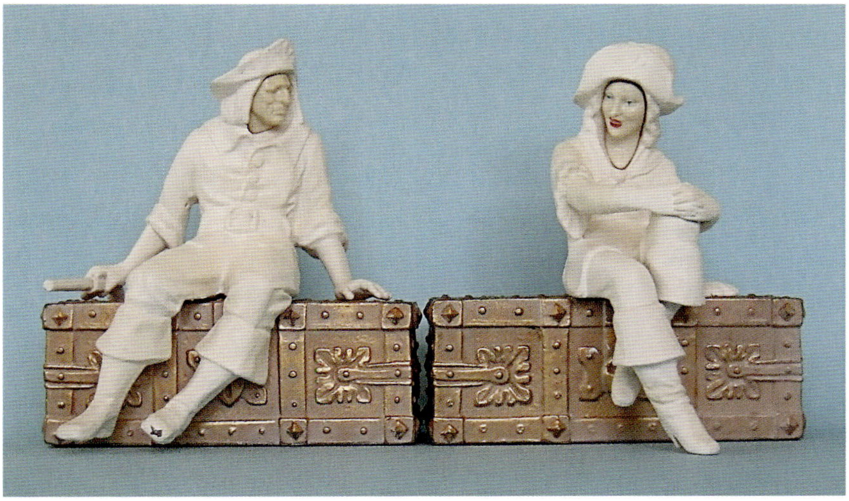

Figure 334. Pirates on Chests. 6.5", gray metal and celluloid. Foundry: Attrib. Hirsch Foundry. Circa 1932. Rarity 5. Art Deco. American Modern. Produced to match the all-white room décor of 1931-33. Bronze-colored pairs are more frequent. $275-420.

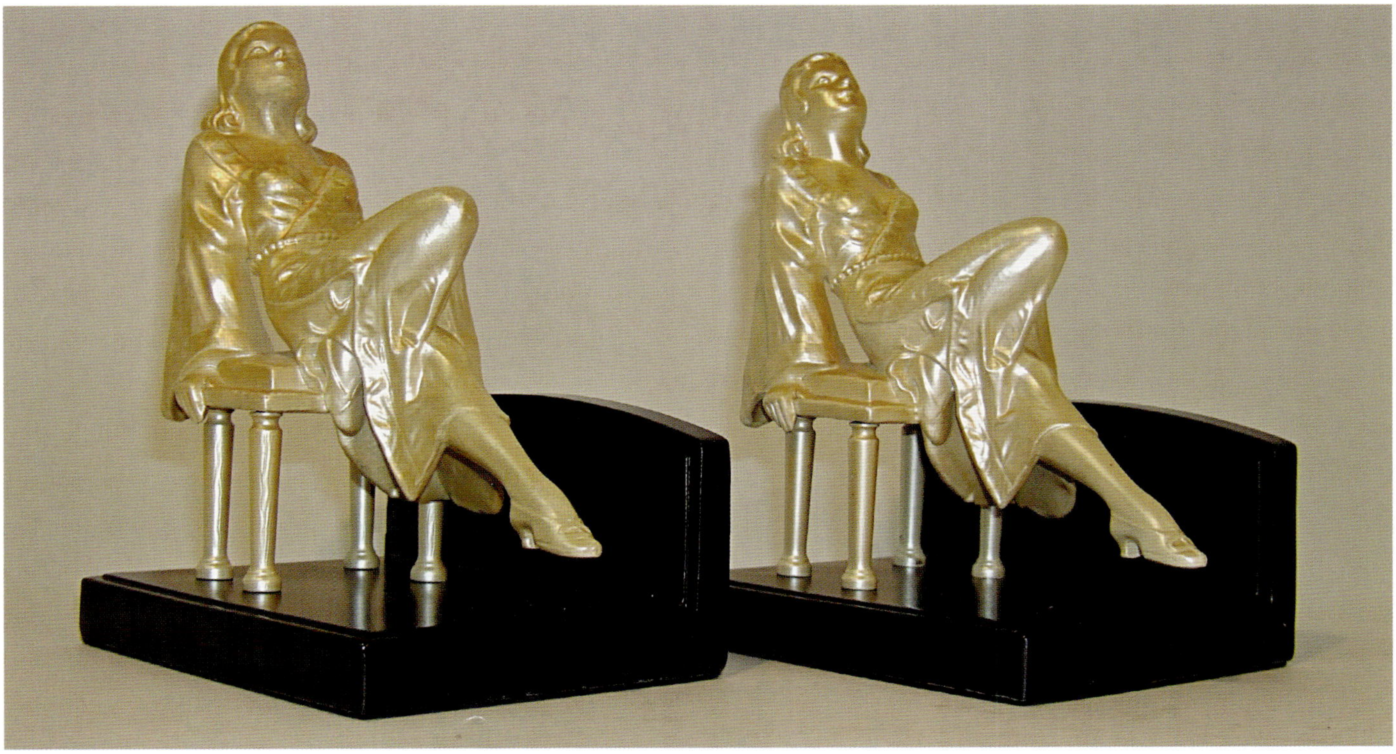

Figure 335. Jean Harlow. 6.75", gray metal. Inscription: Greist, New Haven. Foundry: Greist Man. Co. Circa 1933. Rarity 5. Art Deco. American Modern. Here she matches the all-white room décor of 1931-33. *By courtesy of Charles DeCosta, from his collection.* $600-700.

Skyscraper forms and streamlining were most popular, but there were other variations of American modern as well. For example, WPA Moderne or classic Moderne styling appeared on public buildings in the 1930s, related to Roosevelt's WPA (Works Progress Administration) effort. Images of men and women with the appearance of stripped classical figures were pictured, but were given touches to make them look racy and more modern. Decorations in Rockefeller Center in New York City and Hoover Dam in Arizona display good examples of this style, and souvenir bookends for Hoover Dam show them too (Figure 337). American Modern prospered until the time of World War II, when more somber considerations replaced the focus on fashion.

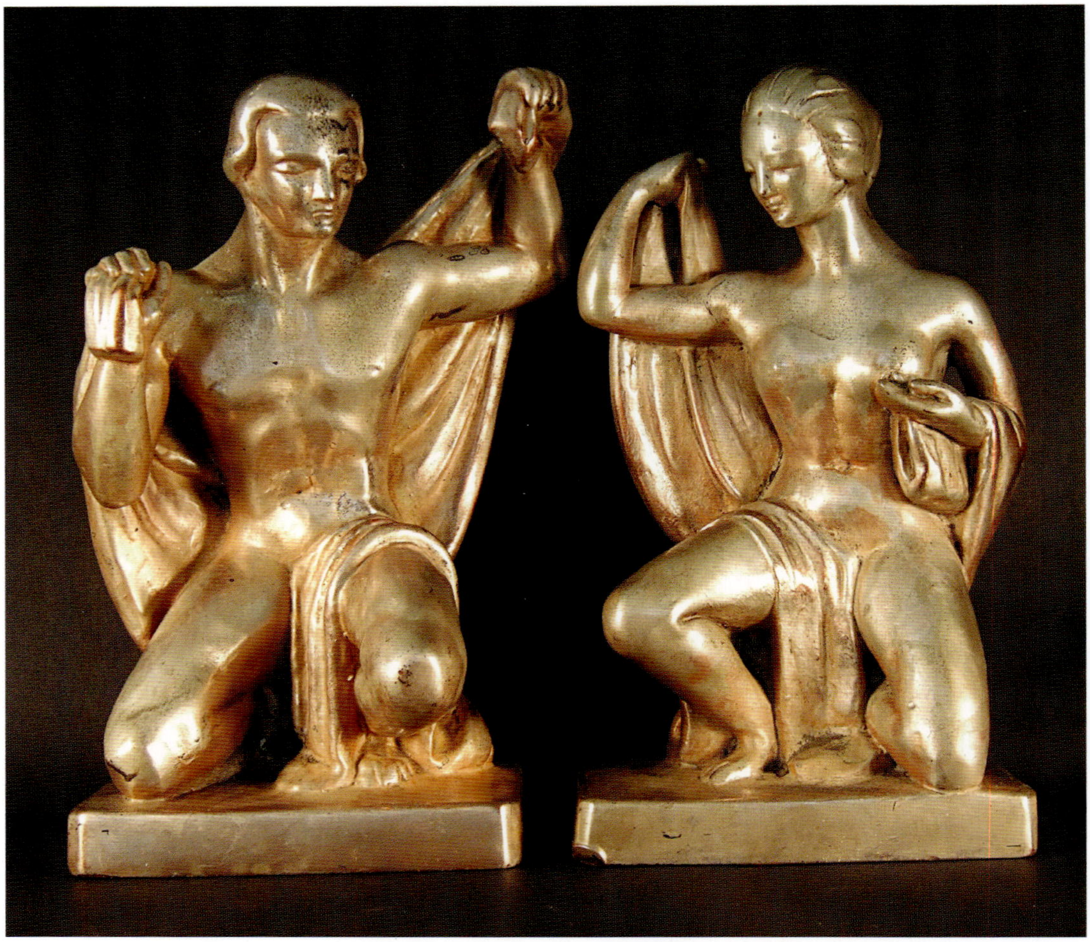

Figure 336. American Classic. 12.75", electroformed bronze. Inscription: Kupur. Foundry: Attrib. Frederick Cooper Studios. Sculptor: Attrib. Frederick Cooper. Circa 1935. Rarity 5. Art Deco. W.P.A. Modern. These are massive bookends, 15 lbs. per pair. $1,400-1,800.

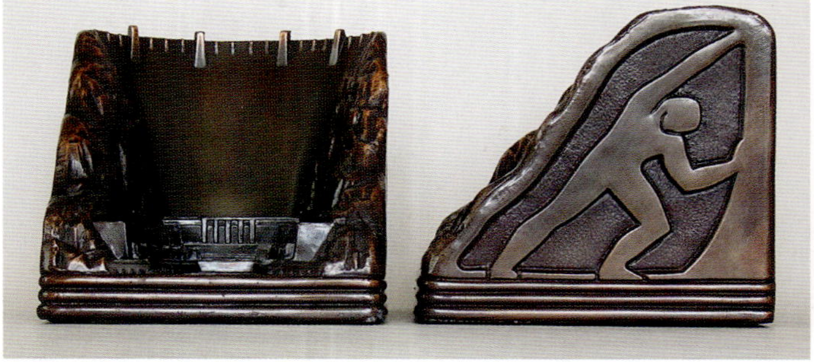

Figure 337. Hoover Dam. 4.5", gray metal. Foundry: Attrib. Dodge Inc. Circa 1936. Rarity 3. Art Deco. W.P.A. Modern. This is the tallest bookend of several issues. Note the silhouetted classical figures on the side of each bookend. There are many Art Deco decorations within the dam passageways. $400-600.

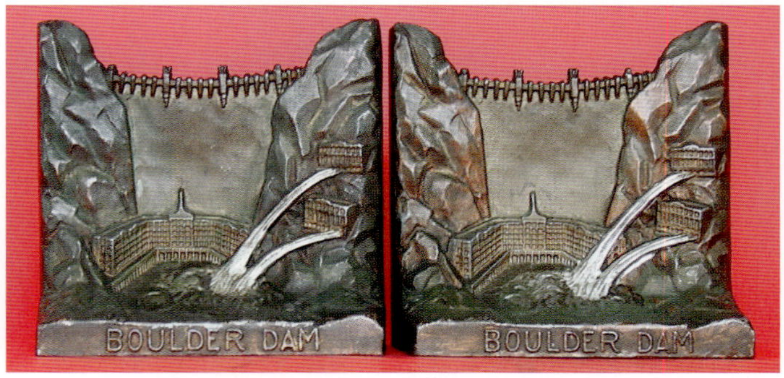

Figure 338. Boulder Dam in Construction. 4.75" Inscription: Paper tag reads Ashcraft Artcraft in Kelso Ca. Circa 1933. Rarity 5. Art Deco time period. $256-384.

Chapter 7

Mid-Century Modern Bookends

By the end of World War II, Art Deco was not an important style. A new style began, which became known as the 1950s style. This style can be seen as a reaction against Art Deco. It avoided geometry, especially avoiding sharp angles, and presented instead with soft, free forms, many frivolous and cute. Surfaces were ornamented and colorful. The 1950s style was eventually combined with the styles of the 1960s and 1970s to give us the style we call Mid-century Modern today. The 1960s contributed functional Scandinavian furniture designs, and liberated fashions like miniskirts and bikinis, which were quite unlike 1950s fashions, and Mid-century Modern objects have become very popular since that time.

New bookends from the 1950s, 1960s, and 1970s were relatively few and tended to look like 1950s material (Figures 339-340). During the 1960s, Op-Art became fashionable. This art was concerned with surface kinetics and effects to confuse vision. It did not remain popular very long, but we found one pair which qualifies. It has a surface on which it is difficult to focus (Figure 347).

The bookends we have seen from the 1980s and 1990s were not distinctive and generally have little appeal to collectors.

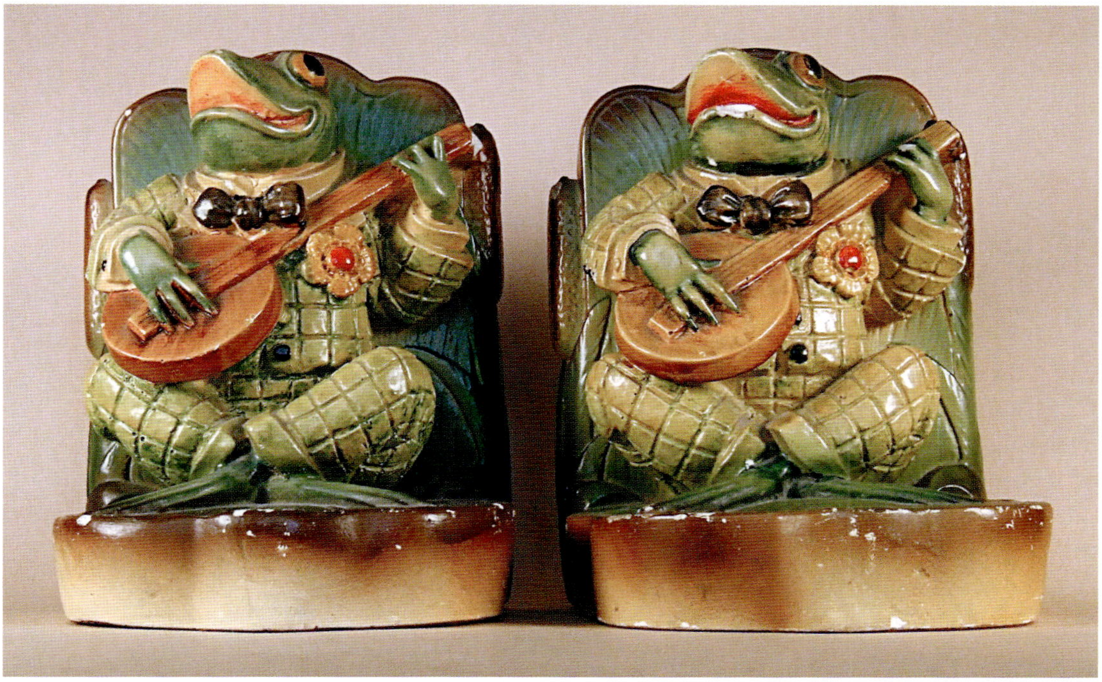

Figure 339. Frog and Banjo. 6.25", chalkware. Inscription: Stern Louis Co. and 1943. Rarity 5. Mid-century Modern. $28-42.

Figure 340. Oval Form. 4", bronze. Inscription: Aubock and Made in Austria. Sculptor: Carl Aubock. Circa 1955. Rarity 5. Mid-century Modern. $400-600.

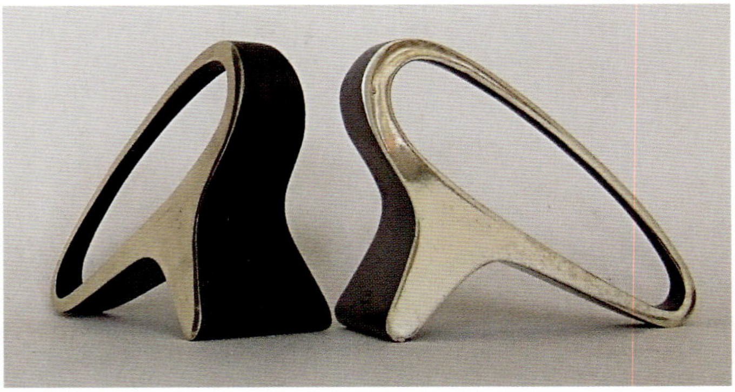

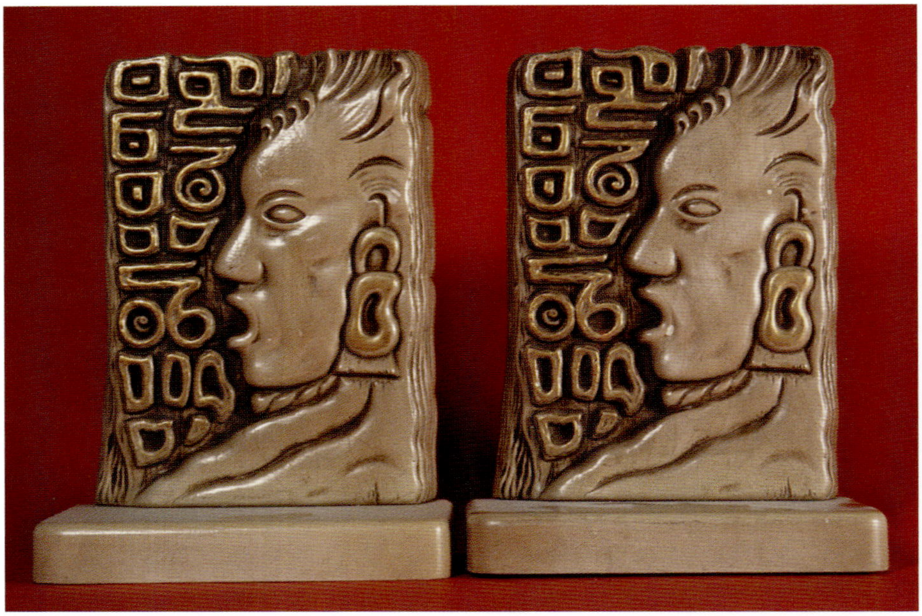

Figure 341. Polynesian. 7.25" Pressed wood. Inscription: Syroco Company label. Circa 1955. Rarity 5. Mid-century Modern. $60-90.

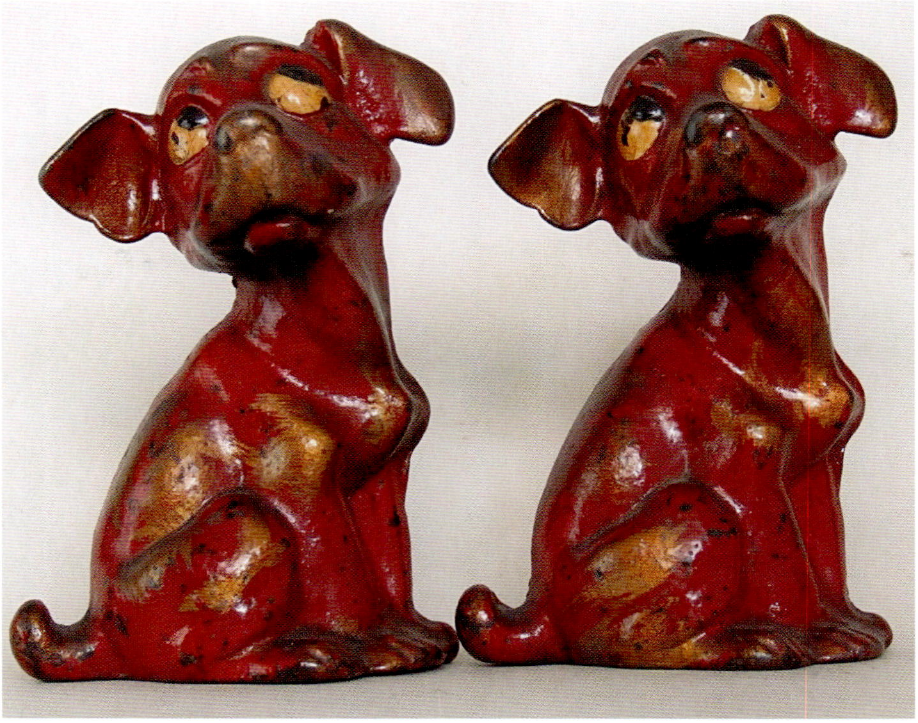

Figure 342. Cute Dogs. 5.5", iron. Inscription: 650. Foundry: Hubley Mfg. Co. Circa 1950. Rarity 3. Mid-century Modern. $120-180.

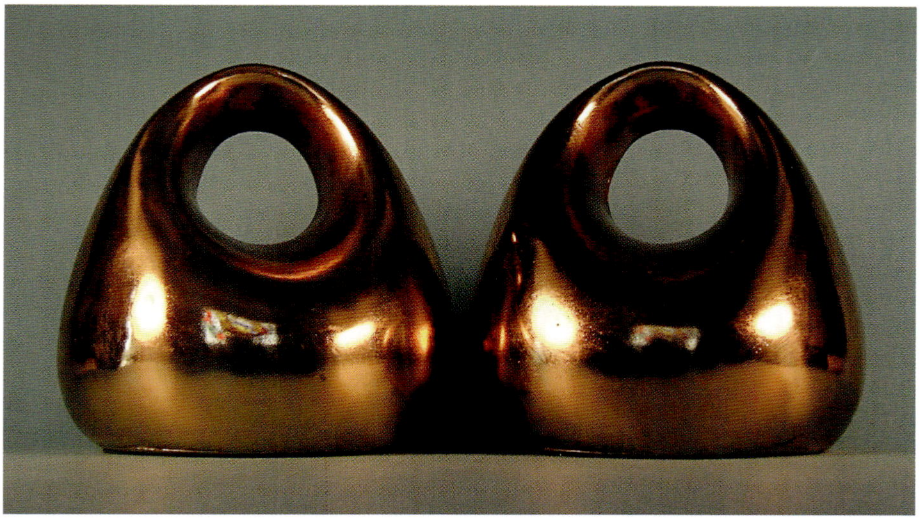

Figure 343. Free Form. 5.5", gray metal. Foundry: Ben Seibel. Sculptor: Ben Seibel. 1960. Rarity 2. Mid-century Modern. $120-180.

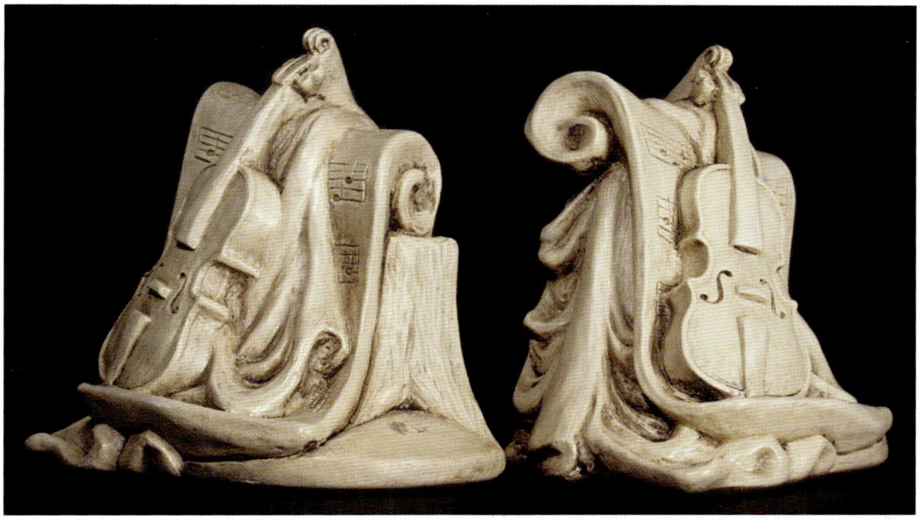

Figure 344. Violin. 7", hardened Plaster. Circa 1959. Rarity 2. Mid-century Modern. $60-90.

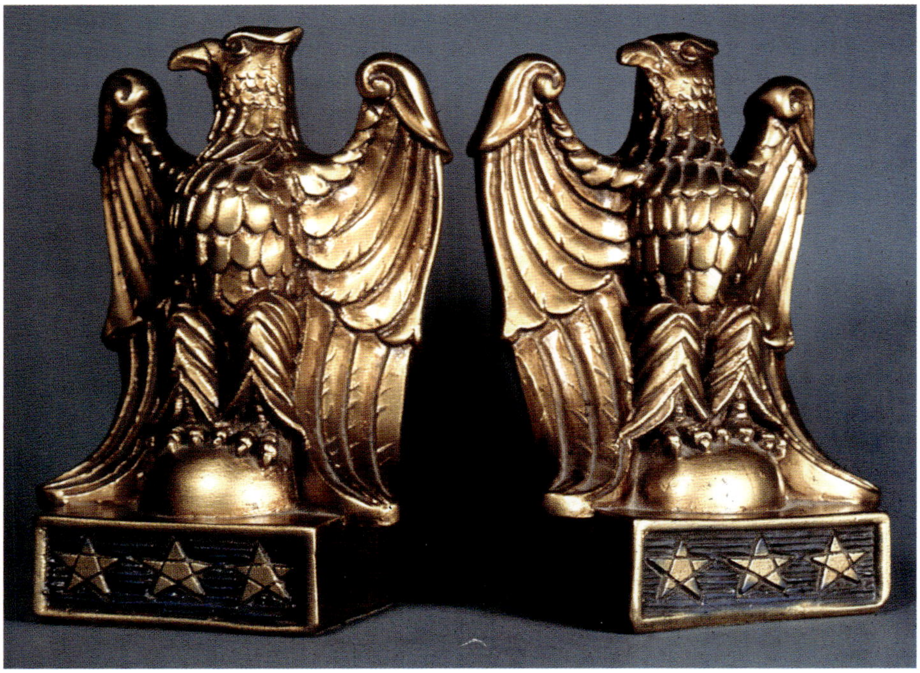

Figure 345. Heroic Eagle. 8.75", hardened plaster. Inscription: Progressive Art Products, 1965. Mid-century Modern. Rarity 3. $60-90.

Figure 346. Scandinavian Abstract. 7", teak. Circa 1974. Rarity 4. Mid-century Modern. $60-90.

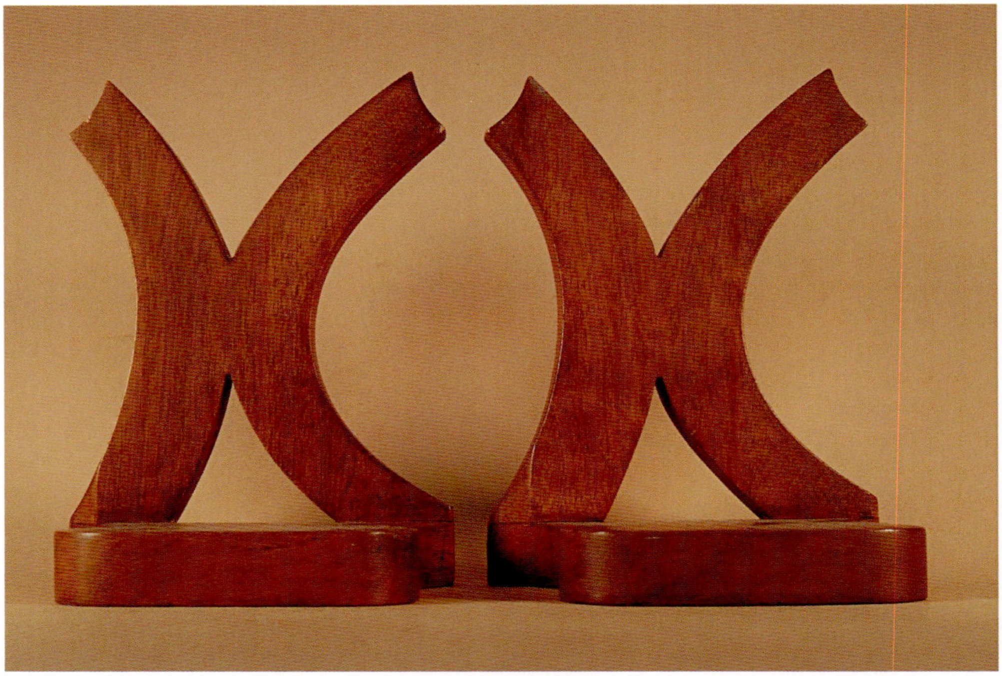

Figure 347. Ripples. 5", iron. Circa 1965. Rarity 5. Op-Art. $260-390.

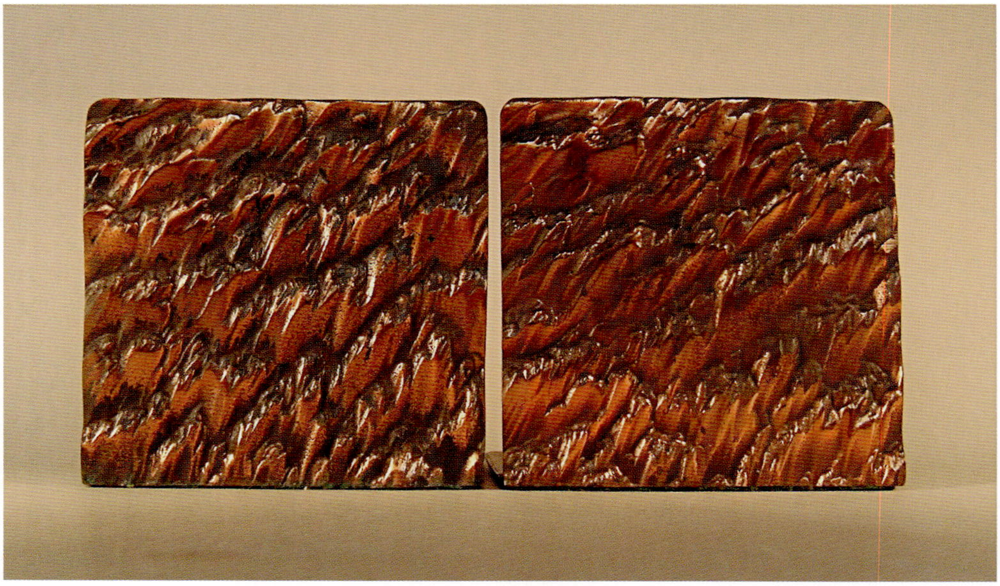

Figure 348. Iron Horse. 5.25", bronze. Inscription: 100th Anniversary1869-1969, Westinghouse Air Brake Co. Cast in Wilmerding Foundry, 1969. Rarity 3. Mid-century Modern. $200-300.

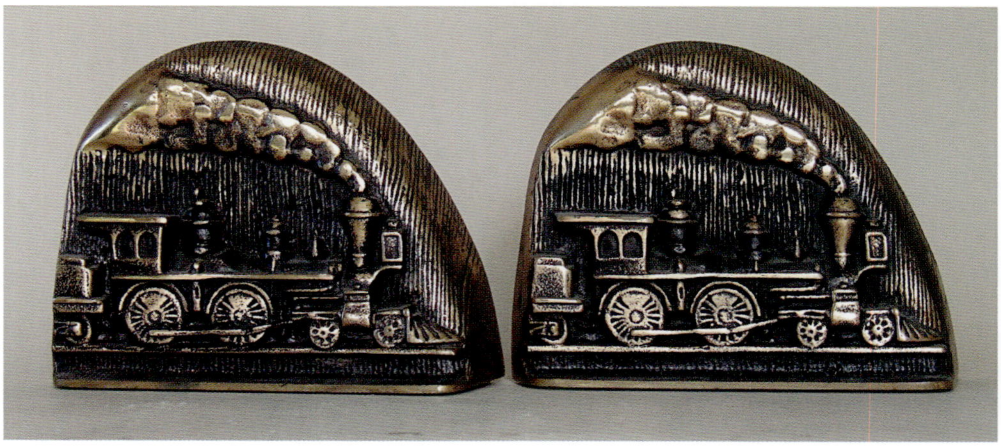

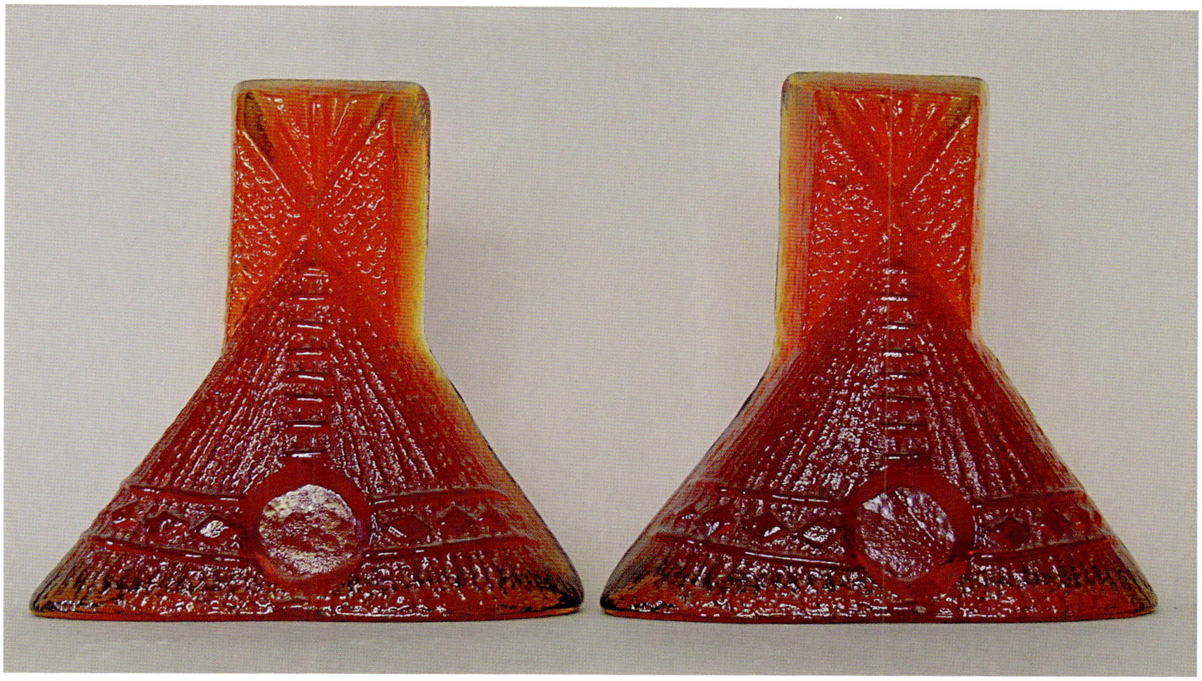

Figure 349. Teepee 6.25" Glass. Foundry: Blenko Glass Factory. Sculptor: Don Shepherd. 1970. Rarity. 2. $80-120. Art Deco. Abstract form.

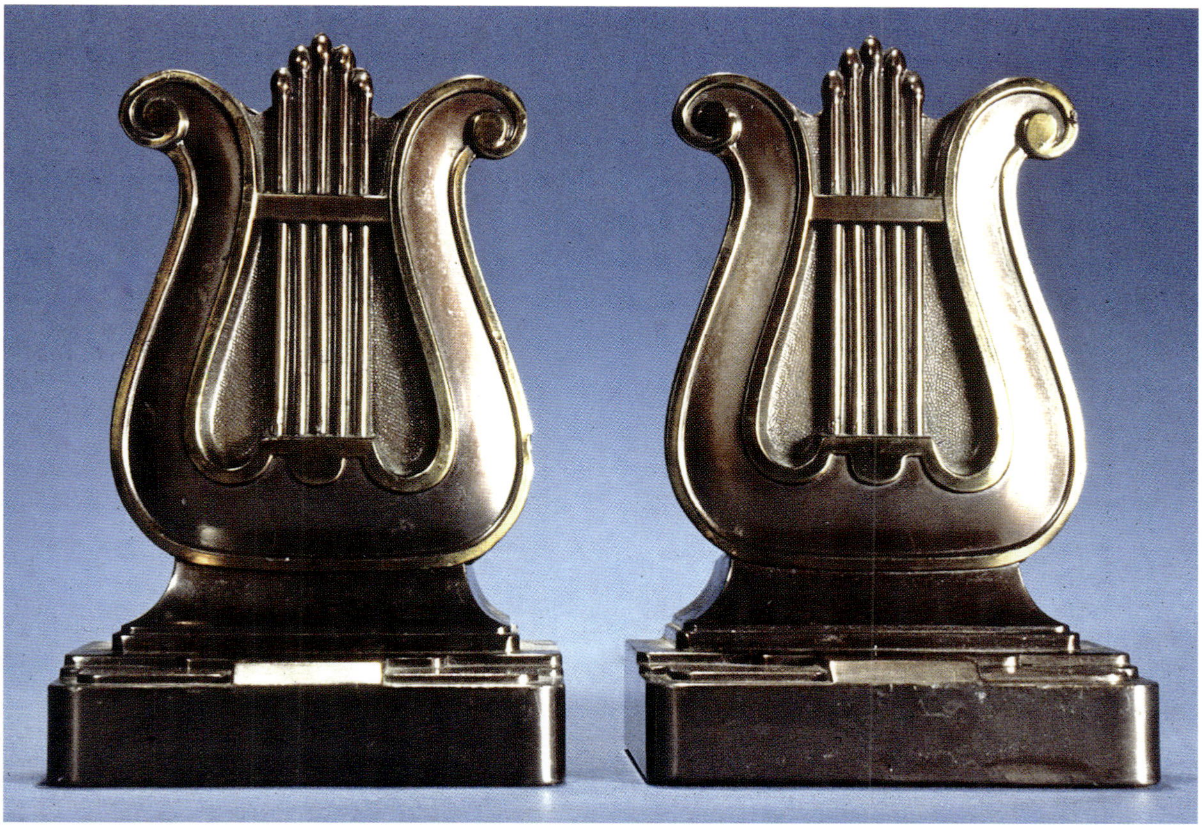

Figure 350. Lyre Form. 6", gray metal. Inscription PMC. Circa 1985. Rarity 4. $60-90. Art Moderne. Probably a reproduction of earlier bookends.

Chapter 8

Twenty-First Century Bookends

There were few bookends in Art Deco times that presented visions of the future, perhaps linked to the Futurism art style (1909-1914). Futurism began in Italy and spread chiefly to Russia and France. This movement projected speed, violence, and technology, and dealt with the problems that would accompany a mechanistic society. The movement clearly foreshadowed the Art Deco concerns with speed and machines. The Futurists embraced youth, vigor, and a new fresh world. Compared to 1909, a new world has arrived and we live in it today.

Futuristic thought was strengthened in America by the rise of science fiction, which has always painted a technological future. There are at least two pairs of early bookends that looked into a science fiction future.

The two pairs were apparently associated with the German science fiction film entitled *Metropolis*, which was directed by the eminent Fritz Lang, and was released in 1927. In the film, a female robot named Hel, wearing head gear, was shown encircled with pulsating rings and was given a human face. The bookend figure is metallic with a celluloid face. Its legs are encircled by rings and it is wearing a metallic helmet. We recognize her as Hel (Figure 351). The hero of the film is named Freder, and he and other characters are forced to manipulate long switches and pointers. The bookends show a man in a nest of long objects which seem to be abstract pointers and switches. He wears futuristic garb and we recognize him as Freder (Figure 352) The movie is now a classic and the restored version can be rented through the Internet.

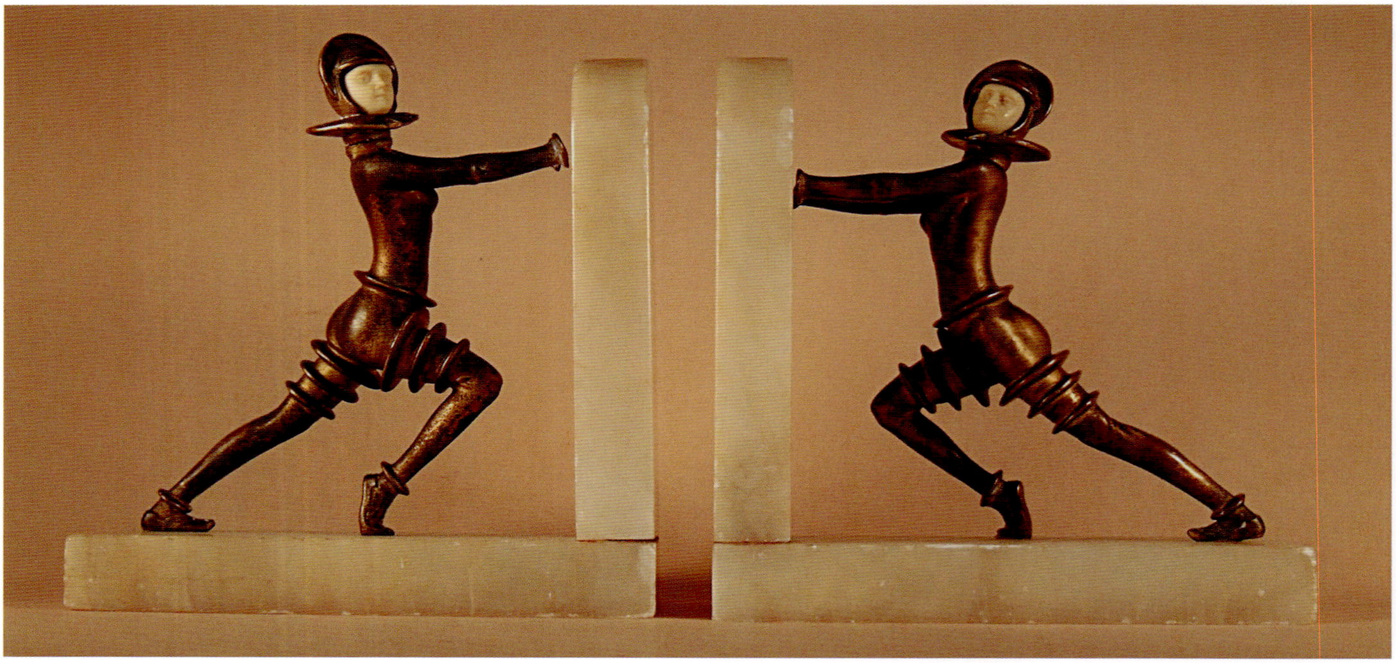

Figure 351. Hel. 6.25", bronze and celluloid. Foundry: Attrib. Hirsch foundry. Circa 1928. Rarity 4. Futuristic. Each bookend should have celluloid face and hands. The hands are missing in this pair. See text above for a discussion of the film *Metropolis*. $400-600.

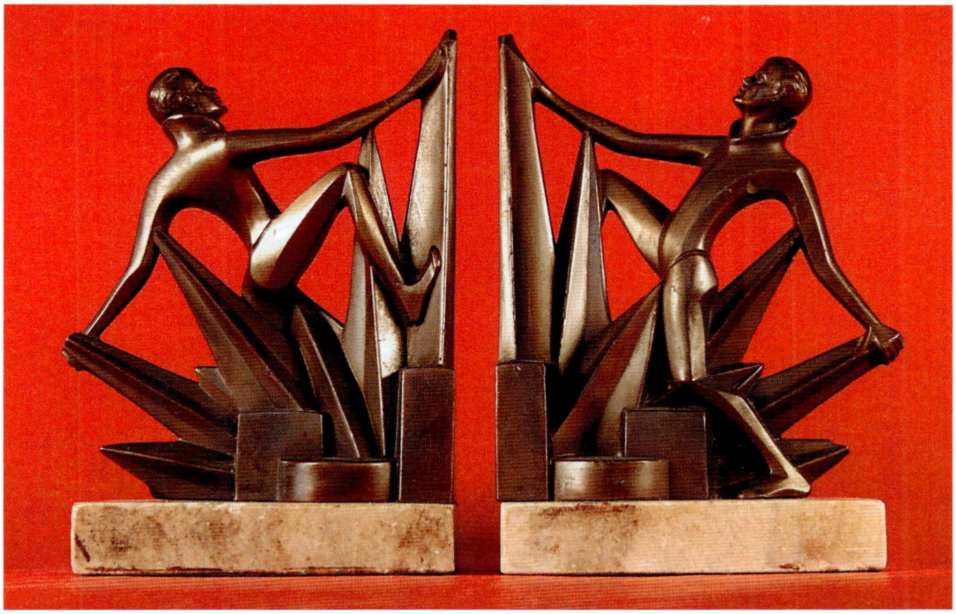

Figure 352. Freder. 6", gray metal, marble. Foundry: Attrib. Hirsch Foundry. Circa 1928. Rarity 4. Futuristic. See text above for a discussion of the film *Metropolis*. $360-540.

The twenty-first century is with us now, but we do not live with a dominant Futuristic art style or any new and dominant fashion. One might have expected to be dressed in futuristic clothing styles by now, but this has not happened. The popular American focus now seems to be celebrity worship and fancy, and recent bookends document these concerns. The most popular subject for new bookends has become movie and comic strip figures that have been raised to celebrity status. Now we find bookends featuring heroes like Spider Man, Wonder Woman, Superman, Harry Potter, and more (Figure 353). Toys frequently become collectibles and antiques. People recognize these celebrity figures as their toys. Many are already expensive collectibles and they will presumably be antiques of the future.

• • • •

We see a bright future for bookends. Bookends are familiar items to most people today, and provide decorative additions to most any room décor as garnitures or book and DVD supports. After all, books and DVDs supported by bookends appropriate to the room décor are far more interesting than books or DVDs supported by flower vases or odds and ends, so we recommend bookends to all interior designers.

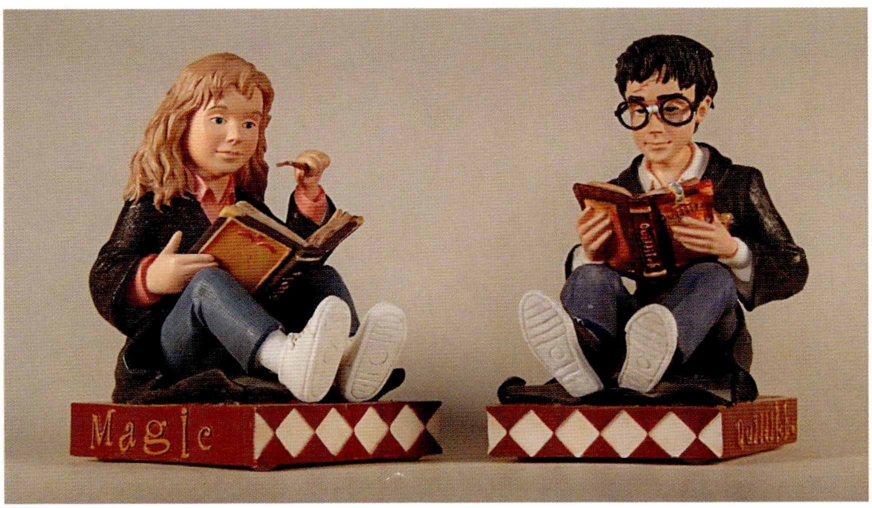

Figure 353. Harry Potter and Hermione. 5.5" Resin. Foundry: Made in China. Distributed by Enesco. 2000. Rarity 1. Aesthetic. $48-72.

Chapter 9

Bookend Manufacturers

The companies that manufacture bookends are important to the value of bookends. Companies with sterling reputations, like Tiffany and Co., for example, are very well known to antique collectors, and the shop mark Tiffany & Company adds value to any object, including bookends. Objects from little known manufacturers must be evaluated without reference to their makers. It is not practical to attempt to list all the companies that have produced bookends, but we can list some of the companies that made appreciable numbers or notable bookends.

Albany Foundry: Little is known about this foundry except it began operations in 1866. The bookends we have seen are all cast iron in low relief and nicely painted.

The W.D. Allen Tool & Machinery Co.: Opened in 1869 in Chicago, it is probably still in business. It is not primarily a bookend foundry but has produced small metal items in the past.

Armor Bronze Inc: Active from 1916 to about 1920 as the National Metalizing Co. and then Armor Bronze Inc. in New York City and again as Armor Bronze Inc. from 1934 to 1948 in Taunton, Massachusetts. They produced bronze bookends by an electroforming process. Many different sets were produced, and all of them are very collectible today, although the Taunton products were less durable than the earlier ones.

Bradley and Hubbard Manufacturing Company (1852-1940): Popularly called B&H, Bradley and Hubbard was based in Meriden, Connecticut. Originally clockmakers, they expanded to producing oil burning lamps and architectural and household objects of many kinds. By the 1890s their name was already associated with high-quality and artistic merit. Most of the bookends that we have seen were made of iron, sometimes with attached gray metal figures, or, rarely, made of bronze. Most are easy to identify because they bear a Bradley and Hubbard logo (B&H) as a shop mark or a company label, but the artists' names are usually missing. Two shop marks were used, one with the mark B&H within a circle, and another with a lamp and the name Bradley and Hubbard within a triangle. Most of their bookends are in the Victorian style, but they did issue some admirable bookends in other styles. Today we find most B&H bookends in very good condition, attesting to their reputation for high quality. Apparently, their paint was baked on and, therefore long lasting. B&H bookends command good prices today for their good reputation and their durability.

California Bell Company: The California Bell Company was started by Mrs. A.S.C. Forbes in 1914. She had been producing El Camino Real bells and possibly other objects since 1906. We attribute some early unmarked bookends (Figs. 217, 218) to this source because their metal resembles that of the souvenir bells from California Bell.

California Clay Products (1923-1932): This company was based in South Gate, California. It produced an assortment of high-quality clay products with at least one design of solid-cast bookends.

Chase Brass and Copper Company (1876-1976): Based in Waterbury Connecticut, it produced bookends from about 1930 to 1941 in Art deco, American modern style. These are readily identified by their logo, an impressed Orion figure, on each bookend. Bookends were made from copper and brass from outstanding designs by Walter Von Nessen and Russel Wright. Chase bookends have a loyal following among Art deco collectors and, therefore, command relatively high prices.

The Connecticut Foundry Company (1919-1983): Having made a variety of cast iron products, there are a great many bookends with the Connecticut Foundry shop mark in circulation, most all of them of copper-flashed iron and cast in low relief. Prices for these are generally low because they are not very decorative.

Craftsman Studios: This arts and crafts shop began in Los Angeles in 1910 and used a shop mark of Craftsman Studios with an anvil and hammer and probably the initials L.A. They moved to Laguna Beach, California in 1925 with the same shop mark but Laguna Beach substituted for L.A. They changed hands in 1932 and then used a shop mark with the anvil and hammer with Craftsman Inc or Craftsman Co. The shop went out of business in about 1955. This information was supplied by Jane Janz.

Crescent Metal Works (1924-?): The company produced gray metal bookends of very attractive designs, and these sell well today.

Dodge Inc: Principally a manufacturer of trophies, this can be seen on most of their bookends today as the two-tone brown shiny finishes usually associated with trophies. Started in Chicago in the mid-1920s, the foundry later operated from Los Angeles and other cities and was still active in the late 1940s. They produced the dog bookends entitled Buddy, with a distinctive mottled brown finish, for McClelland Barclay, the eminent designer. All the Dodge bookends we know are gray metal and the finishes tend to deteriorate.

Enesco: Originally a part of N. Shure Co., a catalog sales company, Enesco became independent in 1958, but is not a foundry. It is a multinational company that distributes gifts and home-décor products as well as figurines and collectibles, chiefly in resin and porcelain.

Flint Faience and Tile Company (1921- 1933): This company operated in Flint, Michigan, and produced a variety of tiles and other ceramic products. They produced at least three designs for bookends.

Forest Craft Guild (1907-1917): The Forest Craft Guild began in Grand Rapids, Michigan, as a metal workshop to make Arts & Crafts objects. From these dates we know that all of their bookends were made at an early time. Their bookends are very rare and command relatively high prices today. Their shop mark was frequently below the felt, which is unusual for bookends.

Frankart Inc: Arthur Frankenberg began producing bookends and other metalware in 1921, and incorporated as Frankart in 1924. He designed and sculpted graceful nudes which were very well received. Frankenberg left the company in 1930 and founded the short-lived Quoizel Metal Art Company. His early bookends were well made from gray metal and have generally survived in good condition, sometimes with some deterioration of the paint. Many of the Frankart bookends produced in the 1930s were pot metal, corroded readily, and are found today in very poor condition or about to deteriorate. Frankart's early good reputation stayed with the company, and today Frankart products have a very good reputation among collectors; the demand keeps their bookend prices high. Reproductions and repainted pairs made in later times are commonplace so buyers must be wary.

The Gift House (1928-1934): This company distributed numerous, chiefly iron, bookends from their New York City location. The bookends were made in an associated foundry, Bronze Met.

Goberg Metallwarenfabrik: This metal workshop functioned between 1909 and 1920 and possibly earlier and later, in Germany and in Rasper, Austria. The shop belonged to Hugo Berger and produced household items chiefly of pressed iron in the Modernist style. Shop marks include Goberg, Rasper, Austria, Made in Germany, and possibly others.

The Gorham Company [Gorham Founders] (1831-present). The Gorham company has a stellar reputation for silver and bronze metalware. itissued over 100 different pairs of bookends early in the twentieth century, chiefly of Victorian style. Bookends marked Gorham are always finely cast and command premium prices.

Greist Manufacturing Company (1894-?): This company opened in New Haven, Connecticut, and produced sewing machine parts and many other objects.

Grenfell Mission: The Grenfell Missions opened in Labrador in 1893 and in Newfoundland in 1894. The missions gave medical care to the natives and promoted industrialization and handicrafts, including carpentry and the weaving of hooked rugs. Today, the early handicrafts of the mission, including bookends, are expensive folk art.

Griffoul Foundry: Active in the 1920s through the 1950s, it produced bronze and probably some iron bookends by a proprietary sand-casting process brought from France and were frequently signed by the sculptor. The more recent bookends are uniformly well cast and finished, and very desirable to collectors.

Heintz Art Metal Shop (1906-1919): This Arts & Crafts metal shop produced L-shaped bronze bookends faced with sterling silver applied decorations. The appearance of the surface of the bronze was considered very important and various surfaces were patinated by secret procedures. Each bookend bore an impressed Heintz logo of the stylized company name within a diamond, which identifies them today. These bookends are desirable antiques and sell for hundreds of dollars per pair today.

J B Hirsch foundry (1907-?): This foundry was based in New York City and produced numerous desirable bookends. Some bookends were marked with an impressed JBH. Hirsch bookends were sometimes produced with bases of metal, black bakelite, or marble, and sometimes with celluloid parts. Celluloid was used primarily in 1931 and 1932.

W. H. Howell Co.: Opened in Geneva, Illinois, in 1862, this company is important because it made bookends as early as 1906 (Figure 120) All the bookends we have seen were cast iron in low relief, and most of them portrayed Western subject material, but the pair in Figure 245 is Art Moderne.

Hubley Manufacturing Company (1894-1978): Well known for their production of iron toys and household items, they produced bookends, nearly all from iron, with a three digit serial number on the rear, and sometimes signed by the artist. In our experience, the three digit number on iron bookends conclusively identifies Hubley. The iron was durable but the paint was not, despite a durable primer coat.

Hummel: Hummel figurines, generally from porcelain, have been produced since about 1935. They became important to a group of Hummel collectors and can easily be found in antique shops today. Authentic bookends bear a variety of shop marks, including the signature MI Hummel, WG, Goebel, a V, and sometimes a bee. Hummel pieces were produced into the 1960s and values can be found in specialty listings. Their popularity seems to be diminishing

Jarvie Shop (1906-1920): Robert Jarvie (1865-?) started the Jarvie shop in Chicago, where he made and sold metal items, including candlesticks, bookends, and other Arts & Crafts-style items marked with the name of the shop. A lot of two pairs of these bookends sold at auction for $10,500 in 2011.

Jenfred-Ware: We only know that this company was active in the 1970s in New York City. It was probably a distributor and not a foundry.

Jennings Brothers: This foundry began in about 1891 in Bridgeport, Connecticut, and was ended in the 1950s. The foundry produced metal household items, including bookends. Jennings brothers bookends were made of bronze plate over a layer of gray metal. Some were silver plated. The designs were admirable and the durability was very good, so Jennings Brothers bookends are well-respected today. Jennings Brothers bookends are marked by a raised lettering J.B., usually followed by a four-digit serial number which is sometimes erroneously interpreted as a date.

Judd Company: Active from 1827 to about 1954, bookends were among the products they made, generally of painted iron. Bookslides, bookracks, and free standing bookends of good quality were produced. Very many Judd bookends have survived, and they can be identified by a four digit serial number shop mark. The four digit number is occasionally preceded by a zero.

K&O Metal Novelties Company (Kronheim and Oldenbusch): Active in New York City from 1895 to 1939, the company made household objects, including bookends. All the bookends from K&O that we have seen were made from gray metal. Most of their bookends were in gaudy colors. The foundry apparently aimed for novelty, as their name implies. Many of the bookends we find today are poorly cast and with deteriorated finishes.

Kathodian Bronze Works (KBW), (Art Bronz): This foundry was active in New York City from about 1900 to about 1916. They made electroformed bookends and other figurines and made light ammunition in a New Jersey plant. Artistic designs and early dates make their bookends valuable. Bookends act as cathodes in the electroform process and this probably accounts for the name Kathodian.

Handel Lamps: The Handel Company was established in 1876 in Meriden, Connecticut. They made very high quality lamps and other decorative household objects. Their lamps are still highly collectible, and their bookends are of interest to collectors as well.

Littlestown Hardware and Foundry Co. Inc. (Littco): This foundry began in Littlestown, Pennsylvania in 1916. The bookends were iron, substantial, good quality, and produced until about 1941.

Marion Bronze: The Marion Bronze foundry was active from about 1922 to about 1971. Bookends were produced by electroforming. Early bookends bore a bronzed finish and were unremarkable. Beginning in the 1950s, they issued superlative bookends, still electroformed bronze, but with faultless enamel finishes, very colorful, decorative, and durable. Many of their bookends were somewhat-modified reproductions, but this does not necessarily detract from their desirability. Their shop mark was a conjoined MB.

Mason Mfg. Co.: Active from 1929 to 1945 in Los Angeles, California, they produced Spanish revival furniture and accessories from alder wood, iron, rope, leather, and paint. This furniture has become very collectible in recent years and sells for high prices. Their product lines are known as Monterey. Their shop mark is a horseshoe, but it does not appear on all pieces.

Paul Mori and Sons: This foundry was active in New York City from about 1915 to about 1930. Their bookends were electroformed bronze. Their products were marked Paul Mori, Galvano Bronze, Gotham Art Bronze Inc., or left unmarked. The bookends were of good quality. Some were reproduced by other foundries so identification may be difficult unless they were marked.

NAL Co.: Nothing is known about this foundry, but it was active at an early date. Figure 47 shows bookends they produced in 1903.

Nemadji: The Nemadji Tile and Pottery Co. began in Moose Lake, Minnesota, in 1923 and closed in 2002. They produced items which they imagined resembled ancient Indian designs.

Nuart: Nuart was a New York City foundry that produced numerous pairs of gray metal bookends in the 1920s and 1930s. Because of its name it is sometimes confused with Frankart. The bookends, and especially the finishes, were not very durable, but pairs that survived in good condition are attractive to collectors.

Philadelphia Manufacturing Company: This company made bookends in Philadelphia and then moved to Lakeland, Florida, in 1972-73, and took the abbreviation PMC. PMC bookends are usually gray metal, not of the highest quality and identified by a shop mark or a company label that specifies PMC. Many PMC bookends are reproductions of those from earlier foundries including Jennings Brothers bookends and may even be marked J.B. with the four digit serial number so collectors must be careful. Many PMC finishes are a shiny gold color and tarnish rapidly so collectors may not prefer them.

Pompeian Bronze Company: Active in New York City in the 1920s and probably earlier, it produced electroformed bookends and then gray-metal bookends generally marked with the company name, the company label, or the initials PB, and sometimes signed by the artist. Their bookends are prized for beautiful lacquer finishes.

Roman Bronze Works (1897-?): This foundry was the first one in the United States to employ the lost-wax technique. It developed into the preeminent foundry in the country for casting for sculptors, and was used by the foremost American sculptors early in the twentieth century. The foundry cast Tiffany's bronze articles and lamp bases as well. Any bookends marked Roman Bronze Works or RBW are automatically very valuable because of their impeccable forms and the foundry's stellar reputation.

Ronson: Initiated by Louis V. Aronson as the Art Metal Works (AMW) in 1886 in New York City, it moved to Newark, New Jersey the following year and eventually produced a number of high-quality household objects, including bookends. The bookends were marked AMW, Ronson (trademarked in 1910), LV Aronson, Louis V Aronson, or LVA. Bookends were carefully made from gray metal and given a great variety of attractive finishes. Today they are very desirable collectors' items, prized for their high quality and colorful appearances. Ronson cigarette lighters are well known and collectible as well.

Rookwood Pottery (1880-1960): This company produced high-quality Arts & Crafts style ceramic items in Cincinnati. After 1960 the company changed ownership and location and again now exists in Cincinnati. Its hand-thrown objects are the most desirable, but after about 1905 they produced chiefly slip-cast objects. Slip cast and solid cast bookends are available for collectors at relatively high prices. Bookends are marked with a shop mark that includes the name Rookwood.

Roseville Pottery Company (1892-1954): Founded in Zanesville, Ohio, it was very successful and produced a great many Arts & Crafts style pots and bookends. Nearly all the bookends are marked with the word Roseville, so identification is straightforward.

Roycroft: The Roycroft metal workshop is described in Chapter 4, page 65. Roycroft bookends are dated by the shop marks (see Appendix)

The Sarsaparilla Foundry: Active in West New York, New Jersey, from about 1950 to about 1999, they made metal objects, including reproductions of Art Deco bookends. The bookends we have seen are good quality, gray metal, accurate reproductions.

The SilverCrest Company: This company was begun by Fredrick Smith, sales manager at Heintz Art Metal Shop in 1919. He purchased Heintz and set up his own company, presumably with knowledge of the Heintz trade secrets. Known as Smith Metal Arts as well as SilverCrest, the company produced, bronze, L-shaped bookends, usually with sterling silver decorative elements on the bookend faces. The Smith bookends could be mistaken for Heintz, and are of equal quality, but Heintz used a shopmark with their initials and SilverCrest used one showing the word SilverCrest. Smith's company was active from about 1919 to the present time.

Carl Sorenson: Carl Sorenson operated a metal workshop in Philadelphia in about 1914. The shop produced copper desk accessories, including bookends, all desirable today. The shop mark was an S within a C and should not be confused with Craftsman Studios.

The Syracuse Ornamental Corporation (Syroco): Begun in1890, their bookends were generally made around the time of the Second World War from a resin mixed with wax and wood flour. The casting was not durable and they do not sell for high prices today.

Tiffany Studios: Tiffany Studios was established in New York City by Louis Comfort Tiffany in 1900. Bookends were produced apparently between 1916 and 1918. Louis Tiffany is regarded as the foremost producer of Art Nouveau items in America, and all bookends and all items marked Tiffany are desirable and expensive. Many Tiffany bookends were L-shaped, low relief parts of desk sets, but a small number were made as bookracks and also as figural forms.

Verona: Little is known about the company that produced bookends marked Verona, but it was possibly the Verona Foundry in Illinois. All of the Verona bookends we have seen were cast iron and only one was polychrome.

Weidlich Brothers (1901-1950): The Weidlich Brothers Manufacturing Company was established in Bridgeport, Connecticut. They became respected for their high-quality silver items and produced high-quality bookends as well. These bookends were bronze, which was plated over gray metal in a format like that seen in Jennings Brothers' bookends. The shop mark on their bookends is WB inside an outline of a shield and should not be confused with the Warner Brother's mark. Today their bookends are found in very good condition and sought by knowledgeable collectors.

Wiener Workstatte: The Wiener Workstatte was active from 1903 to 1932 in Vienna, Austria, New York City, and other locations. Its designers and craftsmen contributed to the Modernist style. Karl Hagenauer worked with this group and his bookends are very collectible today.

Chapter 10

Bookend Artists

Gregory Seymour Allen (1884-1934): Allen was born in New Jersey, but moved to Glendale, California, in 1925. Allen studied under Gutzon Borglum, H. M. Shrady, and Philip Martini. He sculpted bookends for several foundries, including Hubley, Armor Bronze, and Judd. Allen is known as an artist of the West. He particularly liked to portray horses and these appear in many of his works. He is listed in many publications, including *Who's Who in American Art,1936-1939* and *Davenport's 2003-4*.

Carl Aubock (1900-1957 and (1924-1993): There were several Carl Aubocks from the same family who were sculptors and designers in Austria. They produced chiefly Austrian Modernist objects from their own shop, and are well-regarded today.

McClelland Barclay (1891-1942): Barclay studied painting in Chicago and New York City under H. C. Ives, George Bridgman, and Thomas Fogarty, and eventually became the best-known illustrator of the early twentieth century, especially for pin-up art. He produced several different pairs of bookends, usually signed, which are highly collectible today because of his excellent reputation. He started his own foundry in the late 1930s. Listed in *Fielding, Mallett,* and *Davenport's 2003-4*.

Antoine Barye (1796-1875): Barye is considered the finest sculptor of the French Animaliers school. He studied under F. J. Bosio and Antoine-Jean Gros. Barye depicted wild animals for his chief productions and he became very well known. Some of his works were eventually held by the Louvre. A number of his animal sculptures have been reproduced for bookends. Listed in *Bermans, Mallett,* and *Davenport's 2003-4*.

Hugo Berger: Born in the late nineteenth century, date of death unknown. He designed German Modernist items for his metal-working shop, Goberg Metallwarenfabrik, which was associated with Schmalkalden, Thuringia, Germany and Rasper, Austria.

Edgar Brandt (1880-1960): Brandt began his career designing mortars for the French infantry. He graduated to designing and producing wrought iron objects in Art Nouveau style and later became the leading exponent of Art deco metalwork. Brandt received extensive recognition during his lifetime, and his bookends are very highly priced today. Listed in *Davenport's 2003-4*.

Gladys (Edwards) Brown (twentieth century): Brown was a painter, sculptor, and author. She was an authority on Arabian horses and sculpted numerous bookends of horses for Dodge Inc. Listed in *Who's Who, Davenport's 2003-4*.

Henri Crenier (1873-1948): Crenier was born in France and was trained there as a sculptor under Alexandre Falguiere at the Ecole des Beaux-Arts. After emigrating to the United States he received many honors for his work. Listed in *Fieldings, Hughes, Mallett, Who's Who in American Art,* and *Davenport's 2003-4.*

James Earle (Earl) Fraser (1878-1953): Fraser was born in Minnesota and grew up in North Dakota where he became familiar with the American West. He was recognized at an early age for his talent as a sculptor. He studied at the Art Institute of Chicago under Richard Brock and later taught sculpture with leading artists of his time and received many important commissions for public sculptures during his lifetime. Fraser designed the buffalo nickel for the U.S. Treasury. His best known work is *The End of the Trail,* which has been reproduced very many times as bookends, often with wrong titles. *Listed in Bermans, Fieldings, Mallett, Samuels, Who's Who*, and *Davenport's 2003-4*.

Karl Hagenauer (1898-1956): See Wiener Workstatte in list of manufacturers. Listed in *Davenport's 2003-4*.

Harriet Frishmuth (1880-1980): She studied under Auguste Rodin and at the Art Student's League in New York City. Frishmuth became very well known for sculptures of supple, athletic young women. She is listed in *Bermans, Fieldings, Mallett,* and *Davenport's 2003-4*.

Gerda Gerdago (1906-2004): Born in Vienna. She produced many expensive objects in bronze and ivory. Listed in *Bermans, Sculptor,* and *Davenports 2003-4*.

Karl H. Gruppe (1893-1982): Gruppe was born in Rochester, New York. After studying in Holland, beginning at age 12, he studied at the Art Students league with Karl Bitter and eventually became the chief sculptor for the

New York Department of Parks from 1934 to 1937. He worked chiefly in marble and bronze, but also painted portraits. Listed in *Bermans, Fielding, Mallett, Who's Who,* and *Davenport's 2003-4.*

Paul Herzel (1876-1956): Herzel was born in Germany and grew up in Missouri. He studied at the Beaux Arts Institute of Design in New York City. He worked as a sculptor, painter and illustrator and received many honors. His name appears on many Pompeian Bronze and Armor Bronze bookends. Listed in *Fieldings, Mallet, Who's Who,* and *Davenport's 2003-4.*

Anna Vaughn Hyatt (1866-1973): Hyatt was born in Cambridge, Massachusetts. She studied with sculptors H. L. Kittleson and Herman Atkins MacNeil, worked for Gutzon Borglum, and became a master of naturalistic animal sculpture. She won many prizes, and her work is represented in many parks and museums. Listed in *Fieldings, Hughs, Mallett, Who's Who,* and *Davenport's 2003-4.*

Isidore Konti (1862-1938): Konti was born and studied art in Vienna, and moved to New York City in about 1891. He was very successful as a sculptor and most of his works were in classical European subject material. Today his work is still sought by museums. Listed in *Bermans, Fieldings, Mallett,* and *Davenport's 2003-4.*

Jack Lincoln Lambert (1892-1967):Lambert was active in Chicago as a painter, sculptor, and illustrator. Listed in *Who's Who* and *Davenport's 2003-4.*

Freddie Leekya (1967-): Leekya was born on the Zuni Indian Reservation in New Mexico. He is the son of Francis Leekya and the grandson of Leekya Deyuse (Old Man Leekya) the famous fetish carver. Freddy Leekya began making jewelry in high school and has not had any formal art training. He sculpts fetishes and human statuettes from rocks on the Zuni reservation, and sells them through galleries.

Edward Lewis (?-): Lewis is a member of the Leekya family on the Zuni Indian reservation in New Mexico. He attended the Institute of American Indian Arts in Sante Fe. Lewis paints furniture and murals locally.

Max Leverrier (1891-1973): Louis Octave Maxime Le Verrier was born near Paris, and showed great promise as an artist from an early age. He studied in the Beaux Arts School in Geneva, returned to France in 1919 and opened a studio in Paris. In 1925 he was awarded a gold medal at the Paris exhibition. In 1926 he opened his own foundry and cast pieces for leading French sculptors. His foundry produced sculptures of very high quality with exceptional detail and accuracy from a proprietary mix of metals. He sculpted throughout the 1920s and 1930s and produced pieces that are now quite valuable and much sought after. Contemporary signed reproductions of his bookends have appeared on the market and generally cannot be distinguished from the original pieces. Listed in *Bermans* and *Davenport's 2003-4.*

Frank Xavier Leyendecker (1877-1924): Leyendecker was born in Germany and studied in France. He is known principally as an illustrator, and did covers for *LIFE* and other magazines.

Jules Andre Meliodon (1867-?): Meliodon was born in Paris and sculpted and taught in Pennsylvania and New Jersey. Listed in *Who Was Who in American Art, 1975, Fieldings,* and *Davenport's 2003-2004.*

Salvatore Morani (1874-1964): Morani trained as a youth in Italy, at the Belle Academy of Naples and Rome, and came to New York in 1905. During the World War I, he made several important sculptures favoring our war effort. Afterwards, Morani made busts of Franklin and Eleanor Roosevelt for Hyde Park, and made large-scale works for the 1939 World's Fair in New York City. Morani's signature is found on Armor Bronze bookends from about 1914. He is listed in *Who's Who* and *Davenport's 2003-4.*

William Meyerowitz (1887-1981): He was born in Russia and was brought to the United States in 1908. He took classes at the National Academy of Design. under William Merritt Chase and Charles Mielatz. Meyerowitz was very active in artist's associations, and was especially known for his print making. He is listed in *Fieldings, Mallett, Who's Who,* and *Davenport's 2003-4.*

Roland Paris (1894-1945): Paris was born in Austria and studied under Henry Van der Velde (1863-1957), a cofounder of the Bauhaus. He worked in bronze and ivory, and was known for depicting flappers. Very successful, he is listed in *Bermans, Sculptor,* and *Davenport's 2003-4.*

Edith Baretto Parsons (1878-1956): Parsons was born in Halifax, Virginia, and studied at the Art Students' League in New York City with Daniel Chester French and worked as an apprentice to James Earle Fraser. She did memorial fountains, portrait busts and animal figures, now all expensive. She is listed in *Bermans, Fieldings, Mallett, Who's Who,* and *Davenport's 2003-4.*

Max Peinlich: Born in Austria and emigrated to America. After working as a sculptor, Peinlich turned to making jewelry. Listed in *Davenport's 2003-4.*

Howard Pierce (?-1994): Began making pottery and porcelain items in California in 1935, and continued working there until his death.

Serena Plasikowski: No information found.

Ben Kimberly Prins (1904-1930): American illustrator. Born in Holland and worked principally in

Wilton, Connecticut. His work appeared on many national American magazine covers. Listed in *Davenport's 2003-4.*

Brenda Putnam (1890-?): Putnam was born in Minnesota. She studied under James Earle Fraser and later enrolled in the Art Student"s League in New York City. Putnam established a studio in New York City in 1910. She was known for portraits, animals, and cherubs on garden fountains, and her bookends sell for high prices. Listed in *Bermans, Fieldings, Mallett,* and *Davenport's 2003-4.*

John Ruhl (1873-1940): Ruhl trained as a sculptor in New York City and was involved in several important public sculpture projects, including the Lincoln Memorial. Ruhl created bookends for Armor Bronze and others. He won several medals from the Society of the Beaux-Arts Architects and is listed in *Who's Who in American Art* in 1913, *Fieldings*, and *Davenport's 2003-4.*

Ben Seibel (1918-1985): Seibel was an artist and musician. He studied painting under Schanker, sculpture under Amino, and architecture at Columbia University. Seibel designed household articles in New York City from his own shop and designed objects for several companies, including Roseville pottery and Jen Ware.

Louis Comfort Tiffany (1848-1933): Tifffany is a giant among American Art Nouveau and Aesthetic Art-style artists. He is best remembered for designing and producing glass and metal items. His Tiffany Studios made a complete line of interior decorations. All items were of the finest quality, including the bookends, and the bookends deservedly sell for very high prices today. His bookends are marked with the Tiffany name, so they are always recognized.

Walter von Nessen (1889-1943): von Nessen immigrated to the United States from Germany in 1925. In 1927 he set up Nessen Studios in New York City. His early training in German Modernism helped him to become a leading industrial designer in the United States, especially with designs for lamps. At one time he designed for Chase Copper and Brass and gave us several deco bookends. Listed in *Davenport's 2003-4.*

Dirk Van Erp (1860-1933): Van Erp was born into a family of coppersmiths in the Netherlands, and emigrated to the United States in 1886. After making copper pieces for friends, he opened the Art Copper Shop in Oakland, California, in 1908. In 1910 he moved his shop to San Francisco, and worked until his retirement in 1929. After Dirk's death, his son William continued the shop until 1977. Dirk Van Erp is considered the most important metalsmith in the American Arts & Crafts Movement. His lamps sell for tens of thousands of dollars and his bookends are expensive as well.

Carl Valdemar Vieth (1870-1922): Born in Denmark and worked as a sculptor in Connecticut. Listed in *Fieldings*, and *Davenport's 2003-4.*

Alice Morgan Wright (1881-1975): Wright grew up in Albany, New York, and studied sculpture at the Arts Students League. She was a lifelong feminist and animal rights activist. Many of her sculptures were experiments in cubist and futuristic styles. In 1909 she won both the Guzom Borglum and Augustus St. Gaudens prizes in recognition of her work, and her work won extensive international acclaim. She is listed in *Fieldings, Mallett, Who's Who*, and *Davenport's 2003-4*

Francis West: Listed in *Davenport's 2003-4*, but biographical information is lacking.

Bruno Zach (1891-1945): Zach was born in the Ukraine and studied at the Vienna Academy. He went on to produce numerous high-end bronze sculptures. Listed in *Bermans* and *Davenport's 2003-4.*

Appendix

Shop marks

Figure 354-362 show shop marks from some of the foundries that made bookends

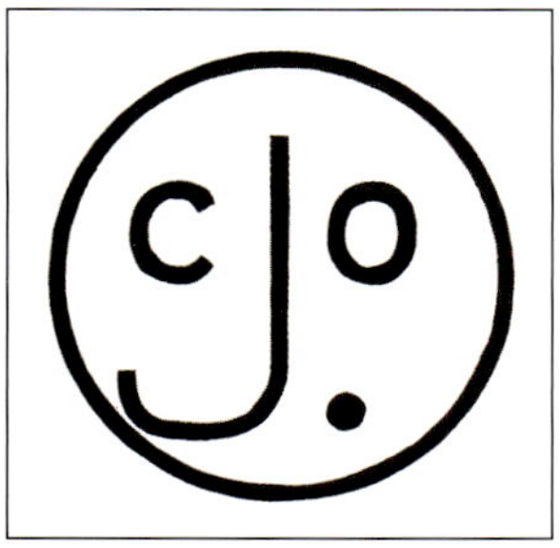

Figure 354. Shop mark of the Judd Co.

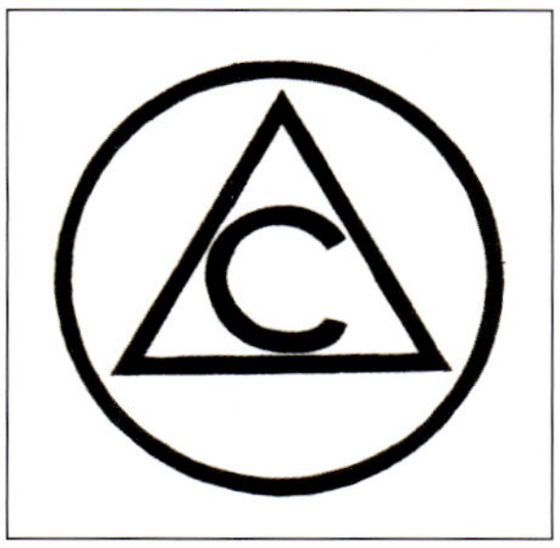

Figure 355. Shop mark of the Connecticut Foundry.

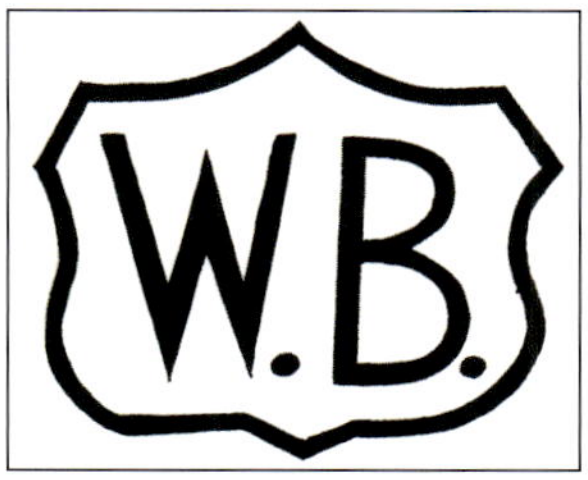

Figure 356. Shop mark of The Weidlich Brothers Mfg. Co.

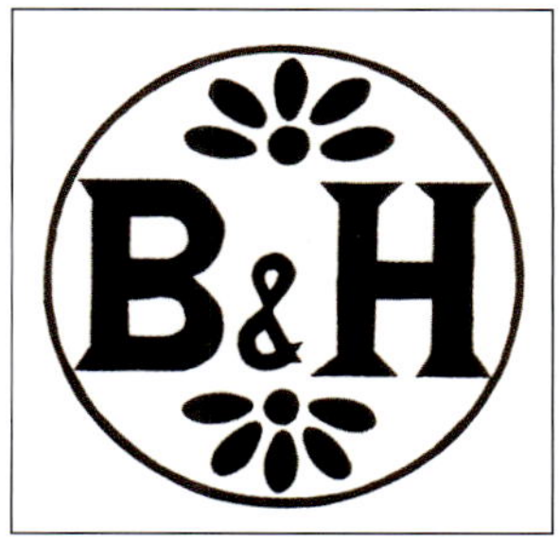

Figure 357. Shop mark of the Bradley and Hubbard Mfg. Co.

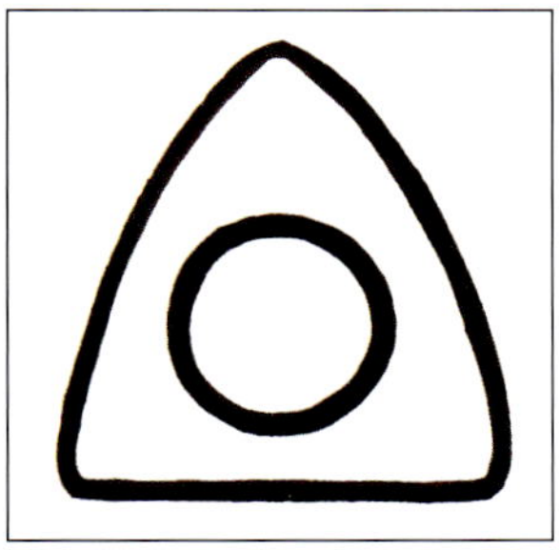

Figure 358. Shop mark of Armor Bronze Inc.

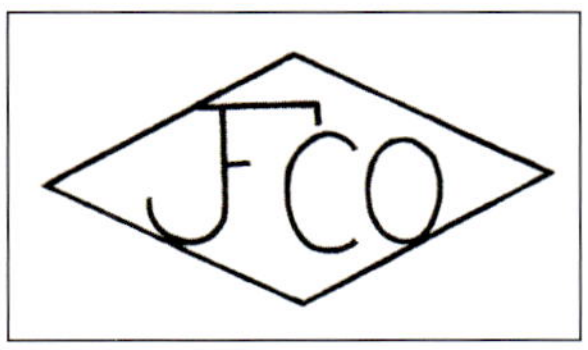

Figure 359. Shop mark of the JF company.

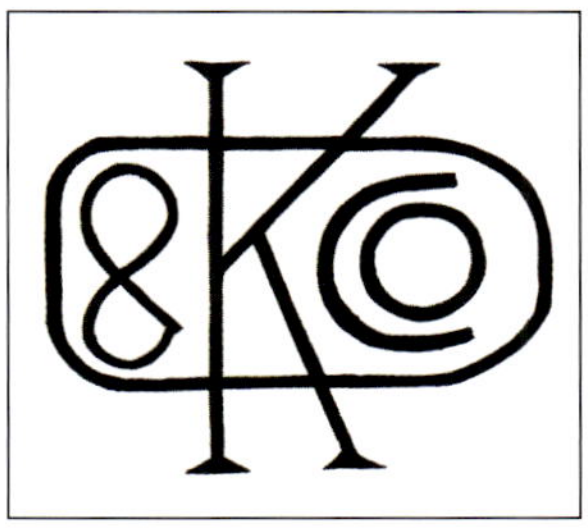

Figure 360. Shop mark of the K&O Metal Novelties company.

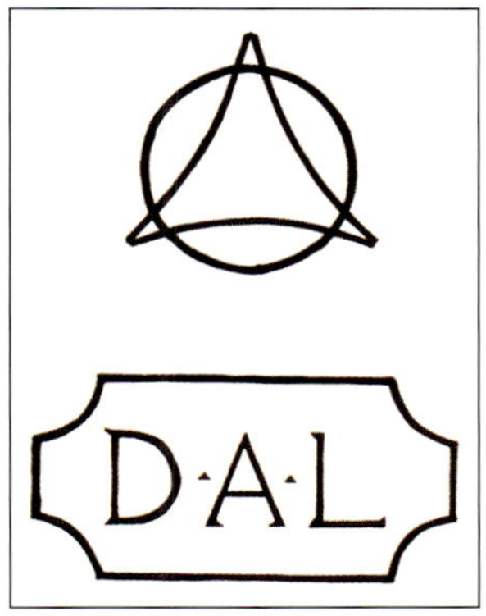

Figure 361. Shop mark of the Decorative Arts League (D.A.L.)

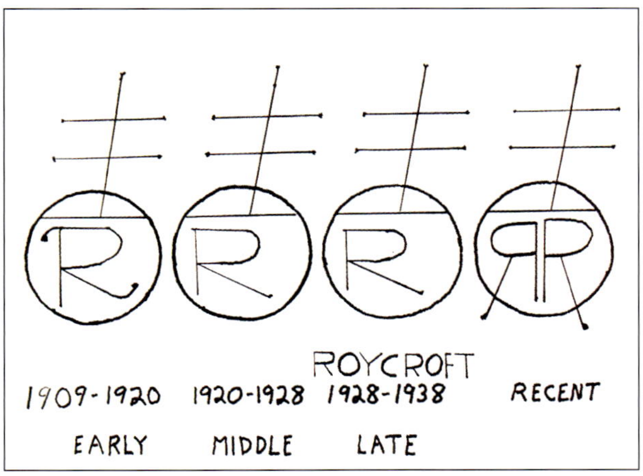

Figure 362. Roycroft shop marks. Early, Middle, Late, Contemporary (Recent). The late mark includes the word Roycroft below it. The recent mark means that the bookend was made after the Arts and Crafts production era at Roycroft. Rare marks can be found at the *Roycroft copper online price guide.*

Bookend Materials

Most bookends in the past have been made from metal, because it was heavy, strong, and easily painted or patinated in some way. Painted bookends could be baked in order to make the paint more durable or sold without first baking (cold painted).

Unfortunately, there have been no chemical analyses of the metals in bookends, so we are sure only of the readily identified ones such as copper, bronze, lead, iron, brass, or aluminum. A great many bookends, however, are made of zinc or zinc alloys or other alloys which cannot be identified with certainty. These are usually metals with a gray appearance, and we simply call them gray metals. Among bookend collectors bronze is preferred, but the type of metal is not the most important criterion for value. A gray-metal or other metal pair may be more desirable than a bronze pair, dependent on other factors.

Zinc and zinc alloys were frequently used for bookends because they gave detailed castings and would not rust. Zinc is frequently called spelter and it is not the same as white metal or pot metal. Pot metal refers to lead and copper mixtures used to make large pots or to uncontrolled mixtures of scrap metal left over from casting procedures. Pot metal objects may sometimes corrode, and pot metal bookends are not likely to be well cast or durable. White metal refers to several metal alloys which appear white.

Non-metal parts are occasionally found in bookends. Ivory is a sumptuous material and old bronze and ivory bookends are among the most costly of bookends today. Celluloid and Bakelite were used before World War II and were considered exotic in their day because all plastics were new and admired. Celluloid in bookends is often described today as ivorine, an unnecessary euphemism. Bakelite is still highly regarded in jewelry and in bookends. Plexiglass is not sought after in bookends.

Plaster of Paris (calcium carbonate) is usually called plaster and is cast to make solid bookends. These bookends, called chalkware, were popular in the early twentieth century, but fell out of favor, presumably because they were easily chipped or broken. Chalkware bookends were produced again during World War II, when metal was devoted to the war effort, and these were frequently used as carnival prizes. Today chalkware bookends are relatively inexpensive.

In the past decade or so, bookends made of synthetic resin (there are a number of these polymers) have appeared, as, for example, Figure 353. The resin is reasonably heavy and durable, although not as heavy or durable as metal. These are castings made from sculptures, generally using vulcanized rubber molds which can copy very fine details. Resin bookends may even appear to be bronze or other metal bookends when the resin contains metal powder. The use of resin has led to exact copies of vintage metal bookends. Collectors should inquire whether bookends are metal or resin before buying bookends online.

Casting Procedures

A relatively small number of bookends have been fashioned by hand. Most have been produced by molds by processes called casting. In general, an artist sculpts the likeness of a bookend from which a hollow mold is made, reproducing the form of the bookend within the mold. After that, a preparation of clay, metal, or some other material is introduced into the interior of the mold and allowed to harden. The mold is then removed and the newly-cast bookend is recovered. The process can be repeated to make numerous castings from the original sculpture.

Sand Casting

Many bookends have been made by sand casting. A bed of fine sand is prepared within a container called a cope, and the sculpture to be replicated is pressed into the sand. More sand, in a container called a drag is pressed down upon the part of the sculpture which is still exposed. (The sand keeps its shape throughout the procedure because it is mixed with molasses or some other material before use.) The drag is then lifted, the sculpture is removed, and the drag is replaced. There is now a space between the sand in the cope and the sand in the drag which is a replica of the sculpture. Molten metal is then introduced into this space and allowed to harden. The metal casting can then be removed. Sand casting leaves a raised seam around the metal casting and impressions of the sand grains in the metal. Seam and impressions are polished off in well-made bookends, but are left in place and can be detected by presumptive buyers in poorly-made bookends.

Slush Casting

A hollow mold with the form of a sculpture within it is produced and there is an opening in the bottom of the mold. Molten metal or other fluid material is introduced into the mold and then it is drained out through the opening. Some of the fluid remains inside the mold and forms a coating on the interior surface. After the material hardens, the mold is removed and a thin-walled, hollow replica of the sculpture is recovered. No pressure is used to force the fluid material against the sculpted interior surface of the mold, so the detail in the replica is frequently not sharp. There is a sizable opening in the bottom of the replica where the fluid was emptied. This is a good clue to identifying pieces made by the slush-casting method.

Most pottery bookends are made by slush casting, which is called slip casting when making pottery items. A slurry of clay and water called slip is introduced into the mold. The finished bookends are light weight, hollow, and thin walled, as expected. Slip-cast bookends may be quite expensive if they were produced by a famous pottery, but the surface detail will frequently be poor nevertheless.

Electroplating

Electroplating is a procedure by which metal is deposited on an object by means of an electric current. The object is immersed in a bath containing metal salts and a current is passed through the bath using the object for the cathode. The object becomes coated with the metal in the bath, which may be nickel, chrome, bronze, silver or other metal. The longer the object is held in the bath, the thicker the deposited coat becomes.

Many vintage bookends were plated with bronze or other metals. Generally, a bookend was cast in gray metal and plated with bronze, nickel, or chrome.The metal coating was durable and attractive. Bookends from NAL Co., Jennings Brothers, and Weidlich Brothers were routinely produced this way with bronze plating. The gray metal provided rigidity to the bookends

Copper Flashing

This process was the same as for metal plating except the plating was extremely thin. It was common for iron bookends to be given a very superficial coating of copper which gave them a copper-colored sheen. Old iron bookends frequently lose all or part of the copper coating and the sheen though oxidation, and take on a dark appearance which is a patina from the copper coating which still remains. Rust begins wherever the copper is completely lost.

Electroform Casting

Electroform casting was very popular early in the twentieth century, and these bookends, which are bronze, are now wrongly called bronze clad or copper clad, rather than properly called electroformed bronze. This process was used by NAL Co.,and by Paul Mori & Sons (Galvano Bronze). The process was also used by Pompeian Bronze Co. and, almost exclusively, by Armor Bronze Inc., by Kathodian Bronze (KBW), and by Marion Bronze.

The electroforming process was chiefly an electroplating process, but the plating was not deposited on a metal casting. Instead, the electroforming process began with an original, full-sized sculpture created by an artist. Replicas of the sculpture were then produced in plaster or some related material, with a hook embedded in the bottom of each one. Each replica was coated with carbon and hung by the hook in a bath of metal salts. An electrical current was passed through the bath which caused a heavy deposit of bronze upon the replica (the cathode). The thick bronze provided rigidity to the finished bookends. These bookends can always be identified by the scar on the bottom of the bookend where the hook was removed (Figure 141). Electroforming is now obsolete.

Lost Wax Casting

A wax sculpture is encased in a heat -resistant material, such as clay, that is hardened and then heated to melt and drain away the wax, producing a mold into which molten metal or other material is poured and left to harden. The clay is then removed to reveal the cast object. This method can produce complex, three-dimensional sculptures in great detail.

Bookend Fakes

In the past decade, many newly-made metal bookends have been offered as vintage. In order to lure buyers, new bronze bookends may be signed with the last name of a famous sculptor and perhaps an initial which may or may not be a correct initial for the sculptor. These bookends are usually in mint condition, which is a red flag, but buyers may believe they have found a bargain.

Figure 363 shows a pair of bookends for example. One bookend is a cowboy and the other is an Indian. The metal is gray metal which is finished to look like a Remington bronze. The bookends are signed F. Remington. Frederick Remington, the famous sculptor of Western subjects, never made bookends like these. This pair is suspect anyway because the Indian's face looks like a white man's face, and the base is a maroon resin which resembles the maroon resin common among imports from China.

New bookends have also appeared from England which are meant to deceive. For instance, there are two pairs of females (Figures 234 and 297) which have been given larger, uplifted breasts (not shown) and are frequently listed on eBay. Also from England, one can find inexpensively-made replicas of sculptures by the famous Josef Lorenzl that have been newly-manufactured as bookends. We do not buy any bookends from England or China.

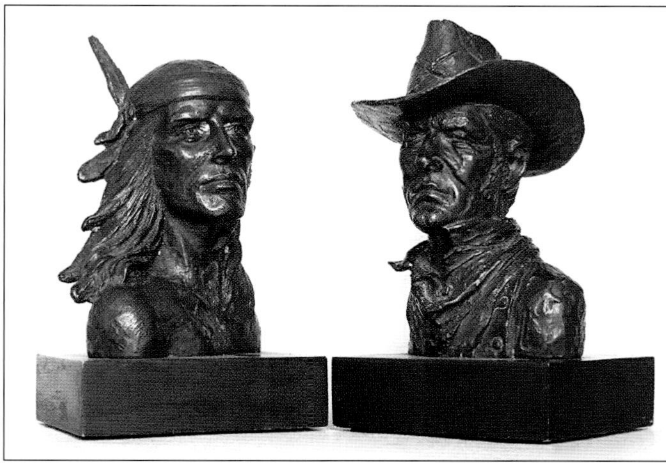

Figure 363. Cowboy and Indian. 6", gray metal, Bronze-like finish. Inscription: F. Remington. Foundry: Attrib. China. Circa 2005. Rarity 5. Aesthetic. Fredrick Remington never made these bookends. They are suspect anyway because the Indian has a white man's face and the base seems to be the dark purple resin common to imports from China. $buyer's choice.

References

Harris, Nathaniel. *Victorian Antiques.* New York, NY: Golden Press. 1973.

Benton, Charlotte, T. Benton, and Ghislain Wood. *Art Deco 1910-1939*. London: V &A Publications. 2003.

Johnson, Donald Brian. *Chase Complete*. Atglen, PA: Schiffer Publishing Ltd. 1999.

McBride Gerald. *A Collector's Guide to Cast Metal Bookends.* Atglen, PA: Schiffer Publishing Ltd. 1997.

Johnson, Bruce. *The Official Identification and Price Guide to Arts and Crafts.* New York, NY: House of Collectibles. 1992.

Schneider, Stuart. *Ronson's Art Metal Works.* Atglen,PA: Schiffer Publishing Ltd. 2001.

Seecof, Robert, Donna L. Seecof, and Louis Kuritsky. *Bookend Revue*. Atglen, PA: Schiffer Publishing Ltd. 1996.

Index of Bookend Subjects and Figure Numbers